AF528658

PANORAMA
OF
INDIAN EDUCATION

PANORAMA OF INDIAN EDUCATION

JANARDAN PRASAD

M.A. (Philo., Soc.) M.Ed., N.D. Art
Diploma in Wood Working
Former Lecturer in Education (Art)
Department of Education (Central Institute of Education)
University of Delhi, Delhi

KANISHKA PUBLISHERS, DISTRIBUTORS
NEW DELHI-110 002

KANISHKA PUBLISHERS, DISTRIBUTORS
4697/5-21A, Ansari Road, Daryaganj
New Delhi-110 002
Phones : 2327 0497, 2328 8285
Fax : 011-2328 8285
e-mail: kanishka_publishing@yahoo.co.in

Panorama of Indian Education

First Published 2008

ISBN 978-81-8457-039-7

PRINTED IN INDIA

Published by Madan Sachdeva for Kanishka Publishers, Distributors, 4697/5-21A, Ansari Road, Daryaganj, New Delhi-110 002; Typeset by Sunshine Graphics, Delhi, and Printed at Nice Printing Press, Delhi.

Dedicated to
respected and reverred
Honourable Mr. APJ Abdul Kalam
Formar President, Republic of India

Foreword

Writing a foreword on a manuscript is an arduous job. It can not be done without knowing about the writer. Shri Janardan Prasad, the author of the book "Panorama of Indian Education" (भारतीय शिक्षा चित्रण), was working in the Central Institute of Education as Lecturer in Education (Art) since 1958, before I joined C.I.E. He retired in March 1994. He is a hard working and self-educated man. From art to philosophy, sociology and education he has left no bearers to cover. His richness of experience, in diverse, yet akin disciplines, seems to have inspired him to write few books on art, audio-visual education, on various fields of education as teacher education and women education etc. etc. and also on wood working, covering educational ventures.

Going through the manuscript of this book "Panorama of Indian Education", I saw formidable arrays of topics which have been covered by the writer in this book. He has tried to visualize and depict the important aspects of education. He tried to mention old Brahmminical Gurukula education. He mentioned its merits and demerits. He tried to depict its prime aim of life building of the youngers. Also he mentioned its demerits as it was sectarian. He has also highlighted the old Indian educational processes. He has mentioned the educational adaptability in Indian caste based social stratification and, its effects on the Indian society.

He also mentioned the root causes of the present Indian social dys-functioning by renouncing the Indian social values—as sociability, truthfulness, simple living and high thinking homogeneity and co-operation, the main reason he pointed out is the present system of formal education which was imposed by the then British India Company Government, on the advice of Lord McCauley in 1833 A.D. for their own ends. The alienistic system of Indian formal education, which is still being followed by the Indians has totally killed the Indian culture. And now the old Indian social values like sociability, morality, co-operation and sharing, love and affection, work culture and sharing have been damaged. The man has become greedy, self-centred and acquisitive. The present education system is only examination based. It has no place for inculcation of good life habits in the youngers which are necessary for their enculturation. And he laid emphasis for the removal of all social stigmas which can only be possible by the reformation of present educational system, then only our culture can be revived. He also laid stress for the removal of gender bias, aesthetic education, sociability and following the teaching professional ethics by the teachers etc. etc. I hope this book will be useful for the educators.

Prof. U.S. Sharma
Former Dean (Education)
Central Institute of Education
Delhi University

Gratitude

I am highly grateful and thankful to a kind and humane person Dr. B. Biswas, former Professor, Industrial Chemical Technology, Harcourt Butler Technological Institute, Nawabganj, Kanpur, U.P., who had very kindly continuously motivated, inspired and encouraged me to self-educate myself, while I was working as a carpentry instructor in Technical Education Department, Department of Industries, U.P. He did so in a pious, non-inclinative way. And due to his kind auspicious inspiration I could do intermediate (U.P. Board), B.A., Agra University, Certificate in carpentry from Government Technical Institute, Gwalior, M.P. and Advance Diploma in Wood Working from Government Wood Working Institute, Jalandhar, Punjab. After all this, I was promoted to the post of Orthographic Drawing Instructor at Government Polytechnic, Tehri, U.P. (Now in Uttrakhand).

Prof. B. Biswas had advised me in July 1958 to leave Government Polytechnic, Tehri, U.P., and join as Wood Craft Instructor at Central Institute of Education, Government of India, University of Delhi and continue my self-study. At C.I.E. I found a very congenial, helpful and kind atmosphere. Many of the teaching faculty members of C.I.E., finding me hard working and diligent encouraged me for self-study. This enabled me to materialise the dreams of honourable Prof. B. Biswas about me. Late Prof. E.A. Pires, Late Prof. P.K. Roy, the then Principals of C.I.E., Late Shri K.D. Bakshi, Late Shri H.A. Gade, Late Dr. G.P. Mehrotra, Prof. R.P. Sharma and Shri S.P. Tyagi encouraged me to continue my self-study. And I could do B.Ed., M.Ed. and M.A. (Philosophy) from Delhi University, Delhi and M.A. (Sociology) from Meerut University. I could do 7 years National Diploma in Fine Arts from College of Art, Delhi (A.I.C.T.E.). Prof. R.N. Mehrotra, the then Head of the Department had advised me to do Ph.D. in Art Education. But my son Dr. Satish C. Sharma, now Prof. Mechanical Engg., Department of Mechanical and Industrial Engineering,

Indian Institute of Technology, Roorkee (Uttrakhand), had advised me to take care of my health. I retired as a lecturer in Education (Art) from C.I.E. in 1994. After my retirement I contributed in the field of education – (1) Wood Working, (2) Education and Society, (3) Education and the Teacher, (4) Art Education, (5) Audio-Visual Education, (6) School Education and Social Development, (7) Women Education and gender justic, (8) Teacher Education and (9) Indian Educationscape. Credit goes to all of these kind gentlemen for their contribution. I have also worked on (1) Vishwakarma Artisans of India, (2) Family, and (3) Indian socioscape. These books are to be published.

Janardan Prasad

Preface

The nature has not gifted all individuals to do all work efficiently. Some are capable to do mental work more sincerely and efficiently. Some can do manual work more effectively and diligently. And some are lacking in both of these capabilities. They can only work as helping hands. But our educationscape is astonishing. It aims at to educate all equally in spite of their individual differences. Our educational authorities, rulers, teachers, parents and social milieu desire that all youngers should be taught all subjects equally in spite of their varied psyche, mental capabilities and interests. And students in spite of their individual differences and interests are forced to get equal education, which is also examination oriented. And all parents desire that their wards must reach to the new heights in their lives and should add new feathers to their family crowns and should pass their annual examination in flying colours and should compete in the job market. As such, they all pressurise their children to study more and more. And for achieving this goal the parents even prohibit their children not to do any homework. They even do not allow their children to wash their *'kachha banyan'* and towel after taking bath in the bathroom. Many parents do not allow their children to come out of their house to play with their peer group. By doing so the parents generate a sense of social dysfunctioning as it creates a sense of unsociability in the young generation. This kind of pressure on the youngers sometimes crosses all limits as the youngers generally go in depression and they even commit suicides.

The Times of India dated 05.03.2006 reported that two students ended their lives for not doing well in their Senior Secondary Examination 2006. One student of Government Senior Secondary School, Sector II, R.K. Puram, New Delhi, who had failed last year and, was appearing again this year, ended his life by hanging himself with the ceiling fan in his room. His father wanted him to take science but the boy was unable to study science. He coped with the desire of his parents and said sorry to them by ending his life on 03.03.2006. Another 17 years student of Senior Secondary School, Tilak Nagar, New Delhi, hanged himself as he was refused admission in XII Class, Senior Secondary Examination, 2006, conducted by Central Board of Secondary Examination, New Delhi. All this has happened due to undesirable examination stress which is one of the present important feature of education panorama of our educational system.

Usually a child does not take such drastic decision to end his/ her life in the sphere of moment. Undergoing conditions of pressure for good examination results which cause acute depression might be the cause of acute depression which entail such unfortunate action taken by some students. Such bad awkward happenings are not limited only up to school education. Some students studying in higher learning institutions like Engineering Colleges, Indian Institutes of Technology and Medical Colleges also commit suicides after their poor performance in their annual examinations. As such, education panorama of education system is very dangerous which very often forces the students to commit suicides. And the main reason behind such bad happenings is the intense desire of the parents to see their children coming out in flying colours in their annual examination so as to compete in their job market. The parents do not assess the capabilities of their wards.

All parents desire that their wards be admitted in top ranking educational institutions. And for seeking admission in the institutions of higher learning the students are forced to get coaching in coaching shops which are run by private persons. Such coaching shops are found in every nook and corner of villages, towns and big cities. Such coaching centres try, generally, for alluring the students for getting the admission in their coaching centres saying as – "An Institution or Academy of Miraculous Solutions to Competition", "A Sure Preparatory Programme to Qualify the Entrance Examination of .....", "Fly High to the Career Sky", and "Study Smart" etc. etc. As such, the coaching shops assure the aspirant students sure admission in the desired courses of study. The parents of the students try to admit their wards in the coaching centres and, also they pay unaffordable coaching tuition fees. This panorama of Indian education or education panorama shows that our educational system prepares the students for cut-throat competition in all fields. And it has no place for enculturation by inculcating good sane life habits and attributes in our youngers for saneful social living. And generally our youngers remain quite unaware about the nice sane social behaviour and good character. As such, keep this aspect in view our educational system needs drastic immediate reformation. And for that a deep visualisation and analysis of our educational system is a dire necessity of the day.

The socioscape of our society depicts the increasing crime ratio in the society. Loot, snatching, burglaries, frauds, unsociability, polytheism and henotheism for material gains and its effects on simple living and high thinking, molestations and rapes of innocent young girls and young ladies are becoming a common social feature. The media generally reports about such unsocial happenings in the society, regularly. All this is happened due to greedy human nature, which has been immensely increased due to acculturation. Acculturation occurs due to cultural diffusion, which occurs due to coming in contact with the foreigners. The cultural diffusion is like the whirlpool waves in water pond caused due to stone throwing in water pond. We Indians came in contact with the Westerners who are materialistic hedonistic, consumeristic, xenophilic and maglomaniac. And we have adopted their culture. This has killed our national culture. Due to this our old value system is not only on dys-functioning stage but on killing stage. We have adopted the class structure and have more or less renounced our old caste system. With the result the sense of sociability, morality and social cooperation have more or less been vanished from the society. Our old educational system laid emphasis on inculcation of good life habits, is totally ignored.

For making our youngers sane and responsible future citizens there is a need of inculcation of good habits and enculturation of our youngers. As such, there is need of full examination of our education panorama and educational structure. Aspects like teaching, examination, life building processes, commercialisation of education, equal opportunities for all intelligent and diligent children, equal opportunities for education for all girls, apprising them for their future life roles as they are anta-property (पराया धन) and also inculcation of good behaviour in both boys and girls are necessary.

For doing all this, the teacher have to play a vital role. During the course of teaching the pupil-teachers should be educated about all aspects of education panorama. The education and teaching are two different aspects which are supplementary to each other though these are necessary. Due to examination oriented, the educational system has been more or less commercialised. Many people earn a lot due to commercialisation of education. In the past Indian education system was not at all commercialised. It was a charitable system for the common good. The society used to donate for the Gurukulas and Madarsas. Teaching was considered one of the most pious donation. The Gurus were dedicated teachers. They were life builders. Now the teaching due to examination system, education has been more or less commercialised. No teaching professional ethics is followed. Most of the teachers do tuitions for their hedonistic gains. Many teachers do side business. Teachers in rural areas devote their time in tilling their lands. Such teachers enjoy school teaching for their leisure.

Like all this the present education panorama has created many social problems and stigmas. Therefore, there is a need of thorough examination of educational system which is alien to our culture. It is, therefore, necessary to highlight the detailed viewpoints of our education panorama for bringing desirable changes through reformation in our educational structure. The writer has tried a bit in this regard by writing 'education panorama'. A few points have been highlighted and not all.

Janardan Prasad

Contents

1

Introduction

Everybody is bound to do some action during his/her life, as Lord Krishna told to Arjuna on the battlefield at Kurukshestra on the first day of Mahabharata War (*Shrimad Bhagavad Gita*: Chapter III, Sloka-3) between Kaurvas and Pandavas. For a suitable viable action for any social work or economic activity some planning is necessary, so that the activity may be carried out on the right track. Then only any work can be done correctly and logically. Without doing this neither the conceived social aims nor the individual aims can be achieved. All socio-economic, cultural, religious, axiological, epistemological and familial aims can only be achieved, if the related activities are assessed in advance and then carried on. This kind of action can be said to be on the right track. So some sort of advance planning is necessary. Without pre-planning the activities cannot be put on the right track. Neither the individual or individuals doing the work can be benefited nor the society as a whole can be enriched. As such, it is necessary to know about the action to be done in detail in advance. And for knowing this an intense *per se*, that is, visualisation, analysation and consequent synthesis of the particular activity, which is to be done, is necessary before doing the activity. And this can be said to be tantamount to making a landscape of a geographical track as done in art. A landscape always depicts all panorama of land, its flora and fauna texture of land and shape of the geographical track. It helps in understanding the geographical region. This principle also applied to all kinds of human activities, such as, socio-economic, cultural, familial, axiological and educational. The educational structure of any society or a country has a wide spectrum. It depends upon the country's political and theological structures of the different societies. Education being an important social activity, as its bases are on socio-economic activities of the society, needs a thorough pre-examination and consequent analysis before its implementation. In every society many socio-economic activities like fabrication of consumer goods, and their consequent manufacturing and production on large scale, is done for human use. These fabricated goods are produced in factories in large scale and are sold in market. Education helps in such activities. But education cannot be fabricated like consumer goods are produced in factories in mechanical way as it is a process of taking out hidden human potentialities. One of the most important educational aspects is that education should be for life building of the individual and for social homogeneity and integrity. Our younger generation are clients of our educational institution, which are the roots of educational structures. These clients are conscious beings and are called students. They are not ignorant clients like that the clients of the recognised professionists—the lawyers, doctors and clerics. Their clients are considered ignorant clients. As such, the education of the youngers cannot be carried on in mechanical way. But the present education is carried on in a mechanical way under the present formal system of education which is also alien. The present education system is a state instrument. The state wants to educate all youngers in a uni-pattern way ignoring the fact that all students have individual differences, and many of them are not interested in learning what is taught to them.

This type of educational system has created many social problems. This has mitigated the work culture, sociability and homogeneity which were imbibed in our culture. It has crumbled down the social institution like joint family, caste, panchayats and community organisations. It has brought cutthroat competition in the society; simple living, high thinking, religiosity and spirituality are no more. Polytheism and henotheism have replaced monotheism which is no more due to human greed and self-centeredness. Youngsters do not pay respect to elders, and sometimes even to their parents. Nuclear families have taken place of the joint families. Due to this the enculturation of the youngers has become impossible. The advance system of communication encouraged cultural diffusion which has brought killing acculturation.

Our present system of formal education was imposed by the British rulers. And the main aim of the formal education was to acculturate the Indians for keeping them slaves forever. The second aim was to prepare the Indians to serve as clerks in British Government offices. For this the English language was made compulsory for all students. The British Government had been so successful that we Indians more or less have lost our national culture. We eat, drink, dress and talk in alienistic way. In spite of rigid caste system, we Indians were homogenous, cooperative and sociable. And now on many occasions it becomes difficult to recognise the boys and girls because they dress in anta-way, when the bodies of the boys and girls are topsy-turvy. In the present system of education the main aim of education which is life building is totally ignored. And our educationists are totally immune to this fact. Inculcation of good life habits—as good behaviour, sound character, good work habits, good healthcare habits, sociability, morality, speaking true, simplicity, spirituality, respect to elders, fair sex and, love to youngers is neither done in the family nor in the schools. Our present formal education only lay emphasis on good examination results. This has also made the parents of the children mad. They lay too much pressure on their children for reading more and, show good shining results. Read and read is the only cry in the four walls of the schools and houses of the children. Many mothers torture their children for good examination results. Many of the mothers are not well educated to teach their children, but they leave no stone unturned to force their children not to mix up with their peer group and play with them. This kind of familial torture for good examination results changes the psyches of the children especially of the young girls and spoil their personality development. The girls are anta-property (पराया धन). They fail to develop the adjustment of psyche which is very necessary for them to adopt in their married life. Like that many adolescent boys become criminals in their future life. As our present system of education is doing the work of social dys-functioning instead of doing social-cohesion and unity. Our future guardians are made mad-materialistic, hedonistic, consumeristic and xenophilic. They become totally self-centred instead of onlookers common interest. The spirituality and sane sociability are no more in the society. All youngers are becoming self-centered, egoistic and greedy. This is why the society is engrilled in unsociability, corruption and crimes. The cases of loots, burglaries, dacoities, cheating, molestation and rapes have become common social feature now-a-days. And the days are not far off when Indian society is going to be barbarous and jungli society.

The Indian society was once considered the cultured and civilised society in the world, as the Indian culture is one of the best oldest culture of the world. Two upper castes—Brahmans and Kshatriyas were educated in Gurukulas. The main aim of Gurukula education was life building. The human life was divided into four parts—Brahmacharya Ashram (1-25 years), Grahastha Ashram (26-50 years), Banprashtha Ashram (51-75 years) and Sanyas Ashram (76-100 years). In Brahmacharya Ashram the youngers used to get education in Gurukulas which were used to be far away from their houses. The Gurukulas used to be situated in jungles on river banks. The *Shishyas* (students) were used to be educated in religiosity, spirituality and sociability. The *Shishyas* and *Gurus* used to live in Gurukulas with *Gurus* under a common roof. They used to live a simple life. The education was totally free. Local people used to contribute for the functioning of ashram kitchen. The students also used to collect food items from the local people. The teaching was considered one of the poise donation. The Gurukula *Gurus* (teachers) used to inculcate good life habits in students as: (1) early to bed early to rise makes a man healthy and wise, (2) taking bath regularly, (3) doing yoga and meditation, (4) participation in daily joint prayers and yajna, (5) to speak truth, (6) to be social and moral, (7) to follow the national culture, and (8) to be loyal to elders, fellow beings and to the nation. After getting *'diksha'* at the Gurukula the disciples (students) were required to go to the countryside and educate the masses through religious and spiritual discourses to be sane and loyal citizens of the country. In total, the Indian education was idealistic. There was no state control and commercialisation of education at all. The state neither used to finance it nor used to impose its dictates. So it used to look the social requirements. The other two castes Vaishyas and Sudras used to educate their children in their vocations non-formally themselves. And their wards used to follow their family occupations. As such, the Indian social stratification had permanent occupational base which lead the society free from competition. There was no examination system in both of these educational patterns—that is familial types—formal and familial non-formal. These two systems of education were quite different from the present alienistic formal system of education carried on in schools and other state run institutions.

The present formal system of education is totally examination based and has now been commercialized by commercial persons. There is a spate of such commercial educational institutions in India. There are large number of public schools and coaching centres which charge high fees from the students. These educational institutions claim that these do life building. But acculturation of the students is done. Now commercialisation of education has become a common social feature. Many teachers spend most of their time in doing tuitions and, they pay less attention to teaching. Many teachers spend time in preparing examination guide books. The students generally read such guide books for the preparation of their examination. Life building has no place in the present system of education, which should be the prime aim of education. In such a situation it has become very necessary to know all aspects of our educationscape.

For this, it is very necessary to study our educational structure very minutely, so that all aspects of educationscape for bringing some reformation in total educational structure, change is inevitable. The present education system needs a change and it should be changed. This can only be changed if its all pros and cons are logically examined and its merits and demerits are found in detail. And a viable educational structure which could protect our culture be searched and adapted. This should be done after detailed discussions and a logical agreement is reached. It is, therefore, necessary to plan a viable educationscape for the country.

2
Human Resources Development

Men and women who constitute a human society are called human-beings. The word human is a derivation of French and Latin words 'humain' and 'humanus', which mean a living being having rational dispositions or qualities or life attitudes which are signs of good saneful social living. The human-beings are rational beings. So, a man being a rational has roots of thinking, reasoning and analysing. This is why a man could exploit the natural resources for his benefits. But in spite of being rational, he has a drawback. He is greedy, acquisitive and self-centred. So human resources development is very necessary for the existence and prosperity of all human-beings, society as a whole, as well as, for the development of a strong and viable nation. If the members of the society are not socialised, moralised, civilised and educated well, neither they can, nor the society, nor the nation and its Government can prosper. And for these ends, human society came into being. It has been looking after the interests of the human-beings and attending to their needs. The human society has been doing this arduous job of human resources development since its inception. It has been providing all kinds of facilities for inculcating the men, for socialising, moralising, theorising, enculturating, educating and preparing the man for earning his livelihood. The society from the very beginning has been a pivot or base of the human resources development of its members. As such, it seems necessary to say something about the society and, its roles for the upliftment of human-beings or in doing human resources development.

SOCIETY

A society is a wider whole, composed of various biological wholes, that is, human-beings. The human-beings or biological wholes, that is, men and women are members of the human society. But these members of the human society are not well-integrated, as body parts of a biological whole, that is, a human-being are intensely integrated. The members of the society, that is, human-beings are not well-integrated, as they have individual differences. They are greedy by nature. Human-beings are considered rational living beings. The nature has gifted them with some special awesome bodily faculties. The human-beings have been rewarded with bigger brains to think, reason and analyse, erect posture to stand and walk and, moveable hands to work and to fabricate new things for the use of human-beings. But in spite of all this the Divine Authority made man very greedy, acquisitive, self-centred, selfish and hedonistic. So, from the very beginning the human-beings have been involved in serious social conflicts which make the saneful social living peacefully difficult. Also the God created many sane and humane living human-beings, who always thought of common good of all. These sane seers always thought of some viable sane institutions which could enable the human beings to live together harmoniously and peacefully. And the prime institution, the society came into being to control the selfish nature of the human-beings.

SOCIETY, THE SYSTEM OF INTER-RELATED PARTS

Various models of society have been highlighted by the social, scientists regarding the development and structural functions of the society. Three main dominant models are:

Evolutionary Model

According to this model, the society goes through a system of adjustment in its development. The evolutionary school of sociology have different forms. Immanuel Kant, Herbert Spencer and Karl Marx contributed to this school thought. The evolutionary model is also known as uni-liner model. According to this model, the societies began as simple societies of tribes which were uni-lingual. After sometime these societies undergo the process of differentiation. The stages they normally cover are: (*a*) stage of food gathering, (*b*) hunting, (*c*) fishing, (*d*) agriculture, and (*e*) mechanised agriculture. These stages are linked with a particular specific model. In this process, there used to remain homogeneity in culture.

Cyclical Theory of Evolution

C. Pratt developed this theory. According to this theory the society or societies emerge at a point. Thereafter there is increase in some characteristics and these go down. Societies are:

(i) a combination of relatively large number of people,
(ii) living together in a definite geographical area,
(iii) have reciprocal relationships with each other. These relationships result in:

Systems of social association entail

- acceptance of desirable mutual interests and goals to be achieved, so that,
- mutual cooperation may be possible which can provide,
- unity to the social whole which can be fostered by,
- sane developed habits of sharing in,
- an independent mode of life held together by,
- established life norms, and
- inter-related social states.

Structural-Functional Theory

This theory is based on science of biology, structure and function which constitute the key of the science of biology. According to this theory the whole society is a whole, is treated as an organism, wherein inter-relationship of the institutions is the main base. The various systems or organs of the society have definite functions.

The structure is a generalised concept of sociology. It is applicable to many aspects of the society. For example, the structural-function theory can be applied to kinship or social continuity or marriage. Some qualities or aspects of two or more persons link them together so they become inter-locked and operate as a system. Structure constitutes the basis upon which the performance of functions depends.

Societies are differentiated on the basis of structural functions (as, Eastern and Western societies, plain and tribal societies). The concept of hereditary functioning may be used to signify all structures of the human societies. The societies also differentiated on the basis of hierarchy of social structures.

Stable relationship is the characteristics of social structural, relationship. There are culturally defined ways in which the individual behaves, which means social structure implies 'relationship'. Action is the basis of relationship, whether it is physical action-kissing or non-physical action like no-kissing in which there is no act, yet the behaviour is indicative of action.

These relationships are endless, but none of these relationships can hang itself, because these relationships have dimensions of time and space etc. For example, father-son-relationship enters into various other relationships like father-mother relationship, mother-daughter relationship, grandmother-mother relationship and relationships with nephew and with siblings etc. etc. These relationships may take different forms of roles, at different stages of time and place. The relationships take a qualitative different form according to these dimensions. For example, son as a student in the class room, relationship of mother and father during day and at night.

We notice that there takes place the clustering roles. This clustering of roles provides the brick works of structure. Social structure is like a system. This system involves certain continuity in respect of its parts. The economy, the policy, education, culture, religion and Government etc. of a society constitute its system. The social system is characterised by inter-dependence and inter-influencing. Every change does not affect the system, but a major change does.

Movements, processes and continuous actions characterise the sub-systems of a system. These sub-systems are not static over a period time. For example, the nature of relationship in kinship group undergoes a change. However, the changes are not unregulated or unrelated. Therefore, there is always a measure of stability in a social system.

Talcott Parsons emphasised on "Family, Socialisation and Process". Morris Zeolite described the social phenomenon as under:

Unit: A unit is an elementary particle from which the whole system emanates.

Society: When two or more units are related to each other, change in one unit results in change in other units.

System: Units are interdependent. These interdependent units contribute the system.

System equilibrium: The nature of relationship is sustained despite change in units. Every system seeks equilibrium over a period of time. And every system has a boundary.

System I	*System II*
Father-Son	Mother-Daughter

Why is There no Change

Reward and punishment is carried on at individual level. The rest of the society is controlled through culturally defined behaviour, that is, servile sane behaviour of the Indian women. Why is it so? Why should not the women behave in some other way?

STRUCTURE OF THE WHOLE SOCIETY

Every social system is beset with certain functional problems.

1. The problem of tension management or problem of pattern maintenance. The problem is as how to motivate the members of the society to perform their roles efficiently. In other words, it means how to help others to conform culturally as per defined expectations. The individual by his nature is not prone to conform to social norms and culture of the society. This gives rise to tension in social system. The relationships in the social system are subject to this kind of tension.

2. There must be ways to keep the deviants or defaulters in control. And for this purpose it is necessary to educate the members of the society to conform to prescribed social norms. This can be done through the mechanism of integration that characterises a particular society. And if human beings are properly educated and, human resources development is done logically, it can play a positive role in the social development. And the members of the society can be sane members of the society.

3. The goal attainment functions of the society are national security, development of resources, including human resources development. Polity of the society, that is, institutional framework and appropriate political system and sub-systems are necessary for this purpose. Each of these functions of the society, serve, as the focus of attention by the social organisations.

Social Institutions and Their Functions

1. The institution of marriage focuses on tension management.
2. The institution of family focuses on familial education.
3. The institution of education focuses on formal education.

Suspension of rude behaviour and, judgment is the main activity in the process of tension management, social cooperation is necessary for this. For this, the institution of marriage is much important in the modern complex society, mother and father have to accept the child and bring him/her up. Whatever his and her weaknesses are, but they have to shower parental love on the child. Mother and father are genesis of human society.

Similarly, the family is responsible for paternal maintenance. The family is urgent necessity for good life habits in the young children. As such, familial education is the pivot in life building. Youngers must be motivated to work. They should be educated about the political, social and social institutions. It requires innovation and motivation. This can be done through socialisation and proper education of both parents and the children. In this the institution of family used to play a prominent role. The family used to inculcate all necessary life attitudes in the youngers. But this situation has totally changed due to materialistic and hedonistic trends of social life. Now joint families are no more. And nuclear families mostly remains busy in the rat-race of money earning. So the parents do not have time for familial education. In the earlier societies, the socialisation was done by the family. Now due to acculturation most of the members of the society have become self-centred. So, there is a need to revive our old joint family system, for which the members of the society are to be educated. Education makes the individual more autonomous in the midst of facts, competition, rivalry and protection etc. These constitute the reflections of the society in respect of human resources development.

The functions of education in the simple society are generally performed by the family through familial system of education. However, the differentiation of function becomes necessary in complex societies. Thus, the social institutions arise to take care of the patterns of fabrication and management in the present complex societies. Earlier this sort of education was taken care of by the hereditary non-formal education. Now the social educational institutions have become necessary for such education.

Bringing up and inculcating of good life attitudes takes place in the family. Formal education is imported in educational institutions. The political system of the country helps in the management of institutions imparting formal education. Ballot power plays a vital role in democracy. Also caste, class and other hierarchical organisations play a dominant role in the formation of Government in a democracy. The institution of society has a varied meanings. An enduring complex and relative behaviour helps the society to meet some of its fundamental problems. The institutions of society are also related to association of the people for the good of the people. It is the pattern of relationship that subsists in a group that, gives a character of the institutions. The pattern of relationship that subsists in a group gives it a character of institution. The patterns of relationships aim to perform certain functions, that is, tension management, bringing sanity and prosperity in the society. Socialising serves as a major stabilising force in the society. In the Indian context, the marriage of man and woman is an universal phenomenon. It is organically necessary and for that social pressure is built to force every woman to marry with a man. The institution of marriage serves the same function in establishing the society, as ethics does in establishing the religion. As such, all social institutions provide continuity and serve as regulating and fulfilling mechanisms. However, conformity to society is not common (Ref. Radcliff Brown).

Family and Education

- Extent of social learning that takes place in the family is culture and its transmission.
- Family has the manifest function of reproduction. However, the rules, rituals, beliefs, traditions, customs and taboos that are associated with the reproductive function of the family, are important for education. For example, the child's rearing patterns leave crucial impressions on the personality of the children. The methods of instructions in class room should follow from these practices in order to be effective.

Socialisation and enculturation take place in family as:

(*i*) Socialising helps in learning the language and at a stage a child is expected to learn language through it.

(*ii*) Child depends on others for protection. According to Burgess 'none of the methodologies are followed in the family and school is suitable place to children.' The children look at the world differently than the adults do.

(*iii*) The 'learning setting' in which socialisation takes place in the nature of home educational environment. In the family the elders impart learning to the children. The learning climate in the family is significant in the child learning process.

(*iv*) The group experience that child gets in the family is significant in learning.

(*v*) The emotional climate of the family is also significant for learning. It depends on personal relationships to the family.

(*vi*) The psycho-drama in the family affects the learning of the child says Burgess. It is important for human resources development. It is determined by the continuum of 'fear', 'hate', 'superiority', 'inferiority and insecurity', and 'protection'. The psycho-interaction between husband and wife and other interaction problems or psycho-drama in the family affect the human resources development. The husband and wife or father and mother should not do such drama before the youngers.

(*vii*) The family as social system is very important for enculturation of the youngers. The family can help in culture development. The family always reflects the social norms of the broader social system. Family and education are miniature of society.

Family and Familial Education

The traditional family was joint family system which is almost non-existent in the modern hedonistic age. The roles, customs, statues and values relevant to the traditional joint family either have totally crumbled or have undergone a drastic change.

1. There was restricted individualism in the joint family. In a joint family each one of its members has to go ahead simultaneously. All members of the family have to develop against unrestricted individualism, that is obtained in the school.
2. In a joint family there used to be self-restraint against the self-indulgence, which is not possible in the hedonistic society.

The security of the members in the traditional joint family, was the responsibility of the society, which is now provided by other social agencies. In this connection Kapadia's study of Mahar's may be referred to:

Values

- Material comfort in the traditional family is treated as a means and not as an end.
- Looking at life at different stages—viz., pre-marriage, marriage as a compulsory stage, post-marriage stage.
- Solidarity within family was in the past. Patriarch was the trusty of the family property and family management in the past. Now joint family is no more, so patriarch is also no more.
- Cooperation was the main value of the family system. In the emergent society, it is egalitarian cooperation. In the traditional society cooperation was based on superiority of the male.
- In olden times there was value of fraternalism with non-family members. The culture of the group sets many conditions when influence the member. And the member learns a lot from the group. This results in the formation of general tendencies of behaviour which we call personality.
- But J.J. Rousseau, a French thinker termed all this a 'rude' social behaviour. He said that "the child is born free but found himself/herself in chains". According to him there should not be any social dictum in the development of the child. The child should grow according to nature.

Personality differ from society to society. These differences and uniformation are due to traditions, value orientations and custom complexes.

Direct Socialisation

- Direct socialisation starts with the birth of the child. Urges, instincts and capacities are susceptible to the process civilisation. However, reflexes cannot be socialised.
- Development of the 'self' is the nucleus of the whole process of socialisation. Communicative interaction is basic to the development of the self.

Interactions are necessary for socialisation which occurs as follows:

1. Authoritative interaction is essential for the parents.
2. Equalitarian interaction is essential for the parents.
3. The child acquires identification through imitation and obedience. These processes make the child aware of himself or herself.
4. Capacity to differentiate one member of the family from the other (as attitude towards mother of the family from the other i.e. attitudes towards father, uncles and sibling etc.).
5. 'Self-identity' or the 'ego' develops in the child. However, the self-remains dynamic one. It goes on changing, developing and adjusting.

Who Socialises the Child?

(*a*) Authoritarian groups, that parents, elderly family members, community member and teacher etc.

(*b*) Equalitarian group: Siblings, peer group, elderly family members. Here rules of behaviour are based on working principles, conflicts, cooperation and sharing constitute basis of socialisation.

Agents of socialisation are:

1. Family, 2. Peer group, 3. Siblings, 4. Neighbourhood elders, 5. Community elders, 6. Voluntary organisations, 7. Religious organisations, and 8. Mass Media.

Social Change

Social change also affects the socialisation of the youngers. Greek Philosopher, Hereclitus said that change is inevitable. The concept of structural differentiation is probably the key sociological concept, in the analysis crescent or increasing social change. It indicates how the social institutions grow in size and, how these institutions function in specialised and distinct manner. And how the sub-systems emerge which also help in social role. Also the processes of cultural diffusion and acculturation bring versatile social change which in the end prove to be killing the national culture. All these social points should be taken into consideration by the educationists while planning educational processes for the human resources development.

SOCIAL VERSATILITY OF HUMAN RESOURCES

For the common social development and, for the revitalisation of Indian social structure it is very necessary to develop the human resources in right direction and tape them for the common good. For doing so education can play a positive role. But until and unless the full 'educationscape' is intensely visualised and analysed the human resources development cannot be done correctly. Human resources are many and innumerable. Every human-being has been made unique by the Almighty God, with special ability, intelligence, diligence, aestheticity, courage, moral sense, specificity in one unique area of action, social character, a sense of cooperation and sharing with his/her fellow beings. Though this seems to be very difficult to happen because of acute indulgence in greed for meeting our materialistic desires for achieving our hedonistic, consumeristic and xenophilic ends. However, when there is a will there is a way. No single individual or party can bring a reformation in any social structure, all social beings and agencies can revitalise a social-structure. The first effort should start for the development of human resources from home. First of all the parents should present good social values themselves before their youngers. They should discard the craze for materialistic and hedonistic aspirations which have infused in them by the acculturation. As such human resources development should never be based on mere material gains. In spite of material gains the development of other human faculties should be taken into consideration. Development of sociability, which has been crumbled by the virus of acculturation and consequent greed and self-centeredness should be given due importance in our educationscape. Also development of morality, homogeneity and humanity should be given prime preference. There should be all round efforts to develop a spirit of cordiality in the youngers towards their family members, respect for elders, neighbours and ladies. Our educational programme should inculcate good life attitudes like—early to rise and early to bed, simple living and high thinking in the youngers. The family, the parents and other family members should initiate the steps for prime human resources development. This can only be done if steps are taken to revive the institution of joint family system, from the nuclear families. The religious institutions can also play a vital role in this regard. These can inculcate a spirit of ethnic unity and sobriety. Of course, the school can also play a vital role in this regard. But it appears difficult as school activities only lay emphasis on teaching for good examination results and no attention is given on life building process. Though schools and other educational institutions can play a pivotal role in this regard through co-curricular activities, but these institutions are forced to concentrate only on good examination results. Also, this responsibility lies on the shoulders of the political masters of the country. They should pay due attention for re-structuring our present educational structure which could have place for humanity, sociability and fraternity. The political masters should have a tag on political bungling as creating vote banks for their own benefits, which generally breeds corruption and unsociability in the society.

Basically, the Indian social structure can be said a homogenous social structure because of monotheistic religious philosophy believing in *Paramatma* (Almighty God) and *Jeevatma*. This duality of soul is described in Sankhya Yoga Darshan of Indian theistic school of philosophy. Therefore, in olden times, the spirit of cordiality, sociability, cooperation and morality was easily developed in Indians, and this entailed simple living and high thinking. And the development of human resources was correctly done by old Indian Brahmanical education. But because of human greed and acculturation, which developed due to Western cultural diffusion, we have totally forgotten our customs, traditions, cultural traits and culture. And no proper human resources development could be possible in the present materialistic and hedonistic age. The harmonious human resources development is essential for sane prosperous social living. Still, there exist many social ethnic groups having specific expertise and talents which could help in the human resources development. It is necessary for the national development. All of the ethnic groups are the levers of our national machinery. If any of ethnic group is left out and proper human resources development is not done, there cannot be harmonious national development. This can be done by upward mobility alone. All other aspects should be given due consideration.

India is a multi-racial, multi-cultural and multi-religious society. There are many castes and creeds and religious sects which reflect diversity in Indian society. Yet common religion, common language covering geographical belts bind all sections of the society. And, yet there is a unity in diversity which should be utilised as main source of human resources development. Indian old culture was based on self-sufficiency and mutual trust which was a kind of big human resources, this should be revived and preserved through enculturation of all sections of the society. And the revival should be done by all collectively.

Finally, roots of any social structure of the society can be traced in its tribal population, races and kith and kins. Until and unless these are thoroughly studied, understood and their human resources are developed, the nation cannot prosper and progress. Original human-beings were tribes. It is the tribes which developed specific customs, skills for making some useable artifacts which laid the foundation of their culture. The tribes have great potentialities. Indian tribes live in hilly tracks and, the tribals like Santhals, Mundas have skills to exploit the hilly resources. Therefore, it is very necessary to develop the tribal human resources for the benefit of the nation.

For the development of human resources, the development of human character, which is an explanatory constituent inferred from habitual or significant action of an individual imbibed in interrelated set of attitudes, is necessary. The character structure develops through experience of the individual. Because of social consequences change in human behaviour takes place. Character formation is influenced by home, family, peer group and by school mates. It is a kind of human resources development. Character may be elevated by social norms as social traits, moral values and sociability observed in the society.

Important aspects of character are (*a*) relatively permanent behavioural configuration, (*b*) good sane habits, (*c*) modes of social defence, and (*d*) morality and sanity.

For all these human resources development in education plays an important role. And the prime foundation of the education, in the present days is the school education. Until and unless the educationists, authorities, parents, the teachers and the community are not fully aware about basic tracts of human resources development neither the individual nor the society can be benefited. Lack of knowledge about all these keeps the society in lurch. First of all the mother who is the prime teacher should be made aware about it. Due to good examination results the examination phobia should also be reduced for human resources development.

3

Education

Education is a process of bringing up or moulding the youngers for living a congenial, homogenic and comfortable social life. Man or woman cannot live alone in isolation. He or she has to live with his fellow beings. All living beings are not sane individuals. Safe and secure living of human-beings can only be possible if the individual knows to adjust with his fellow beings. And for this appropriate bringing up of the youngers is very necessary. This can only be possible through suitable education. So, since times immemorial the man has been bringing up and educating his off-springs for living a sane and comfortable social life. And since times immemorial the educational objectives have been based on this principle. In all ancient civilisations like Mohanjodaro and Vedic civilisations in India, Greek civilisation, Hebrew civilisation, Chinese civilisation in China educating the youngers has ever been a prime social activity. In all civilisations educational aims were framed according to social needs and, education was first started in familial way. Education was imparted in family in which the mother was the prime teacher of the child. Even in Gurukulas in India familial type of education system was followed. All *Shishyas* (students) and *Gurus* (teachers) used to live under the common roof of the Gurukulas. In a sense the Gurukula was a bigger joint family in which balanced parenting was done. And the students were moulded in right form. In other words the Gurukulas were moulding houses of the youngers wherein there was no room neither for too much love nor for too much torturing. The main aim of Gurukula education was to mould the life of youngers. The youngers used to live in alienistic way living away from the parents. Some Gurukulas were named on this principle as Taxila. Taxila means a moulding place. Still in many areas the familial education is in practice. The main aim of education in the tribal areas is to mould the child according to their tribal culture.

Education is recovery. Mere passing of information can never be education. Joetibhai Desai said that "a child can never be taught, he/she can be brought up". So education is a process of bringing out the hidden potentialities of the child. Therefore, for educating the youngers a process should be applied which may innovate and motivate them to think, reason, analyse, comprehend and learn by upsurging and bringing out hidden knowledge. While doing so the teacher should apply innovative teaching methods giving a chance to the students to think and reason, which should be carefully nurtured and passed on to the younger so as enable them to think and prove their sincerity, integrity, devotion and eradication in learning and knowing things. For detailed knowing about knowledge it is necessary to know further.

GENESIS OF EDUCATION

By studying dictionaries and encyclopaedias we come to know the etymology of the word 'education'. The English word 'Education' is a derivation from the Latin word 'Educare', meaning to help in 'coming up' or 'to raise' or 'to dig out', or 'to bring up'. Likewise the Sanskrit word, *'Vidya'* has come out from the Sanskrit word 'Vidh' (विध), meaning raising (उभारना). The word *'Siksha'* has come out from Sanskrit word 'Sikhs' to bring up from within. Also the Arabic word *'Talim'* = Ta+alim which means 'self-learning' from within.

From the above descriptions it can be inferred that education is a process of leading out or bringing out what is already within. But the question arises what is to be brought out and from where it is to be brought out or raised? There are mythological descriptions and interpretations in our Hindu Vedic mythologies and Greek mythologies about the concept of 'education' which also have been repudiated by later empirical thinkers. Aryans believed that human soul is immortal. It does not die when physical body of the person dies. In Hindu Sankhya-Yoga Darshan (सांख्या योगा दर्शन) it is stated that every soul which embodied in a physical person is part of the 'Bigger Soul' which is termed as *'Paramatma'* or a 'Transcendental Being". So, there is duality of soul. One is 'Transcendental soul", that is, *Paramatma* (परमात्मा). Another is *'atma'* (आत्मा) or individual soul which is embodied in every physical persons' body. The 'transcendental soul' or *'Paramatma'* (परमात्मा) is equated with God and is considered 'Immortal'. And every soul or human soul (आत्मा) is also considered 'immortal'. It is believed that every individual soul is part of Bigger Soul, that is *'Paramatma'* or a 'Bigger Whole'. When the body of man or woman gets exhausted and become old, the *atma* (आत्मा) or individual soul leaves the human body and goes to another body. This process is termed as transmigration of the human soul which is called as rebirth (पुर्नजन्म). As such, human soul is immortal.

The *'atma'* or 'soul' which is called (जीवात्मा) while embodied accumulates the experiences gained by it through the sense organs of the body, in which the human soul (जीवात्मा) is embodied. What we remember, what we had experienced and was stored by the soul. According to Greek thinkers the recovery of these accumulated experiences, which had been stored by the soul in the previous embodied life and which are to be further supplemented through experiences, is a process of education. This recovery is done through educating or getting out these experiences through the process of teaching done by the teacher.

It is also believed that the Greeks knew about the immortality of the soul (आत्मा) from Indians. It is, believed, as described by a mythologist, it may be true or a mere hunch or a pure imagination, that during the rule of Greek King Pericles (543 BC), the Spartans used to create troubles for their neighbours, as many countries are still doing in the present days. War ultimately erupted between Greeks and Spartans which continued for 27 years (431-404 BC). This war is known as Pelosenean War. King Pericles made military service compulsion for all able bodied Greeks (between the age of 18 years to 40 years) by imposing emergency through the law of conscription.

Individual differences existed in human-beings always. As such, some Greeks liked to fight, and some did not. Some went to war front willingly. Some did not like it. Those who did not dare to go to warfront tried to escape. There was one Greek Sophist (name not known) who escaped from military duty and fled to Egypt, where he tried to know why people fight each other. Getting no satisfactory reply, he was advised to go Taxila in Bharat (now in Pakistan). From Egypt he went to Iraq (Mesopotamia), from there he came to Taxila Via Aryana (present Iran) and Gandhara (present Afghanistan). Both these countries were Aryan countries and had blood relations with Bharat (India). He stayed at Taxila for about eight years. He studied all Indian theistic philosophical schools—Sankhya-Yoga, Naya-Veshiska, and Vedant-Advit Vedanta, all Hindu scriptures and epics and also aestheistic schools i.e. Buddhism, Jainism and Carvaka, all Upanishads, Arynakas, Brahmas, *Ramayana, Mahabharata* and *Shrimad Bhagavad Gita*. He participated in all Gurukula activities at Taxila and finally he knew that the human soul is immortal as various Indian theistic philosophical adhere to.

According to India, the human soul is immortal, permanent, invisible, indestructible, imperishable and, is part of the permanent soul which is called *'Paramatma'* (परमात्मा). All individual souls (जीवात्मा) are parts of a bigger 'whole' that is *'Paramatma'* or 'God'. Therefore all individual souls are immortal. The 'Prime' or supreme soul is present in all bodies, as such, all human-beings are true representations of God and are equal. This is why the Indian society in spite of rigid caste system, different religions, faiths and cultural patterns, has unity in diversity. Karl Marx has praised the Indian society. The individual's soul or *'Jeevatma'* (जीवात्मा) takes work from the human body. It acquires the experiences through the body sense organs and, accumulates these experiences with it. Bringing out these experiences from the human soul (जीवात्मा) or brain is called 'Education'. As for digging earth some instruments like spade (फावडा) are required, for bringing out human acquired old experiences some methods like telling, teaching, educating and using of teaching aids are required.

The Greek Sophist after staying at Taxila about eight years, and knowing that the human soul is immortal and never dies, this is why Arjuna after listening sermons of *Shrimad Bhagavad Gita* from Lord Krishna fought and won Mahabharat War; the Greek Sophists went back to Greece to participate in Pelosenian War. He went to King Pericles and offered himself to go to the warfront. He told to the King Pericles that 'neither the human soul dies nor destroyed. Only human body dies. Therefore, there is no reason to be afraid of war. With this adoration the Greeks got encouraged. They fought the war against the Spartans. They not only defeated the Spartans but totally eliminated them. And the terror of Spartans was eliminated for ever totally.

This message was picked up by other Greek Sophists and thinkers. They started thinking why individuals' soul (जीवात्मा) or

Jeevatma does not die and is immortal. Socrates (470-399 BC) was an original thinker, speculator and philosopher. He used to think, reason, speculate and discuss all ontological, teleological, epistemological, meta-physical, axiological and sociological problems with his disciples in the street corners. Plato, Crito, Hereclitus, Isocrates, Paremdas and Theatetus were some of his disciples with whom he used to discuss all such important matters. His wife Xentippe did not allow Socrates to permit entry of his disciples or any outsider in his house. If, anybody dared to enter in the house, she used to pour a full pot of cold water over his head. Socrates was very conscious to know about the reality of Indian concept of immortality of the soul (जीवात्मा), so he discussed such ontological question with his disciples in the street corner before his house.

Indians merely said that human soul is immortal. It cannot be destroyed. But no concrete proof about the immortality is available in Indian scriptures. Also, no concrete proof has been advanced by the later seers in this regard. The Greeks were eager to know why the soul (जीवात्मा) does not die along with the human body? Socrates discussed this ontological aspect at length with his disciples and finally come to believe that the human soul is actually immortal. Later on, after the death of Socrates his disciple Plato compiled the dialogues of Socrates with his disciple. These dialogues covered all problems mentioned above relating to truth, beauty, justice, ontology, epistemology, axiology and education. The dialogues, phaedo, meno and republic covered the concept of education. The dialogue 'phaedo' covered immortality of the soul and education to some extent. In dialogue 'phaedo' three proofs have been advanced for the immortality of the soul (1) Law of Contrariness, (2) Law of Form, and (3) Law of Reminiscence which also depicts some light on education.

Law of Contrariness

Everything in this world comes and goes. One who was born and brought up will positively die. Like sun rises in the morning and sets in the evening and, every day is taken by another day, every night is followed by another night. And also all living beings, plants, flora and fauna come and go. The life of a person comes and ought to go. As such, life follows death and death follows life.

There is a continuous circle of coming and going. And this circle always entails contrariness. There is some transcendental element which keeps this coming and going on. It gives life to physical world. This transcendental element is nothing but soul (जीवात्मा) which is part of the omnipresent, non-visible, non-destructible and immortal, that is, 'Bigger Soul' or *Paramatma* or God. The human soul being part of the God or *Paramatma* (परमात्मा) is immortal.

Law of Form

Since everything in the world is temporary, illusionary and perishable, this temporariness has a permanent base or image elsewhere. This idea is analogous to Indian idea of 'Maya' and Stirtha (Permanence). The things or lives which we see in this world are all temporary, illusory and perishable. And a permanent base of these things or lives is elsewhere, which is invisible, permanent, omnipresent and is transcendental. This idea of permanent form is analogous to Indian idea of 'Supreme Soul' (*Paramatma* परमात्मा) or Almighty God which is imbibed in all individuals or living beings as 'souls' (जीवात्माएँ). In other words all individual souls are parts of a bigger whole that is Supreme Soul (*Paramatma* परमात्मा)—the God. The individuals' soul which is part of Almighty God given the human body of which real form is elsewhere.

Law of Reminiscence

We remember many things. How do we remember? What is the power or mechanism that makes us to remember? It is the soul (जीवात्मा). Since the soul does not die, it keeps the gained experiences stored with it. It is due to the enlightenment of the soul we remember all past experiences gained through the body sense organs. The soul which is permanent, imperishable, undestroyable and immortal makes the individual to remember. The process is nothing but remembrance of the past experiences. It is a recovery of knowledge which is already with the soul.

In India Naya-Veshiska Darshan (theistic Indian school of philosophy) a more advance convincing argument is available in this regard. The Naya-Veshiska Darshan argues that we only remember till we are alive. A dead body cannot remember. We remember what we had experienced through our bodily sense organs in the past and, which was stored by our soul. The movement the human body dies, the sense organs of the body, that is, -eyes, ears, touch, taste and smell do not work. Neither the sense of the human body work nor the head remembers. The soul transmigrates to another body. It takes all of its gathered experiences. As the human body grows, the soul activates to remember. Therefore, the human soul is the prime source, believed for remembering, which is the main tool of education. Till the human soul resides in the human body we can see, hear, touch, taste and smell and can remember. When the body dys-functions and ultimately dies, the force governing the body, that is, soul goes with the body's acquired experiences. Taking out these acquired experiences is 'education', which is done through remembering. In dialogue 'Phaedo', the Greek thinkers also had opined that till the soul transmigrates to another body it remains in the Hades, that is, cremation ground (श्मशान भूमि).

Various thinkers have defined 'education' on these lines, though they do not attribute creditability to the soul for all of learning and education. Even Plato did not attribute direct creditability to the soul for the emergence of education. He said that the education is result of sense perception (*per se*) plus comprehension. Sense perception leads to comprehension, learning and education, which occurs due to gaining of knowledge. Aristotle laid stress on the analysis of the matter. Rene Descartes believed in innate ideas and laid stress for thinking, reasoning and analysing for taking out the innate ideas which are possessed by the human body at the time of birth. So, he had laid stress for thinking, reasoning and analysing for education which could be possible by taking out the innate ideas. He believed that he existed because of 'Cogito Ergo Sum', that is thinking, reasoning and analysing. British empiricist philosopher John Locke repudiated the rationalistic theory of innate ideas advanced by René Descartes. He believed that the mind of the child at the time of birth is blank like a 'Tabula Rasa' (a slate). As the child grows, he/she perceives physical things and acquires primary and secondary ideas through perception. As such, John Locke believed that the individual is born without any previous experiences or knowledge. He perceives and gathers knowledge. At the time of birth the child's mind is blank. As such, John Locke's thinking is against the hidden knowledge stored by the human soul. So the teacher while teaching the students should provide sufficient experience sincerely and strictly. And John Locke termed this process as 'hardening' in education. And on this assumption many thinkers like Comenius, Pestalozzi, Froebel and John Dewy etc. etc. advanced varied teaching methodologies. A few quotations of thinkers given on education are given below:

> "Education is to equip the man to understand truth, beauty and goodness". —*Socrates*

> "Education is a training which makes you, "to hate what you ought to hate", and "love what you ought to love". —*Plato*

> "Education is the creation of a sound mind in a sound body". —*Aristotle*

> "What sculpture is to a block of marble, education is to the soul". —*Addition*

> "Education is defined as natural harmonious and development of man's innate powers". *Pestalozzi*

> "Education is defined as process of development which consists passage of human being from infancy to maturity, the process by which he adopts himself gradually in various ways to his physical, social and spiritual environment". —*T. Raymont*

> "Education is the development of capacities which enable man to control his environment." —*John Dewey*

> "Education is to create humbleness of mind." —*Dr. Arnold*

> "Education is to know what one does not know and behave well." —*Johan Ruskin*

> "Education of the child should be according to nature." —*J.J. Rousseau*

"Child's education should be based on play".
—*Madam Montessori*

"Child's feelings should not be hurt. Education should lay stress on emotional development of the child". —*Fredrick Froebel*

"Herbert Read famous art theorist has also exposed the same view on education as advanced by *T. Raymont*".

"Education is manifestation of perfection already in man".
—*Swami Vivekananda*

"By education I mean all round drawing out of the best in child and man, body, mind and spirit. Literacy itself is no education". —*M.K. Gandhi*

"Education is thought that leads to bodily expression".
—*R.N. Tagore*

As such, viewing the above opinions, it can be assumed that education is a process of development of talent or innate potentialities or capabilities enshrined in the child or student. Mere pouring of information or imposing one's acquired knowledge to the students can never be education. Every student or child has his/her innate capacities and capabilities. The development of these capacities and capabilities is education. The child or a student is not an ignorant client. The nature has gifted every child or student with especial unique mental capabilities and capacities. In comparison to other living beings human child or student has been rewarded with bigger brain to think, reason, analyse and comprehend and to take decision for action. He has been rewarded with moving hands for acting and flexible feet for walking. Other living beings—animals, birds, beasts, insects and bees lack all these. The child or student cannot be dictated to accept the diction of the teacher, as a patient accepts the prescription of a doctor or a client of a lawyer accepts the legal advice of the lawyer. Also an ignorant client of cleric accepts his dictum. Therefore, it is essential to educate the child or student in a proper, logical manner and in congenial atmosphere while teaching so as to develop his/her innate capacities.

PANORAMA OF INDIAN EDUCATION

Any phenomenal scape is the embodiment of multiple aspects of a phenomena. In other words a scape is a whole or a combination of various aspects of any phenomenon or a discipline. A phenomenon, be it a social or economical or historical or physical always has a multiple aspects which give it a shape or a form, is called 'scape'. The term 'scape' is usually used for the artistic and architectural activities, done for making a *'landscape'* or a *'seascape'* or a *'nightscape*, or a 'cityscape'. As such, a pictorial presentation in any field of is a 'scape'. But a scape can be found in various disciplines like sociology, economics, theology and education etc. etc., so there is a need to study the scape of any discipline very carefully and then take a suitable action.

Etymology of Scape

As already mentioned an artistic presentation is called a scape. As per Blackie dictionary, the word 'scape' is an adoption of Greek word 'scape' meaning 'a radical stem bearing a fructification', 'a balanced stem', 'a sort form having multiple shapes'. On the basis of this description the artists name the artistic pictorial presentation of a geographical perspective of a piece of land or a geographical track as 'land scape'. On this ground the artistic views of many of geographical or physical scenarios are called as 'landscapes', 'seascapes', 'nightscapes and cityscapes'. When detailed aspects of any other disciplines as sociology, economics, politics, theology or education are presented, these are called scapes of the related disciplines.

Such pictures of geographical tracks or views, called 'land scapes' or 'seascapes' or 'cityscapes' are generally made either on a thick white cartridge paper (72 lbs variety) or on a convese in two dimensions. Such pictorial views are made to show the flora and fauna, hilly tracks, plane tracks, trees and forests, water pools and deserts. These are called land scapes. Such land scapes depict virtual scenarios of three dimensional geographical tracks. So these are mere representations of the reality and are virtual. All real physical things are three dimensional, whereas their two dimensional representations are virtual. All artistic land scapes or sea scapes or city or architectural scapes are always first done through sketching, and therefore these are completed by colouring and composing.

Like artistic scapes made by the artists, many sociologists, economists, theologists, politicians and educationists presented many scapes related to their disciplines. As such, a 'scape' be it a 'landscape', 'seascape', 'nightscape', 'city scape', 'socioscape or educationscape' presents the related aspects of the particular scape always has a wide spectrum. And for dealing the particular discipline there is a need to study the 'scape' or whole aspects of a particular discipline. Then only one can proceed further.

The discipline of education has a wider and varied spectrum as, promotion of other disciplines can only be possible through the knowledge of education. It is a process of life building of the youngers who are our future guardians. So the discipline of education has a wider and varied aspects which make the 'educationscape' more vivid and important. But it is unfortunate that only few educational aspects of 'educationscape' are given due attention, and other important educational aspects are generally ignored. This tendency makes the 'educationscape' a fractured scape.

The Greek Philosopher, Hereclitus said everything is in flux —be it a biological aspect or botanical aspect, or sociological aspect or economical aspect or educational aspect, a drastic change will take place surely in due course of time. As such, the human-beings should be prepared to face such change, so, the youngers should be educated accordingly to face such changes. He/she should be mentally prepared to meet the changes. As such, the education of the youngers should not be restricted to subject teaching-learning only. It should be comprehensive. The education programme should have all life building measures and inculcation of good life habits as 'early to bed early to rise' to speak true, to live a simple life, to develop work habits, to educate the children to respect the elders, fair sex and to love the youngers and animal life. The youngers should be made aware about the national culture and for that they should be enculturated. Any how inculcation of hedonism, Xenophilism and meglomanism should be totally avoided. The children should be advised not to take fried, spicy and junky foods. So education system should be very comprehensive and logical.

The educationscape has been facing such social fluse from the very beginning. In the beginning the resources of human-beings were very limited. The man used to live in bushes in the jungle, and his needs were very limited. The man used to aspire things which were very necessary for his existence. The man is a rational being. The nature has gifted the man with such body faculties—as bigger brain to think, reason and analyse, moving hand to act and do work and fabricate things for human use and, also erect posture to walk see and observe the flora and fauna and natural resources. Besides all these gifts the nature has made the man very greedy and self-centred which adhered the man to exploit the natural resources for his as well as for human benefits. The human beings usually have individual differences, which made the man competitive. So the human beings have ever been trying to exploit the natural resources for their benefits. The human needs have also been increasing which expanded the educational infrastructure. All this multiplied the educationscape continuously from the very beginning. From the inception of the society the man has ever been developing the socio-economic, political and theological scapes which have increased the educationscape too.

With the passage of time the man added many wings to his crown. Many social, economic, and cultural avenues increased. With the development of science and technology many industries were developed which made the man rich. Many social institutions came into being. The man who once was living in bushes in jungles like animals shifted to comfortable houses in villages, towns and cities. And the man became rich and affluent. The affluency entailed many problems. It entailed hedonism, consumerism and xenophilism. All these brought cultural diffusion and acculturation in the human societies which changed the human behaviour topsy-turvy. Earlier the man believed in monotheism and spirituality. Simple living and high thinking were the life mottos of the man. The man used to believe in common good. He used to share the happiness as well as grief with his fellow beings. The present man has become totally topsy-turvy. He has become totally egoistic, self-centred, hedonistic, consumeristic and xenophilic. This has entailed self-centredness, unsociability, immorality and corruption. So the base of education has been widened for individualistic development which has entailed cutthroat competition in education as well as in the society. In olden times the education aimed at life building, base of which common social development. Now, the base of education is solo-development which is entirely based on good examination results and competition. The present educationscape is totally formal. The formal system of education is totally state controlled and is mechanically operated. All students have to walk on the same track in spite of their individual differences. What is missing in Indian education these days is 'human touch' say educationists. The children are neither treated as individuals nor are allowed to become independent thinkers. For good examination results the parents pressurise their wards too much to do more study which spoils their personality. So the children suffer from hyper-tension, and many of them commit suicides, undesirable behaviour, heart ailment and depression are becoming a common feature in the younger generation these days. The parents alone cannot be blamed for this nasty situation. The administration is also responsible for this bad situation. Also some means of affluency in the society is responsible. Some mothers spoil their children. They provide fat and junky foods to their children as a gift of love. Too much of love is poisonous. There should be balanced love. It would provide balanced parenting. The parents should avoid T.V. serials seeing otherwise their children would follow them.

Our Gurukula system of education in Hindus and, Madarsa system of education in Muslims were once considered a source of life building. These were temples of inculcation of good life habits in the youngers. These institutions used to do mental enrichment of the youngers. Now the schools can never be said life building institutions. They only prepare for annual examinations, which usually create tension in the minds of the students. Our present generation is becoming unsocial, immoral, non-diligent, hedonistic and non-cooperative due to the affluency and, present system of education. The present children do not pay due respect even to their parents. This is because there is no place for the inculcation of good life attitudes neither in school education nor in the family. Other elders of the extended families are totally ignored. Our present education is totally examination based. It does not create a sense of human touch in the youngers. The youngers should be prepared to be ideal citizens. The children should be prepared to assert themselves. They must be taught to appreciate beauty. The work habits should be developed in the children at family as well as at school levels.

The present examination system is cruel and killing system. The students cannot be truly assessed by examination. They can be assessed through observation which can be possible through close rapport between the teachers and the students. But can the teacher assess the students in the present examination fever? No, the teacher should be prepared to do the correct objective observation of the students. Then only the students can be relieved of examination pressure. And social milieu can be transformed. They can become ideal citizens. It is, therefore, revamping of the present educationscape is most necessary. For this, reformation of our whole educationscape and its related structure is very necessary. Then only the reformation of our educational structure can be put on right track. For doing the reformation all objectives of education as deciding of all educational aims, teaching and other educational activities as preparation of curriculum, syllabus, curricular, co-curricular and extra-curricular activities, sports, health care habits and respect to elders and love youngers should be given due place in education.

AIMS OF EDUCATION

Genesis of any individual or social activities always lies in the aims which are to be achieved by doing the activities. All human-beings and living beings do some activities aiming something to be achieved. So, aims for the social activities to be done for the common good, are to be decided in advance and, then the activities are to be done. Education is the most important social activity. It has a very wide spectrum of the development of human-beings and the development of sound social infrastructure. So the educational aims are to be decided carefully and rationally according to the social needs. Different societies have different needs so the societies should place their educational aims according to their needs. In the present materialistic hedonistic age the society has no say in framing the education aims. Some selected elite class members and some bureaucrats are assigned the job of deciding the educational aims by the rulers. Our present formal education structure, which is alienistic, is totally examination oriented. And teaching is also done for good examination results. The shining examination results are not total education, it is much more. It is a life building process. So educational aims should be based on life building of the youngers.

Before considering what to teach and, how to teach for educating the students, the teacher should be aware about the versatility of educating process and should be aware about the broader educational aims to be achieved? In other words the teacher should be aware about the aims of education. Educational aims should always be framed keeping in view the national needs. National needs are always determined keeping in view the changing social patterns, social structure and total social phenomena of the society. Greek Philosopher, Hereclitus said that everything is in fluse in every moment, so every society is changing at every moment which needs change in educational pattern of every society. Socio-economic, political patterns and cultural heritage weave the social structure of any society and the state. If the economic conditions of the people of any state are not good and, the people are jobless and poor, the first educational aim of the state should be to relieve the citizens from this tragedy. And educational programme should be job oriented for the younger generation, so that, they may be able to earn their livelihood for saneful living. As a matter of fact every state should try to create the viable conditions for economic development of its citizens. And economic development should be laid on logically honest foundation. Along with training in economic activities the younger generation should be educated in axiology, sociability, morality, adherence to truthfulness, work habits, simplicity and about the national culture considering the varied social needs of the different people, different thinkers have suggested different aims of education. They suggested educational aims:

Aristotle	: "Humble mind"
Neitze	: "Magnanimous mind"
Christ	: "One who enjoys love"
Immanuel Kant	: "No action of which love is not motive can never be virtuous"
Brutus	: "Duty"
Confucius	: "Family"
Bertrand Russell	: "Neither dogmas, nor scepticism but belief"
M.K. Gandhi	: "To create conditions for upbringing"

J. Krishnamoorthy : "Conditions for enculturation and love for nature"

As such, divergent views and opinions have emerged in different societies regarding educational aims. Different societies subscribe to different aims of education according to their social needs and social structure. An economically backward state will always subscribe to educational aims which will help in its economic development. A fundamentalist theocratic orthodox state will make education religious oriented. In many Muslim countries the teaching of religion is compulsory school subject. A secular state like India where so many communities are living together and believe in different faiths will have a secular notion of religion and will not allow teaching of religion in schools. This becomes necessary to maintain unity in diversity. A communist country would like to perpetuate its communist ideology and, the school curriculum will not have any place for religious education. It will try to highlight the economic disparities in the society. A capitalist country would like to adapt 'Laissez Faire' theory for the economic development. As such, their educational aims will be based on competition and democratic ideals. A terrorist state, like sparta as Spartans did in the past, and still a few countries in the present world using terrorism for preparing their citizens for terror. The main agenda of the Spartans education was to educate their youngers in terrorism for usherping the property of others. They fought with Greek for 27 years, 2500 years ago, known as Pelosenean War. There are many terrorist countries who are still using terrorism as a tool to achieve their ends. For that they educate their citizen to be terrorists. A democratic country will always like to mould their would be citizens to be democratic. And these countries always frame the educational aims to strengthen the democratic structure in their countries. As such, if we peep into the historical development of the world, we find that educational aims have always been in a flux from society to society and from state to state or country to country.

Earlier, traditional educational structure was classical in nature and, conservative methods of educational aims as well as process of methods of teachings were used. Man was supposed to be religious and spiritual. He was supposed to read religious scriptures and was required to follow religious codes of conduct.

In India Brahmans were supposed to read Vedas and other religious scriptures like — Upanishads, Arynakas, Brahmans, Shruties, Epics like *Ramayana*, *Mahabharata* and *Shrimad Bhagavad Gita*. They were supposed to educate people about the religious, axiological and social knowledge, in order to make the common people aware about '*Karma*' (कर्मा), *Moksha* (मोक्षा), *Dharma* (धर्म) and '*Adharma*' (अधर्म), so as to make people aware about good '*Karma*', so that sanity may prevail in the society. Likewise, Athenians were asked to learn 'Homer'. The Chinese were asked to study Confucianism to make the family structure strong by respecting the elders. The Christians were asked to read Bible. Also the Muslims were asked to read Quran and Hadis to be sane. The Indians were taught to believe that only good sane actions can give '*moksha*' or deliverance from the material life. As such old Indian education laid great emphasis on simple living, high thinking and on religiosity and spirituality. The *Gurus* always advised the *Shishyas* (students) not to commit *adharma* (अधर्म) (a non-religious action) so that sanity, humanity, truthfulness and cooperation may prevail in the society. The Chinese used to perform many rituals in honour of their past ancestors (पितृ श्रद्धा एवं पूजा). Likewise, in all societies there are some religious codes of conduct for the citizens for maintaining the social harmony in the society. All such codes of conduct were also imbibed in educational aims in all societies for maintaining the social harmony in the society. All such codes of conduct were also imbibed in educational aims in all societies for maintaining social harmony in the society. All old societies had prescribed certain religious codes for their citizens. These codes were included in their educational aims. This was done for maintaining peace and harmony in the society. This has developed an exquisite refined sense of aestheticity, brotherhood and equality in the olden societies. The old societies were not materialistic societies. Greeks were energetic and Chinese were lazy. Generally in olden times the people used to devote their energies to promote art, culture, homogeneity, science and in examining the natural resources, which entailed thinking, reasoning, comprehending, analysing which lead to self-learning. Politics and patriotism offered them a practical outlet of energy. Greeks proceeded very well in this regard. When a Chinese failed to achieve desirable results in this regard, he used to retire and go to hills where he used to write poems on the pleasure of country life.

Chinese education produced stability in the cultural field, as art activities were done more. But in the field of science little progress was done. Perhaps it was due to scepticism. Passionate belief either lead to progress or disaster but not stability. Science when it attacks the traditional beliefs, has its own scientific beliefs and creates an atmosphere of literacy criticism. Same happened to Indians for a longer time, as they stuck to such beliefs that could not lead to progress. They fought each other. With the result they became slaves and remained slaves for thousand years. The religious dogmatism created conditions that other religions converted them to their religion in large numbers. The result was a long chronic national weakness. The megalomaniac beliefs in the upper castes made the Indian society weak and disunited. This is why the foreigners ruled India for such a long time. This happened due to Indian inadequate educational aims. In a pugnacious world energy is very necessary for self-conservation. Utilisation of energy resources cannot be possible without the knowledge of science. So the educational aims should be so framed which could promote science. Without science and mathematics progress is not possible. Also, along with science some important elements of humanities should be taught without which the future guardians will not be able to defend the democracy.

In olden days traditional education was confined to a very small percentage of population, be it Greek, Israel, China or India. With the passage of time the countries felt the need of universal education and adopted new process of education, that is, education for all. Modern Japan has a tendency to make Japan a great nation. So, this motto is the supreme aim of Japanese education. Japanese educational aim is to train the manpower in such a way that it may prove great before all great powers without sacrificing their own culture. Therefore, the Japanese education could produce a devoted, sincere, active and religious workforce, which could adhere to their Shinto religion. And due to this fact Japanese could emerge as one of most powerful industrialised nation in the world out of the debris of Hiroshima and Nagasaki. The Japanese could explicit a national character.

Western empiricist countries tried to erode the cultures, cottage industries, trade, religions and social structures of many Eastern Asian countries and African countries for their own industrialisation. They tried to westernise these nations through cultural diffusion and acculturation, which they materialized and achieved through imposing their own formal system of education. As such, mostly all East Asians and Africans were accultured through the process of alienistic formal education. Because of this these countries lost their social customs, traditions, cultural traits and educational structures to some extent. India became an acute prey of this acculturation feature. China resisted the penetration of western culture for a long time. Finally, the Chinese were also affected by cultural diffusion, but they could protect their cultural heritage by and large. So China could emerge as a big nation.

There are many organisations in many societies which still function as pioneers of dogmas and outdated beliefs. These organisations do not come out of the net of dogmatism. Their dogmatic beliefs do not permit them to move forward, progress and become human. These dogmatic societies do not accept the modern realistic educational aims. So such societies remain culturally and economically backward and do not progress. These societies do not realise the bases of socio-economic development and do not progress. Due to the dogmatic beliefs they do not hesitate to harm others.

So the educational aims in all societies are framed according to the needs of the societies. A nation having democratic form of Government would like its all citizens to be purely democratic and humanistic. The educational institutions, by applying democratic norms, as having elected student bodies, try to achieve this educational democratic aims. A society having a speculative bent of mind will always allow free expression and free democratic discussions. And educational institutions in such a society also follow the same pattern. All this lay the foundation of a democratic ideal society. And democratic ideals become the core of educational aims. Such societies will be ideal societies and, their educational structures and processes will be ideal ones because of idealistic social aims. Hegel, Neitze and Swami Vivekananda were the profounder of such educational aims and related educational structure. Nations having Communist Governments—which are generally one party Governments, always would like to prepare the obedient citizens who could not disagree with the Government policies. Such Governments lay down such educational aims which suit to the communist system. Countries where exist capitalist economy would like their future citizens competitive and acquisitive. In such a situation axiological aims go to the background. There remains a wide divergence between people — some are very rich and some are very poor. So, such Governments always adopt a pragmatic approach while laying down educational aims and, design their educational structure accordingly. As such, educational aims are always decided according to particular socio-economic needs and related social structures.

In the present age of industrialisation of which science and technology are prime instruments, the educational aims give preference to teaching of science and technology. And the school is the temple of learning where the students are taught these subjects and are prepared to participate in the process of industrialisation. The teacher is the beacon light for achieving this educational aim. He is an instrument for bringing scientific technological change. A nation cannot prosper if its future guardians are not properly educated. If we look to the nature of a man and woman, ontologically and biologically we find that they are well-equipped by nature of exploit the natural resources for their benefits. The drawback of the man/woman is that, he/she has maximum animal nature in spite of his/her being a rational being. So the educational aims should be so framed that the greedy nature of the human-beings may be controlled. The man should be educated to follow rationality first and then become competent to earn his livelihood honestly, and earnestly confirm himself/herself to sociological norms, so as to keep his greedy nature under control.

It is true that every nation tries to improve its economic conditions for the betterment of its citizens. But such a development should entail some moral values and norms which may carry on a logically honest foundation of just economic development. So, along with training in economic activities the youngers should be educated in social ethics. The future guardians should be made fully aware about the corruption and truthfulness. The educational aims should give prime importance to this fact.

In olden times, the joint family was the epicentre of true education and enculturation through which the life building of the youngers was done. The elderly men, women and grand parents used to make the younger aware about this menace of corruption telling them about *'Sukarma'* (सुकर्मा), *'Dharma'* (धर्म), *'Adharma'* (अधर्म), *'Netikta'* (नैतिकता), *'Anetikta'* (अनैतिकता). This was done by telling the youngers stories of Jatkas. These teachings are more or less absent in the present society, because of dys-functioning of joint family system and disappearance of sound community life. The nuclear family system has dragged the joint family system in dustbin. The present period of over ridden with materialistic activitism. Both the parents generally remain busy in the rat-race of money-earning leaving their kids at the mercy of crèches and day care schools. The grand parents also live separately. As such, the parents expect the schools to discharge their parental duties which is not possible because the educational aims of the schools are to prepare the students for annual examinations.

All this is due to cultural diffusion and acculturation which has made the people very greedy and acquisitive. Now the members of the society have become totally greedy, acquisitive, consumeristic, hedonistic, self-centred and corrupt. And all this happened due to the virus of acculturation. There are individual differences. Sometimes, climatic and geographical conditions make man greedy and acquisitive. This is why, there is a cultural variation in human societies. Many people of various societies are very greedy. Some are not. When these people interact there happens cultural diffusion which takes the form of acculturation. East Asian and African countries became the victims of acculturation which took place due to cultural diffusion between their culture and Western culture. But this is also true when the people of a country loose their culture they loose everything. So this is very necessary that the younger generation should be made aware about the national culture. This cannot be done by the parents, as mostly the parents have become hedonistic, xenophilic and consumeristic. They also make their children hedonistic, consumeristic and xenophilic by providing them junky fast foods and fashionable wears. Simple living and high thinking is no more in the society. Also, according to Greek Philosopher, Hereclitus, change is inevitable. One phase of change is over. Now, the other phase of change should also take place. And the responsibility falls on the shoulders of teachers of the school. So, the educational aims should be so framed that the younger generation may be made aware about national culture. For this it is necessary to inculcate viable values in the youngers. They should be made aware about axiology, for generating morality, sociability, truthfulness, punctuality, cooperation, respect for elders and love for the youngers. But it is very difficult job for the school teachers, as the present alienistic formal system of education is badly examination oriented. There is no provision of religious discourses or religious teachings in schools due to secularism. Job avenues need teaching of science and mathematics. Only very few students take philosophy, sociology. There is no provision of teaching philosophy and sociology in schools at secondary level. These two disciplines can give knowledge of morality and sociability to the students and, make them homogenous and moral and, also spiritual. These may help the future guardians to become honest citizens in their future life. They will also know the importance of society and saneful social living. Also if the society provides healthy social atmosphere then the citizens may be safe. Therefore, it is necessary to root out the tendency of personal greed, corruption, and unsociability from the society. For this end the educational system should be viable which could stop acculturation.

Everybody is a social human being. He/she has to live in the society. Even the beasts, animals, birds, insects and bees from their societies and, maintain these. An individual is part of a big whole, that is, the society. A part of a big whole cannot function alone. As the parts of a biological whole function. Only the bigger whole makes the functioning of the parts possible. As without soul the human body becomes redundant and dead, an individual if does not go along the social whole, that is, society, he/she is isolated and becomes redundant and dys-functioning, an unwanted person in the society. Therefore, the education should be aimed to make the youngers aware about the social whole, that is, society. Such an august educational aim cannot be achieved by the teacher alone. All social and educational agencies should strive for it.

While framing the educational aims one should fully know about complete social perspectives of the society. What type of men/women the society really needs. Does it need greedy and acquisitive persons, who only run after money and believe in exploitation of others. Or does the society requires just, rational, moral, social, spiritual, sharing, cooperative individuals who will never ride over the needs of others? For the evolution of correctly honest, social, cooperative atmosphere, renouncing and self-conscious persons who could visualise and understand the different social structures as—the capitalist, socialist, feudalistic, communistic, socialistic, terroristic, secularistic and theocratic and arrive at a decision to know which is best. And suitable educational aims should be framed accordingly for the education of the youngers of the country. We should elicit lessons from the past and present happenings. And how the educational system was affected in the past and how it can be affected now? And how our social fabric may be affected by a system of education. Keeping all these perspectives in view we should think of framing the educational aims, which could help us to restore our culture and, can boost us for future progress and economic development for preserving our national identity. No matter, if need be, our present educational structure be drastically changed to achieve our desired national goals.

One of the prime aim of education should be the personal, social, economic and economic development of the individuals. Personal development should be so that a person should treat the society as his/her mother. And this aim demands education for cohesion, fraternity, sociability, morality, truthfulness and cooperation. This will help in building a strong cooperative society. A corrupt and greedy person can never be useful for the society. The present alienistic formal system is so badly examination oriented that is affecting the parenting of the youngers. Every mother generally pressurises her child/children to read more and more. They evade even inculcating good life attitude in their children. As such, the development of the youngers demands the national aims. A few of these are given below:

- To instill a spirit of self-introspection. A person should know what is good or bad for him/her in tune of social integrity, national cause. The person should realise about herself/himself about good or bad. Also the individual should know about reality.
- To instill social acceptability. For this, a set of some personal values, character, moral attitudes, spirit of honesty and integrity desire for active participation in social affairs in the country for common cause, social participation, spiritual awareness, respect for elders and women, urge to help the weak animal, birds and finally to ward off egoism, self-centredness, corruption and megalomaniasm.
- Aims of education should not be limited up to teaching subjects. The students should be made aware about political system and political awareness. They should also be made aware about political requirements. The political

corruption engulfs the whole society and it badly affects the lower strata of the society.

- Though our country is secular, but we witness a number of communal riots in the society. Many of our politicians play communal games in politics covertly. Our education should also aim at inculcating religious tolerance, cooperation and religious harmony and tolerance.
- An individual is not only a physical being or an object which has only a form. He/she is a conscious being. A conscious being requires some concepts and ideas, through which human experience is properly set for sane use.
- Our education should be aimed at for the development intenshionatity and capacity in a person to generalise things.
- The educational aims should inculcate a spirit of tolerance, sharing, cooperation and commitment to the common causes and goods by adhering to social values and social welfare.
- The educational aims should be so designed that the students may be enculturated through educational process. It should discourge acculturation through cultural diffusion.
- The education should at preparing the students for saneful future living.
- The educational aims should also try to create an aesthetic sense in the students by inculcating creative spirit in the students, so that, the future guardians may become inventors in future. A creative man always remains generous and kind. For achieving this end, there should be sufficient provision for creative work.
- The teacher can contribute a lot but not alone. There should be sufficient arrangement for co-curricular, extra curricular activities as games and sports and social service programmes. The students better learn through perception. The co-curricular activities should be given equal weightage with curricular activities. The co-curricular activities should cover creative cultural programmes relating to all social aspects of the national culture, social living and social cohesion. In addition to the co-curricular activities the students should be given a chance to go on picnics, educational tours and excursions.

SOCIO-ECONOMIC, CULTURAL ROOTS OF EDUCATION

All living beings — animal, birds, insects, beasts, bees and human-beings come to this world for a limited short period. All are mortal. Their souls (जीवात्मायें) being parts of Almighty God are immortal and permanent. Human souls gain experience through body sense organs and take these experiences while the souls leave the bodies. And taking out or, educating these is called 'education'. All living beings are born due to 'unity in bio-diversity'. This unity takes place when a male and a female are united together through the institution of marriage. The male and female unite and, give births to the future guardians, that is youngers. They bring them up and try to prepare them to live a sane happy life. For this, social homogeneity and self-sufficiency are very necessary. Though one who is born will have to die surely. The parents should prepare their offsrpings to live a happy, homogenous and sane social life.

Because of rational and greedy nature a human-beings, neither one can live alone, nor can live in limited or restricted 'unity in bio-diversity', i.e., husband and wife (married life). It is, therefore, very necessary for all human beings to live together a collective homogenous and saneful social life with his or her fellow beings. It is necessary for his/her safety and security. The society is a collectivity or a whole of different human-beings who are members of the society. Human-beings are biological wholes. In a biological whole all body parts are so composed and integrated that the parts are bound together to exist till the human body is alive. This union of the body parts makes the existence of the human body possible. The social whole or the society is not like a biological whole in of which all body parts are bound together. All members of the society have to reciprocate with his or her fellow beings. This reciprocity gives strength to the members of the society. It is necessary to control the greedy nature of the men or women. All members of the society have different psyche. Many of them are self-centred and greedy. Many are rational beings who take care of weak and poor. Such rational individuals try to protect all. So they have laid down certain social behavioural conducts and rules of conduct and character. All should speak true. All should be social and moral. All should cooperate with each and share happiness and grief of all social beings. For all these activities, some activities are done. And carrying out such activities, some social traditions, social traits, specific behavioural norms for the citizens are developed. The individuals become creative. They try to create and invent new things. Art and craft are developed. Some folk art are also developed. All these activities give a form to national culture. And citizens should follow the culture sincerely and faithfully. Specific social religiousity and spirituality also help in the development of the culture of a nation. The society as a whole and *its collectivity* helps in such activities. Such activities are necessary to control the individualistic psyche of the members of the society.

Above all, for doing all these activities and, for covering the life journey, the survival of an individual is most essential. For survival an individual needs food, clothes and shelter. In the childhood all these needs are met by the parents of the child. But when a child becomes adult he or she will have to earn for his/her sustinance and survival. So, earning for livelihood is one of the most important essential human activity. Therefore, an individual should be made to earn for his/her livelihood. An earning man/woman can only be self-supporting. As such, a young should be prepared to be self-supporting. So the roots of human education lie in the socio-economic and cultural scapes of the society. And an individual should be educated to meet his/her socio-economic and cultural needs, and educational structure should be prepared for these important educational needs.

Education of the youngers should be based on the socio-economic and cultural bases of the society. And it should start from their childhood. The parents must be fully aware about these socio-economic and cultural bases. Especially the mother who gives birth to a child, brings him/her up and inculcate life attitudes in the children, should be educated about these important life roles by the elderly ladies at her parental home. Earlier the elder members of the joint family used to do this auspicious job. But now due to hedonism the joint families have been totally crumbled and nuclear families have come into existence. The elders have no role to play for inculcation of good life habits and enculturation. Either the grand parents are forced to live separately or they themselves live separately from their son or sons and daughter-in-laws. It is seen that elders are generally disregarded. The young members of the extended families do not give any respect to their familial elders. In nuclear families both the husband and wife generally do jobs to meet their hedonistic needs. They have their younger children at the mercy of crèches or day care schools. Such institutions are becoming hob-nob of commercialisation of education. As such, life building procedure is totally missing in our familial education which was earlier the main foundation of education.

Life building was the prime aim of Indian old Gurukula education, as well as, Madarsa education. The students were taught religiously, spirituality and sociability. The main base of Indian old education was enculturation of good sane life attitudes and habits. Too much of love is poisonous. Generally, many mothers shower too much love on their children. This is very dangerous. To avoid this familial alienation is necessary. So to avoid too much love and affection the youngers were sent to the Gurukulas which were far off from the students' homes. These were situated on river banks in jungles. At Gurukulas the students were served simple food. They were required to go to the bed early and rise early in the morning. After rising, they used to go to the jungle for natural calls. They used to take bath in the moving regularly. After this they were required to attend common yoga and meditation classes. And after this they used to attend the common *'yajna'* and *'sandhya'*. After this *'Shishyas'* used to take refreshment. After this the students used to sit under a tree with the *Guru* who used to teach them religion, spirituality and socio-economic and cultural requirements. The teaching was done through verbal communication by the *Guru*. But it was not solo or one way communication. The teaching used to follow a free discussion (वाद विवाद) between the *Guru* (the teacher) and the *Shishyas* (the students). Like this, the education in Muslim Madarsas was totally based on life building. The students were taught religiosity, spirituality and axiology. These Madarsas were totally secular in the past. As such, the old Indian education was totally based on life building of the younger.

Change is inevitable. The old pattern of Indian education has also changed from religiosity and spirituality to consumerism and hedonism. This happened due to extreme acculturation of the Indians. Our present system of formal education aims at material gains. All students are taught in uniformal way. They are prepared to achieve the material gains in their lives. There is no place of religiousity, spirituality and axiology in our present educational system. Our present education is purely examination oriented. Examination system eludes spirituality and axiology. It is only aimed at material gains. And such materialistic education is taught in mechanical way. Material gains should also entail axiological social gains. Affluency in the society has also changed our educationscape. The mothers, mostly provide junky and fast foods to their children. Both the parents lay stress on good examination results and force their children to read and read. They are ammune to socio-economic and cultural needs of the society. In the family atmosphere inculcation of good social habits is totally missing. Generally parents see TV serials up to late hours in the night. Their children also follow them and go to bed very late and rise very late in the morning. Monotheistic spirituality is missing from the families. Generally people become polytheistic and henotheistic for attaining material gains. And they arrange *kirtans* and *bhojs* (lungers) for gaining material benefits. As such, our socio-economic and cultural panorama of the society has totally changed. Caste system has been changed into class system as many castes have been sanskritized. In such a situation there is an urgent need to examine our educationscape and to reform it.

For the improvement of any system or structure for any social activity, it is necessary to examine the working of existing system in detail. This should be done keeping in view the contemporary requirements. And then find out the merits and demerits of the existing system. For doing so it is also necessary to examine the old system or structure, if there was any in the past, and compare it with the existing system or structure. It would not be correct to assume that our old system of Gurukula education had no demerits. Denial of entry to the two casts — Vaishyas and Sudras and to women even some of two upper castes—Brahmans and Kshatriyas was one of the major demerit of Indian Gurukula system of education. Whereas, life building through inculcation of good viable life attitudes, moulding their lives to sociability, morality, homogeneity, which were key for the personality development and character development of the *Shishyas*. The products of the Gurukulas were supposed to devote their whole lives for the social homogeneity and harmony. They used to do this through religious discourses given to the social milieu. They used to tell the people to be religious, spiritual and honest. So people used to be honest and sincere to the society. In spite of rigid caste system, the products of the Gurukulas used to devote their whole lives for the social development.

The present formal system of education is lacking all these social objectives. It generally creates an elite class which always becomes maglomaniac. They always think of their benefits. If any one is highly educated, he always tries to lead an alienistic life. It is also seen that some times such persons avoid deep mixing with their kith and kins such persons generally talk or keep closer contacts with the persons of their calibre. Such condition was not found in Gurukula products. Also the present system of formal education does not encourage the hereditary vacations. The non-formal system of education has been totally wiped out. As such majority of the highly skilled artisan class people are becoming sanskritised. The caste bias may be one of the reason of sanskritisation. All of the lower castes want to adopt white collar jobs. These are demerits of the present formal system of education. The present system of formal education has also merits, all people irrespective of caste are entitled for formal education. There is no gender bias. But demerits are more. It kills work culture. It has no place for work and enculturation. Rather it promotes acculturation and commercialisation. As such the present system of formal education has more demerits than merits. One of the most merit is that it is based on equality. And there is no gender bias. It, therefore is necessary to reform the present system of education keeping in view the socio-economic and cultural needs.

EDUCATIONAL *MODUS-OPERANDI*

Any kind of activity, be it social, economic, political, axiological or educational needs a *'modus operandi'* or a working process of achieving the desired ends in any field of action and, some measures are to be adopted for it. The word *modus* is a derivation of French and Latin words, 'modulus' meaning a 'measure' or 'action to be taken' to achieve the desired ends by doing some activity. The word *'operandi'* is also a derivation of Latin word 'opera' meaning an operation or action to be taken for a work to be done. All socio-economic activities which are to be done by the public organisations or Government organisations for the betterment of masses have some *'modus operandi'* having some ends in view overtly or covertly. So all sorts of educational processes have some *'modus operandi'* to be applied to achieve the desired ends.

Educational processes are: (*i*) Familial education, (*ii*) Informal education, (*iii*) Non-formal education, and (*iv*) Formal education.

(*i*) *Familial education* has no pre-conceived form of education to be achieved, but has a '*modus operandi*' for the life development of the child. The child is born and brought up in a family. The parents and all other family members take due necessary care to bring up the child. The child also observes his/her parents and family members from the first day of his/her birth. He/she continuously observes his/her mother, grandmother and other family members and learns a lot from them. There is no imposition of tough rules over the child. There is a shower of all kinds of love. And the child learns through his/her perception (*per se*). His/her emotions are built up in the family. The child becomes passionate. Passion though is a bad regulator but through familial education it is changed into a powerful spring. It is the family background which makes a man/woman a sane person. The child from the very beginning continuously observes his/her elders doing some work. And in due course of time he or she grows and imitate the elders and learns to do some work and learns in informal way.

(*ii*) *Informal Education:* Informal way is a process of education in which no pre-conceived aim is fixed. But the youngers follow the already existent form of life — as how to live, whether a simple life or hedonistic life, to follow life patterns of the elders, as simple living and high thinking, early to bed early to rise, to take care of health by following health care habits, to be religious and spiritual and to follow sane life living habits. Since it was feared that the parents and elders shower too much love on the youngers, the youngers after attaining the adolescence age were used to be sent to Gurukulas, where they used to learn many living styles in formal way. Also the youngers used to learn a lot in informal way from the community elders as sociability, morality, cooperation, dedication to ethnicity and community. Now due to killing acculturation which has risen the human greedy nature to the extreme, all members of the society are in rat-race of money earning. Even wife and husband both do jobs. Joint-family system has been totally crumbled. Mostly all people live in nuclear families. They do not maintain any relationship and reciprocity with their parents and family elders. They have become totally consumeristic and hedonistic and, believe in living a happy single life, the way of informal education has also been fractured. The informal education remain only limited to taking to fast and junky foods. No desirable social norms are inculcated in the youngers.

(*iii*) *Non-formal Education*: Everybody is bound to earn for his livelihood. For that the youngers are bound to learn to do some work. India is a caste based society. All castes follow different vocations. As a matter of fact Indian social stratification is hierarchical. Every body is supposed to follow his hereditary occupation.

The roots of the caste based Indian social stratification lies in 'Varna system' which was the product of Rishi Manu's mind. Rishi Manu wanted to see the Indian society well-integrated, homogenous and competent to face all socio-economic and cultural situations. As such, Rishi Manu had visualised a logical social stratification on the pattern of homogenic human biological whole in which all body parts functions in harmony with each other, as in human body some body parts like head, heart, lungs, liver, kidneys, pancreas work in harmony and keep the body alive. So, he visualised a social stratification like human biological whole. He thought a social stratification on the pattern of (*i*) human head, (*ii*) human torso, (*iii*) human legs, and (iv) human feet. He named, this kind of social stratification as 'Varna system'. The members of the society who were supposed to be epistemic and able to do mental work earnestly and to proficiate in the field of knowledge were designated Brahmans on the pattern of human head. The Brahmans were supposed to follow the professional ethics, which entails (*a*) to be epistemic and add to his knowledge, (*b*) to be sincere to the whole society, and (*c*) to be non-inclinative. (*i*) The Brahmans were supposed to study the Indian Vedic Scripture like, all four *Vedas*, all 122 *Upanishads*, all Shruties, Epics and *Shrimad Bhagavad Gita* and make the masses aware about the religiosity, spirituality and sociability. As such, the Brahmans were supposed to live a very simple life of austerity. They were not supposed to be greedy at all. As such, the Brahmans were supposed to be the torchbearers of the whole society and a noble 'Varna'. (*ii*) Next to Brahmans were those who supposed to protect the members of the society. They called 'Kshatriyas'. They were equated with the 'torso' of the human body. They were supposed to rule the nation and manage the rule of law. They were supposed to manage the human affairs and give justice to all people. (*iii*) Those who supposed to look after the economic needs of the general public were supposed to do agriculture work for producing cereals, cater animals for producing milk products and do business were called 'Vaishyas'. They were equated with the human legs. All three Varnas were termed 'divijas' that is twice born. And finally (*iv*) who used to serve all the three divijas that is—(*a*) Brahmans, (*b*) Khastriyas and (*c*) Vaishyas were put on the lowest ebb of the society and were called 'Sudras'. The Sudras were equated with human 'feet'. All the four Varnas were supposed to do their duties very sincerely. But the individual differences always take place. The Varna system was purely ability based. It was not birth based. The persons who had capacity to exhibit their epistemic capabilities were allowed upward 'Varna-mobility', it is believed, Maharishi Balmiki is one of the example. With the passage of time the Varna system ability based social stratification, which was established by Rishi Manu and, was developed for establishing a sane social stratification was crippled by greedy upper Varnas during the *Mahabharata* period. Many Rishis also did so for benefiting their off-springs. Maharishi Vyas who had survived for 157 years and had seen his seven generations; it is assumed had contributed to the perpetuation the birth based caste system. As such, Varna system was totally crumbled and was changed to birth based thousand years back.

The birth based caste system entailed caste based vocations. A caste had to follow a particular hereditary vocation which was followed by its ancestors. An off-spring of the Brahman was supposed to learn Sanskrit and read *Vedas* and other Vedic scriptures. A son of a Rajput Kshatriya was supposed to learn how to use arms. Likewise a son of a Vaishya used to follow the occupation of his parents. A son of a carpenter or a blacksmith would have to learn his family occupation. And for this the youngers were trained non-formally in their family occupations.

Non-Formal Education

Non-formal education is a system of education which does not require a stipulated curriculum or a trained teacher. A younger of an artisan family or other service class like barber or waterman will have to follow his family hereditary vocation or occupation. For learning his family vocation he would have to work with his elders while they were doing their family vocation. A son of a carpenter or blacksmith or tinsmith or coppersmith and also the son of a barber or waterman would have to work with his elders while they were doing their family vocation. The younger was not required to attend a formal vocational course in a technical institute. The parents of the young and the Government were not required to spend money on the vocational training. During the vocational training the youngers used to remain in their home. They used to have a wide spectrum of learning. They had to visualise a lot of raw-materials. They used to see the elders doing complicated fabrications and acquire skills. As such, the youngers used to be highly skilled artisans, expert in doing complicated fabrications. They were not required to knock the doors of the employment exchanges. They used to get regular employment in the society.

The Indian non-formal system of education became prominent due to hereditary caste structures and became famous in the world. When the East India Company British Government was planning to impose British type of formal education on Indians in 1832 A.D., the then Go/erner, British Government of erstwhile undivided Punjab had strongly opposed the imposition of formal education on Indians. He had argued that this would kill the Indian culture and work culture. He had emphasised the retention of non-formal education which according to him was best in the world. However, the formal education was imposed on Indians which has also rooted out the non-formal education. The concept of purity and pollution adopted by higher castes and consequent degradation of artisan castes, forced the artisan castes to adopt formal education, discard the non-formal education and adopt sanskritisation.

Formal Education

Etymologically, the meaning of the word 'Formal education' is giving a form or shape to education according to the desired and prescribed social norms by the society or by the state. The word 'form' is a derivation of the French word 'forma' meaning a 'shape', 'extreme appearance of a body or structure', 'a phenomenon', 'to give a shape or to mould' and 'to do make up'. It can be said that, 'formal education' is a process of providing a shape to an educational structure of a country as per needs of the society and the rulers of the country for achieving the desired socio-economic, cultural and political ends. According to Platonic conception education is a self-discovery or upliftment of hidden potentialities of a man/woman and, thereby enrichment of knowledge, truth, beauty and goodness. According to Emile Durkheim it is an influence exercised by the adults and, as a result of it, arising out certain physical, mental, intellectual and moral states of mind which are necessary for a sane society. Max Weber says that society is an area of competition, conflicts and struggles and education prepares the man/woman to combat all these. Karl Marx thought that education is the only possible measure through which social upbringing is possible, through the development of social institutions. Other sociologists considered education as a process of social up-bringing. These views of modern sociologists and educationists are, more or less, matching with the convictions of the *Gurus* (teachers) of old Gurukulas. They said that the education is a way to prepare the child to live in the society according to some sane social norms. The functionalists consider education as a caretaker and dispenser of cultural resources of the society. The culture can be revised, raised and enriched through formal education.

The main aim of the present form of formal education is to equip the youngsters with the knowledge of 3Rs which are considered necessary for socialisation, social control and for seeking employment. And formal education is expected to achieve these ends systematically and explicitly. The joint families and community were doing and accomplishing these social aims in a differentiated manner before the society become complex. Due to the slippage of educational and cultural functions of primary educational agencies like family and community and, also due to the emergence of machine age the institution of school came into existence and the formal education came into being. Before the industrialisation, the education was transmitted to the youngers by the social institutions like family and community in informal and non-formal familial ways of educating, as mentioned earlier. As a matter of fact the child starts learning, through informal and non-formal ways, from the parents, family elders and community members. Skills acquired through these educational process are permanent and continue life long. Also, through informal and non-formal education, the youngers get some knowledge they can get from family members.

If we further peep into and, look to its perceptivity we find that word 'formality' has emerged out of the word 'Form', means an action, that has been done for a mere obligation, having no intense desire to do for a viable good result. Likewise, the 'Formal Education' which being imparted in schools entails a kind of formality which is done as a mere obligation to ward off the responsibility of imparting 3 Rs to the young generation. It does not entail any life building aim of making the youngers aware about sociability, morality, dedication, diligence and developing traits of character building. In formal education the prime importance is given to the study of subjects for the preparation of annual examination, as formal education is entirely examination oriented. Whereas, the non-formal education imparted by family members and informal education transmitted by the peer group extents these qualities because of instinctive character of these.

Rise of Formal Education

Years ago, Augusta Comte said that 'old society is dying and new society is emerging'. Before this utterance the education was imparted in informal way through familial methods of education. In many pre-literate tribal societies, an age group used to undergo and, still in many tribal areas youths undergo tuitions in religious teachings and practices through symbolism under the care of a specially selected adult who had/has proficiency in henotheistic or polytheistic religious practices. Likewise the youths used to acquire skills in many activities from their parents and elders in non-formal way. Also, for acquiring or learning skilled activities, different from their parental activities, the youth used to acquire proficiency either from skilled persons or through the craft guilds in non-formal way.

As already mentioned, in India Gurukula Asharmas situated on the river banks were considered temples of familial type of informal education and a bit of formal learning. The main aim of Gurukula Asharma education was life building of the youth. Since in homes the parents used to shower too much love, to send the youngers to Gurukula was considered good for inculcating good social values in the youngers. They used to develop good life habits as—early to bed early to rise, simple living and high thinking, to adopt good life health habits by doing yoga, to be religious and spiritual and to live a saneful social life.

First step towards formal education was going for apprenticeship in craft guilds in Western European countries. The learners used to live in the craft guilds with guild masters or journeymen. Due to the development of science and technology machines were invented which entailed industrial development first in England and later on in other countries of Europe required proficient person in different industrial areas. It also required skilled tradesmen. All this required some sort of educational structure which could train such workforce. So the schools for educating the workforce were established where elementary education was imparted and knowledge of 3 Rs was given. Initially such schools were established by the businessmen and industrialists for educating their own children and also the youngers who could be employed in their own industries. Later on, there arose a need for vocational schools, common schools and basic schools which were later on called grammar schools. All these schools were run to give a 'form' to the youngers.

In olden times, the academies like Platonic Academy in Greece, Vidyapeeths in India for higher learning Taxila, Nalanda, Ujjaini etc. etc. existed, where some sort of formal education was imparted. As such, some sort of formal education was imparted in India, Greece, China and at some places in Europe also. Also some sort of extra-schools like Padha (पाधा) schools in India were teaching Mundi Hendi. Madarsas in Muslim community used to teach Islam religion, teaching about 'Holy Quran' and 'Hadis' to youngers to make them sane and humane. Also in Christian societies the Holy Bible and 3Rs were taught. The full development of formal educational set up came into being, rather boosted after the development of writing. In the beginning, first of all it was a monopoly of priestly class, upper classes and upper castes. The priests promoted the diversified schools for their children. The lower castes and classes were not having opportunity to send their children in such schools established by priests and rich classes. In Greece, the society was stratified in four categories—the nobles, warriors, philosopher/teachers and artisans. The nobles and warrior were considered superiors to other two classes, as in India the society was stratified in four Varnas and, Brahmans and

Kshatriyas were considered superior Varnas and still are considered better in the Indian society. The other castes—Vaishyas and Sudras were degraded. In Greece the artisan castes met the same fate. In Europe the society was stratified in feudalistic manner which was based on exploitation of the poor by the rich. So, in Europe the feudal class enjoyed the fruits of formal education ignoring the poor serfs.

In pre-industrial days the schools were widespread in China and, in less elaborated form in India, which were called *Pathshalas* and, in many parts of the Islamic world. The Western world was not having such elaborated schools. The reason might be climatic conditions there. So the formal education came into being there after industrialisation and of their trade expansion in eastern Asian countries. There are evidences that even in primitive societies, where some work techniques existed, that there existed schools for educating the people for maintaining the records and chronicles for correspondence. This helped these societies to enculturate the youngers.

Initiative first came from the craftsmen for the development of formal education and development of schools for learning 3Rs for keeping accounts, preparing useful orthographic illustrations and for preparing catalogues and booklets for widening the scope of their craft business. After the industrial revolutions many of these crafts enlarged their establishments and took the shape of industrial units. And in due course of time they felt more need of skilled trained workers. And they established schools for imparting education formally. First of all, such schools were established and run by private organisations or establishments. These organisations prepared a *'modus operandi'* — such as, curriculum, for imparting education formally in these schools matching their requirements for the industries. When the number of such schools increased the state extended its control over these schools. As such, the state exercised its power to influence the implementation of formal education. The state also influenced the industrial units to chalk out the school curriculum for formal education as directed by the state. And bit by bit the state control over the schools increased. and the schools totally followed the state directions and became the units of the state.

Theoretically the educational institutions like schools, industrial schools, polytechnics, engineering colleges and universities should never be under the state control. These should have autonomous character and should be under the scanner of the society. "When one once in power always wants to be in power" is an old adage. So the rulers want to adopt such measures which keep them in power for ever. So the rulers always try to impose their will on the educational infrastructure too. They always try to implement their agenda through the educational system. This situation applies to all types of ruling infrastructures, be it democracy or aristocracy or monarchy or theocracy. A democratic state would like to have an educational infrastructure which may promote democracy. An autocratic state would like to have an autocratic system of education. A theocratic state would like to have religion as a compulsory subject in education and that too, the religion of the rulers. Many aristocratic countries do not allow the girls to attend the schools. A monarchy would like to prepare the obedient citizen. In such a situation the schools and educational institutions functioning is controlled by the rulers who always tries to impose their will through the imposition of textbooks etc. This trend always hinders the logical epistemological development of the youngers. Their individual development is marred or restricted. All this restrict the common necessities like enculturation and inculcation of sociability, morality, sociability, truthfulness, development of character in the youths in the society. All these can be developed through arranging co-curricular activities, extra-curricular activities along with the co-curricular activities in the school since the formal education is examination oriented, this does not happen under the new scheme of formal education.

In the present materialistic age hedonistic allurements is a common feature. As such, the main aim of the school formal education remain to prepare the students for competing in the job market. The schools prepare the students for good examination results. The students are also pressurised to study more and more to get good marks. Due to the dire competition for getting employment in the society, the parents—especially the mothers not only desire that their wards should come in flying colours but, they pressurise their youngers to read more and more. They do not want to miss anything in this regard, and, evade enculturation and inculcating of good habits in the youngers. Actually they remain ignorant about the real education of their children. The present system of formal education is based on differentiation and competition for economic gains and exploitation. As such, the present system of formal education considerably is a license for employment and not a way for the life building of the youngers. This has brought the virus of cutthroat commercialisation in the field of education too. Many private schools such as 'public schools', preparing and coaching schools have emerged as a business organisations want to clinch the money from public.

On the whole, it is also true that the present system of formal education helped the Indian people making them literate in large numbers. Because of this, we Indian could be united and could achieve independence. National development could be possible. It gave equal opportunities to all irrespective of, castes, creeds and of economic status which was denied earlier. But, it can also not be denied that formal education totally ignored enculturation and cultural development.

4

Educational Processes

Any kind of activity, be it social, economical, cultural, theological, axiological, mechanical or educational entails a functioning process. Even the human life which has a long continuum entails a process. The child is born, brought up encultured and prepared for living a healthy sane social life. He/she is prepared to share bio-heterogeneity and to live a life of bio-diversity in unity. As such men and women who are biologically topsy-turvy live together life long. The man passes through varied stages of life—as, a child, a young married householder and finally as an old man. The man/woman continuously learn throughout their life stages. Likewise, education is a life long parental system of perennial learning. The educational systems of various societies are affected by biological, social, economical, cultural, political, theological and axiological factors of the different societies. And the different societies adopt different educational structures and processes. This requires careful study of the past history of the society and its educational structure is to be studied. And also the study of current conditions of the society is also needed. Then only appropriate educational process for the society can be thought and adopted.

The process of learning in the whole animal world starts from the very stage. Generally, education is imparted from the very beginning—informally, non-formally in familial way and, finally in formal way. If we peep into the human educational history we find all these educational process. And for good education of the younger it is very essential to know about all these educational processes.

(*a*) Familial Education

Familial education starts in the family at a very early stage of the child. Familial education is imparted first informally and thereafter when the child grows non-formally. In old cultures and civilisations was very prominent. The main aim of familial education was to enculturate the youngers and prepare them to follow and perpetuate the national culture. In old cultures and civilisations like Indian Mohanjodaro and Harappa cultures, Dravidian culture and Aryan culture, Greek culture and civilisation, Hebrew culture and Chinese culture and civilisation were based on familial education, which aimed at to perpetuate the culture. The mother of the child used to play a prominent role in familial education. She used to bring up the child and inculcate in him/her desirable necessary life attitudes as—to be punctual, honest, hard working, to respect the elders and fair sex to love the youngers and to have a sense of self-introspection. All these desirable life attitudes were to be inculcated informally, for which the mother and other family members used to present desirable ideal way of living. And the children used to follow the ideal way of living. It is seen that not only the human beings, but also animals, birds, insects, bees and beasts used to educate their youngers informally. So the youngers used to learn a lot from their parents informally through perception (*per se*). Still in many tribal societies the informal education is in the core of their education system. The mother and the family members of many tribals in India still prepare their youngers to follow their tribal culture. The youngers when they learn how to talk used to be allowed to mix up with their peer groups. They used play with their peer groups, talk with them, attain sociability and learn many things pertaining to their social life. As such, informal education is a process which does not require any formality and aims at sociability, axiology, religiosity and diligency. Now in the modern scientific age informal education has been totally wiped out as the parents are generally busy in earning for meeting their hedonistic needs. They do not have time to enculturate their children. Due to greed the old joint family system has been totally crumbled. Community elders who also used to play a prominent role in imparting education informally also remain busy in doing their own works. As such, the younger generation has been denied familial education to large extent.

(*b*) Informal Education

Informal education is an educational process which is based on inherent form of life styles, living and culture, instead of prescribed educational form which is based on prescribed academic achievements. A form means a shape or a structure. When education is designed to give a particular shape or structure or form which is similar for all youngers, that system of education can be said formal education. But when the children are prepared to learn and follow an established life norms and social and cultural patterns and they learn by observing and imitating the family members, community elders through the process of imitation. Such educational process is called 'informal education'. In informal education the youngers are not required to go to an established educational agency like school or college. They observe and perceive their elders, family members, parents and community. Members doing some family work and duties and, they follow them and learn. The youngers are also encultured through informal way of education. As such, the youngers learn many things through observing their elders. The elders often do not give prescribed instructions. Nor they force the youngers to do particular things; the youngers only observe their elders and learn the necessary living conditions, life styles and culture traits. The youngers learn many things which, neither they are able to learn through observing or imitating their elders, nor their parents and elders make them aware about such secret knowledge. The youngers only learn from their peer groups of their age. As girls learn many things about their future married life from their peer group. So informal education plays an important vital role in the life building of the youngers. But now the role of informal education has been fractured due to desire of influency of the parents. Most of the parents are always eager to earn more and more money for meeting their hedonistic needs. Because of this desire many parents do not follow an idealistic life. They renounce the monotheistic religiosity and generally adopt henotheism and polytheism for gaining material gains. Their youngers also follow their path. The real life attitudes are not inculcated in the youngers so the youngers are deprived off the deserved informal education. And the parents of the youngers think that the school should also discharge the duty of imparting informal education which is impossible.

(*c*) Non-Formal Education

The non-formal education is also a process of familial education.

The youngers are involved in hereditary vocations and are trained by the family elders non-formally. There is a set programme of training of the youngers. The youngers are regularly involved to participate in doing hereditary trades and work with their elders. As such, the youngers continuously work with their elders. They observe and follow the working methodologies of their hereditary vocations. As a matter of fact it is a familial apprenticeship. Working with their elders the youngers visualise and observe a wide spectrum of raw materials, tools and working methods. The non-formal education is imparted by the family elders. Through non-formal education the youngers learn a lot through *per se* and observations. They become highly skilled and specialised in all kinds of fabrications relating to their family trade or vocation. In India all artisan castes and service class train their youngers in their family occupations non-formally. Because, India is a caste ridden society, occupations are followed on caste lines. A son of a carpenter or blacksmith till now used to follow his hereditary occupation. As such, the wards of the hereditary artisans used to be highly skilled and proficient in their family trades in comparison to those who are trained in industrial training institutes. As such, the wards of the artisans used to learn in a perspective spectrum in which they used to observe their elders while they are working. They used to observe their working techniques, application of tools and right use of raw materials. One of the top most advantage of hereditary non-formal education was the availability of regular employment. Hereditically non-formally trained artisan did not require to knock the doors of employment exchanges for jobs. But the upper castes always disregarded the working artisans castes, even though their race linkage may be with upper castes like Brahmans and Kshatriyas; but working artisans were considered 'Sudras'. Due to this the concept of purity and pollution was imposed on them. Though most of the skilled artisans were intelligent than the upper castes, but due to social degradation they adopted sanskritisation. And most of the wards of skilled artisans evaded their family vocations. This trend also affected the non-formal education in India. They shifted to another occupations. The hereditary trained skilled artisans are very less in number in the society now. Indian non-formal system of education was not only liked by the Indians. It was prevalent in other countries like China, Ceylon and some Asian countries. In Europe the artisans were trained in guilds. But Indian system of non-formal education was much appreciated by the Westerners. Karl Marx had appreciated it. When Lord Macaulay was trying to impose western type of formal system of education on Indians in thirties of nineteenth century, the then Governor of Punjab (now half of the Punjab gone to Pakistan) Lahore had objected the imposition of formal education on Indians. He supported the old Indian system of education of Gurukulas and Madarsas. He had argued that the Indian educational institutes were aimed at to enculturate the Indians. And the Indian non-formal system of education was the best as it was aimed to prepare the artisans as a best fabricating force and earn livelihood. Now the non-formal education system is more or less crumbled due to formal training institutes, in which students of all castes are admitted and are certified. Due to certification those who are non-formally trained are not employed in factories and workshops.

(*d*) Formal Education

Formal education is a system of education which is designed or planned to achieve a pre-conceived common socio-economic aim. Under the formal system of education a set of pre-conceived achievements are decided in advance. And all youngers in spite of their tastes, capabilities and interests are allowed to get education. Subject content which is to be taught is decided in advance. For teaching the subject content in a specified curriculum is prepared by the experts. Such content is taught in state managed educational agencies like Government run schools, aided schools and other educational agencies like colleges, universities and technical institutions. Generally the states decide what to teach and what not to teach. The society as a whole has no say in formal education in the present times. Whereas in olden times the situation was topsy-turvy, the state had no control over educational institutions. The society as a whole used to run the educational institutions like Gurukulas and Madarsas.

Now all educational institutions are instruments of the state and all follow formal system of education for achieving stipulated national educational aims. What are these educational aims will be discussed later on. First it is necessary to know what is a 'form'. A form is structured or fabricated shape. The word form is a derivation of French and Latin words 'forma' meaning a configuration of physical things or shapes given by man or woman composing different things together. An educational form is a desired educational shape. The formal process is also applied in many fields—such as forming social, economic, cultural, political, theological structures. And educational form or formal education is designed to achieve the desired structures. In social structure, formal system is applied to make the society a sane society. In political field the politicians apply a form to develop a desirable loyal followers. But in education field the rulers want to apply measures which could create army of loyal followers to adhere and follow the ideology of the rulers. Recent dilemma of publication of books in NCERT for school children has exposed this tendency. The rulers wants to make the youngers to follow their schemes. For achieving this end the school of formal education is a tool for shaping the future guardians as per need of the day. As such, formal system of educational process is an applicable system of education for desired ends and under formal method of education. The educator tries to shape the future guardians according to the suitable norms which may achieve the desired ends.

The theory of formalism emerged in early twentieth century. First impact of formalism can best be seen in creative things and artistic aesthetic things. When an artist creates an artistic thing he/she gives shape to it. In the beginning the shape or form was given by the artist for his/her emotional satisfaction without any inclination or for material satisfaction. The art form is a combination of some symbols. The symbols are composed together to depict some ideas in shapes. The shapes have virtuality. It can be said that a form is a structural shape. In other words a form may be said a new creation. Later on the concept of formation covered the materialistic things and hedonistic fields. Because of industrialisation art forms were commercialised which brought change in art formalism. This change occurred in other areas also. And due to flux in the formality in socio-economic and cultural fields the rulers and administrators also designed the system of education through which they could materialise their objectives. As such, in education social, cultural and spiritual objectives are generally ignored. In the present formal education materialistic and hedonistic objectives are thought and school activities are planned accordingly. School curriculum is also planned accordingly in advance, and the students are taught accordingly in schools. The present system of formal education is the latest process of education which is done through teaching. The teaching is done by the teacher. The syllabus of the school is so heavy that it keeps both the students and the teachers very busy. The teaching process applied in schools is more or less information posing process. The teacher is always at the giving end and the students are at the receiving end. Whereas, the teaching should be a two way interactive process through which the teacher could ignite a thought process in the minds of the students. The school should create a situation which may expose the students to an epistemic atmosphere and, the students may be innovated and motivated to think, reason, analyse and they can learn through enquiry. Thinking leads to reasoning. If we took to the epistemological aspects of education, education is nothing but bringing out which is already within the learner. And thinking helps in the process of educating.

Therefore, it is essential that while teaching the students, both at school and university level should be aimed for educating the students, for bringing out the hidden potentialities of the students. This can be done through bi-polar communication involving the students in activities. At the school level it is very essential, because activity based teaching always motivates the students for thinking and reasoning. For education thinking is very essential. Necessary care should be taken that the students should be encouraged to express. Good education is that which is based on deductive process and the students are allowed to contribute in the knowledge development. Such process of education will always satisfy the ego of the students. When a student contributes and does a new thing in the class room during the course of teaching process, he/she is not only satisfied but is over thrilled and overwhelmed with his/her achievement. This also helps in the personality development of the students. For such an educational recovery it is necessary to use some tools skilfully. What are these tools? These are nothing but audio-visual aids. The use of teaching aids always entail rapport between the teacher and the students. Education is a two way process which always requires active participation of both the teacher and the students. It is, therefore necessary that both the teacher and the students should actively participate during the teaching.

In formal education teaching is necessary. All teaching processes involve the communication of ideas. This is done through telling or teaching, sense perception and also by reading the written material. Our sense organs are the gates of knowledge. All of our sense organs help us in understanding the environment around us. Hearing and seeing are most important sense organs. We understand and learn by both of these sense organs. By seeing we learn quickly. So providing direct experience in formal education while teaching for educating the students is most essential. This helps in completing the multi-educational process of learning, that is, motivation, stimulation, comprehension and learning possible. Perception further helps in establishing a channel between the learner and the things which are worth of learning. The assumption "what we hear generally we forget and what we see generally we remember", is considered important for education as reminiscence is one of the most tool for education.

If we look etymologically, both the concepts—the teaching and education, though have different meanings but are supplementary to each other and, go in hand in glove. Without teaching education can never be possible and, without education teaching is fruitless.

For this end deductive approach is to be applied while teaching, which would entail correct use of teaching methods and proper application of teaching aids. For this revitalising of the present school curriculum will be necessary. Our present approach of formal system of education is only examination oriented. The life building approaches in our present formal system of education are totally missing. Whereas the old Indian system of education, that is, Gurukula education and Madarsa education laid stress on life building. Along with subjects learning and knowing on which the present formal education lay stress essential epistemical approaches, aspects like self-searching or introspection, socialising and moralising, good behaviour, believing in truth and beauty are also totally missing in our present formal educational processes. There should be a space for enculturation in our present formal educational process which can only be possible if teaching is made activity oriented.

What is seen in the present society is that the man is mad after material gains. The axiological aims are always ignored. Our formal education system only aims at good examination results and not for making the future guardian as sane citizens. This is why we notice loot, burglaries, molestations, rapes, chain snatchings and murders in the society. Our formal system of education is blind to these problems. And the society is going to be criminal society day by day. This situation has emerged due to blind modernisation which entailed greed and xenophilism, Westernisation which has entailed blind acculturation which killed our culture, simple living and high thinking, monotheistic spirituality, sociability, brotherhood and cooperation. Due to this, our old social institutions like joint family life, brotherhood community life and moral life are also disappearing day by day. Now we are bankrupt in our process of cultural development as our enculturation process is disappearing day by day. Our formal system of education only aims at preparing the younger generation for annual examinations and producing them in mechanical way as nuts and bolts are produced in factories.

If our present formal system of education is not reorganised and, our educational aims are not reformed we will totally loose our culture which has been largely damaged to a large extent by alienistic system of formal education imposed by Lord Macaulay nearly one hundred seventy three years ago. So our present formal system of education needs immediate reformation.

The teacher is the main functionary in the process of modern system of formal education of our children. The education is as old as society. The present teacher is the successor of our old *Gurus* of Gurukulas, who were the enculturators, social and national builders. They were true epistemic. Our present teachers should be grateful to the old *Gurus* (teachers) and should follow their teaching professional ethics. This would be paying the due respect to them. The present teachers working under the formal system of education should be epistemic like our old *Gurus*. They should proficiate, should acquire proficiency in the field of teaching. They should care their clients, that is students. They should be non-inclinative as our old *Gurus* (teachers) were. For doing this our present teachers should try to gain knowledge of the subject content they are going to teach. They should lay emphasis on self-learning by the students. They should use better teaching methods which may lead to motivate the students for self-learning. The teachers should keep in mind that they are not servants of the teaching institutions. They are the life builders of the future guardians. They should realise that the area of their job is much more wider. It is not limited to teaching only. They should try to bring social harmony and, should enculturate the students. This can be done by inculcating good life attitudes in the students. They should be prepared to adopt good behaviour, sane character. The students should know sociological, economical, cultural and axiological values. The teacher should apprise the students about simple living and non-hedonistic living.

Now-a-days there is a wave of instantivity in achieving material gains at every stage of life. This is because of advancement of science and technology and, thereby unprecedented increase in production of consumer goods resulting a way of hedonistic, consumeristic and xenophilic way of life. So, the educational processes have been very badly affected, which has entailed changes in social, economic, cultural and theological aspects of life. For material gains the man has totally forgotten the social, religious, cultural and economic aspects of life. The man has become more or less self-centred and greedy. Daily prayers are now missing. These are replaced by weekly or periodical satsangs on the Western style of weekly prayers in churches as was designed by St. Calvin in the wake of industrialisation—"work hard throughout the week and attend church once a week on Sunday". For material gains the man, day by day is loosing humanity and is adopting animal nature of irrationality. The man is becoming more and more greedy, irrational, self-centred, orthodox and fundamentalist which generate undesirable tension in the society as well as in the whole nation. The modern formal system of education is responsible for this social change. The modern social change generates unbearable tension in the society as well as in the nations. What is happening in the world we all know. The modern Spartans, that is, terrorists have spread their wings throughout the world. The old Spartan were limited only up to Greece. The terrorists are taking the lives of many innocent people. The terrorist activities in Chezes in Russian school had taken the lives of 400 innocent school children. Like that many countries including India are victims of terrorism. True and sane education can solve all such barbaric problems not only in India but in many Asian countries like China, Japan, Indonesia, Sri Lanka, Thailand, Pakistan, Fuji and Mauritius.

Uptil early twentieth century the formal education was imparted by the teacher to the students directly. The mode of communication was verbal and that too was one way. The teacher was considered a man of knowledge, a man of character having limited needs necessary for his subsistence. As such, the teacher was devoted to his profession. He used to acquire knowledge by reading library books and from his own experience. Though, there were chances of interaction between the teacher and the students, but due to alienistic system of formal education which was purely examination oriented it was minimum. As such, more or less the students used to be passive listeners. And there was very little scope for the students to think, reason and analyse what was taught to them. On the contrary our old Brahmanical Gurukula Education was totally based on *'Vad'* and *'Vivad'*, that is systemic combined discussion between the *Guru* (teacher) and *Shishyas* (students). As such, our present system of formal education has no place for regular discussions. Also it is considered killer of informal and non-formal systems of education. As it is examination oriented it is bookish. Its products are receivers and crammers. Our formal process of education has also made our teachers and educational administrators totally formal. They have to perform their duty in mere formal way, as other Government servants do. They can in many ways be compared with workshop mechanics who deal with lifeless unconscious materials.

Not only the teachers and educational administrators have become formal but, the parents have also become formal. They have forgotten that it is home where the education of the children starts in informal and non-formal ways and, it is their duty to perform. They only aspire to earn more and more. Husband and wife both go out of home for doing jobs. With the result they have to push their young children to crèches and day care schools. When the children come home tired they try to use the electronic media—T.V. and radio for mitigating their fatigue. Our educational system's process cannot be improved until the parents craze for more earning is stopped and the mother gets more time for necessary familial education. The mother should carry on the familial education till the child is ready to bear the burden of living alone.

No doubt, the present formal educational process is goal for good performance in examination, which is necessary for getting employment in present technological competitive industrial age. But one should not forget that an individual, besides an earning member, is also a member of big social whole, that is, society. An individual can only survive if the social whole, that is, society survives. For the survival of the society there should be certain social rules, regulations, customs, traditions, institutions, culture and cultural traits. An individual cannot survive without these social requirements. Without these the man will go back to barbarous age. In entire animal world, the nature has rewarded the human-beings with some special human faculties, that is, bigger brain for thinking, reasoning, analysing, comprehending and planning for the future. Nature has given to human-beings moving hands and erect posture for acting and walking. But the man has also been loaded with too much of greed and acquisitiveness, so to educate the human-beings for saneful living is essential. Our educational process should have a provision to educate the youngers for warding off the present social evils like unsociability, material desires, corruption and self-centredness. Our educational process is examination oriented. It should devote to generate social harmony through love and affection. Our educational aims should be designed to achieve these goals. It should generate socio-cultural homogeneity in the society for harmonious living. It should also prepare the youngers for economic self-sufficiency. Also education should create conditions for individual dignity, social integrity, honesty, social security, freedom to adhere individuals own traditions, customs, religious beliefs. The dominant sections of the society should not impose their will on the weaker sections of the society. Education should also generate a sense of tolerance, a sense of simple living and high thinking.

Acquisitive, possessive and individualistic human personality is the gift of capitalistic society. This has damaged the humanistic values. Proper education can relieve our youngers of this human evil. The education process should nurture a spirit of diligence, professional ability and competence and also a spirit of human care in younger generation. All these create a social consciousness in the youngers. The explosion of knowledge added more burden on the teachers as well as on the youngers. In view of all this, the quality of education needs reformation and improvement, and the teacher will have to hear the burden of it.

The teachers have to work in hostile educational atmosphere including cynism, despair and unrecognition. Even the students do not respect their teachers in many cases. These days the teaching profession do not get due recognition in the society. In spite of all this the teacher should be proud of teaching profession, then only their teaching process can be successful. Professor Amrik Singh says that modern teaching community suffers from self-inflicted wounds. The educational, historical and evolutionary conditions added the miseries to the teaching community. Main trouble lies in teaching and learning processes. The teaching community should look to the innovative and creative teacher and, great personalities like Sarv/Shri R.N. Tagore, Aurobindo, C.V. Raman, Dr. Radhakrishnan, J.N. Kapoor, Pandit Madan Mohan Malviya, Mahatma Gandhi, Dr. Zakir Hussain, J. Krishnamoorthy and many recent creative thinkers like Swami Ram Dev and Swami Shradhanand who contributed a lot in the field of educational processes. Also the teacher training institutes like Central Institute of Education, Delhi established by Maulana Abdul Azad in 1949, should be established more in the country. These educational institutes should follow the foot steps of Late Professor A.N. Basu and Late Professor (Dr.) E.A. Pires, former Principal of Central Institute of Education, Delhi. The education should be self-propelling force. Edward Shills in his paper 'Academic Profession in India', remarked that Indian community has its incapacity to do hard work in doing persistent academic work and to build up an academic community. They tacked academic professional ethics which could have brought a social change.

As such, the teacher is the builder of the nation will have to play a vital role in revitalising the present rottened, alienistic, and unsuitable formal educational process, so as to bring a dynamic, desirable social change in Indian society through appropriate educational process of teaching. The teacher is the epicentre of the development of the youngers. He/she can revive the Indian culture.

But the teacher alone cannot bring reform in the present crippled alienistic formal process of education. The rulers, the parents, the administration and the whole society should examine the present educational process and, find out the merits and demerits and should take necessary steps to reform it. It is the result of our present educational process that youngers fail to do anything in sports. It is because that our educational process is purely examination oriented and, due to this games and sports activities are generally neglected in schools. Likewise many other activities like arts and crafts activities which are necessary for enculturation are ignored due to examination pressure. Due to examination fever, co-curricular and extra-curricular activities do not take place in schools and students remain unaware about the national culture.

EDUCATIONAL AGENCIES AND INSTITUTIONS

Educating the human beings and their off-springs is very necessary for their development and sustinance and for the existence of the society. For this end, the human beings have been continuously educating their off-springs from the very beginning since the inception of the society. Not only the human beings but all living beings—animals, birds, beasts, insects and bees etc. also have been educating their off-springs from the very beginning, though their educating is limited to informal educating, which is done for their existence. There is an epistemic difference in the education of human-beings and other living beings. The informal education in other living beings, that is, animals, birds, beasts, insects and bees is restricted for their existence. Whereas, the spectrum of education of the human-beings is much more wider. The human-beings, that is, men and women are rational beings. The nature has gifted the human-beings with bigger heads, moving hands and erect posture. The human-beings can think, reason and analyse the physical phenomenon and act accordingly. They always thought of new things. And the man has ever been inventing new things and has been fabricating the new things for the human use. And the man has been educating his off-springs for doing so through informal and non-formal process of education. The animal could not do so. They only educate their off-springs in informal way. As the time passed the man searched new avenues for exploitation of the natural resources for human use. In the beginning the man was living in bushes. He improved his standards of living and shifted to villages, towns and cities. And for doing so, the man educated his off-springs through informal and non-formal ways of education in his family. Necessity is the mother of invention. It promoted the development of science and technology, which helped in the fabrication of new things. The new industries came into existence for the fabrication of new things, new knowledge was required, and for the application of the new knowledge some agencies and educational institutions were required. The human-beings, being rational beings always thought to prepare their youngers for reaching to new heights. They always thought to give good education to their youngers. So they always contributed in the development of educational institutions. At home, they educate their children in informal and non-formal ways in the beginning. Thereafter, they sent their off-springs in *Pathshalas* and Gurukulas. Due to the development of science and technology the field of fabrication of material goods increased which necessitated the formal education. First the necessity of formal education was felt by the industrialists. They established schools which were later on taken over by the Government. In due course of time formal education structure become pan-national necessity for the socio-economic development of the nation. And new educational institutions came into being. And for all educational agencies and institutions specific educational structure emerged for the socio-economic development. In brief it can be described as under:

Social Educational Agencies

(*a*) *Family*

The word family is derivation of Latin word 'Familia' meaning a household, a body or whole or group of persons living together life long under a common roof. Their food is cooked over a common oven. All family members live long together happily. The family or a common household is managed by an elder, who takes care of all family members. All adults generally male members earn and contribute in the sustinance of the family. The head of the family used to look after the needs of the family—as bringing up by inculcating necessary social life attitudes as, developing good health care habits, doing work, speaking true, respecting elders and fair sex and loving the youngers. Actually the family is a genetic whole. The youngers are married in other families on different totems principles (Gotra गौत्र). The marriages are arranged on patriarchcal principles. Only in some tribes matriarchcal marriages are arranged. This unity in bio-diversity of a male and female make the birth of a child possible, who in due course of time becomes young and adult and becomes member of the society. The family plays a vital role in bringing up the child which, it does through informal and non-formal education. The elders of the family play a very positive role in life building of the youngers, which they do by inculcating good habits, good life attitudes as good behaviour and character. This, generally is created by inculcating good life habits—as speaking true, respecting elders and ladies, loving youngers, to be social, to develop good health care habits as early to bed early to rise and to develop spirituality. All this was done by elders of the joint family. Indian joint family system was considered an auspicious social institution which used to do the upbringing of the youngers very sincerely. It was praised throughout the world as it was considered better than the nuclear family. Many foreigners had praised the Indian joint family system for its educational roles. During the British rule, when Lord Macaulay was trying to impose the British formal education system in 1832 A.D. on Indians, the then Governor of undivided Punjab had praised the Indian joint family system as it used to do life building of the youngers through informal and non-formal education. He had objected the imposition of formal education. Mr. Albert Comer a disciple of Dr. Sarvapalli Radha Krishnan, former President of India had praised the Indian joint family system. He had expressed his views in 1954 before the writer when he was in India to see the Indian socioscape. He had stayed with the writer in Govindpuri, Modinagar, U.P. where, the writer was told about the Indian joint family system. American first lady Mrs. Hillary Clinton had praised the Indian joint family for its life building and education roles in 1993 and, had advised the Americans to adopt the Indian joint family system and discard nuclear family system. Another American lady Mrs. Dr. Arthur William Earl of New Jersey had also praised the joint family system for its positive life building roles. As such, the Indian joint family system had been playing a very posture role in life building of the youngers. But now as Hereclitus, the Greek Philosopher, said social change is inevitable the Indian joint family system has been crumbled down and nuclear family system has taken place of the joint family system. Both the parents generally remain busy in the rat-race of money earning. They go out of the house and leave their young children at the mercy of the crèches and day care schools and there is no place for informal, non-formal education and life building of the youngers in the family.

(b) Community

The word community, is a derivation of Latin word, 'communittas', meaning 'common possession or employment', common variety of things, goods or individuals having common ways of living in the society having common social traits, cultural traits, culture standard or a way of living or people of the same race. The term community is the development of the word 'common' which is a derivation of Latin word 'communus' and French word 'Commns' meaning 'living together', "ready to be in service of the neighbours, to live in fraternity". As such, people of a community generally have common law, character, culture, cultural traits, customs, fraternity and cooperative ways of living. So the people of a community care for each other. A community is a big whole or a combination of different families living in nearby localities. Many people categorise community a combination of people following a common profession or vocation or work.

As such a community is a combination or a big whole in which many people of different castes or creeds live together. They share happiness and grief of the neighbours and, help each other. Indian society seventy years ago, in spite of caste heterogenity was a united social common whole. All people used to help each other. The elders of the community used to treat the youngers of other families as their own youngers or wards of their own. And in any difficulty they used to help each other. Educated members of the community used to educate the youngers of their neighbours. In the village of the writer (Village Bhalaniagaj, Distt. Haridwar, Uttrakhand) there were three freedom fighters named (1) Late Maharshi Shri Harish Chander ji, (2) Late Shri Babu Malkhan Singh ji, and (3) Late Pandit Babu Ram Sharma (Munda). They were vibrant freedom fighters. But in addition to this their main aim was to bring social reformation. They were named as '*Swatantra Sangram Sainani Tickari*' (स्वतंत्रता संग्राम सैनानी तिकड़ी). They had monitored the freedom fighting movement of the nearby area. They used to fight the untouchability in the village, illiteracy, orthodoxy. They had tried to develop village cottage industries. They had tried to inculcate good life attitude in the youngers. They had tried to involve the youngers in religious reformation by making them Arya Saarbajis. They had tried to inculcate good habits in the youngers. They had tried to educate the village girls. The girls' school opened by them is now Rashtriya Inter Co-educational College in which approximately one thousand girls are studying. They used to educate the youngers. Late Pandit Babu Ram used to educate the Muslim girls about their religion by teaching them about Quran and Hadis. The writer's neighbour Pt. Bhagrit Lal Sharma used to teach the children of the *Mohalla* including the writer. As such, the elders of the community used to play a vital role in the life building of the youngers. But now due to crumbling of joint family system and material change the elders of the community do not get time to do so. Also the parents of the youngers do not like any intervention of the outsiders in the life building of their children.

(*c*) *Religious Institutions*

In olden times the religious places like temples, Gurudwaras, Thakurudwaras, Mosques used to play an important role in educating the youngers. The *Pujaris* of the temples used to educate the people about the spirituality, morality, sociability, sanity and cooperation. And the religious places were also used by other educated persons. The Gurukula educated persons were required to make the people aware about religiosity, spirituality, culture, sanity, morality, sociability, truthfulness and, they used to do so through religious discourses which they used to give at religious places for moulding the life of the youngers and adults. The ladies and girls were also educated at religious places.

(*d*) *Religious Educational Institutions*

In olden days in India, some aged persons who were epistemic, religious and spiritual used to leave their families in their Banprashtha or Sanyas Ashramas and to go in jungles for living a solitary life. They used to make a small ashram where they used to live a religious and spiritual life. Such persons used to live alone in separate Ashramas. Such persons used to pray Almighty God, in monotheistic way, do meditations and give religious discourses (धार्मिक प्रवचन) and also used to educate people about sociability, morality, truthfulness, sanity and good life attitudes. In such Ashramas some elderly ladies with young girls used to come to listen religious discourses. A group of young boys and girls were also taught by the Rishis of the Ashramas, without any inclination.

In due course of time some religious bodies like 'Vaishnites', 'Sanatan Dharamis', 'Arya Samajas', 'Radhaswamis', 'Nirankaris', and 'Sikhs' established their schools, and, also some minority schools were established for educating the younger generation of all castes. After sometime such schools came under the scanner of the state. And the state brought such schools under its complete supervision. The state imposed some common rules and regulations on such religious managed and minority schools for proper functioning. But this cannot be denied that the religious organised and minority managed such schools did not contribute in the field of education in secular way.

(*e*) *Gurukula Ashramas*

The main aim of Indian Gurukula education system was life moulding of the youngers which was not possible in the family. As 'unity in diversity' is very necessary for social existence. And also unity in bio-diversity is very necessary for human existence. When a male and female are united from two different totemic sides, the births of the youngers become possible who become members of the society. The unity of 'love and affection with harshness and strictness' of the youngers is very essential. If this is not done and, the children are only loaded with too much of love they are generally spoiled. This what we see in the present affluent hedonistic section of the Indian society. The old Indians were intelligent they had visualised this social fact. And they thought of a viable human life structure. They had divided the human life in four parts: (1) *Brahmcharya Ashram* (ब्रह्मचर्याश्रम), (2) *Grahastha Ashram* (गृहस्थाश्रम), (3) *Banprastha Ashram* (बनप्रस्थाश्रम), and (4) *Sanyas Ashram* (संन्यासाश्रम), on the pattern of Indian social stratification in four Varnas (1) Brahmans, (2) Kshatriyas, (3) Vaishyas, and (4) Sudras like the composition of human body (1) head, (2) torso, (3) legs, and (4) feet. All these human life periods entailed renunciation. In the first period of life, till they are adolescents the children were supposed to live in the family along with their parents and other family members, where they were educated in informal way. But it was observed, and it is still seen, that the mother and some other family members generally love their youngers too much. And too much love is poisonous, so the old Indians thought of separating their youngers by sending them away to distant places where they could learn viable life social attitudes, as sociability, morality, good life habits as, early to bed early to rise and to learn religiosity, spirituality, good life health care habits. So the idea of establishing Gurukulas in jungles on the river banks might have emerged. Another purpose of establishing the Gurukula was to perpetuate the joint family system which was considered the epicentre of inculcating good life attitudes and development of good behaviour and character.

Indian Gurukulas were established to bring cohesiveness and amity in the society. These were like very big joint families in which *Shishyas* of many varied families of different kith and kins were living together with *Gurus*. The relationship between the *Guru* (teacher) and *Shishyas* was like affinity between the father and sons. The activities of the Gurukulas used to be designed to inculcate all necessary good life attitudes for establishing social homogeneity. These life attitudes used to be as—to believe in simple living and high thinking, early to bed early to rise doing all daily necessary activities as national call, taking both, morning walk on the river bank, doing daily health care by doing exercises, yoga and meditation. And after attending common prayer and yajna and doing *pranayam* and meditation. And after owing these activities going to Gurukula Ashrama's dinning hall and take simple light refreshment. And after taken pure vegetarian refreshment the *Shishyas* (students) used to go to their *Guru* (teacher) under the shadow of a tree to listen his sermons on religiosity, spirituality, sociability and other subjects as *itihas* (history), sociology, philosophy and Sanskrit language etc. etc. after listening the *Gurus* sermons a vad vivad (debate and discussion) used to follow between the *Guru* and *Shishyas*. After this, the students and the *Guru* used to take lunch. In the afternoon the *Shishyas* (students) used to go nearby villages to collect food items for the Gurukula kitchen. Some used to go to the jungle to collect wood for the kitchen. Some used to collect grass for the Gurukula Ashram for the Gurukula Cowashram (गौश्रम). The state had no control over Ashramas. The Ashramas were financed by nearby villages. And famous Gurukulas like Nalanda, Taxila, Vallabhi etc. etc. were run by the nearby villages. One senior *Guru* used to manage the Gurukulas. The *Gurus* were pure professionists. They used to follow the teaching professional ethics. They were very sincere to their conscious clients. They were very episteme and non-inclinative. They believed that *Shikshadan* (education donation) was the poist donations. They used to sustain by living in ashram, only getting food.

As such, Gurukulas were the noblest educational institutions of India which were crumbled down by the alienistic system of formal education. Any some ideal thinkers tried to save the institution of Gurukula. Swami Shardhanandji had established Gurukul Kangri, Haridwar. And on this pattern many Gurukulas were established by many pious men in the country. Most of such Gurukula Ashramas like Gurukula Narsen, District Haridwar are functioning well and are inculcating good life habits in the *Shishyas* (students). Recently two Ashramas (*i*) Sanskriti Vishva Vidyalaya at Rishikesh and Patanjli Yoga and Ayurveda Peeth at Bahadrabad District, Haridwar were established by public organisations and, Uttrakhand Government recognised these vidyapeeths as state universities.

(*f*) *Madarsas*

On the pattern of Gurukulas there are some Madarsas in Muslim countries, and functioning in some Muslim dominated areas of other countries. The main aim of Madarsa education like Gurukula education, is to make Muslims aware about Quran and Hadis related religiosity and spirituality. Also to make the Muslims aware about the religiosity, spirituality, honesty, kindness, sociability and brotherhood. The Madarsas are generally secular, as these only propagate Islam but do not interfere in other religions. In India Dar-ul-Ulum, Deoband is one of the famous Madarsas of the world. Students (Muslims) from different countries come to study at Daruband Deoband, District Saharanpur, U.P. Like Gurukulas, the Madarsas are also supported by the local people. In Madarsas, the students live in Madarsas with the Maulvis under common roof. They have also to follow some life building rules—like early to bed early to rise, to pray five times by performing *Namajs* and to *Juma Namaj* on Fridays at noon. Dar-Ul-Ulum, Deoband is still famous in the world for its secular religiousity, and nationality. In 1946, 1947 Maulana Madni, Head of the Dar-ul-Ulum, Deoband had openly opposed the partition of India. He had advocated for the secular religiosity. His main aim was to teach the Muslim students Quran and Hadis and make them aware about the tenets of Islam. He was for inculcating some good life habits as to pray God by performing *Namaz* five times a day, to make the students sane, non-materialistic, honest, sociable, kind and cooperative. As Deoband was the ideal Islamic centre for learning. But now a Maulvi of Allahabad who had planned bomb blasts at Hanuman Mandir, Varanasi and at a Varanasi railway station on 7.3.2006 added a black spot on the face of Dar-ul-Ulum, Deoband. U.P. Like that Madarsas in many countries have crossed the all limits of Spartans in spreading terrorism throughout the world. The Madarsas should realise, this dicotomy of injustice being done to the innocent people by the terrorists. They should educate their students not to cross the limits of humanity and social sanity.

(*g*) *Schools*

The man has ever been trying to add something to his wings for his comfort. He developed science and technology. And with the development of science and technology the industrialisation took place. With the passage of time the industrial revolution came into being. The man developed new tools, machinery and industrial infrastructure which required skilled manpower for the fabrication of consumer goods. Also the managing hands, trained hands for marketing the manufactured goods were required. First of all industrialisation took place in England. Earlier the consumer goods were fabricated and manufactured by the skilled artisans on a small scale. These artisans were trained by artisan guilds. For newly emerged industries a large number of skilled artisans were required. The artisan guilds were unable to train the required good number of skilled trained artisans. The consumer goods produced in newly emerged industries were capturing new markets. So it was necessary to develop these industries. This was not possible without skilled trained hands or artisans and to employ proficient managing hands. So, the industrialists thought of opening of some institutions which could train some required skilled technical hands and some hands for managing their industries. Such institutions were named as schools.

Etymologically the word school is a derivation of Latin word 'Sehola', which means, 'a leisure discussion', 'a philosophical thought', 'a place where persons are instructed in species of learning', 'an educational or technical establishment where higher learning is achieved through instruction. Followers of teachers are those who hold and follow common social, economic, religious doctrines. And such schools are as Socratic school, Platonic school, Vedic religious school like Vaishnites, Shankrites, Arya Smajis, Radhaswamis, Nirankaris in Hindus, Shiaites, Sunnis, Sufis in Muslims, Catholics and Protestants in Christians. There are schools in the field of art, which are called 'school of paintings—like Italian School of Painters, Bengali School, Pahari School and Rajasthani Schools of Paintings and also Madhubani School of Painting etc. etc.

The contemporary institution of school in the field of education aims at formal education. In addition to formal there are systems or ways of education as familial education and non-formal education and informal education. And the human-beings have been educating their youngers through these systems of education. With the passage of time the population increased which changed the human psyche also. The human-being rational beings are also greedy. In the pursuit of industrialisation the capitalists of the Western countries invested their money for acquiring the tools, machinery, capital goods and raw material goods. First they attracted the citizens working in the craft guilds to work in their industries. But the number of such artisans was small. To meet requirements of their industries they thought to train new hands who could be engaged in their industries. So they started the institution of school, and industrial schools for giving them formal education in 3 Rs as well as training them in specific trades to meet the requirement of their industries. The skilled trades were like carpentery, blacksmithy, tinsmithy, coppersmithy, fitting and fabrication. In due course of time, due to intensification of industries, which required a big trained workforce many separate schools and industries were established by the industrialists. As such, the institution of school first came into being in England and, later on it spread in other European countries. After sometime the institution became a pan-universal phenomenon. But in India and in some other East Asian countries a type of formal education was already in existence. It was imparted in Gurukula Ashramas and Buddhist monastries, to some extent. While in search for markets for selling their products as consumer goods in the world these industrialist capitalist countries captured some countries and made their colonies, where, in due course of time, these capitalist countries tried to impose some sound elements of their social structure, social values, ways of living and cultural traits. These countries used their system of education as a tool for achieving all these. In India on advice of Lord Macaulay, the then legal advisor in East India Company, British Government imposed their system of formal education in 1833 A.D. to annihilate the renowned and famous Indian culture. Many members of the Governor General's council had opposed it. But Lord Macaulay argued that it was necessary to kill the Indian culture for keeping the Indians as their subjects for ever. And for implementing this scheme, formal education was imposed on Indians and the institution of School came into being.

In order to exploit and harness the natural resources of the captured countries, the imperialist industrial countries always imposed their formal system of education. For this end these countries always tried to change the social structures of the captured countries. They did so in the garb of modernisation and development of their subjects. This alternative reform movements in their colonies or occupied countries were aimed at to destroy the indigenous social system and cultures in the third world through cultural diffusion in the first phase and thereafter alluring their subjects to their culture. This way these industrialist countries made the subjects of their colonies loyal to them. All sectors of these countries—such as, human resources, environmental system such as family system, community system and educational system were badly affected. And the formal system of education, which was imparted through the institution of school was considered appropriate best tool for bringing this flux.

In the beginning, the covert aim of colonisers by providing formal education, was to make the subject of the colonies loyal to them. They also needed a loyal, obedient workforce, because to bring the servants from England was not economical. To achieve this end Lord Macaulay thought to acculturate the top section of the Indian society, that is, 'divija' higher castes and kill their paramount culture slowly. For this end, the system of formal education was imposed on Indians, was implemented through the institution of school which functioned as an instrument of state. The scheme of Lord Macaulay worked as a slow poison, which killed the Indian culture bit by bit. And now Lord

Macaulay might be eating Indian sweets like *Kalakand* (Indian milk cake) in his grave. As the science and technology took a speedy pace and, which entailed industrialisation, the formal education strengthened its roots and became increasingly differentiated. So the institution of school became prominent and got increasingly state protection, validity and ultimately became state instrument.

Earlier in India, the education was not a state responsibility. It was an enterprise of the society, be it managed by Dharmsangthans, or by Churches or Mosques. Legal validity given to the school by the state made the school drifted from the society. The society lost its say with regard to education of their children. The school management went to the hands ot the bureaucrats who decide what to teach and what not to teach? The school activities like curriculum construction became the domain and monopoly of very few. Even the teachers of the school have no say in this activity. Whereas, in old Indian education system in Gurukulas, it was the teacher (*Guru*) who used to decide what to teach? The *Guru* used to prepare his disciples (*Shishyas*) to face the life situation, and adjust themselves in the social milieu after learning it in Gurukulas. The present system of formal education, which is imparted in schools and other educational institutions, has no basic foundation of education. The main reason of this is that the schools are isolated from the society, even though these are run by public money under the Government control. The present educational institutions are tools in hands of bureaucrats and few elites and, the society has no say in functioning of these schools. Most of the colonies of the Western imperialists became independent one after another. But the institution of school imposed by the alien rulers remained intact doing the same job as it was done during the rule of foreigners. The present rulers looked to earlier foreign rulers as their torch bearers and beacon lights. They thought that the Indians can be relieved from economic backwardness and poverty by following the alien system of formal education. Human psyche of greed and self-centredness made them to accept the formal education ignoring the needs of nationality, national culture, morality and sociability. The Indian caste structure, in which the upper castes promoted purity and pollution, degraded the lower castes. This degradation also promoted the formal education under which all lower castes could avail opportunity to get education. And generally all people thought that the modern alien system of formal education can only deliver the goods and can relieve them from poverty and economic backwardness.

As such, the third world visualised the deliverance from age old poverty through industrialisation and modernisation, which can bring economic growth and social change. So the socio-economic structure introduced by the colonisers remained intact as it was introduced. Old Indian indigenous way of harmonious living based on self-sufficiency, and which was the core foundation of the Indian economy started further crumbling. In India pre-independent cottage industries had a glorious hoary background of Indian economy future crumbled. It became a part of heterogeneous feudal economy which is based on centralised feudal capitalistic economy. Old Indian Gurukula and Madarsa education more or less crumbled due to formal school education system. Products of schools and universities got preference, though they are produced in mechanical way as nuts and bolts are produced in factories. In the present alienistic formal system of education imparted in schools, universities and other institutions, neither there is a consideration of individual differences nor for enculturation which is necessary for life building. Our cottage industries which had a hoary past have been totally vanished due to bookish formal education. This has also crumbled our age old non-formal education. Teachers' primary role is life preparation of the students for saneful living by inculcating in them life values like sociability, morality, simplicity, truthfulness, sanity and cooperation is totally missing. The present formal system is purely examination oriented. This has brought cutthroat competition in the society. Respect to elders, sympathy for weak and women are totally, more or less, missing. The joint family system, which was the epicentre of enculturation and good education, has been crumbled down due to human greed. Our elites, elders and community members can be blamed for this and not the teachers.

Organisational, professional and pedagogical values of our educational system, of which the school is the edifice are totally alien and do not meet our social needs. It could only create an euphoria of modernisation which entails acculturation. Modernisation in which we believe is tantamount to imitation of Westernisation. It aims at renouncement of our old social values, beliefs, traditions, cultural traits, religiosity and spirituality. In other words it is nothing but acculturation by adopting heterogeneous social system based on feudalistic social structure and, renouncing our age old homogenous social system. It negates our age old social and cultural values given to us by our sane ancestors. The present school education fails to enculturate our youths, rather than it acculturates them and, creates a class system in our caste based society.

Lord Macaulay while introducing the new type of English formal education for Indians not only had in his mind to prepare clerks for East India Company British Government, instead he had meticulously thought of killing of Indian culture, cottage industries and trade. This imagination has been so successful that we have lost our dress, food habits, speech, customs, cultural traits and what not. Also, this cannot be denied we have also been immensely benefited too. We learned English which removed the barriers of our regional languages. We got united and achieved our independence but at a heavy cost as our country was divided. A nation which looses its culture looses everything. Our political leaders and educationists could not visualise this fact. The emergence of a special kind of elite class which always remains doomed in maglomanity also promoted the formal school education, because it provided them and their wards good job opportunities. Those who know and speak their mother tongue and national language do not get a chance to speak on educational matters. So the educational administration of school system became the monopoly of English speaking elite class. It is this class which invented public school system. The public schools created rich English speaking class. These schools have openly commercialised the education and promoted acculturation openly. English speaking products of the public schools consider themselves superior than the masses. The bulk of bureaucrats, administrators, engineers and army officers come from this class to govern the rest of the majority. It is said that only 1 to 2 per cent people can speak and write English in India. It is this class which fosters English education and adopts Western cultural styles to reap the fruits of employment and power. Now the public school has been so commercialised that even uneducated persons have opened public school. In the village of the writer an illiterate barber had opened a public school which functioned till he was alive.

The present formal system of education in technical trades is imparted by special technical trade institutes like industrial training institutes which has replaced and crumbled the age old non-formal hereditary system of education. The non-formal hereditary system was hereditically transmitted on caste lines. It used to create a permanent way of social stratification in the society. Through non-formal education man used to be more skilled than the present trained in industrial schools. The man used to go through a wide spectrum which learning family trade. He used to visualise a lot of raw materials, variety of tools and working techniques. The industrial training institutes can not do this in a short period of time. The caste based non-formally trained artisans still have deep roots in the Indian society, but due to industrialisation and formal training they have lost their base because of certification by the I.T.Is. Without paper qualification or certification, the hereditary artisans are denied employment in workshops. As such, some of the vocational artisan castes have been totally wiped out of their hereditary vocational roles. And they migrated to cities and towns for earning their livelihood.

The politicians, though reap rich harvest from age old caste structure in winning elections and capturing power, they totally ignored the social transition of caste system. Though some castes are still doing some works of fabrication but, the merits of their vocations are ignored. Their children do not get chance to go to the schools. The veil of purity and pollution is still so dominant that even illiterate upper caste youngers and elders consider themselves pure and megalomanious. They do not pay respect to highly educated lower caste people. In south, they even avoid the shadow of the Schedule Castes and Tribes. And our education system has failed to make the people aware about this kind of social degradation. The lightly skilled artisan castes remain backward in the society, as only certification from industrial schools, art schools, and polytechnics pay dividend, not ability and skills. As such, hereditary skilled artisans generally remained unemployed, and only industrial schools trained artisans are employed in workshops. Consequently production at national level in production units falls. Also the falls work culture gets fumbled. Those who are not skilled and are employed in production units, exist due to buttering. As such, this fact cannot be denied that the alienistic formal system of education is responsible for this lacuna.

In olden days the main purpose of education was life building. Socialisation, moralisation and inculcation of sane good life attitudes was the main purpose of education. Now, the home atmosphere is totally hedonistic they earn throughout the week go to the temple once a week is the present social ethos like protestant Christians do. Religious prayers are totally banned in schools, because of secularism. Under the formal education there is no place of enculturating religiosity and spirituality, so there can no place for character building and sane behaviour development. The tragic result that we often read in newspapers, that mother-in-law gets murdered her daughter for dowry, son murderes the father for property and crimes like chain pulling, loot, burglary, bribery and corruption have become common feature in the society. Not only the big metropolis like Delhi, Mumbai, Chennai and Kolkata but the small towns like Ghaziabad and Muzzafarnagar are becoming the dens of criminals. As such, the crime index is rising day by day. Before, independence there was no fear while walking in the night in both rural and urban areas. One had to fear the beasts like wolves etc. now the beasts and wolves are found no more, but human beasts and wolves are found in abundance. One cannot walk after sun set in both urban as well as in rural areas. Urban areas like Delhi has become the dens of criminals like rapists, burglars, chain pullers and dacoits. It is because of our alienistic system of formal education which has no place of axiology. And the schools are blamed for it. So our formal system of education needs reformation.

(*h*) *Higher Education*

Like formal education, many Indian universities were the gifts of our British rulers. To bring administrative officers and bureaucrats from England for East India Company British Government in India was neither economical nor viable. So they thought to prepare a loyal obedient Indian administrative work force for the Government offices. The Indian officers were available at cheap pay packets in comparison to English officers. So they thought to educate and prepare the Indians for Indian Civil Service (I.C.S.) training in England. For this end, the British Government established a few important universities in India. First they established Calcutta University. Thereafter, they established Madras, Bombay, Lahore (now in Pakistan) and Allahabad universities on the pattern of English universities. These universities conducted courses in humanities and in science and mathematics. The products of these universities were inspired to seek admission in Indian Civil Service (ICS) Training Institute, London. And many Indians got admission in this institute. Shri Subash Chandra Bose, a renowned vibrant freedom fighter was an alumnus of this Institute. Besides getting cheap administrative force the British Government aimed at to perpetuate the acculturation process in India through Indian I.C.S. officers and to kill the Indian culture totally. Largely the Indian administrative force proved to be loyal to the English masters. They also proved to be helpers in their acculturation process. Later on the British Government opened other central universities like Delhi University in the country. All of these universities, later on established, aimed at to produce a white collar job workforce. These universities did not give importance to enculturation. These universities produced graduates and post-graduates who considered themselves elitists. They used to shun hand work. They renounced their family vocations and generally aspired and tried for white collar jobs. This tendency eluded the youngers from their primary roots, that is family vocations. And the caste structure under which a large section of society used to follow their family vocations. They after getting formal education only aspired for white collared jobs. And due to purity and pollution, fever ignited by upper castes, the artisans castes tried to Sanskritise themselves. The teachers working in the Universities were different from the old *Gurus*.

The East India Company British Government also had few engineering colleges. They had established Thomson Civil Engineering College, Roorkee for preparing Civil Engineers for monitoring the Ganges Canal in Uttar Pradesh. They had an another college on the pattern of Thomson Civil Engineering College at Pune to look after construction needs in Maharashtra. They had also established Michel Engineering College, Lahore (now is Pakistan) to train Indian engineers to supervise the mechanical fabrication needs in India. For the civil and mechanical infrastructure there was a need for some draftsmen, wood work supervisors in India, so the English rulers established College of Art, Calcutta, College of Art, Madras, Mayo College of Art Lahore (now in Pakistan), Mayo College of Art, Jaipur, Government Wood Working Institute, Bareilly, School of Carpentry, Allahabad, U.P.,

College of Art, Lucknow which has wood working as a separate subject, Government Wood Working Institute, Jalandhar, Punjab. Also some institutes were established by private organisations like Shri J.J. School of Art, Bombay. The teaching was done in these institutes in formal way and enculturation was not done.

After independence, the Government of India paid special attention to technical education. It established four Indian Institutes of Technology at (1) Kharagpur, (2) Bombay, (3) Chennai, (4) Delhi in the first instance. After sometime Indian Institutes of Technology, (5) Kanpur and (6) Indian Institute of Technology, Guwahati were established and finally (7) Roorkee University (Thomson Civil Engineering College) was given the status of Indian Institute of Technology, Roorkee (Uttrakhand). Now there are seven I.I.Ts. in India which have international status. Like the I.I.T., some private organisation opened the Indian Institutes of Management in India at Ahmedabad, Mumbai, Delhi and Kolkata etc. also large number of teacher training institutes came into being. Many of these institutes are functioning purely on commercial lines, though some of the teacher training institutes have viable training infrastructure. And teachers are produced in mechanical way as nuts and bolts are produced in factories. A few years back some universities had opened B.Ed. correspondence courses, which had totally vitiated the teaching profession. Many products of these commercial institutes did not know even about the viability of teaching aids like important aids—as charts, models and chalk-boards. Only the would be teachers were trained or educated in theoretical aspects in which they were examined and given B.Ed. degrees.

The commercialisation of education made the admission difficult not in Government higher educational institutes but also in private commercial institutes. Another reason for this difficult admission was that most of the parents want that their children should get higher education in educational institutes of repute. These educational institutes admit the students through admission tests. And for the preparation of these admission tests the aspirant candidates have to prepare for the tests. For this preparation many coaching centres earn a lot of money. These coaching centres charge all of the aspiring candidates for preparing them for the admission tests. For that these coaching centres charge good tuition fees. The parents of the candidates pay the fees after cutting of their necessary other expenses. As such, the coaching programme which has commercial stint also helps in cutthroat competition in the field of higher education. Majority of the candidates do not succeed in getting admission in higher educational institutes. In old system of Indian education this kind of competition was not there. Only those candidates who were epistemic and wanted to gain academic achievements used to go to institutions like Nalanda and Taxila, rest used to follow their hereditary vocations.

5

The Present School

The school is one of the most important educational institutions of any educationscape. It is the soul of every educational system. Because it is the school which prepares an educational foundation of the youngers to education, from lower level to higher level. The number of schools is highest in all sort of educational institutes. First of all students have to take school education, then only they can aspire for any kind of higher education. The school education is the base or foundation for all types of higher education and, for living a saneful social life. In the present industrial age the institution of school is a common feature in all societies. If we peep into the historical development of education, we will find that the institution of school is a common feature in all societies though in varied forms, in every culture and civilisation. The purpose of the school education was different in olden days than the present day school education. It was aimed at life building. As such, the youngers were educated for saneful social living. The parents, family elders and school teachers (*Gurus*) used to prepare the youngers for a specific social, religious and spiritual life. They used to inculcate good life attitudes, sane behaviour and health care habits. This was done to establish or promote a specific social, spiritual or religious way of life in the society. As such, many philosophical schools as (1) Platonic schools, Socratic schools and Aristotalian schools in Greece, (2) Vaishnite schools, Mathas and Ashram schools, *Pathshalas*, Buddhist and Arya Samaj schools etc. etc. in India, (3) Buddhist and Conficious schools in China, (4) Hebrew schools in Israel and Muslim schools, which were called Madarsas, in Islamic countries. The aims of these schools were quite different and were based on life building. The present day institution of school is an instrument of the state. It aims to implement the educational motives of the state through formal education and placing the ruling party on permanent ruling track. Whereas, the olden days schools were not governed by the state. Of course, these schools were supported by the society but they used to function for common social good independently. It is, therefore, very necessary to do a deep study and analysis of the working of the present day and past schools' functioning. For this, first it is very necessary to go into the etymology, analysis of the functioning of the present day schools and, present social climate and its effects on school education.

If we look etymologically, the word 'school', is a derivation of the Latin word 'Schole', which means 'leisure discussion', 'a philosophical thought', 'a place where persons are instructed in areas of learning, 'an educational or technical establishment where higher learning is achieved through instructions', 'followers of teachers and thinkers who hold specific common, social, economic and religious doctrines as already mentioned, like Sogatu school, Vashnite school, Sanskriti school, Arya Samaj school, Radha Swami school, Nirankari school, etc. etc. and also schools of creative arts like Italian school of painting, Madhubani School of Painting, Pahari School of Painting, Rajasthan School of Painting and many such schools as Sir J.J. School of Art, Mumbai, School of Art, Kolkata, School of Chennie, Mayo School of Art, Jaipur and Schools of Art, Lucknow, Chandigarh and Delhi etc. etc.

The contemporary educational institutions of schools only impart formal education. There are other systems of education like (1) familial education, (2) informal education, and (3) non-formal education. Though, the institution of school existed in all times, the genesis of the present system of school education, which basically does or imparts formal education can be traced to industrial revolution. Which first took place in England when the Capitalists tried to industrialise the cottage industries for the commercial use. They mechanised the cottage industries for exploiting the natural resources to the maximum for human use and, make money out of it. Necessity is the mother of invention. Many men invented many new things. They developed tools, machines and, also developed new infrastructures for fabricating and manufacturing new things for the use of human-beings in the society. As such, the man developed new techniques for exploiting the natural resources for human use. This enabled the industrialists to manufacture more things than required locally. They started searching of markets for their manufactured goods. First of all they captured the markets of their captured countries.

In this pursuit of industrialisation and consequent commercialisation, the capitalist industrialists of the West had invested their money for developing the necessary industrial infrastructure—that is tools, machinery, capital goods and varied raw materials. They also attracted the artisans who were working in their own guilds and recruited them as experts journey men (technicians) in their industrial establishments. Their number was not sufficient to cope with the requirements of new emerging industries. For meeting such requirements new workforce who could be engaged in these industries was needed. Old educational structure manned by clerics was, basically religious and spiritual could not train the required workforce for the new emerging industries. As such, these industrialists first started schools for imparting formal education in 3 Rs. As well as, after this they opened some industrial schools for training the youths in some trades like blacksmithy, tinsmithy, coppersmithy, carpentry, fitting and fabrication. In the long-run due to intensification of industries a big workforce was required. So the schools for imparting education in 3 Rs and, separate industrial schools for training youths in technical trades were increased. As such, the institution of schools for imparting formal education first came into being in England. Later on it spread in all European countries, which in the long-run became a universal phenomena for imparting education in 3 Rs and industrial trades to the youngers. In India, and in some Asian countries like China an unique type of semi-formal system of education was in existence. The aim of such system of education was different from the present system of formal education. In India, Gurukula Ashramas, Buddhist Monasteries, Jain Mathas and Muslim Madarsas used to train the youngers in religiosity, spirituality, morality and sociability. The main aim of education was life building.

While in search of markets for selling their industrial products as consumer goods, the capitalist countries captured many countries in the world, and made these countries as their colonies, where they tried to impose their culture patterns and cultural traits through cultural diffusion and acculturation. For this the capitalist industrialist countries tried to impose some elements of their social structure, as cultural traits, ways of living and values. And for this end some capitalist countries tried to impose their formal system of education. As already mentioned on the advice of Lord Macaulay, the then British Government in India run by British East India Company imposed formal education in 1833 A.D. on Indians which is still being followed by the Indians. This has killed the Indian culture to a large extent. Now, we Indians are having nothing of our culture. The acculturation, due to Western cultural diffusion, has been so strong that we Indians lost every element of their culture. We do everything in western style. It is (acculturation) this has which killed our social values as sociability, morality, cooperation, work habits and sanity, only we have been rewarded with self-centredness, greed, corruption and shameful crimes like loots, dacoits and rapes. The Indian culture which was popular in the world is no more and we are half alien. This happened due to alienistic formal system of education imposed on us by our British masters.

The Western capitalist industrialist countries always desired to build a marketing base of their industrialist products in under-developed countries. For this end, they also tried to occupy these countries, and for making the people of these countries loyal, these countries always tried to acculturate them to their culture. For doing this they always tried to impose their educational system, for changing their original elements of social structure, values, ways of living and cultural traits. In India on the advice of Lord Macaulay, the then law member in Viceroy's Council of British East Company, the British Government had imposed, the present formal system of education in 1833 A.D. on Indians which is still going on unchecked. The results of formal education are well-known to all of us. The Indian culture which was famous in the world for its hospitability, sociability, cohesion and cooperation, religiosity and spirituality, social integrity and simple living and high thinking is no more.

The Western capitalist industrialists always desired to build loyal colonies in order to exploit the human resources for their own benefits, and also make the captured colonies their business hubs. They always exploited the natural resources of their captured colonies for this purpose, they always tried to bring the social change in the social structures of the captured colonies by modifying their ways of living according to their cultures. This they did it in the garb of modernisation. Their alternative reformation movement was based on acculturation of their subjects through cultural diffusion, which was aimed to destroy the indigenous cultures of these countries systematically. These occupied countries had very good social systems, sub-systems and social structures of their own which had no money incentives. The people of these countries used to believe in simple living and high thinking, religiosity and spirituality and co-operation and homogeneity. First of all these capitalist-industrialist countries tried to change the mind-set of their subjects from simple living to hedonistic living. They employed a few of their subjects on Government jobs and, few in their industries. As such, people started becoming loyal to them. Such people adopted their cultural patterns, which in the long-run got boosted and, acculturation of majority of the Indians became a common social feature.

In the beginning, the overt aim of these capitalist colonies was to impart formal education to their subjects for moulding them subjects who could follow their language and culture willingly and could help them in their administration, serving as clerks. But the covert aim was, as Lord Macaulay might have perceived regarding India, was to mitigate and finally kill the indigenous culture through cultural diffusion and acculturation. The formal education was considered the best tool for killing the indigenous culture through cultural diffusion and acculturation, for achieving their political end. And the institution of school was considered the best instrument for imparting the formal education. As the science and technology developed, which boosted industrialisation, the formal education imparted by the school got a speedy boost. The human greedy nature played a vital role in the development of school formal education because majority of the people wanted to be economically well-off. For the economic gains they sacrificed many of their social values, and culture and adopted Western economic values. The education was increasingly differentiated which increased competition in the society. This increased the importance of the school day by day. The institution of school got more and more state protection. And for the degraded lower castes which had no educational avenues due to rigid orthodox caste structure the institution of school proved a boon to them.

Earlier, the education was not a state responsibility. It was a common enterprise of the society, be it managed by community or by a religious authority or by a non-Government agency. But when it was taken over by the state, school drifted from the society. As such, the society lost its say regarding the education of their children. The school management went in the hands of few bureaucrats who decided what to teach and what not to teach. The educational planning activities like curriculum construction became the domain and monopoly of very few. Even the teachers and principals of the schools had, and still have no say in this important educational activity, whereas in the olden times the teachers (*Gurus*) used to decide what to teach? It were they who used to visualise how the youngers would adjust in the society and would lead to a saneful social life. It were the old teachers who used to prepare the youngers to perform their social roles well after leaving the Gurukula Ashramas and adjust in the social milieu. As such, the present institution of school has no systemic role of social education. The present schools devote to the preparation of annual examination. There is no place for sociability and morality like elements in the present day school formal education. This is because the school functions as an state instrument. As such, it is a tool for materialising the dreams of the ruling parties. And for this purpose, the desired formal education is imparted. The state only lay stress on the removal of economic backwardness. Of course, it is necessary, but it should not be at the cost of killing of national culture. Education's primary roles, like preparing the youngers for saneful living by making them aware about the social, physical and cultural environments and, educating them to adjust in the society by inculcating in them social, moral and cooperative values, which is totally missing. Only, the emphasis is laid on material gains which has entailed cutthroat competition in the society. The old concept of homogenous cooperative social living is totally absent. Nothing is inculcated in this regard in the school education.

Therefore, it can be said that the formal education imparted in schools could not and, cannot provide viable education for life building. It can only prepare the youths for examination. Now-a-days, the best youth is considered one who could secure highest marks in annual examination and compete in the society for material gains. The parents, the community, the school administration and media try to give upbeat to this trend as we notice in daily newspapers. As such, the contemporary schools prepare our youngers to aspire for securing higher marks in annual examination for getting white collar jobs in Government offices and in other public organisations and nothing else. There is no place of axiology, sociability, character building, work culture and enculturation in the present system of school formal education. Not only this, the so-called public schools openly acculturate our youths to Western culture, cultural diffusion is not bad but it should not be at the cost of our national culture. The age old religious teachings, which used to make the individual spiritual and help in character building are totally missing in our present formal system of education. The so-called secularism also boosted this trend. Age old value systems which was handed over by our seers and our elders has totally disappeared from the society due to the present alienistic formal system of education imparted in our schools. Due to human materialistic greed and self-centredness dys-functioning of joint family system encouraged this trend. New materialistic system has strongly entrenched in our hearts. To achieve the material gains has become the individuals' prime life aim. This has entailed greed, self-centredness, corruption and non-sociability. The neighbour does not have time to talk to his neighbours. Respect for elders, sympathy for the weak, poor and fair sex and feeling of sharing cooperation are no more in the society. The joint family system has totally been crumbled and, nuclear family system has emerged which is totally self-centred and materialistic as, the members of the family (husband and wife) follow more or less Western value system. Our elites and educationists are totally immune to pay attention to this awkward social situation. They think that the teachers and the school should do what they are not doing.

Organisational, pedagogical and professional roles of the present educational system of which the school is the edifice are alien and do not serve to our educational needs. It could only create an euphoria of modernisation. Modernisation in which we believe is tantamount to invitation or imitation of the Westernisation. It aims at the renouncement of our old values and beliefs, customs, traditions, cultural traits and age old social and moral values. In other words, it is nothing but adoption of heterogeneous social system based on feudalistic social structure which forces us to renounce our old homogenous structure. It negates our old social values and culture which were/are the gifts of old seers and elders.

The present school education fails to enculturate our youths, rather it acculturates them and creates a class structures in our caste based social structure.

As already mentioned, Lord Macaulay who had conceived the idea of formal education through school while introducing the new type of English education for Indians. He not only had in mind to prepare the Indian clerks for East India Company Government but he had meticulously planned it for killing the Indian culture and cottage industries. His conception has been so successful that we Indians have lost our language, dress, food habits, old traditions, customs, cultural traits and what not? Lord Macaulay might be eating Indian milk cake and enjoying in his grave.

Also we have been benefited by English type of formal education. It could bring unity in diversity and, we could achieve independence, but at a high cost. The country was divided. A nation which looses its culture and national social system looses everything. Our alienistic system of formal education helped the English rulers in killing of Indian culture but Macaulay failed to realise that it could drag them out of India. Our political leaders and rulers, could not realise the bad aspects of the present alienistic formal education. They ignored the fact that it is the killer of our culture and, they allowed it to continue, thinking that the formal education would relieve us from economic backwardness. The other tragedy which encouraged the formal education was the emergence of English speaking elite class. This class constitute nearly 1.77 per cent of the total population of the country. But the English speaking people constitute a top brass of educationists, bureaucrats, army officers and other administrators. They rule the majority of people. These top brass people are generally the products of public schools. Those who know and speak their mother tongue were not and, are not given chance even to advice in educational matters. Even in educational institutions the persons are teaching or doing hand work are considered backwards. The school education administration has become the monopoly of English speaking elite class. It is this class who motivated and helped in the establishment of English speaking public schools which created an English speaking class of rich people. And it is this class which encouraged the acculturation openly. The English speaking people, who are the products of public schools is a small minority of the Indian population. They consider themselves superior and megalomaniac from rest of the population of the country. Bulk of the bureaucrats, administrators, army commanders, police officers, engineers, office staff and educators come from this elite class to govern the country. It is this class which foster English education and adopts Western culture and become totally accultured. Generally this class reaps the fruits and employment and power. The public schools fostered ugly competition in every sphere of public life. And due to this school education has been commercialised to some extent.

The present formal education in technical trades like blacksmithy, tinsmithy, coppersmithy, carpentry, fitting and in fabrication is imparted in special trade schools, polytechnics and industrial training institutes which have replaced all indigenous hereditical non-formal system of technical education. The system of non-formal education was a boon for Indian hereditary artisans. It used to develop a definite station in their lives. Earlier through the non-formal education in technical trades, skills were transmitted hereditically by the elders in all castes. It used to create a solid permanent social stratification on the caste bases in the Indian society. A young man used to be hereditically trained through apprenticeship, and to be made highly skilled in his hereditary vocation. There was no need of trade training schools. And the state was not required to spend on such training. Under the process of non-formal education, there used to be a wide spectrum of learning. The young used to visualise, observe and use all kinds of tools and raw materials. He used to learn by imitation, observation and continuous practice. There was not any formal programme of training. Now the industrial training institutes, which were established by the Government just after independence for training the youths formally in technical trades. But the I.T.I. trained persons are not so skilled as the hereditary non-formally trained artisans are. The reason behind this is that neither the artisan trainees have such wide spectrum for learning the skills nor the instructors working in the training institutes are highly skilled as the caste artisan generally are. Because of industrialisation which entailed mechanisation, the caste based technical vocations lost their eminence due to lack of certification. Due to this skilled hereditary artisans do not get jobs in Government and other workshops. They generally remain unemployed. Because of this, many of the hereditary skilled artisans have been uprooted from their villages. They have migrated to cities, towns for doing some petty jobs for their survival.

The politicians, though reap the harvest of caste structure in winning the elections, have totally ignored this fact. Though some artisan castes are still doing some wonderful jobs, their proficiency in their trade skills is ignored. And reason for this is their lack of formal education in technical trades. Their children, because of their financial weak position, also cannot get formal education in their hereditary trades. So, the artisan castes remain backward in the society. Under the present system of formal education only certification is possible from industrial schools, art schools, polytechnics and wood working institutes which pay the dividends and, not the ability and proficiency in trade skills. Due to this fact the artisan castes youths generally remain unemployed. And consequently the national production comes down. Also the development of culture fumbled. Those who are not skilled in technical trades, get employment and exit. Buttering, favouritism and also corruption increase in the society. So, this fact cannot be denied that the alienistic system of formal education is responsible for these state affairs to some extent.

In olden days the socialisation of the child was initiated from the home through some *sanskaras*. Now the home atmosphere of the child has totally become hedonistic and changed. Nuclear families are in the rat-race of money earning for meeting their hedonistic, consumeristic and xenophilic needs. Religious prayers have no place neither at home nor at the school because of secular policy. Now, where to learn religion. Religiosity is necessary for imbibing spirituality, morality, social values and character building in the youngers. The result is what we read in newspapers—the son murdered the father for grabbing the family property, the mother-in-law murdered the daughter-in-law for not brining sufficient dowry. Crimes like chain pulling, pick-pocketing, burglary, bribery, corruption and rapes have become the common features in the society. The youngers do not respect the teachers, elders and ladies. Big cities like Delhi are becoming dens of criminals. As such, the crime index is increasing in the society day by day.

Before, independence there was no fear of dacoits while walking in the night in the jungles. One had to fear the wolves and beasts. Now the jungle beasts and wolves are no more. There are many human beasts and wolves. One cannot go to his agricultural fields after sun set. The capital city like Delhi has become a rape city. Kidnapping, loot, snatching have also become common feature in rural areas too. Also, many heinous crimes like rapes, money matching, day burglaries, chain pulling, pick-pocketing and looting have also become a common feature in small towns, villages and cities. What is the reason for this ugly social situation, it is because of our alien system of formal education which is only examination oriented and does not inculcate good life attitudes in the youngers and also does not enculturate them.

Basically, all of our youths aspire white collar jobs. After getting university degrees they roam for the jobs. Very few of them got jobs as there is a cutthroat competition in job market. Under our present formal school education, neither the students' attitudes and aptitudes for working are based nor, they get any chance to work with their elders on their farms, home, workshops and shops. The concept of Sanskritisation which has emerged due to social degradation of lower castes by the higher castes is another factor to promote no work culture. From the very beginning, due to Varna system which was converted to birth based caste system, the hand workers have ever been looked down with contempt by the higher castes. And this attitude promoted Sanskritisation. The Sanskritisation motivates the lower castes to adopt the pattern of living of higher castes. While unemployed youth find it easy to commit crimes to meet their hedonistic requirements. The result is brooking of criminal society.

The greatest tragedy is that after fifty eight years of our independence from the foreign rule, the politicians, bureaucrats and educationists are still immune to the present state of acculturation. They are still glued to the alien formal system of education. They had cremated the new scheme of basic education, along with the dead body of the father of the nation. No doubt the present system of formal education is also useful in the present scientific industrial age, but it should not be allowed to kill our national culture. As such, acculturation should be checked through enculturation.

TYPES OF SCHOOLS

Now-a-days, there are various types of schools which are functioning under Government as instruments of the state. Such schools are as under:

1. Pre-primary schools,
2. Primary schools,
3. Middle schools,
4. Secondary or High schools, and
5. Senior Secondary schools or Intermediate (schools) colleges.

Besides these there are many coaching and preparatory schools which are run by private businessmen for earning money. Such schools are called as 'creches', day care schools and preparatory schools. Besides, these they are large number of preparatory schools which prepare the students for appearing at the entrance examination for the higher institute of learnings at I.I.Ts, I.B.M., I.M.M. and for civil service examinations.

Besides these schools there are schools which impart technical or skilled education. Such schools are as under:

1. Schools of Art or College of Art,
2. Wood working institutes,
3. Industrial Training Institutes,
4. Polytechnics
5. Fashion Design schools, and
6. Other skill related schools as leather craft schools, paper machie school and puppet making schools.

Some detailed description about the schools:

1. *Pre-primary Schools*: Mostly pre-primary schools are lower kindergarten and upper kindergarten schools. Very few these schools are run by the Government. Most of these schools are run by private persons which earn money by these schools. Mostly schools, 'creches' and 'day care schools' are run by the housewives. Most of them are not trained in pedagogy. Not only women but many greedy

persons do this job. In the village of the writer an illiterate barber who was running a barber shop in Saharanpur, U.P. had opened such nursery schools in the village. Also the people like to educate their kids in schools. The barber had employed two or three unemployed youths who were also unaware about pedagogy. However, the barber earned a lot of money. After his death the school did not function. For many people such schools are good source of income. Mostly all such schools admit kids of 2½ years to 4½ years of age group, who after getting in these schools seek admission in primary or lower class in public schools.

2. *Primary Schools*: Mostly primary schools are run by District Boards in rural areas and the municipalities in the town and cities. The kids of 5 to 6 years of age group are admitted in these schools in first class. In primary schools the kids get education up to 4th class.
3. *Middle Schools*: After this the children seek admission in middle schools in 5th class. In middle school education is imparted up to 8th class.
4. *Secondary or High School*: After passing 8th class the students go to secondary or high school and get admission in 9th class. The students study in 9th and 10th classes. After passing 10th class examination or secondary examination, which is conducted by the state senior secondary examination board, the students get secondary or high school examination certificate.
5. *Senior Secondary School*: Secondary schools are considered most important because after passing senior secondary or intermediate examination the students can seek admission in university colleges or in technical institution.
6. *Public Schools*: So-called public schools actually are not public schools, but these are schools for the children of rich business class and elite class people. The general public cannot peep into these schools as these schools are very costly. These schools charge very high fees. As such poor class people cannot afford to admit their children in these schools. In England such schools are called 'grammar schools' and, 'Government run schools' are called public schools. The public schools in India generally affiliate with the Central Board of Secondary Education, Delhi. The

medium of instruction in these schools is English. The dressing pattern of these schools is alien. The students of these schools speak in English. So it can be said that these schools generally acculturate the students to Western culture. There is no chance of enculturation of the students. It can be said these schools create a cultural lag in the country. About two per cent population of the students study in these schools who get better chances of employment. Majority of the bureaucrats, educationists, army officers and many politicians are generally products of these public schools, who become elites. So, there is a craze to study in the public schools.

But out of these schools there are also some schools which try to enculturate their students. Though such schools are run by socially motivated business class, these schools also charge high fees. One such socially motivated school is Ganga International School, located in the garb of nature on 22 acre plot of land at Hiran Kudna, one kilometer away from Hiran Kudna More, Rohtak Road, Delhi 110 041. It was established by honourable Lala Shri Gangan Bishan Gupta. The school is unique in its functions. It is situated in jungle out of the city and is like Gurukula, Kangri, Haridwar which was established by Late Shri Swami Shardhanand ji, Gurukula, Narsen, District, Haridwar, Uttrakhand and Rishi Schools situated in jungles on the river banks in Andhra Pradesh and Ganga banks in Varanasi, U.P. are of this category. The Rishi schools were established by famous thinker and educationist Late Shri J. Krishnamoorthy who was fed up with the alienistic formal education and consequent acculturation. For enculturation of youth Late Shri J. Krishnamoorthy had opened the Rishi schools. Life building was also his aim.

Perspectives of School Education

Since the rise of human society there existed agencies which used to educate the people. The human-beings are said to be rational beings. But there exists individual differences amongst them. Some of them are very intelligent. Some are diligent. Some are greedy, whereas some are not. Some have unique psyche. Some always think of common good. Some are self-centred.

They do not hesitate in cheating others. Some have sane personality while some others are rubbish, who can do anything for personal ends. Some human societies have been facing such many serious social problems since the rise of their societies. And in many societies the sane persons have been educating people to be sane from the very beginning. In the some societies epistemic, knowledgeable persons used to make the common people aware about the social evils, and educate them through religious discourses for living a sane social life. They used to arrange social gatherings for such social education in the beginning, which in the long-run took the shape of specific schools. Such schools were found in India, China, Greece and Israel. These schools were arranged for common good without any material inclination. In India such schools were arranged at Rishi Ashramas, which in the long-run took the shape of Gurukula Ashramas. Gurukula Ashramas like Vallabhi, Ujjain, Taxila etc. were such schools. Main aim of such schools was life moulding the young individuals. There was not state control over such schools or Ashramas. These were purely run by the society. In Greece such schools used to discuss and impart theological, ontological, and axiological knowledge to the students. The Socratic School, Hippocratic Schools in Greece and, Vaishnitic, Vedic, Buddhist and Jain schools were schools in India. In China Buddhist schools and Confucius schools were also found which aimed at life building of the youngers. Later on when Islam religion emerged such schools called 'Madarsa' were established in many Islamic countries. The main aim of the Islamic Madarsas was also life moulding of the youths by making them religious and spiritual. These schools did not interfere in other religions.

As Hereclitus said, change in every sphere of life is inevitable. With the passage of time change also took place in, educational fields throughout the world. The world's old civilised countries like India, Greece, Latin Europe, Hebrews, China could not be escaped from the educational change. Man by nature is greedy. With the development of science and technology the man improved his fabricating methods for making things for human use. This increased the specialisation in working methods which required the adaptability of new educational methods. The human greed increased day by day.

The man became self-centred and increasingly believed in material enjoyment which entailed hedonism and xenophilism. The man invented many new things for human use. As such, many industries emerged. Things were produced mechanically which needed markets. And in due course of time industrialists searched the markets for their industrial goods which they made the countries their colonies. These industrialists killed the cultures of these occupied countries through acculturation, which they did by imposing their systems of education.

Therefore, it can be safely assumed that the present system of formal education which is being imparted through the institution of school could not provide education for life building which was done by the Indian educational institutions like Gurukula Ashramas, Mathas, Sikhsa Peeths and also by Muslim Madarsas. The present system of formal education only aims at preparing the youths for annual examination which is necessary to face the changing social situations, which occurred due to human greed. The examination system has also killing effects. Many youths commit suicides. Yesterday (24/5/2006) a young girl committed suicide as she could not secure expected marks in the CBSE's senior examination 2006. The best youth is one who secures highest marks in examination. And present best school is one whose all students pass the annual examination and, come in flying colours. In C.B.S.E. Senior Examination 2006 only all students could pass in flying colours C.R.P.F. School, Rohini is one of these. The parents, community, the schools, the administrators, whole society and the media give heat to this trend. As such, it can be said that our schools only concentrate on the preparation of the students for annual examination. The present aim of education is to prepare the youths for white collar jobs and nothing beyond this end. There is no place for enculturation of the students in school curriculum. So-called public schools openly acculturate our students to Western culture. The school dress of these schools is an open indication to cultural diffusion and acculturation. Of course in the present age of science and technology cultured diffusion cannot be stopped, but it should not happen at the cost of killing of national culture. Because of our present system of alienistic formal system of education, age old religious teachings have disappeared from school education and from familial education, which was necessary to generate character building, development of sociability and morality. It is argued that it has happened due to secularism and materialism. Dysfunctioning of joint family system has also added fuel to this social fire. To achieve only material gains has become the prime aim of human life. And this is the prime perspective of our school education. To think how can our school education meet the new emerging challenges of social flux, and root out this social evil is major question for the consideration of our educationists.

Our organisational, professional, sociological, economical and educational needs cannot be met from our present alienistic formal system of education. The present institution of school is the edifice of all kinds of education, until and unless the school education is improved the perspectives of Indian education cannot be improved. The present day school education creates an euphoria of modernisation. Modernisation, in the present form is tantamount to imitation of Westernisation. It aims at renouncing of our old beliefs, values, traditions, art, cultural traits and age old social homogeneity. It is nothing but adoption of heterogeneous alien social system based on feudalistic exploitative social structure, at the cost of our old homogenous social structure. It negates our old social values and eliminates our national cultural development.

Also the present formal technical education has rooted out our old system of non-formal education. Our present day school education centres around only teaching academic subjects and, all students in spite of their liking to other educational areas, have to study the academic subjects. Majority of the students run after university education. And after getting university degrees they roam for jobs. Very few of them get jobs because there is a cutthroat competition in the job market. The present system of education does not have any space for developing work culture. So, neither the present day school students have any chance for the development of parental skills nor they can develop any other work attitudes, as the present day school education does not have such provision. Therefore, our school educated youths neither can work at the parental shops or workshops nor at the agricultural fields. The concept of Sanskritisation in Indian society is another factor which promotes this kind of awkward social situation. From the very beginning due to 'Varna' social stratification and consequent rigid birth based caste system the hand worker has ever been looked upon with contempt by the higher castes which promoted Sanskritisation. The Sanskritisation motivates the backward castes to shift to the life patterns styles of higher castes to look like them. While youths unemployed some try to do crimes to meet their hedonistic requirements the result is brooking of a criminal society. If school education logically reformed, as per social requirements, it can play key roles in social development. As such, the educationists and administrators should look into this aspect.

6

Institutions of Higher Education

In olden days, mostly the Indians were rationalistic, monotheistic religious, spiritual, epistemic and tolerant. They used to believe in simple living, high thinking, tolerance and cooperation. This is why old Indian seers could develop six theistic Indian philosophical schools—'Sankhya-Yoga', 'Naya-Veshiska', 'Vedant—Advit Vedant' and religious scriptures like *Upanishads*, Shruties, Arynakas, Brahmans and epics like *Ramayana*, *Mahabharata* and *Shrimad Bhagavad Gita*. And due to freedom of expression and a sense of religious tolerance some atheistic schools of philosophy like (*a*) Carvac, (*b*) Buddhism, and (*c*) Jainism could also emerge and prosper. And in the later days some specific theistic schools like Sikhism, Nirankaris, Radhaswami's, Aryasmajs and Vaishnites could emerge. Religious tolerance has been the main quality of Hindu religion. Hindu religion is one of the oldest religion of the world. It never infringed on other religions. About 2500 year B.C. ago many Hebrews (Parsis) had migrated to India and had settled in Mumbai and in other coastal areas; they were not disturbed by the locals at all. The Hindu Kings neither forced the migrants to adopt Hinduism, nor pressurised those who adopted new religions like Buddhism, Jainism, Islam and Christianity, to retreat to their original religion Hinduism.

Newly emerged religions—Buddhism and Jainism had established their own educational institutions of higher learning like Nalanda University, which had attracted many scholars from many Asian countries like China, Japan, Korea, Vietnam, Thailand, Myanmar and Ceylon. The Hindus never asked the visitors from these countries to adopt Hinduism. Before Nalanda many institutions of higher learning like Taxila (now in Pakistan) Vallabhi, and Ujjaini etc. existed where scholars from the whole world used to come to study religiosity, spirituality and good governance. They are historical records of the foreign scholars who had come to study at these institutes of higher learning. The citizens of many countries like Indonesia, Java-Somatra, Fiji, Mauritius had adopted Hinduism. And they were attracted to these institutions of higher learning in India. The Hindus never had overt or covert policy of religious conversion.

Main aim of old Indian higher education was moulding of life of youths by inculcating in them good life habits and, developing spirituality, religiosity, morality, sociability for the development of good behaviour and character. This was necessary for cooperative social living. The life motto of the products of Indian institutions of higher learning was to spread this message throughout the world by delivering religious discourses to general public while living in family life (गृहस्थाश्रम).

But the human greed and self-centredness of men and women made the Indians slaves. The Indians remained disunited. First the human greed and self-centredness made them to fight amongst themselves. Consequently the Muslims captured and ruled Indians for about one thousand years. Later on, the Western traders entrenched, captured and ruled India for approximately two hundred years. During this period the Indian Institutions of higher learning faded away. And the foreign rulers imposed their form of school education and, later on the higher university education, which are being followed till now.

UNIVERSITY EDUCATION

The universities had come into being before than the schools which provide formal education. The universities had not limited curriculum as, the present schools have. The man has ever been speculative. He has been trying to know as much as possible. The earlier schools could not provide much opportunity to know much and provide avenues for higher learning. When the schools could not provide avenues for advance learning, some scholars upgraded, some schools as centres of higher learning, which later on got the patronage of church and the state. And such centres of advance learning were called universities.

The term university is a derivation from the Latin word 'universata', meaning a 'community' or 'corporation' which devotes to learning. The full title used for the term university was 'universita magistorium-et scholarim'. At the end of 14th century A.D. the term 'universita' began to be used with exclusive meaning of law, fully recognised community of teachers and scholars, and gradually the term 'Studium Generale' (a centre for instruction for all) replaced the above term. The charters allowed schools, other than cathedral schools, to be opened and licensed and, to be operated under their teachers. Such schools were also granted recognition by religious authorities. After this reformation charters were increasingly granted by secular authorities also. Under these charters, institutions of higher learning, or so to say the upgraded schools of higher academic status, were empowered to confer degrees. And today, all over the world the universities receive royal or national charters which enable these universities to confer degrees and enjoy other privileges to promote education in the higher branches of learning. In such a way the universities came into being or in existence after the schools.

As already mentioned, prior to these universities, there existed some centres of higher learning in the world. There were academies and phobias in ancient Greece and Rome. The centres of higher learning like Taxila, Ujjaini, Valllabhi and Nalanda etc. etc. in India, which were of international repute and had attracted scholars from all over the world. But in India there was no state or religious control over these institutions of higher learning. In Arab world and, also in China there were centres of higher learning. These centres were neither established under the royal charters nor these had state patronage. These came into being with the efforts of the scholars and with the support of community and society. In Muslim world still there exist examples of such centres of higher learning. These are Dar-ul-Ulum of Deoband (India) and Dar-ul-Ulum Cairo (Egypt). These are still being run by the Muslim scholars with the support of community and society having no state control. These are still attracting scholars from all over the world. Their character of action is also of non-interference in other religions, so to say these institutes of higher learning are secular in nature.

Originally, the universities restricted to the study of law, theology and medicine. As long as in 9th century A.D. medicine was at Sabrino University. During 12th and 13th centuries A.D., other great Italian Universities maintained the tradition of teaching law, theology and medicine. There was also revival of legal studies at Paris and Bologna. These become recognised centres of civil and canon law. Paris university organisation influenced all central European universities including Cambridge. The Oxford University grew out of a school opened by William Champeauna during the first decade of 12th century A.D. About the same time many eminent scholars gathered at Paris and with the reputation and inspiration of them Abelard (1142 A.D.) did much to make the University of Paris famous, organised in four faculties—theology, canon law, medicine and arts. Its administrative control passed into the hands of oligarchy, teachers and officials, while teaching function passed on to the associated colleges. By 14th century A.D., there arise some 40 colleges under the secular or sectarian control, thus forming a federation like that existing in universities of Cambridge and Oxford, London. Each college or hall had less independence than the colleges or halls in London had.

The number of universities in Europe grew rapidly during the 14th century A.D. The secularisation of Paris University occurred as a consequence of French Revolution. In 1773 A.D. a decree of the revolutionary conventional abolished the universities and colleges of the ancient regime, and new system of university organisation was promulgated by Napoleon Bonaparte in 1808 A.D. The system of education under the University of Paris was to be controlled and directed by the State. Each of seventeen regions was to have certain faculties. These became regional universities in 1896. The year after religious authorities were allowed some freedom to re-establish faculties under their control.

The development of universities for technological studies, within the university framework came very late, as the institutions imparting instructions in technical studies were considered inferior to the institution imparting education in philosophy, medicine, law and theology. The institute imparting instruction in technical studies, 'Technische Hochschulen', in Germany was the first institute quickly reached to the status of a technical university in 19th century A.D. Thereafter, everywhere, most significant even was the rapid advance in studies of natural and technical studies. Technical universities grown up in Europe and, in several parts of the Commonwealth countries. Meanwhile, the progress in the development of technical universities has been startling in different forms in Europe. The original settlers were quick to establish colleges for the preparation of clergy. Harvard, Yale, William and Mary, Princeton, Kings Brown (later Colombia), Rutledge, and

Dartmouth were all established before 1750 A.D. A more liberal programme of liberal studies was introduced by Benjamin Franklin in the University of Pennsylvania. The older universities retain, even today, some of the conservatism of the European universities; but the circular offerings have been modified by the pressure exerted by large state universities. These institutions were originally established with the aid of federal funds to meet the agricultural and industrial needs of the country's expanding economy. Grants were sanctioned for technological studies. This enabled the universities to introduce a wide range of professional courses at the highest level. The professional and vocational courses which were considered of low grade at one time became more popular. But still majority of the students opt for other courses. In U.S.A., it is estimated that only about 8 per cent opt for technical courses and join technical educational institutions, 23 per cent opt for professional courses like education, four per cent go to applied-biology, 12 per cent to business and commerce and the rest opt for humanities. One reason for this situation might be that admission in technical institutions becoming difficult day by day. And the number of the higher agricultural and technological institutes, which enjoy the status of universities is increasing. Also there are many other professional and vocational institutions which are getting attention world over, such as, poultry, dairy and milk products, book publication, journalism, marketing, quality control, dance and drama, folk arts, forestry, fisheries so on and so forth.

All Common Wealth Countries, including India, followed more or less the British pattern of school education and university education believing it would relieve them of age old poverty and economic backwardness, ignoring the bad effects of acculturation. And in the name of modernisation all newly independent countries adopted English as medium of instruction ignoring their mother tongues. As such, the English has become an universal lingual Franca. This has resulted in mass universal acculturation.

Indian schools, universities and a few technical institutions were established on British pattern. First of all Calcutta University was established on the pattern of London University. Thereafter the Universities of Madras, Bombay and Punjab (Lahore, Pakistan) were established more or less on the same pattern with affiliated colleges. Panjab University (Lahore, Pakistan) in the first instance was to cover Delhi, Punjab, North Western Frontier Province and

Sindh (now all in Pakistan). With the growing demand the universities of Allahabad, Lucknow and Agra were established during the British period. The Agra University was an affiliating university. It covered large parts of U.P., Madhya Pradesh and Rajasthan. The universities of Lucknow and Allahabad were unitary universities. The English masters also felt the need for establishing some technical institutions. When they were fabricating Ganges Canal from Haridwar to Kanpur, U.P., for irrigation a large civil engineering work force was required and they established Thomson Engineering College, Roorkee, U.P. (now I.I.T. in Uttrakhand) and also a Government workshop at Roorkee. The Thomson Engineering College was upgraded and was given the status of university in 1948 first after the independence. On the pattern of Thomson Engineering College, Roorkee, Michal Engineering College was established at Lahore (now in Pakistan) of which specialisation was Mechanical Engineering to meet the demand of mechanical fabrication. An institute of civil engineering was also established at Pune in Bombay Province to meet the civil engineering fabrication demand of the Western India. After sometime Harcourt Butter Technological Institute, Kanpur, King George Medical College, Lucknow, Sarojini Medical College, Agra, Government College of Art, Lucknow, Government Wood Working Institute, Bareilly and Government Carpentery School, Allahabad (later on upgraded as Working Institute after independence), U.P. And also Mayo College of Art, Jaipur, Mayo College of Art, Lahore (now in Pakistan), School of Art, Calcutta, School of Art, Madras, Wood Working Institute, Jallandhar, Punjab were established. Many Indians also established many such Institutes as Sir J.J. School of Art, Bombay was one of them. With the efforts of Sir Syed Ahmad Khan Muslim University, Aligarh was established at Aligarh. With the efforts of Pandit Madan Mohan Malviya, the Banaras Hindu University came into being. Gurudev Rabindra Nath Tagore had established Vishwa Bharti University in Bengal, which is now a university of international repute. Mahatma Shardhanand and Hansraj had tried to revive the Gurukula Ashram education, and he had established Gurukul Kangri Ashram, Haridwar which is a deemed University. The Government of India, with the collaboration of some advanced foreign agencies established Indian Institutes of Technology first at Kharagpur, and later on at Madras, Bombay, Kanpur, Delhi, Guwahati and at Roorkee. Later on institutes of higher learning in the field of agriculture were established, at least one in every state. A Central Research Institute in the field of Agriculture was established at Pusa, New Delhi. With the efforts of Dr. Zakir Hussain, Jamia Millia Islamia, New Delhi was established in twenties of twentieth century. With the efforts of Maulana Madni, Dar-ul-Ulum, Deoband was established. After independence many medical institutes like All India Institute of Medical Services at Delhi, Medical Institute at Chandigarh and at many other places were established.

Also after the independence many state Governments established many industrial training institutes for training the youths in technical trades. This was done for developing a workforce for the Indian industrial establishments. In these industrial training institutes technical training was given in formal way. These training institutes have uprooted the artisans who were trained non-formally hereditary in their homes.

7

Social Flux and Educational Adaptability

The word 'flux' is a Latin word meaning 'the flow of a tide', or 'flowing or passing from one stage to another stage', or 'a change'. And flexibility means the quality of the flux or change. The word 'adapt' is also a Latin word meaning, to correspond, 'to remodel' 'to adjust in the social situations'. The term 'social change' means flux in social situations. The flux in social situations need adaptability for sound and sane existence in the society. The social change always entails economic, axiological, cultural, consumeristic, educational and theocratic changes. If these changes are viable and good the man becomes prosperous. If the social changes are not good, these entail poverty and backwardness. The Greek Philosopher, Hereclitus was the first thinker to highlight the concept of 'flux' or 'change' in the human world and physical world. He said that all things in the physical world—i.e. the physical phenomena, human-beings and social institutions are in flux at every movement. An individual changes at every movement as his/her heart beats at every movement. A river flows and changes at every movement. The sun rises in the morning and sets in the evening. It entails night. So also the night follows the day. A child is born, grows, becomes old and dies. Likewise, every social infrastructure changes with the passage of time, and it takes new form. Education is one of the most social infrastructure changes with the passage of time. So, the educational infrastructure which existed in the past is no more. The changing social situations need a thorough assessment of educational structure and requires necessary educational adaptability. Without adaptability the social subsistence is not possible. Adaptability can only be done according to the human needs and requirements. And education can be a tool to meet these requirements. So for suitable educational adaptability, it is necessary to do necessary social assessment and improvement.

SOCIAL CHANGE

Social change occurs due to the significant alterations in social structure, that is, living patterns, social actions and interactions and, their consequences and manifestations on the total society. All these embody rules of conduct, values, cultural traits and symbols. The social change is prevalent and is a permanent feature of life—that is contemporary, past and future life. Role of social change in modern period is greater than olden days. Change is essential for biological, social, economical, epistemical circles in human life. Social change provides continuity to the social existence also.

Paradoxically the rate of social change has accelerated in the real world of experience, that is, scientific disciplines, which could be possible due to the science and technology. Main impetus to the rate of social change could have occurred/gained due to the greedy nature of human-beings. The man is never satisfied with his achievements. And if something new is gained, it positively entail change in human life. This encompasses all kinds of change in social life, that is, change in human living patterns, leadership, localisation to centralisation, simple living to luxurious living, change in occupational structure—that is cottage industries to mechanisation and industrialisation, specification and bureaucratisation and discontinuance of old manual methods of fabrication. All these happened due to particular inventions.

Social Change and Cultural Change

Social change is that which mainly refers to human behaviour and cultural change which refers to some culturally meaningful symbols produced by human-beings. There is interplay between complex normative patterns of behaviour which we call institutions. These provide rational for social control and human activities in general.

Cultural change requires some social actions, and social change is likely to have some cultural counteractions. However, change in some cultural sub-systems—for example, language, the arts, theological and philosophical systems may be viewed in vertical abstractions from concrete human behaviour. Similarly fluctuations in speaking, fashion, dressing, eating and in behaving may be viewed autonomous.

In order to identify social change we must first of all (1) identify the social structure to which these principles are to be applied, (2) specify time for meaning the change, and (3) to know the psychological perspectives of the human-beings which generally motivates the social beings to change. Without analysing these three conditions nothing can be said about the emergence of social change. There cannot be a single cause of social change in any system or sub-system. Things which are to be identified are (1) individual varieties as of simple nature or of hedonistic nature. The hedonistic human nature generally does not evade in complying the nature of other hedonistic persons. This entails cultural diffusion which results in acute acculturation; (2) technological innovations; and (3) population growth. Such enquiries of specific change lead to social theories of social change.

Moor (1963) said that for small scale social structures in general—face to face groups or formal organisation we can safely assume that social change will originate through formal familiar mechanism as the normative requirement for role performances. Large scale social systems, such as whole societies are less easily studied. But it cannot be denied that the present flexibility in social structure, declining sociability and socialisation lead to know the social flexibilities which do not usher for adjustments in the sociability. This requires educational adaptability. Education adaptability, taken as per social needs, can save the society from degradation and social fall.

To meet the ugly face of social change proper educational infrastructure and proper adaptability is very necessary. Such educational programme should aim at the inculcation of ideal life and social values. And our present alienistic formal education lack such values due to examination pressure.

In 19th century predecessors of modern sociology were pre-occupied with the dynamics of social change. Fredric Le Play attempted to establish canons for systematic description of social types. He attempted to trace the paths of history. Auguste Comte was most ambitious. He invented the laws of three stages—

theological, metaphysical and positivist to which all world civilisations were supposed to confirm.

Evolutionary Theory of Social Change

The directionality of social change may be due to increasing social complexity which came due to structural differentiation in the society may be said a major trend of evolutionary theory of social change. It was influenced by the biological theory of Darwin. Herbert Spencer, Lewis Henery Morgan and some others used Darwin's notion as selective notes for both cross section diversity of societies and cultures and the supposedly segmental stages of social organisations. By the end of 19th century evolutionary theory was dominant factor in social thought. Williams Grame's writing show this trend in spite his tilt to realities. Emile Durkheim whose life long devotion has been for explaining social phenomena in terms of the balance of an independent social system has caused him to identify with what which became the functional approach to the society.

Marxist Theory of Social Change

Even Marxism was a variant of evolutionism particularly in its adherence to notion of sequentional stage of social organisation. The Marxists tried to show how social change came by laying great stress on interaction due to technology which affected social organisation. It spread evolutionary approach because of its belief that one stage of organisation followed by another stage through the operations of the processes that were imperial and unsocial.

Functional Theory of Social Change

Functionalism is an attempt to explain the social phenomena by other social phenomena that are contemporary or quasi-simultaneous. In this respect it rejects the 'quest' for origins. Some of its proponents (i.e. Emile Durkhiem, Radcliff Brown and Malinouski) also tended to suppress all queries about the actual dynamics of social change, while exchanging their views in genetic terms. For them, the demonstration of inter-dependence between different elements of social structure came to mean the search for self-equilibrating mechanism in the society.

From functionalism, contemporary theory is not only a depiction of notions of systematic linkage which may be sequential, but through the concept of 'dys-function' some notion of tension and incipient change also emerged. However, with the renewal, the analysis of social change probably owes more to the undeniable facts of contemporary life particularly to the aspects of modernisation. Although the 'Functional System Models' have served rather well as predictors expected eventual changes in the elements of social structural changes in the elements of social structure held to be related to economic development. All modern societies have some kind of social structures which can lead unwarranted determinism. This mode of analysis has developed comparative states. Pre-existing heterogeneity becomes homogeneity in due course of time. It promotes functionalism.

However, it cannot be denied that social change is a universal factor. It occurs every where in every society entailing certain problems, for which functional equilibrium system is also needed, for which appropriate educational adaptability is needed for the younger generation. The educational programme should also be so designed which could tackle the social tension management. It will require the empirical hedonistic study in the society. This will help in avoiding social conflicts, which arise due to disparities between the members of the society.

Problems of Detection and Measurement of Social Changes

Social change takes intensive time for observation. Educational institutions and also educational authorities cannot do this because of the pressure of examination system under the present alienistic formal system of education. The study of happenings of social change should be undertaken by the Ministry of Human Resources Development, for which a 'Study Panel' should be formed. The panel should notice and record the changes occurred in brief periods. For longer period there should be a historical study. Historians' interest often does not coincide with those of sociologists. Historians have rarely made use of qualitative techniques of data reporting, whereas the sociologists are interested in constructing or recording actual rates of social change. As such, much of the past history look, immune to this aspect of social change.

The Problem of Magnitude of Social Change

What is changing is a primary question? The identification of elements or constructs of social change for observation and analysis is theoretical matter. Opinions may differ as what constitutes a significant social change. Tiny alterations in a small package may be points of interests to sociologists. But how much 'social change' is to be significant and what criteria is to be applied to meet the 'social change' challenge is to be studied by the study panel of the system constructs are studied by the functionalist 'Study Panel' seriously some solutions can be found to the problems caused by social change. If all parts of the society are taken to be independent, a dilemma that change may be viewed through differentiations or variations or the entire social whole to have a gestalt view. As such, the problem of analysing the social change is not simple. The structural looseness of the society is evident and verified. It is, therefore, possible that small changes may alter social system by cumulative degrees.

Social Change in India

Social change in India has brought many damaging social situations. It can be said a 'functional social change', as the Indian society was originally socially stratified on biological functional basis. The Indian society was socially stratified in four Varna—(1) Brahmans as head of the society, (2) Kshatriyas as torso of the society, (3) Vaishyas as legs of the society, and (4) Sudras as feet of the society. The well-functioning of the society can only be possible if there is homogeneity in all groups. The Varna type of social stratification was done on the basis as harmonious functioning of human biological whole. As all body parts in the human body function harmoniously, it was assumed that Indian social stratification based on 'Varna' system would also function harmoniously and would provide permanent employment opportunities. So the old Indian social stratification was done for a logical harmonious functioning of the Indian society. But in due course of time it was converted into a rigid birth based caste structure, which totally blocked the upward movement of the lower castes. And due to this the Indians faced the serious degrading situation in the world. In the beginning the ruling upper caste Kshatriyas fought each other. And due to this the foreign Muslim invaders captured the country and ruled India for nearly one thousand years. Later on, the Western imperialists, the British, made the Indians slaves and ruled India about two hundred years. During this period they tried to kill the Indian culture totally, which was once famous in the world. They did so by imposing their formal system of education with English as a prime subject. This had created the cultural diffusion which acculturated the Indian to Western culture totally. And due to this, we Indians lost every aspect of our culture. Now everything has changed. We speak in foreign English language. We dress in foreign style. And sometimes it becomes difficult to identify the gender whether a girl or boy. We eat fast and junky foods. Our life styles have totally changed. We were the believers in simple living and high thinking. Now we sleep late in the night and rise late in the morning. Indian culture was based on equality and homogeneity in spite of rigid caste structure. Karl Marx had praised the Indian culture. He said that the Indian culture was one of the best cultures of the world as it was based on nice sociability and equality. Now the class structure has also emerged in India. A car owner would always like to talk with a car owner. It has added fuel to the old birth based caste structure. Social inequality has very much increased. And this has happened due to blind acculturation of the Indians. No social harmony is seen in Indian society. Indian sociability and reception have totally gone. Joint family system has been totally crumbled. Mostly people remain in the rat-race of money living nuclear families. The family elders are also totally ignored by the youngers. The parents are unable to inculcate good life attitudes and habits in youngers. With the results the youngers do not develop good work habits. The corruption has become rampant. Nothing can be got done without greasing the palms of the concerned officials. Metropolises, cities and towns have become the dens of criminals. The criminals roam scot free in the day to visualise the targeting spots. The young girls who were once considered pious and were worshiped are openly raped. Even father and uncles do not hesitate to rape their own girls. These are all outcomes of the social change. Everyone aspires to be modern, hedonistic and consumeristic at the cost of simplicity and spirituality. A nation which looses its culture looses everything including independence. We have faced a very disgraceful situation for a long period in the past. May God keeps us independent in our future. And for this adaptability of sound system of education which might revive our old national culture is necessary.

SOUND SYSTEM OF EDUCATION

Sound system of education, which is to be adapted, should be so designed which may eradicate all social evils entailed by foreign imposed acculturation. Of course, the knowledge of science and technology is very necessary in the present modern industrial age, but it should not be at the cost of our cultural development. The present formal system of education is totally alienistic. It is examination oriented which breeds cutthroat competition in the society. It totally ignores the enculturation of our youngers. It makes the parents mad for good shining examination results. In the past the old Indian education was totally life building oriented. It had no provision of examination system. As such our present system of formal education needs drastic reformation, which should be aimed at positive enculturation. It should give attention to the following points on which educational adaptability should be based.

1. Life Building

The main aim of education should be life building, which has a wide spectrum. The youngers should be prepared to live a sane social life. For that some good life attitudes, habits are to be inculcated. They should behave well with the members of the society. They should speak true. They should be cooperative and helpful to fellow beings. They should develop a habit knowing about their environment. In other words they should be epistemic, and develop a sense of self-introspection and working.

2. Unity in Diversity

India is multi-religious, multi-racial and multi-ethnic country. As such the youngers should be educated to adjust with the persons of all religions. They should be made tolerant to live in an atmosphere of unity in diversity.

3. Development of Work Culture

The main drawback of our present system of education is that our youngers evade doing hard work. It is because they mainly concentrate on reading. They are not also innovated by their parents because of examination phobia. The schools also devote to the study of academic subjects. The family and school both should develop work habits in children. For this school should organise some co-curricular activities in the school, and should also have provision of doing hand work, like art and craft activities.

4. Reformation in Examination System

To meet the challenges of social change, it is necessary to bring reform in examination system. The present examination system leave many students in depression. And many students commit suicides. In old Indian Gurukula education and hereditary non-formal education there was no examination system. And in spite of the products of these were very epistemic, proficient and skilled. So examination system should be reformed.

5. Sociability

The modern system of education has brought a drastic social change. This change has made the individual self-centred and hedonistic, which has killed the Indian national culture of which sociability was the main factor. Now the individual has not time to talk with his neighbour. As such, the modern education should make the youngers sociable.

6. Morality

Morality is the essence of life. The modern education should inculcate moral values in the youngers.

7. Spirituality

The spirituality is the soul of social life. The spirituality does not mean religiosity, spirituality is a kind of spirit to deal with fellow beings honestly and nicely. A spiritual person is always theistic and knows what is good or bad. He does not harm anybody.

8. Homogeneity

The Almighty God has rewarded the individual with some biological facilities as bigger brain to think, reason and act rationally, hands to do a lot of work and, feet to walk and visualise natural phenomena. But he has made the man very greedy. This is why mostly individuals are self-centred. And many do not hesitate to harm others. This creates unhomogeneity in the society. The teachers should also educate about this fact.

9. Respect to Teachers, Elders, Women and Children

In olden times the teacher was well-respected in the society. Now the teacher being financially weak is not respected even by his/her own students. There should be provision in our educational system that the students should give proper respect to the teachers, elders, women and children.

10. Enculturation

And finally the main aim of education should be to enculturate the students. The school authorities should make the students aware about the Indian culture and should enculturate them through co-curricular activities done in the school.

8

Education Systems: Old versus New

There is an old adage that 'old is gold'. According to Greek Philosopher, Hereclitus change is inevitable. Everything is in flux at every moment, 'a new is to be old and an old is to be new positively'. So every social phenomena, physical things, their structures, social structures and educational structure are bound to be in the wrap of social change, as day is taken over by night and night follows by day. So, also the social phenomenon has also changed. Earlier the man was religious and spiritual and believed in simple living high thinking, dedication and diligence, truthfulness and cooperation. Now the present man has become totally materialistic, consumeristic, hedonistic and totally self-centred in spite of being rationalistic. All this entailed corruption, crimes, loots and rapes etc. what is the reason behind this humanistic and social change? Of course, human greedy nature may be one of the prime cause. But it cannot be denied that change of educational process may also be one of the important factor which has changed the human psyche totally topsy-turvy. As such, it is very necessary to visualise the old and new educational systems comprehensively and then take necessary steps to reform our present existing educational structure accordingly.

OLD INDIAN EDUCATIONAL STRUCTURE

Out of all living beings, the human beings are considered rational beings. As the nature has gifted them with bigger brains to think, rationalise and act rightly, erect posture to walk and observe the natural phenomena and moving hands to act and utilise natural resources. But the nature has made the human beings very greedy, acquisitive and self-centred. As such, most of the human beings are very greedy, acquisitive, corrupt and self-centred. A human being (man and woman) never hesitates in harming his own kith and kins for his/her self-interest. A human being hardly feels happy if any his/her blood relation prospers. This is the chronic psyche of a human being. And in the past the man never hesitated in torturing his own blood relations, kith and kins and also siblings for his self-interest. And many devastating wars like *Ramayana* episode, *Mahabharata* war and many later wars were the result of human greed and, self-interest. Also the flux of ability based 'Varna system' to dogmatic birth based caste structure or social stratification was changed due to human greed in India. The man has never hesitated in harming his own blood relations for his personal interests. This type of human psyche has ever been a common feature not only in India but in the whole world. Recent murder of a young B.J.P. M.P. Late Shri Pramod Mahajan by his own younger brother Shri Navin Mahajan is one of the ugliest example of human greed and self-centredness. Many such cases has been occurring not only in India but throughout the world.

But, the Almighty God has ever been blessing every society with rational seers who have ever been trying to reform the human greedy behaviour by educating the people to be sane good persons. This they did by educating the people through the religious sermons and making them religious and spiritual. These seers tried to provide an educational infrastructure for the Indian society which was based on 'Varna system'. The seers first analysed the human psyche and thought of an appropriate educational structure. Their first priority was social homogeneity. For this it was necessary for citizens to be human, kind and cooperative. This was only possible when the citizens remain free from greed, and to be social moral. The seers thought that the future guardians should not be showered too much love by the parents and family members. So they thought the youngers should be taught or educated at a distant place from the house of the children. If we peep into the educational development of old youngers all of them used to study either in the Rishi Ashramas or in Gurukula Ashramas. All imminent personalities like Shri Ramchandra, Shri Krishna, Kauravas and Pandavas were educated in Rishi Ashram which were situated on the river banks in jungles. The youngers of two upper 'Varnas', that is Brahmans and Kshatriyas used to be educated in 'Gurukula Ashramas'. The Gurukula Ashramas were bigger Ashramas like the big joint families. There was no state control, over these Ashramas. The nearby villages used to support these Ashramas. Nalanda was supported by nearly one hundred villages. Likewise, Taxila Asharma (now in Pakistan in ruins) was also supported by nearby more than one hundred villages. The students (*Shishyas*) used to live under common roof with their *Gurus*. They used to take very simple food which, used to be purely vegetarian. The *Shishyas* (students) used to collect food items from the nearby villages. Some of them used to collect fuel wood from the nearby forests. And some of them used to cut grass for Ashram cows. In this way the work habits were inculcated in the *Shishyas* of the Ashram. The *Shishyas* (students) used to live a community life. The main aim of Gurukula Ashram education was life building of the *Shishyas* (students) who were required to follow a life process in the Ashramas, early to bed early to rise, to go for natural call in nearby jungles, to take morning bath, to do some exercises by doing yajnas, to attend a common prayer and yajna in the Ashrams. And after doing this they used to take simple vegetarian breakfast. After taking the breakfast the *Shishyas* used to follow their teacher and sit under the shadow of a tree where the teacher used to teach them verbally applying a bi-polar system of communication involving the *Shishyas* in questioning, debate and group discussions. Life building of the *Shishyas* (students) was done through generating religiosity and spirituality to make the *Shishyas* harmonious, social, moral, cooperative and active social workers. Also the students were taught to avoid greed and self-centredness. The *Gurus* of the Gurukula Ashramas used to observe the teaching professional ethics very sincerely. They were very epistemic. They used to study continuously Sanskrit, Astronomy, Mathematics, History, Sociology and religiosity which they used to teach to their *Shishyas* (students) continuously. They used to be very sincere to their students. And they were very non-inclinative. They used to lead a very simple and harsh life and sustain themselves on Gurukula kitchen. For adding to their knowledge store house they used to exchange their views with their colleagues and students. They used to arrange debate and discussions (वाद-विवाद).

The prime aims of old Indian Gurukula Brahmanic-Vedic education were very wide and vivid. The main aim of old Indian education was the life building of the *Shishyas* and to develop their ideal personalities. The individual's life was stratified in four parts or Ashramas (*a*) *Brahmcharya* Ashram (1-25 years of age), (*b*) *Grahasth* Ashram (26 to 50 years of age) (*c*) *Banprasth* Ashram, and (d) *Sanyas* Ashram (75 years of age and onward). Therefore, the Gurukula Ashram was not only aimed at educate the *Shishyas* but to make them aware about the life situations and, to prepare the youngers to face the life situations. They were prepared to be homogenous and helpful to other members of the society. Life attitudes for becoming social, moral, religious, spiritual, cooperative and to be dedicated and diligent were inculcated in them by the *Gurus* (teachers). One of the important aim of Gurukula education was the development of sociability, amity and homogeneity in the *Shishyas* (students). For this the *Shishyas* (students) were educated in religiously and spiritually. They were made monotheistic and not henotheistic and polytheistic. The *Shishyas* were prepared to be sincere to the whole society in spite of rigid caste based, that too birth based, social stratification. They were prepared to be social, moral and truthful. The *Shishyas* (students) were required to follow these spiritual dictum throughout their lives and do social service. During the *Brahmcharya* Ashram the youngers first used to live with the parents and other family members in their early age. And after this the *Shishyas* used to study continuously Sanskrit, Astronomy, Science, History, Sociology themselves. The main process of education was based on self-learning.

Brahmcharya Ashram was a period of strictness and dedication for the youngers. They had to follow certain strict rules in their early life which used to make them true sane social persons. Unwanted parental love was totally skipped from the parents and *Gurus* loved them. They have to lead a common community life in Gurukulas where all kinds of life norms were inculcated in them. Present type of hedonism and consumerism was not at all seen in Gurukula education as, is seen in the present materialistic period. After completing the *Brahmcharya* Ashram, that is, reaching the age of 25 years and completing the Gurukula education, the *Shishyas* used to get *'diksha'* at a Gurukula function. The *Shishyas* used to return to home. They were married and live married life, that is, *Grahasth* Ashram up to the age of 50. After this they used to live a life of renunciation or *Banprasth* Ashram from the age of 51 to 75. And after this a person had to follow *Sanyas* Ashram.

This stratification of period used to inspire a person to lead an axiological sane social life.

The Gurukula Ashram education was totally free from the state control. It used to be linked with the society. The Gurukulas were managed by a team of *Gurus* of which a senior most *Guru* was given the status of *Acharya*. As such, the Gurukula education was totally free and, was not an instrument of the state. Like Gurukulas, there were Muslim Madarsas which were running on the pattern of Gurukulas. The Madarsas were also free state control and was not instrument state and were secular in nature. The main aim of Muslim Madarsa was to make the Muslim population religious, spiritual, tolerant and secular. The Madarsas were also supported by local Muslim population. But now it is blamed that some Madarsas in some Muslim countries are being used to spreading terrorism. This is because of human greed and lack of spirituality and homogeneity in the local population.

Of course, the aim of Gurukula education was to prepare youngers to live a religious, spiritual and homogenous sane social life. And for this the youngers were prepared by inculcating good life attitudes, conduct, social and cultural traits, good character and sound behaviour. They were saved off of the too much motherly love. The Gurukula Ashram education was totally dedicated for sane social life building which is totally lacking in our present system of formal education. These were the worthiest merits of our old Gurukula Ashrama education. But, it is also clear that it was limited to two upper castes—(1) Brahmans and (2) Kshatriyas. These two castes had only enjoyed the Gurukula educations. Other two castes—Vaishyas and Sudras and also women were not allowed entry in Gurukula Ashram. As such, it is this rigidity which can be said caste based, is one of the biggest demerit of old Indian education. Also in Muslim Madarsas women were not admitted. But on the whole it can be assumed that old Indian system of education was better than the present system of formal education.

INDIAN SYSTEM OF NON-FORMAL EDUCATION

Up to 1832 A.D., only two upper Hindu castes—Brahmans and Kshatriyas were having the opportunity of Gurukula Ashram education as per Hindu Varna system, or Varna social stratification, which was converted into rigid birth based social caste stratification. The other two lower castes, that is, Vaishyas and Sudras, the service castes, were denied this educational facility. Also the artisan castes which are said to be the adi-Brahmans and were said to be the off-springs of the 'Lord Vishwakarma', the Lord of creation and aestheticity were also denied Gurukula Ashram education. The two Hindu upper castes—Brahmans and Kshatriyas adapted the principle of 'purity and pollution' to keep away of education the lower castes and artisans. Because, most of them were doing manual work, they were dragged to the lowest social status in the society. This social degradation of artisan castes and other two lower castes made them humble and mentally weak. They were not even given chance to defend the country by serving in the army. This made the nation weak and the foreigners had occupied the country and ruled it for at least one thousand years.

The two lower castes—Vaishyas, Sudras and artisan castes used to train their youngers in their hereditary vocation themselves non-formally. Non-formal education is a process of education in which the learner works with his family members or father and contribute in fabrication of things for human use. Non-formal education does not have a pre-conceived plan of educating the youngers. It is a sort of apprenticeship the learners learn through observation and by doing practical work. The artisan used to keep their youngers with them while they were doing their family vocations, and train them in their hereditary trades or vocations. There used to be a wide spectrum for learning hereditary vocations. The youngers used to observe a lot of raw materials, sets of tools and their use in fabricating things. They used to do a lot of practical work and attain high proficiency in the family vocation or trade. The students who learn doing different trades in Industrial Training Institutes and Polytechnic in formal way do not attain or acquire skills in the trades for becoming skilled workers.

For learning reading, and writing, the wards of the lower castes and artisans, there used to be some local *pathshalas* run by 'padhas' (teachers) who used to educate the wards of the lower castes and artisans in reading and writing which was necessary for running their family occupation. It cannot be denied that higher vedic Brahmanical education was only imparted to upper castes in formal as well as in informal way in Gurukula Ashramas. For the lower castes and artisans to gain proficiency in hereditary trades or vocations was utmost important. The Vaishyas used to educate in their youngers in special business language 'Mundi Hindi' themselves or sometime in special 'Mundi Hindi' *Pathshalas*. On the whole it can be said that the old system of Indian education, though it was sectarian was better than the present formal education as, enculturation and culture building was done quite efficiently through it.

New System of Formal Education

All Indian system of education, that is, Gurukula Ashram Education, hereditary non-formal education and Madarsa education continued in full flame up to 1832 A.D. Muslim rulers did not interfere in the old Hindu system of education, though they had established Madarsa which also function on the pattern of Gurukula Ashrama education. The main aim of old Indian education was to make the youngers religious, spiritual and social for making them humane, cooperative and dedicated to social integrity. And for this educational aim was to inculcate good life attitudes which could root out the human greed and materialistic nature for making the society humane and homogenous. The Gurukula educated people were required to make the general public aware about it through religious and social discourses, while they went leading a married life in *Grahasth Ashram* (गृहस्थाश्रम).

The Muslim rulers had conquered and lived in India as Indians for ever. But the western rulers, Portuguese, French and British had come to India as traders for selling their industrial goods. First they settled on seacoasts, and later on bit by bit they spread in whole India. They had visualised and analysed the Indian social spectrum very deeply. They found that the Indians were stratified through rigid caste system in which the two upper castes were in advantageous position and other two castes were in disadvantageous position. While doing trade they occupied most parts of India. Portuguese had occupied some seacoasts of Southern India as Goa, Daman and Diu. French had occupied some parts of Eastern India on the Seacoasts adjoining to the present Tamil Nadu. The British had occupied almost all of the rest of India. British East India Company had played a dominant role in occupying India. And by 1830 A.D. it had more or less consolidated its occupation. They were governing from Calcutta.

The Viceroy was monitoring the governance, who had an advisory council of seven members. The Viceroy viewed the whole situation and thought of taking some steps for consolidating the British rule over India. Winning the loyalty of Indians was the first priority of British East India Company. They thought of giving some employment to the Indians. For them, to bring clerical staff from England to India was not economical. They thought that some Indians from upper and lower castes can be employed in British Government offices as clerks on white collar jobs. They thought that this would help the Indians economically and they would become loyal to the British East India Company Government. This was not possible without educating the Indians in their educational pattern. As such, the Viceroy put up a proposal to introduce Western type of 'Formal Education' in India in 1832 A.D. The majority of the Viceroy council members had opposed the proposal. They had argued that India had a viable educational system which could enculturate the younger generation. Also, they had pleaded that Indian 'Non-Formal System of Education' was best in the world. They pleaded that the imposition of Western type of formal education would kill the Indian culture, which was unique in the world, and also Indian Cottage Industries. But Lord Macaulay who was law member in the Viceroy's Council of British East India Company had strongly supported the Viceroy. He had argued that if they had to keep the Indians under their control, the Indian culture was to be killed and the Indians were to be accultured through cultural diffusion. Then only the Indian could be loyal to the British East India Company Government. And for that acculturation of Indians it was necessary, which could only be done through cultural diffusion. And cultural diffusion could only be possible through imposition of English type of school and college education. All viceroy council members agreed and British type of formal education was introduced in 1833 A.D. in India by the British East India Company Government in spite of opposition of many Britishers including the then Governor of Punjab, Lahore (now in Pakistan) who had also argued that the British type of formal education would kill Indian culture, non-formal system of education and cottage industries. Then present alienistic formal education system imposed by Lord Macaulay has been so successful in materialising the dreams of acculturation of Lord Macaulay that we Indians have more or less lost our cultural traditions, customs and traits that Lord Macaulay conceived. He might still be eating *'Kalakand'* (Indian milk cake) and enjoying in his grave. Rigid caste social structure, concept of purity and pollution and consequent social degradation might have contributed in it.

Advantages of Formal Education

In the first phase, the British East India Company Government in India opened at least one High School or one Intermediate college in each district of every province in which all students irrespective of castes, creeds and religions were admitted. This was an auspicious gift to the Indian people. Earlier only two upper castes had the opportunity to get Gurukula Ashramas. In Muslim Madarsas only few youngers of the Muslims used to get theocratic education. The school curriculum of formal education was prepared on British education pattern in which the social milieu has no place to suggest about education. The curriculum was prepared by British bureaucrats. At some places girls' schools were also opened. This was a kind of educational innovation which was appreciated by all and, a wave of joy spread throughout the country. As old Indian education imparted in Gurukula Ashramas was restricted to two Indian upper castes—the Brahmans and the Kshatriyas. Also, as the Muslim minority got equal chance of education they were very happy. The aim of formal education was to prepare a white collar jobs work force for the British East India Company Government, so it was examination oriented. As all liked to get a Government jobs they worked hard to come out flying in colours in annual examinations. The teaching of English in schools under formal education got a prominent place, rather it was made compulsory. Besides helping in job procurement, the British type of formal education it helped Indians to come closer to each other. Indians were speaking different languages, were not united. India is a vast country having people speaking different languages, having different faiths and cultural patterns were unable to communicate with each other in absence of a common language. The English language provided a uni-communication media which enabled Indians to unite against the British imperialists and finally forced them to leave India and got independence. Lord Macaulay had failed to visualise this aspect of formal education. But on the whole it cannot be denied that the formal education helped India in human resources development to some extent, though artisan castes were dragged into a very disadvantageous position.

Disadvantages of Formal Education

Disadvantages of formal education are also many in many fields of human life in India. When an activity is done for some human and social advantage, generally it entails some disadvantages also. The British rulers when thought of imposing their pattern of formal education on Indians they had viewed both—advantages and disadvantages of it. Main advantage they had viewed to prepare a white collar job workforce for their Government which, they thought would kill Indian culture and would make the Indians loyal to them. This was the greatest disadvantage for the Indian social milieu, which authorities and, how these activities added to the disadvantages to the Indian social milieu needs a detailed examination. Some of these activities are mentioned below:

1. School as an Instrument of State

From the times immemorial, since the inception of the society, education has been an instrument of change and a source of life building, social development through the development of socio-civil organisation. Through education of social attitudes, culture and moral values can be possible. Be it development of human rational qualities or development of human potentialities education has always been an instrument of change. So, there has always been a demand for a viable educational structure in the society, which always entailed a suitable educational infrastructure. An educational infrastructure needs schools and educational institutions, qualified and trained teachers and some educational equipments. Since the need of education was felt it was evaluated. (*a*) How does education creates conditions for the development of a balanced personalities of the youngers, (*b*) well-sound healthy social conditions to be created for living harmoniously in the society, (*c*) a homogenous value system to be developed in the society, (*d*) to prepare the youngers to earn his/her livelihood judiciously and honestly, (*e*) to prepare the individual to help in the national development, (*f*) visualising right consumption of consumer goods justly in the society. And all these educational aims can be achieved if education is imparted correctly for saneful living in the society keeping the interests of social collectivity. As such, if we look to the social aspects of education, it may be said it is a process of:

(*i*) Personality formation of the individual,
(*ii*) An instrument of social structuring,
(*iii*) Enculturation for cultural development and its perpetuation,
(*iv*) An instrument of training for a vocation,
(*v*) A preparation ground for social stratification,
(*vi*) An instrument of social mobility for a viable social change,
(*vii*) An instrument of mutual understanding, adjustment, cooperation, sharing for common cause,
(*viii*) An instrument of elite formation,
(*ix*) An instrument for the development of sound entrepreneurship,
(*x*) An instrument for the development of good life attitudes, motives, incentives towards social development and social harmony,
(*xi*) To prepare the youngers for self-introspection and self-assessment, and
(*xii*) To develop a sense of respect towards elders, senior citizens, ladies and children.

To achieve all these, different agencies contribute. Sometimes all these agencies sincerely cooperate in achieving all these objectives. Finally agencies, like family, community schools, universities, technical institutes, technical apex bodies like U.G.C., A.I.C.T.E., N.C.T.E., N.C.E.R.T, S.C.E.R.Ts., Inter-University Boards, State boards usually work for educating the young members. But all these educational agencies should have a rapport with the society. If social rapport or social coordination is not there, all these agencies cannot function nicely and these become the instruments of state and do not remain social organisations. In this period the state has tight control over the educational infrastructure and the society has no say. Generally all schools function under the Government control in which mostly all youngers are educated in an uni-pattern in spite of their individual differences, tastes and capabilities, as per states' prescribed norms. And it cannot be denied that not only schools but all other educational institutions are instruments of state. As such, the schools and other educational institutions generally remain under the scanner of the state. And the society has no say in the functioning of the schools and other educational institutions. Not only the Government run schools and aided schools but all private public schools come under the scanner of the State or Central Government. These schools teach what has been prescribed by the state. As such, these schools and educational institutions remain isolated from the society. This is happening under the present formal system of education, which has entailed many social problems. A few social problems are mentioned below:

(*a*) *Non-religiosity and non-spirituality*: There is no space for religiosity in the present system of formal education. Being a secular country, India cannot afford or provide teaching of religion in educational institutions. India is a multi-religious and multi-cultural country in which people believing in different faiths, traditions, customs and cultural traits reside. And not to teach religion in schools and educational institutions is necessary for 'unity in diversity'. But moral education can be given in educational institutions. This can be done through some related co-curricular activities. The another reason of our youngers to be non-religious and non-spiritual may be hedonistic attitude of the people who always remain busy in the rat-race of money. And this happened due to cultural diffusion and acculturation.

(*b*) *Economic competition*: The main aim of our present system of formal education is to prepare an army of white collar jobs. This is the gift of foreign rulers whose aim was to acculturate the Indians, and raise a loyal force of workers. The formal education introduced by them only creates cutthroat competition in the job market. For that good performance in annual examination is very necessary. Competition in job market increases pressure on the youngers to study more and more. And due to this many youngers commit suicides.

(*c*) *Commercialisation of Education*: Increasing competition in the field of education for good examination results, the education has been largely commercialised. Many coaching and guiding centres have emerged in the nooks and corners of the villages, towns and cities. And many uneducated persons have opened such preparing or coaching centres. They employ unemployed educated youths as tutors and earn a lot of money.

(*d*) *Dys-functioning of Social Infrastructure*: One of the major damage the society faced due to the formal education has been the dys-functioning of the social institutions. The most important social institution 'the joint family system' has been totally crumbled down due to human greed. Most of the married couples, being hedonistic and consumeristic want to lead an independent life in a nuclear family. They want to remain busy in the rat-race of money earning. They leave their kids at the mercy of day care centres or crèches. This is because they have been totally accultured due to alienistic formal system of education which has no room for life building measures. As good life attitudes are not inculcated in the youngers. They are made self-centred so they think of their interests and not the interest of others.

(*e*) *Corruption and Crimes*: Earlier societies were corruption and crime free. The people used to believe in 'simple living and high thinking' fraternity, cooperation and sharing. Self-interests were not the priority. Due to greedy nature of human beings and, also because of acculturation, the man has become extremely greedy, self-centered and hedonistic. For meeting his/her hedonistic needs he/she can do anything. This is why the modern society is engulfed in corruption and crimes. Nobody is safe. Burglaries, loots and chain pulling have become a common feature. If anybody sees these happenings he does not dare to help the person who is being looted. In the past the girls were considered pious and were worshiped. Now they are not safe. They are raped in every nook and corner of the cities. The man has become barbarous and jungli. This is the result of our modern system of education which promotes newness in fashion.

(*f*) *Unsociability*: Sociability is most essential for cooperative social living. An individual cannot live alone. He or she has to live in the social collectivity that is, society. But now the individual is becoming unsocial day by day. The reason behind this tendency is hedonistic craze. The man/woman remains busy in the rat-race of money earning. He/she leaves the house early in the morning comes late in the evening and counts the earned money. He/she has no time to talk with the neighbours. Only talking takes place in business deals. Another reason of unsociability is the elitist tendency of our present educational system. One who gets good education becomes megalomaniac and thinks that he knows everything. Such person does not talk even with his colleagues. So this creates an alienistic atmosphere in the society which breeds unsociability and aloofness in the society.

(*g*) *Examination System*: The present system of formal education is purely examination oriented. Of course examination is necessary for evaluating the educational capabilities of the students. It is also very harmful. It breeds unnecessary pressure on the students and also on the parents. We see that many students commit suicides for not getting good marks. Due to examination pressure many desirable life attitudes are not inculcated in the students. Many mothers become mad for good examination results. All these fracture the personality of the students. They always think of competition and not cooperation. In the past we did not have examination in our educational infrastructure. In Gurukulas the students were not examined. Neither in non-formal education the examination had in any place. So there is a need for reforming the present examination system.

(*h*) *Diversity in Unity*: The present formal system of education has distorted the Indian concept of 'Unity in Diversity'. It has divided the people and diversified them in the name of religion, elitism language and culture etc. etc.

(*i*) *Respect for Elders and Fair Sex*: Our present formal system does not inculcate a sense or feeling to respect their elders and fair sex. Actually this is the duty of the family. Since the joint family system has been totally crumbled due to human greed, self-centredness, consumerism and hedonism. The parents do not inculcate a sense in their younger to respect elder members of the extended families. The school curriculum is over laden with the teaching of subject contents for passing out examination, the teachers neither teach to the students to respect elders nor the school authorities try to inculcate habits to respect the elders and ladies. This can be done by arranging related co-curriculum activities in schools.

(*j*) *Acculturation*: The major gift of the present new system of education is acculturation. Acculturation takes place due to 'cultural diffusion'. Cultural diffusion occurs due to mingling of two or more cultures. Due to cultural diffusion acculturation takes place which is adoption of another culture by the people of a country. Acculturation is a killing virus which kills culture of the people who try to adopt culture of another country. A Russian sociologist said that 'acculturation occurs due to cultural diffusion'. Cultural diffusion is like a whirlpool in a water tank. When somebody throws a stone in a water tank it creates a whirlpool in water. When smoking started in Brazil it spread throughout the world. Even the then Queen of Britain imposed a ban on smoking in Britain, it could not be stopped. Still many British people smoke. Many imperialists tried to acculturate their subjects to consolidate their power. British rulers did so in India by imposing their system of formal education. But many countries like China could stop cultural diffusion and consequent acculturation.

But if we compare our both old system of education and new system of education, we find that though old system of education was sectarian as it used to accommodate only two upper castes. And two lower castes and women were barred from the Gurukula education. In spite of this old Indian system of education aimed at life building of all Indians. The youths educated at Gurukulas were trained to inculcate all values in all Indians through religious and spiritual discourses. They were prepared to be social, moral, cooperative and onlookers for the good of all Indians. The old Indian education used to spread an ethos of simple living and high thinking and to stop consumerism and hedonism.

9

Commercialisation of Education

Commercialisation is a process of application of tenets or rules of trade or business done for earning money. As such, commercialisation is an inclinative process done for the fulfillment of one's greed. The term commercialisation is the development of the word commerce. The word commerce is a derivation of the French and Latin words—'Kom-merse' and 'com-morcium' meaning 'togetherness of business and trade'. As such, the word commerce is a combination of two words. The French word 'Kom-merse' is a combination of two words *'kom + merse'* and also Latin word, 'commorcium' is also a combination 'com+morcium'—both mean together with business. As such, the commerce is an activity pertaining to trade based on money earning. So, commercialisation is an activity which is always based on money earning and, is always inclinative. The sociologists said that a commercial activity can never be a profession as a commercial person does not follow any professional ethics. A profession is a relationship between an expert and an ignorant client. The sociologists recognise only three activities as profession. The lawyers, doctors and clerics are recognised as professionists. They even hesitate to recognise the teacher as a professionist as the client of the teacher is a conscious client and not an ignorant client. But this argument is not logical as to handle a conscious client is not an easy job. The sociologists said that a commercialist can never be a professionist as he does not follow professional ethics at all. A professionist should be expert and well-educated. He/she should always enhance his/her knowledge. He should always be very sincere to his clients. And he/she should always be non-inclinative. As such, any activity based on money earning can never be a profession. If a teacher is doing tuitions or any other commercial activity she/he can never be a professionist.

Commercialisation can be categorised as (*a*) hard or real commercialisation, and (*b*) soft commercialisation. In hard commercialisation or real commercialisation a businessman has to spent sufficient amount of money on business infra-structure, such as, sufficient space for building, tools and machinery and skilled workforce. For doing all this the businessman must know about the business well he is going to do. He must be intelligent, diligent and sincere in his business work. Then only he can reap the fruits of his business activities. Still many risks loom large in hard commercialisation. Many national and international events can affect the hard commercialisation outputs, such as, effects of inflation and international competition etc. etc. Another type of commercialisation is only based on sale of manufactured goods as edible things etc. etc. In this area also fluctuation in market goods affects the business. And also many risks may occur in this type of business. But in soft type of commercialisation such economic risks are less seen. The soft type of commercialisation is a kind of perennial source of income. Therefore, now many businessmen also like to invest in soft type of commercialisation, which is, investing money on the development or opening of educational institutions. In the beginning the businessman has to spend a good amount of money for the development of the necessary infrastructure for an educational institution. First of all he has to buy an viable piece of land. He has to build suitable school building having all necessary requirements, such as, class rooms, library hall and rooms, art room and science laboratories. Also attractive office rooms, principal's room, spacious reception hall hovering attractive reception counter are constructed. In addition to all a spacious boarding house with a kitchen and a good dinning hall and, also a canteen are provided in the school building. In addition to all these spacious playgrounds for hockey, cricket, volley ball and a swimming pool etc. also provided. All these infrastructures attract the attention of the rich parents, who in due course of time want to admit their wards in such schools. Such schools used to charge very high tuition fees. After doing all this, the school organiser has to obtain recognition of the Directorate of Education and State Board of Education as C.B.S.E. Delhi. The main thing of opening such so-called public school is to do soft commercialisation through teaching in such schools which are commercial schools in true sense. Only very rich people can afford to admit their wards in such schools. The main aim of such commercialised public schools is to teach and prepare the students to appear in annual examination with a hope to come out in flying colours and add feathers in the crown of the school. Now, the functioning of such commercialised schools is becoming a common feature in the country, as such, school of showing good examination results. The organisers of such school earns a lot of money. The source of income in such schools is perennial. There is no risk of fall in income. And the organisers of these schools utilise the income in many covert form. The functioning of such soft commercialised school has become a common feature in the country. The ostantous character of such schools only force the students to acculturate. And there is no space for enculturation in these schools also. Many rich people who are not educated at all also open such schools and earn money. There are at least 1200 such commercialised public schools in Delhi also. Not only business families but many illiterate persons open such schools. In the writer's village an illiterate barber had opened such school out of which he earned till he was alive. He had engaged some unemployed educated youths as teachers. This school had also harmed the functioning of village primary school and intermediate college.

Now the soft commercialisation of school education has spread its wings further. Many soft-commercialisation business organisers also opened many technical education institutes, that is, engineering colleges, teachers training colleges and medical colleges. And many universities have also emerged which only promote but boost the commercialisation of education. If one goes from Delhi to Haridwar for taking bath in Ganga, he/she will see large number of such soft-commercialisation in the form of engineering colleges, Dental colleges, teaching colleges on both sides of the national highway. This sort of soft-commercialisation has bought a big chunk of fertile agricultural land for establishing such commercial educational institutions. This is not the situation in a particular area. All areas in the country are having such soft-commercial educational institutions.

For this sort of soft commercialisation pertaining to education has brought many foreign soft-commercialisation universities. These universities allure the students and charge very high fees, just 35 to 50 per cent higher than the other regular institutions. B.Ed. colleges run by another state university charge 42 thousand to one lakh rupees from the B.Ed. students; whereas Delhi university run institutes charge only Rs.1200 to Rs.1500 as fee for one academic session. The soft-commercialisation of education has become a hurdle for the poor students.

Also, there are many non-governmental organisations which are still working for the betterment of the common people. Shanti Niketan, Rishikesh, District Dehra Dun recently has established a 'Sanskriti University' in the campus of Shanti Niketan. Main purpose of this university recognised by the Uttrakhand Government, is to revive the Indian national culture. This aim of the Sanskriti University has been applauded by the people in the whole country. Shanti Niketan has also established another 'National Patanjli Yoga University' at Bahadrabad, District Haridwar (Uttrakhand). Main purpose of this University is to promote yoga throughout the country and in the world. These educational institutions are not commercial at all. These are being run on the pattern of Gurukula Ashramas. These are good examples for the people of the country to revive our educational structure on national pattern by opening such educational institutions in all fields of knowledge.

In the past also some sane, kind hearted and pious people used to establish educational institutions for the betterment of common people. One of such pious great person was late Swami Kalyan Dev ji. He had taken *sanyas* when he was eight years old. He survived for 129 years. He died in June 2004 A.D. Throughout his life he worked for the development of education in Western U.P. and in Haryana. He had established 333 lower and higher educational institutes in Western Uttar Pradesh and Haryana. With the support of business community he had established all these institutions. Out of these educational institutions, there are many degree colleges, post graduate colleges, intermediate colleges, Charak Ayurvedic Colleges and few technical schools. The writer had the opportunity to study from 5th class to 8th class at Raghomal National Industrial School, established by him at Bhagwanpur District, Haridwar, Uttrakhand, from 1939 A.D. to 1943 A.D. Late Lala Shri Raghomal was a very rich person. He had agricultural land in 52 villages of District Haridwar. But he had not successor—son or daughter. He came into contact of late Swami Kalyan Dev ji who advised him to establish a school. And he established a school and donated all of his agricultural and other property and, died in the campus of his school. Swami Kalyan Dev ji never adorned his name at any educational institutions. He died in S.D. College Muzzaffarnagar, which he had established by getting donations from the business community. The management of the institutions kept him in his old age and gave him due care. In the village of the writer Arya Inter College and Polytechnic were established by late Shri Maharshi Harish Chandraji in similar way.

Reviewing all of the aspects of the soft-commercialisation through the establishment of private educational institutions is very necessary and decide whether it should be allowed to continue or not in future. This kind of soft-commercialisation through the establishment of private educational institutions is very harmful for the social structure of the society. But only Government cannot stop this kind of commercialisation of private schools. The community also cannot do it as many members do not want to interfere in such unsocial activity. Only the pious, sane persons like late Swami Kalyan Dev ji can stop it by doing actions by establishing educational institutes with the public support.

10
Formal Education

There are various processes of educating the youngers as (*a*) familial education, (*b*) informal education, (*c*) non-formal education, (*d*) formal education. Familial process of education is a process of educating the children in familial way of living. Informal way of education is a process of education when the youngers learn through interaction with his/her peer group. They talk with the peer group, disclose their hidden emotions. In other words such interaction provide a chance of catharsis and knowing something which they do not learn neither from parents nor from other family members. In other words through informal education the youngers know about some secret things as sex. Many things are not revealed by the parents and family members of the children which they learn from their peer group. Through peer group the process of sociability also develops among the youngsters. Non-formal process of education is a process thereby the youngers learn skills hereditically for doing family vocation, which they follow life long. In non-formal education the youngers start working with their elders and learn doing some skilled works by imitating their elders. It is a kind of hereditary apprenticeship. For all these processes of education there is not any pre-decided action plan or programme for the learners. Their activities go on unusual and non-pre-planned way. And there is no stress on the learners. There is no examination or assessment processes. But in formal process of education, which is different from familial, informal and non-formal processes of education, there is pre-planning. Keeping in view how the learners are to be moulded and prepared for a specific purpose, and what objectives are to be achieved, the educational activities are pre-planned in advance. So the process of formal education needs a detailed pre-planned elaboration in advance.

The word 'formal' is an objective of the word 'form'. As already mentioned, the word 'form' means a shape. Every physical thing, living being, flora and fauna and every structure, be it a social structure, or economic structure, or cultural structure, or educational structure has a form or shape. This form has always inherent objectives to be achieved by giving a specific shape. And such activities are called formal activities. When an educational programme has a preconceived aim, it is called 'Formal Education'.

Etymologically, the meaning of word or concept of 'Formal Education' means giving a form or shaping the youngers or moulding the youngers, who are our future guardians, through a specified educational structure. This is done as per prescribed norms of the society or state. As such, we can say 'Formal-Education' is a pre-conceived educational process of a society or a state or a country to achieve the desired appropriate suitable socio-economic and cultural gains or aims. According to Platonic conception of education, education is a self-recovery or upliftment of hidden potentialities of a man/woman and thereby enrichment of knowledge regarding truth, beauty and goodness. The concept of 'education', as already mentioned is a derivation of the Greek word 'Educare' meaning to dig out or to develop. According to Durkheim it is an influence exercised by the adults and, as a result, it is a process of arising out certain physical, mental, intellectual and moral states which are demanded by the society. Max Weber says that the society is an area of competition, conflicts and struggles, thus education is a preparation to face all these situations. Karl Mannheim thought that the education is only possible means through which social upbringing for living together in the society could be possible. Karl Marx described education a process to combat all social needs and evils. Other sociologists considered education as a tool of social upbringing. The views of the modern sociologists are more or less matching with the views of our *Gurus* (teachers) of Indian Gurukulas. They said that education is a way to the youngers to live in the society according to social norms. The functionalists consider education as a caretaker and dispenser of cultural resources of the society. The culture can be revived, raised and enriched through formal education. But this is not happening with the present form of 'formal education'. The main aim of the present formal education is only to equip the students with the knowledge of 3 Rs which are considered necessary for socialisation and social control. In the present habits in the younger generation, traits like good behaviour, accountability, enculturation and spirituality are necessary for the good character development in the youngers. Whereas, to counter systems like familial education, informal education and non-formal ways of education, which are to be imparted by parents, elders, and peer group, entail all these qualities because of their instinctive character. But these are also fading, due to hedonism, from the society.

RISE OF FORMAL EDUCATION

Years ago, Auguste Comte said that 'old society is dying and new society is emerging'. Before this view of Auguste Comte, the education was imparted in familial, informal and non-formal ways. In many pre-literate tribal societies an age group still undergoes for tuitions in religious beliefs, religious practices and spirituality through symbolism under the care of a specially selected elder who has proficiency in henotheism, henotheistic rituals and prayers. Likewise, the tribal youths used to acquire skills in many activities from their parents and family elders in non-formal way. Also for acquiring skills in many related activities, which are different from their family vocations, youth used to acquire proficiency from other skilled persons, that too in non-found way.

As already mentioned earlier, in India going to Gurukula Ashram, situated on river banks in jungles, for education, was also a kind of semi-formal education, but with different social objectives, that is preparing the youngers for sane social living. First step towards formal education was undergoing in apprenticeship, and going for that to craftsmen guilds was necessary and remaining there with guild masters or journeymen for a specified period. This practice existed in Europe. Consequently, due to invention of machines and development of industries, first in England and thereafter in Europe, there arose a necessity of workforce, proficient in different fields like accountancy, workshop practices etc. etc. The community religious schools were found incompetent in educating and producing a viable workforce for new emerging industries. So the industrialists first established schools for imparting education in 3 Rs to the wards of the industrialists. Later on, the need of vocational education was also felt. The common schools were established in which the children of the community were admitted and these schools were called grammar schools in England.

In olden times, there existed academies like—Academy of Plato in Greece, Vidyapeeths in India like Taxila, Nalanda, Vikramshila, Vallabhi, Ujjaini and many other Gurukulas show that there existed some sort of formal education in Greece, India, Israel, China and at some place in Europe too. Also some sort of extra schools like *Padha Schools* (पाठशालाएँ) in India were imparting instruction in businessmen's language which was called Mundi Hindi. Madarsas in Muslim countries and church schools in Europe were to give instructions in religions to the youngers to make them aware about the teachings of 'Quran' and Hadis in Muslim countries and, in Christian countries the youngers were educated about the 'Holy Bible'. In India the '*Shishyas*' (students) were taught about religiosity, spirituality and sociability in Gurukula Ashramas. Full development of formal education came into being after the development of writing. In India the writing came into existence about five thousand years or more, ago. In the beginning it was the monopoly of priestly class. In European countries the writing was developed later than India, Greece and China. The priesthood promoted the diversified schools for their children. As in India, the lower classes in Europe were not having opportunity for education for their children, as these schools were established by the priests for imparting education to their children in formal way. The reason for this discrimination was that the persons in position always tried to command and avail the facilities for their own benefits. Who were powerless always could not avail the facilities for the development of their children. In Greece, the society was stratified in four categories—nobles, thinkers, sophists and artisans, like India. The upper three classes got chances of education. As we all know the Indian society stratified on Varna system which was converted into rigid caste system. Only two upper castes used to avail the opportunities of Gurukula Ashram education. The two lower castes used to educate their off-springs in non-formal way. Still the upper castes are opposing 27 per cent reservations for OBCs. In Greece the artisans used to face the same situation as was in India. In Europe the society was stratified in heterorganic manner—the upper class feudal and the lower class workers and serfs. Such social stratification was based on feudalistic style which entailed exploitation of the poor by the rich. So the feudal class in Europe always enjoyed the fruits of formal education. The hand workers and serfs did not enjoy it.

In pre-industrial age the schools were wide spread in China and in less elaborated form in India and in Islamic world. The Western world was not having such schools for imparting formal education. The reason may be the climatic conditions of the Western world. The formal education appeared in the Western world after industrialisation. There are evidences of existence of simple technologies even in primitive societies. Such societies had some sort of formal education for educating the people for keeping records and corresponding with other people. Such schools helped the primitive societies to enculturate their youth.

For educating the craftsmen and other workforce first the schools were established by the industrialists. It was necessary for making the workforce for keeping the accounts and business, records by the clerks and, doing good fabrication by the artisan—craftsmen. After the industrial revolution many craftsmen enlarged their establishments which needed trained workforce. So many schools were established for which a formal process teaching was designed. Day by day the number of schools increased, a common teaching programme was designed, for which a common curriculum was also designed. And the number of schools increased too much, the state extended its control over these schools. And the schools became instruments of the state. The state exercised its power and tried to impose a formal system of education which could be suited to its needs and interests. For this end the state imposed its will on the educational institutions. So the state always designed the educational structure favourable to it. A theocratic state always liked a pattern of formal education which may promote theology. Likewise all states want to promote their ideology through the formal system of education. A theocratic state restrict women to walk freely. A monarchy would like to impose a scheme of formal education which could promote and practice monarchy. In such a situation the educational institutions are not allowed to function independently and the development of epistemological atmosphere is marred. In a autocratic state the interests of autocratic ruler are always protected. In a democracy freedom of speech and right to information are always promoted through formal education. And sociability, morality, cooperation and the development of national culture through enculturation should be the agenda of formal education along with imparting academic education. Along with all these the students should be made aware about socio-economic and political conditions of the nation. But the examination phobia becomes a main hurdle in achieving all these ends.

The school and other educational institutions have also their own limitations to carry on such an elaborate arena of formal education. In the present materialistic and hedonistic age, allurement of material gains has made the results of the examinations, very important and, the teachers have no time to inculcate good life habits in the students and enculturate them. All energy is devoted for preparing the students to do well in annual examination. The excellence in annual examination has become the prime priority of the whole society. And due to this there is cutthroat competition in the society these days. The examination phobia has become a very important common social phobia. Schools and teachers are rewarded and punished on the basis of annual examination results. The parents have become mad for the good examination results. Also the students work hard for showing good results. Some time the students commit suicides. A girl was told by her fellow student in Ghaziabad on 27.5.2006 that she failed in her secondary examination 2006. The girl immediately committed suicide. Her result showed that she had secured 95 per cent marks in her annual examination. The parents also torture their wards for good performance. The teachers also earn money by doing tuitions. The teachers and school authorities lay emphasis on teaching examination subjects. They do not realise the parameters of real education. The present day formal education has become a commodity, a license for employment and a source for the economic life development. Many types of schools, such as public schools, Government schools, coaching schools, day care schools are functioning in the society. There is a need to make all these schools aware about real education. As such, the system of formal education should mould the life of the students to live sane social life. It should also inculcate sociability, morality, cooperation, tolerance, truthfulness and national integrity along with the subject knowledge. The school curriculum should have a process for all these.

11

Effects of Present Educational System

When a system for any kind of operation is developed in any area, be it, socio-economic, political, cultural, theological or educational it may entails good or bad effects on the total social infrastructure of the society. And out of these activities educational activities play a kinetic effect on the total social infrastructure. Because, educational infrastructure of a society is the liver for its socio-economic and cultural development of the society. As such, total infrastructure of a society is affected by educational structure.

India is one of the oldest society of the world. It had a renouned educational structure for maintaining its homogenic socio-economic structure and for enculturing the people. This educational structure had semi-formal system of education imparted in Gurukula Ashramas situated on the river banks in jungles. The *Gurus* (teachers), *Shishyas* (students) used to live under a common roof of the Gurukula Ashramas. The *Shishyas* (students) were kept in the Ashrama for warding off too much parental love and to socialise them. But only the wards of two upper castes—Brahmans and Kshatriyas were admitted in the Gurukula Ashramas. The wards of Vaishyas and Sudras and women were not admitted in Gurukula Ashramas. The main aim of Gurukula Ashram education was life building of the future guardians of the nation by inculcating sociability, religiosity, spirituality and by developing necessary good life habits in them. Another aspect of education aimed at socio-economic development. It was based on vocational system of non-formal education under which vocational castes used to train their wards in their hereditary vocations themselves. The youngers from the early age used to work with their elders while they were doing vocations. This type of educational structure continued till the foreigners occupied India. Muslim invaders ruled India approximately eight hundred years. And the English ruled about two hundred years. During the Muslim rule the Indian education was not badly affected as many of the Muslim rulers believed in non-interference in the Indian religious educational institutions like Gurukula Ashramas. Another reason was that most of them had settled in India and made India their motherland. Though a few of them wanted to change the theological picture of India by converting majority of the Indians to Islam. Since the Muslim rulers made their home they adopted tolerance and adaptability. But the westerners were businessmen; they viewed the total Indian social infrastructure from business angle. As such, they had adopted policies to make the Indians loyal and obedient subjects. And for this they had imposed their system of formal education for acculturating the Indians to their Western culture. The alienistic system of formal education has badly affected the Indian socio-economic and cultural systems to large extent. A few of the effects are as given below:

Acculturation

Acculturation is a social process of drifting from the national culture to an alien culture. The acculturation generally occurs due to cultural diffusion. And cultural diffusion occurs in the modern scientific age. The cultural diffusion is like an occurring which cannot be stopped by a mechanical device. When smoking started in the world many countries had banned smoking. The queen of England had also banned smoking in England but in spite of this smoking could not be stopped. Like smoking the system of formal education spread throughout the world. The Viceroy's Council of East India Company, British Government in India, on the advice of Lord Macaulay thought of imposing the British type of formal education in 1833 A.D. The overt aim of the British Viceroy's Council was to provide a big white-collar job force for the East India Company, British Government, as to bring such a clerical force from England was neither viable nor economical. Their deep-rooted covert strategy was to make the Indians loyal to them. Though majority of the members of the then British Viceroy Council were not in favour of imposing the British type of formal education on Indians. They had pleaded that the British Government should not play with the Indian culture, which was good according to them. Also many other British East Company Government officers objected to this proposal. The then Governor of Punjab, Lahore (now in Pakistan) had also objected. He said that the Indian system of Gurukula Ashram education and Indian system of non-formal education were best in the world. But his argument also did not bring any result. Lord Macaulay had argued that "if the British people want to keep their hold, the Indians were to be accultured", which was only possible through the British type of formal education in India. Then only the British can keep the Indians as their slaves forever. The argument of Lord Macaulay was accepted and the British type of formal education in which teaching of English was given a prime place. This alienistic system of formal education has made the Indian social situation topsy-turvy. It has not only ruined, but has totally killed the Indian culture through acculturation. We Indians have totally lost every traits of our national culture. Now we eat, dress, speak and behave totally in British style. Because of acculturation, we Indians have totally renounced the important Indian life motto of "simple living and high thinking", which was to check the greedy temper of the man. Now we totally have become greedy, self-centred, megalomaniac, hedonistic, consumeristic and xenophilic. This has changed every aspect of our culture. All this has happened because of our deep acculturation. The dreams of Lord Macaulay about the acculturation of the Indians has come out true, and now he might be eating milk cakes in his grave. All this social change has happened due to deep acculturation which could be possible through the alienistic system of formal education which we are still pursuing. The killing virus of acculturation has also entailed many other killing social evils which may be described as under:

(*a*) *Non-Religiosity and Non-Spirituality*

The Indian culture is one of the oldest cultures of the world. In the past we Indians were pure religious and spiritual, less greedy and, cooperative in spite of rigid birth based caste system social stratification. Mostly the Indians were monotheistic in spite of some atheistic sects as Buddhism, Jainism and Carvacs. Monotheistic Indians used to pray the Almighty God two times a day in morning and in the evening. The Muslims used to pray five times in a day. This was done in a non-inclinative way. In *Shrimad Bhagavad Gita,* the Lord Shri Krishna had told to Arjuna not to pray Almighty God for any personal or material gain. The man is supposed to do his duty without expecting any result. The result of action should be renounced. Though the man is a rational being but is greedy also. We Indians became more and more greedy due to acculturation which happened due to formal education, which has no place for enculturation. Under monotheism the man believes in one Supreme God, who is the creator, sustainer of the physical world. As such, in olden times, the Indians were not henotheistic and polytheistic. They also used to pray some auspicious Gods and Goddesses, but as the source of Almighty God. Now, we Indians have adopted henotheism and polytheism. The daily prayers are not done because the man is intensively remain busy in the rat-race of money earning. He earns throughout the year and his family members arrange half-yearly and yearly *satsangs,* in which they distribute *prasad* and sometimes they arrange community lunch or *lunger* (लंगर). This is done on the pattern of protestant Christian Calvinic dictum, "earn throughout the week and attend church on Sunday". As such, there is no religiosity and spirituality in the Indian society now. In school education there is no place for religiosity and spirituality due to our national policy of secularism. There should be some place for morality in education. The school authorities should try to inculcate morality in the students through some functions as morning assembly, though it is not sufficient.

(b) Non-Sociability

Non-happening of the good relations among the members of the society is termed as 'non-sociability'. The term 'sociability' is a derivation from Latin word 'sociabilies' which is the development of the Latin word 'socio' out of which term society was developed by Auguste Comte. The word 'socio' means maintaining good sane relationship with the social fellow beings. And for maintaining good cordial relationship with the fellow-social beings a keen desire for amity and sociability is a quality or manner or same behavioural quality of human beings. A man/woman is to be earnestly sincere to the social whole, that is, society. He/she is to be human, non-self-centred, non-egoistic, non-megalomaniac, considerate for all, that is, for elders, youngers, fair sex and should be aware about the contemporary social situations. For social harmony he/she should maintain a close rapport with the neighbours, should maintain a cordial, sympathetic and reciprocal relationship with all fellow-beings in the society. He/she should behave very nicely with all members of the society. It is necessary for the betterment and security of all members of the society.

But in the present materialistic hedonistic age, the man/woman always remains busy in the rat-race for money earning for materialistic and hedonistic gains. He/she believes in 'eat, drink and be marry'. The present man/woman has become totally carvac (चारवाक). This is why the present individual remains busy in achieving mere material gains and has no time talk with his/her fellow-beings in his neighbourhood. This social situation has become a common feature in rural, as well as, in urban areas. About seventy years back when the writer was a child the people in his village had a very close rapport. They used to share the happiness as well as grief of the people. Now in the villages also people have become totally self-centred. They also remain busy in their own ends. In the towns and cities the people remains busy earning money in the day and counting that money in the night. They do not talk to their close neighbours. The main gift of the present formal education is meglomanity and eliticism. The highly educated people consider themselves extremely megalomaniac. The lecturers, readers and professors working in universities and in other institutions of higher learning do not like to talk to the people below their rank and sometimes even with their fellow elites. Such an awkward situation has emerged because our youngers are being prepared only for gaining material gains under the present alienistic system of formal education, which is only aimed at for preparing the students for good examination results. No inculcation of good life habits and enculturation is done due to examination phobia. As such, unsociability is also the gift of acculturation, which is the prime gift of our alienistic present system formal education which is alien. The sociability is not only 'the domain of the human society'. All living beings maintain nice sociability. In the animal world the sociability is also nicely maintained. It is, therefore, very necessary that all members of the society should be educated not to be non-social but should be social. This can only be done if the younger generation, the future guardians of the country, should be educated to be social sincerely. Then only the non-sociability, which is the gift of materialism, hedonism, consumerism and xenophilism and which are the gifts of acculturation can be checked. Our present educational system needs reformation to check these evils.

(c) Disunity

Due to human greed and self-centredness the social disunity is seen in the society. Unity is very necessary for the survival of the biological wholes as well as for the existence of physical phenomena. All physical phenomena exist because of its unity with earth, sky and flora and fauna. Biological unity of male and female make the social existence possible. Unity is done through the social institution of marriage. Similarly all animals in the world exists because of their unity. Animals, birds, bees and beasts though cannot speak but they keep themselves united through other means of communication. Likewise, all other things made out of physical things like wood, iron, copper and tin are given unity through fabrication or joining together through joints. A carpenter or a tinsmith, or a fitter, or a blacksmith or a weaver always fabricate things by joining some parts together. If a joint of a fabricated thing becomes loose the thing become dys-functional. And all physical things are fabricated out of non-conscious material. If the parts of these things are not correctly joined the unity of the manufactured thing becomes shaky and ultimately it becomes dys-functional. The human body is a biological whole, in which all body parts so integrated that, these functions in harmony with other parts and make the human existence possible. If one part of the body goes wrong and becomes dys-functional the whole human body becomes crippled. The society is also a collectivity of individuals, who are biological wholes. But the society cannot be equated with a human biological whole. The members of the society have individual differences, interests, tastes, desires and are self-centred. Their psyche is different, and it is difficult to keep the individual beings united. And unity of the members of the society is also very necessary. The society has also some sane persons who lay down certain social norms for the social unity. They had established institutions like family, community, marriage etc. etc., so that, all members of the society may remain united. The human beings are rational beings. But they are greedy and self-centred. The human self-centredness, is the gift of western cultural diffusion and consequent acculturation. The acculturation has brought a social change. The man becomes more greedy and self-centred, which has entailed disunity in the society. The nuclear families have emerged and disunited the kiths and kins. The son does not hesitate killing the father for usurping his earned property. Some wives get their husband killed for their hetro-biological satisfaction. The youngers do not respect their grandparents and other elders. Mostly ladies dys-functions the joint family. And for all these have human greed, self-interest for meeting hedonistic needs, are reason of it. A disunited organisation or a society or a nation cannot survive for a long time. And we Indians have faced such an awkward situation of living under the rules of foreigners, because of disunity. We should learn a lesson from it.

As such, it is necessary to take some steps to remain united, we should prepare our youngers, the future guardians, to remain united. Our education can do this job efficiently. Though the teachers in the schools and other educational institutions are busy and overloaded in teaching for preparing the students for examinations. However, only passing the examination is not education, the education is much more. It is a way of life building, and social unity is one of most important aspect of human life. Preparing the students for social unity also should be a prime educational aim. Inculcation of good attitudes in the students for social unity should have a place in the school as well as in other educational institutions' curriculum. Social unity is very important for the national integrity. Some ideas about the social unity should be developed in the students through morning assembly and through some relevant co-curricular activities. These co-curricular activities should be organised house-wise. The students would learn about unity and cooperation.

(d) Corruption

Cultural diffusion of the Indian culture with the western culture which resulted in mute acculturation of the Indians also entailed killing corruption. The term corruption is the development of the corrupt. The word corrupt is the deviation of the Latin word 'corruptum', meaning 'to change from sound state of mind, to purid or pubriscent state of mind', to impair, 'to change from pure to worse', 'to bribe or grease the palm'. So corruption is an act of falsity through rooting out correctness or trueness through false means. Because of acculturation and consequent desires for affluency for hedonistic living, the mindset of majority of Indians changed to earn money by fair or foul means. The concepts of simple living and high thinking, religiosity and spirituality have been totally renounced. And majority of the Indians are involved in rat-race of money earning through any means. Now the materialistic ends of the individual can go to any extent. Greasing of the palms of the concerned persons has become a common feature these days. In doing so favouritism, side-tracking mediocrity, cheating usurping others' rights, occupying public property, misusing of allotted public property have become the common forms of corruption in the society these days. The virus of corruption has spread its wings so wide in India that it is very difficult to get anything done without greasing the palms of the concerned persons. And many people boost the corruption by bribing the concerned officials for getting their work done early. They bribe the concerned persons willingly and happily. As a matter of fact giving bribe and taking bribe are heinous crimes. They both should be punished. If our education system prepares the youngers not to give and take bribe, the social evil can be controlled. But our present educational structure is quite immune to this serious social problems. It has nothing to do for checking the corruption in the society. It is over busy in preparing the students for the examinations. Also the parents do not inculcate any good life attitudes in the youngers for battling with the corruption in the society. If the teachers take some steps and if these steps are not augmented by the parents, no good result is expected. However, the schools and other educational institutions should take steps to make the students aware about the essence of morality. This can be done by the good behaviour of the teachers and staff, arranging some related co-curricular activities and through morning assembly talks.

(e) Development of Good Life Attitudes

One of the major drawback of the present system of education is that it lacks life building of the students. There is no provision of inculcation of good required life attitudes in the youngers. Good life attitudes, such as, (1) early to bed, early to rise, (2) after this doing regular life activities as going for natural call, taking bath, to do prayers, meditation and yoga, (3) believing in simple living and high thinking, (4) to be cooperative, (5) to respect elders, fair sex and love youngers, (6) to love siblings and youngers, (6) to develop work habits, (7) to have sense of ethnicity and kinship, and (8) to be very humbles. All these qualities are missing in the present younger generation. Their life styles have gone totally topsy-turvy. They sleep very late and also rise very late. They have been made to take junky and fast foods by their mothers. Their work habits are more or less nil. They even do not wash their *'kachha banyan'* after taking bath. Our education should have a provision for all these life qualities.

(f) Development of Self-introspection

The educational system should have a provision to make the students self-introspective.

(g) Revival of Qualities of Old System of Indian Education

For the life building of the youngers, it is necessary to adopt some qualities of old Indian Gurukula Ashramas Education.

12

Curriculum

The curriculum is sort of working road map for any educational institution—be it a school or college or technical or medical institute or any institute of higher learning like I.I.T. or IIM etc. etc. Functioning of any organisation or an institution be it a family or business unit or school or an industrial training institute or any other educational institution can only be possible if it has a wisely well pre-planned or chalked out working plan. And above all this, it should be followed sincerely. Since schools, colleges and other educational institutions impart formal education to the students, these institutions should proceed as per prescribed curriculum. The pre-planned curriculum, can be said a teaching plan. And all teachers, lecturers and professors have to proceed according to the prescribed curriculum. As such, the role of every teacher in every educational institute is always tagged with the institutions curriculum, pertaining to the subject to be taught to the students. As the teacher has to proceed or teach according to the school curriculum, he/she should not only be aware about the curriculum contents, he/she should be fully prepared to teach according to the curriculum. The preparation needs sufficient knowledge of the subject content, proficiency in presentation of content before the students. This can only be possible when the teacher is fully aware about communication methods.

ETYMOLOGICAL INTERPRETATION AND DEFINITION

The term of curriculum is a derivation and development from the Latin word 'curricula', meaning 'a running', 'a race'. The term curriculum is generally applied in educational context. It refers to a specified content or course of study to be taught at a school or in educational institution or technical institution or in an university. Theoretically and, in practice the term curriculum is used to mean a teaching plan for materialising the learning possibilities of the students studying at an educational institution. The learning activities entail teaching, providing experiences through perception and acting. This can only be possible if the students are innovated and motivated for self-learning. And infusing in them general awareness about the subject content, is necessary for self-learning. As a matter of fact self-learning is real education. So the school teachers, and if possible the university or college lectures, should provide a wide spectrum of subject related experience to the students for gaining knowledge themselves about the subject related things and about the world and, vicinity the students are living. The students should be made aware about the national culture. The students should be enculturated about the national culture. This is to be done in addition to the teaching of the subject content. As such the teachers of the schools and of other educational institutions have an arduous responsibilities to discharge to make the future guardians of the nation responsible, competent to earn their livelihood and to live a sane rational social life.

In true sense, the term curriculum can be referred to the total structure of ideas and related activities needed for the sound life building of the younger generation of the nation. As such, the school education as well as, all other educational institutions need a well-planned and stipulated educational programmes to meet the needs of life building of the youngers, so that they may be successful in their lives. And the schools or other educational institutions should strive to achieve the desired stipulated educational national aims. As such, the school education and, the education at higher level should be aimed at to achieve the life building process of the youngers. The students should be given opportunities to learn the subject contents like language, humanities or social sciences, mathematics and science. And in addition to the subject contents the students should be given opportunities to learn good life attitudes. Such attitudes can be easily inculcated through arranging some co-curricular activities. Usually in school teaching and college teaching more attention is given to subject content teaching due to examination phobia. The students should be given a chance to learn the subject of his/her choice and to learn some activity which the students could follow in his/her future life for earning his/her livelihood in the later stage of life. A student has to live in the society as member of the society throughout his/her life. Therefore, the school education or college education curriculum should have place inculcating some social life values in the students. These values should be spirit of sociability, sharing, cooperation, brotherhood, morality, tolerance and urge to respect the elders, women, love for the youngers and an intense desire to follow the national culture. Covering of teaching of subjects comes under curriculum and inculcating the life values such as to be honest, diligent and to follow the enculturation comes under the co-curricular activities and, other activities necessary for sociability can be covered under the extra-curricular activities. Activities like sports and social service activities come under extra-curricular activities. The school education and college education should provide all required opportunities to the students for learning subject content and for some activities necessary for enculturation. Opportunities for learning and gaining experiences to the students will lead them to gain desired learning outcome. And for these ends it is necessary to provide some means of instructions which include class studies, guidance and counselling programmes, community services and creative artistic activities/programmes.

Curriculum as defined in Spen's Report 1938 (England), in strict sense, is a statement or of course of study, methods of teaching or processes of instructions for all experiences which a pupil acquires under the guidance of a teacher in the school or in other institutions of learning. So the curriculum is a planned scheme of directed learning which occurs in the four walls of an educational institution and, the group of students irrespective of their tastes and individual differences share it. Directed learning is a training which a pupil has to learn and, what is considered for him/her necessary. Such learning is given by the teacher in a planned way as per curriculum prescribed by the authorities.

WIDE AND VARIED VIEWS OF CURRICULUM

Some people use the term curriculum to refer the content which is to be taught by the teachers in a school or in some educational institutions. Others say that teaching and learning methods comprise curriculum, while others assume that it is students' achievement or attainment and, how it is assessed. While some say that the curriculum is moulder of beliefs, values and understandings that are passed on the students in an educational institution not through formal education of teaching, but unconsciously through the institution, total programme and climate, that implicitly and explicitly generates awakening in the pupils' life attitudes, that is, habits of regularity, punctuality, cohesion and cooperation, we feeling, sharing, simplicity, motivation and deference to the authority elders and fair sex.

As such, curriculum is a path or a road through which a student covers his/her journey to reach a desirable destination in the life or attain a goal. It is a deliberate process or path whereby an individual or a team identify desirable educational aims and objectives for particular learners and, design appropriate courses of study and suggest methods, ways of media of communication. The school and other educational institutions implement the curriculum, designed for a particular course in order to achieve the desired educational aims.

Genesis of Curriculum

Looking to the genesis of the term curriculum for school and higher education one has to trace the steps which led to the emergence of formal education. Before the industrialisation education of the child was the responsibility of the parents and elders of the community and society, who used to educate them in familial, informal and non-formal ways. The state had no control. The children of the well to do families used to employ the teachers for educating their children. The Sophists were such teachers in Greece. In India also some well to do families used to follow this practice. Guru Rabindra Nath Tagore was taught by such teachers at his home. The teacher used to come to the house of the child and teach all subjects. As the working class was not able to afford to employ teachers for teaching their children at home, they used to train their children in their own occupations themselves, this type of education is often, called non-formal education. And, in India all artisan class and other working class used to train their children in their family occupations. The higher castes—Brahmans and Kshatriyas used to send their children in Gurukulas for educating them. The education in Gurukulas was aimed at to inculcate a spirit of social responsibility, competency, sociability, morality and epistemacy. So this kind of education was called "*Panchmukhi Siksha*" (five-faced education). With the emergence of industrialisation and, consequent development of formal education, such old traditional system of education based on religiosity and spirituality became redundant, as this could not produce trained skilled hands to man the industries. So, the responsibility of educating the youngers was shifted from family to society managed institutes like Gurukula Ashramas, *Pathshalas* and Madarsas to the educational institutions like schools, where the group of students could learn collectively. In the beginning the schools were financed and managed by the society and industrialists. But with the passage of time the schools were purely managed, financed and handled by the state. The state maintained the schools as instruments of the state. As such, the school curriculum was so designed which could be in the interest of the state. This also relieved the parents of the children from their duty of familial education. They could do their jobs easily at home or in factories. Intensive industrialisation entailed modernisation and urbanisation which necessitated skilled specialisation. So one teacher concept of teaching was also found insufficient and ineffective, so it became redundant in due course of time. School education became a necessity. It became a paramount agency of teaching and preparing the students for examinations. At school, many teachers could teach instead of one teachers. It also provided job opportunities for educated youths. After passing out examinations and consequent certification the students could be able to try to find out jobs either in Government offices or in industries. As such, to cope with employment requirements, first the youths were given school education in subjects like language, humanities, mathematics, science and thereafter the student could get higher education in colleges, engineering colleges or in medical colleges where, the students could learn to do some activities like fabricating, orthographic drawing and business management. For all this a planned school education structure, as well as higher education structure were/are needed for which proper school curriculum was/is to be planned accordingly.

Curriculum Building

As Auguste Comte anticipated, when he gave the new term of 'sociology'—'old society is dying and new society is emerging'.

He had anticipated and suggested the new science of 'society' to deal with the new emerging social problems. As such, the industrialisation has brought many surging social problems about which the youngers are to be made aware of. Since, due to materialism and consequent modernisation, consumerism and hedonism both the parents are in rat-race of money earning, and they can not do familial education and inculcate necessary good habits for enculturation. It is assumed that what is skipped by the parents should also be done by the school teachers in addition to subject teaching. Of course this is an arduous job. But the school or other educational institutions cannot do it at their own as the schools have to follow the curriculum designed by the state. As such, the state curriculum development authority designs the curriculum through which, the school or other educational agencies could generate a sense of epistemacy in the students to learn necessary subjects for appearing in annual examination. And it is necessary to know ontological, sociological and axiological problems and educate about all these problems. Earlier such knowledge was transmitted by the elders of the family. The earlier school was one teacher-one pupil school and the pupil had to accept what was being taught. There was no curriculum. The present school of education has to play different roles. There are many specialisations and specialist teachers who specialise the students in different fields. The students are living in a technological world where he gets information from many sources. In this situation the making of primary school curriculum was not a difficult job. With the passage of time changes in curriculum construction came slowly. Thinkers like Froebel, Pestalozzi, J.J. Rousseau, Madam Montessori, Rene' Descartes, Comenius and Margaret Macmillan influenced the pedagogic thinkers, who tried to construct the curriculum accordingly. In England, until Hadow Report (1726) school education meant only grammar school education which was purely academic theoretical and dominated by external examination. Only intelligent upper class children could have assess to it.

The broadened term of curriculum has emerged due to blind industrialisation. The educationists felt that the child is a total process and not only a mental process, which implies that the school should have a programme for the development of the whole child rather than only classroom teaching. People learn more through participation rather than passive assimilation of knowledge of subject content. As long as, 'assign, study and receive' is an accepted formula for the greater part of the child development, the curriculum could only be conceived as for those courses subjects that were/are lined up for the students to take up. But as the theory of mental discipline discarded, belief and in the development of whole child began to be realised in practice the curriculum, as a broad basis of total programme of activities is conceived for the survival of the child. Such a programme is to be implemented by the schools or any other educational institutions. Providing the wide and varied activities are generally called extra-curricular activities, though generally considered secondary activities but, are necessary to ward off academic boredom. But, still emphasis is laid on teaching subjects. The extra-curricular activities are generally sidetracked, and only arranged if these activities do not hamper scholastic studies of the students. It is believed that these activities may sidetrack and hamper students' studies which may affect the examination performance of the students. So the subject is still dominant in school teaching as well as in college teaching. As such, the school curriculum, is still prepared mechanically to prepare the students as mono-moulds for passing the annual examinations, killing their interests initiatives. This practice keeps the students continuously away from nature, social milieu and even from the parents. Only master strategists plan curriculum at the instance of those who are prominent in curriculum building process.

The curriculum should not only be framework of subject content courses and related matters. Other things which are going to unfold many useful experiences to the students and, may enrich their personalities should be included in the curriculum. The activities are to be selected in advance before the re-opening of the school. And the teachers should start interacting with the students just after opening of the school or educational institution. Everything according to Hereclitus everything is in flux, so social phenomena is also change and educational institutions be changed.

One of the most glaring fallacy in curriculum construction is that the educators are prone to statistical goals. They ignore the students' psyche and interests. They plan curriculum for common life for common good, for general common training and for common good and for general citizenship; and for that they prescribe the scale of success — the success in examination in taught by subject contents. But individual differences of the students depicting their abilities, varied interests, capacities of sociability, morality and enculturation are always totally ignored. Only attention is paid on subject teaching. Indian old system of education was aimed at inculcating all these in the youngers. These were main base of educating the youngers.

While planning the curriculum the teachers, prominent intellectuals, senior citizens and social workers should always be involved. As such, the curriculum should never be prepared in camera, as generally is done. There should be continuous research in this regard as suggested by Prof. Stephen M. Corey in his book *'Action Research'*. The curriculum is generally for general group which is experienced by the whole group equally in spite of individual differences. It should cover a programme of life building and sustenance. Educationists should examine the social perspectives, then decide about the educational goals which should be covered by the curriculum. General subjects and specialised subjects should be distinguished very carefully and should be taught earnestly.

Various committees and commissions were formed in the past for curriculum development and implementation in United Kingdom of which the educational patterns we are still following. These committees have cautioned about curriculum construction.

1. Hadow and Spen Reports and Education Act 1944 (U.K.) established education as an activity for all, with monotonous curriculum.
2. Newsom Report 1963 (U.K.) about the future of curriculum. It said that the present form of curriculum does not create a sense of reality in the students.
3. Again in United Kingdom, Head Masters Report 1967 suggested that the Head Masters of the schools should be involved in curriculum construction. There should be a provision for creative arts in school curriculum construction. Also there should be a sufficient scope of curriculum enrichment. This can be done if some innovative teaching methods are applied in teaching, such

as using of teaching methods and application bi-polar methods of communication in teaching.

Curriculum Planning

Edward A. King has rightly said that:

(*i*) Curriculum is an instrumentality for translating hopes for materialising child education into concrete reality.
(*ii*) Curriculum is necessary for eliminating a lag between mechanical and social progress.
(*iii*) Curriculum is necessary for helping an individual student to achieve greater success in a living-in society.
(*iv*) Curriculum construction is necessary for creating a democratic society.
(*v*) Curriculum should be so framed that the pupils should be able to understand the social problems.
(*vi*) Curriculum should reflect measures necessary for establishing permanent peace in the society.

As such, for curriculum planning, there should be a continuous permanent study and research so as to achieve the long term viable social goals.

Identifiable Concepts of Curriculum

(*i*) Identifying social and national objectives.
(*ii*) Developing the educational programmes according to these objectives.
(*iii*) Identifying teaching and learning situations.
(*iv*) Identifying the aspects which may unfold the students' personality and may enrich it.

Following should participate in curriculum planning:

(*i*) State-wise leadership groups.
(*ii*) Local leadership groups.
(*iii*) Representatives of general public.
(*iv*) Representatives of the learners and teachers.

Following should be the bases of curriculum construction:

(*i*) Social milieu, social philosophical issues including ethical, moral, economical and psychological problems.

(*ii*) Culture of the nation.

(*iii*) Economy, chances of employment and thereby social mobility.

(*iv*) National objectives, based on social flux and desirable educational adaptability.

(*v*) Psychological based steps to be taken pertaining to mental health, sociability keeping in view the individual differences of the students.

(*vi*) Information about sociological bearings entailed by mechanisation, industrialisation, modernisation, urbanisation and sanskritisation emerged due to following the western ways of life and consequent acculturation.

(*vii*) Castes, creed, class, communalisation, untouchability, concept purity and pollution and its effects on education. Reservation of some seats in educational institutions and its effect on merit.

(*viii*) Exploitation of the poor by the rich and by the politicians.

(*ix*) Steps to be taken for enculturating the students through artistic and cultural activities.

(*x*) Role of the educational institutions in the changed social situations.

(*xi*) Secularism *versus* religiosity.

(*xii*) Social services training.

Following areas should be the instructional fields:

(*i*) Core subjects like mother tongue, related language, human social studies, mathematics, physics, chemistry, biology, botany etc. etc. and one or two foreign languages.

(*ii*) Creative activities like fine arts and crafts, group discussions and debates.

(*iii*) Co-curricular activities—these activities should be arranged regularly on specific days and on specific occasions as Teachers' Day, Gandhi Day, Tagore Day, etc. etc. And also religious festivals as Janmashtmi, Diwali, Christmas Day, Basant Panchami, Id-ul-Fitr and Guru Nanak Birth Day etc. etc.

(*iv*) Parents' Day—special decoration should be done by doing

Alpna, Rangoli and moveable etc. etc. If possible a talk should be arranged on balanced parenting on Parents' Day.

(*v*) Educational institutions' foundation day should be arranged. And on this occasion some dignitary should be invited to preside who should address the gathering. Special reception should be arranged and a cultural programme should also be arranged.

(*vi*) Generally it is seen that due to examination phobia, games and sports are ignored. These should be arranged regularly and should be compulsory for all students.

(*vii*) The programme of every school and educational institutions should start with morning assembly. The morning prayer should start with an introductory talk by the Principal. All teachers and many students should address the morning assembly.

(*viii*) All important activities like examination, use of teaching-aids, co-curricular activities, extra-curricular activities should be clearly mentioned in the curriculum.

(*ix*) Steps to be taken for enculturation of the students should also be mentioned in curriculum and

(*x*) At the end of the session, a valedictory function should be arranged for the final year students.

Taking into consideration all these points the curriculum should be planned. There should be a core committee to review and implement the curriculum. The committee should suggest ways and means for the improvement and implementation of the curriculum, keeping in view the social needs and health of the students. The committee should coordinate with the related agencies in this regard.

13

Purpose of School and Higher Education

Every social activity is always done with a specific purpose. And, school and higher education is done with a specific purpose. Main purpose of education is to mould the lives of the youngers or, so to say doing their life building, so that they may live a sane social life in future. The term 'sane' is the derivation of the Latin word, 'sanus' meaning 'sound', 'a mentally sound biological whole', 'non-damageable healthy, mentally sound body having regular exercise of reason and other logical mental faculties. So sanity is a state of individual saneness. Inculcation of sanity in the youngers is the prime duty of the parents of the youngers and the teachers. Of course, the off-springs of the human-beings are rational being like their elders, but they are also greedy like many of their parents and other elders. So the main purpose of the education should be to control the greedy nature of the youngers. It should be done through familial as well as formal education.

Main aim of Indian old system of Brahmanical education, which imparted in Gurukula Ashramas, was to mould the life of Shishyas (students) to live a sane social life in their future lives. And for this purpose the youngers were separated from their parents and made to live a social life in a bigger family in Gurukulas. The *Shishyas* used to live a community life in a bigger home, the Gurukula Ashram, wherein the individualistic temper of the *Shishyas* used to be changed to common temper for living cooperatively with their fellow *Shishyas*. The *Shishyas* used to be separated from their parents and family elders to live a social life in Gurukula Ashram. It was done to save the youngers from the too much parental love which could be dangerous for their life building. There is an adage that "too much parental love may be poisonous and dangerous". Such love makes the youngers unsocial, non-cooperative, non-diligent, lazy and desirous of tasty and junky foods. In Gurukula Ashramas the Shishyas used to live in their first stage of life, that is *Brahmcharya* Ashram. In Gurukula Ashramas the *Shishyas* were bound to live a simple, austerous and social community life. They used to take a very simple vegetarian (सातविक भोज) common food. From the very beginning the *Gurus* (teachers) used to inculcate some desirable life attitudes in *Shishyas* (students) necessary for living a sane social life. The *Gurus* and *Shishyas* used to live under the common roof of the Gurukula Ashramas. The *Shishyas* (students) used to eat very simple common vegetarian food (सात्विक भोजन). They were not given special love and affection as given by their parents in the family. The *Shishyas* were required to do some Gurukula duties like collection of food items from the nearby villages. They were also to collect fuel wood from the jungles. Also the *Shishyas* were required to cater the cows. There used to be a work schedule in the Gurukula Ashramas. The *Shishyas*, after taking dinner used to go bed. "Early to bed, early to rise makes a man healthy and wise" was the dictum of the Gurukula Ashram. After this the *Shishyas* used to go out in the jungle for natural calls. They used to take bath and attend collective *pooja* and Agnihatra (हवन). After this they used to attend yoga class, which used to follow religious discourses given by the *Gurus*. And thereafter they used to take simple refreshment. After that the *Shishyas* used to follow their Gurus for attending their lectures on religiosity, spirituality, morality, sanity, homogeneity, truthfulness, sharing and cooperation. After this, the *Gurus* used to teach Sanskrit, *Itihas* (history), *samaj shastra* (sociology), astrology, etc. etc. The main purpose of the Gurukula Ashramas was to inculcate good life attitudes as mentioned above for the life building of the Shishyas, so that, they may lead a sane cooperative social life. After the Gurukula education and completing the *Brahmcharya* Ashram at the age of 25, they were to enter *Grahasth* Ashram and lead a sane social life. They were supposed to educate the general public about sanity. They used to inculcate good life attitudes in them and mould their lives.

Now the situation of school and higher education is totally quite different. The education imparted in the educational institutions is based on mere teaching school subjects for preparing the students for examination. The schools do not try to inculcate good life habits which may prove good for their future life in leading a sane social life. As a matter of fact only passing of examination cannot be true education. True education is much more and its aims are also versatile.

The present school and higher educational structure should visualise the whole social situation which emerged due to social flux caused by cultural diffusion and consequent cultural change caused by the killing acculturation. Now the educationists, politicians and general public should realise the damage the present alienistic formal education system has done to the India social structure. No doubt this system has benefited a lot to the Indians. But at what cost? It has totally mutilated and damaged our national culture. We have lost every aspect of cultural traits of our national culture. If the culture of any nation is lost, its everything even independence is lost. In such a situation the existence of the nation becomes fractured. So, it is necessary to look into this aspect and reform our present national educational structure. Of course it is true that in the present scientific industrial age the knowledge of science, technology and other related subjects is utmost necessary, which should also be assessed, evaluated. But this should not be done at the cost of our national culture. As such, our educational curriculum should provide an opportunity for viable enculturation. The enculturation can only be possible by inculcating good life attitudes like—sociability, religiosity, spirituality, morality, axiology, simplicity and sense of self-introspection. The parents cannot do this as they are too much busy in earning for meeting their domestic hedonistic needs. This can only be done through school education. The schools can do it by presenting model educational infrastructure as same socially and, by educating the students through morning assembly and related co-curricular activities programmes.

EDUCATION AND SOCIO-ECONOMIC DEVELOPMENT

Socio-economic infrastructure is very necessary for the existence of all human-beings, who are parts of the social whole, that is, society. Without the development of socio-economic infrastructure the human-beings cannot survive. Not only for the human-beings, it is necessary for the animals, beasts, birds, insects and bees also.

This is why the human-beings have been continuously developing and improving a viable socio-economic infrastructure in the society. And the society is a bigger whole or an organisation of such social structure. The human-beings are rational living beings. In spite of rationality they have animal nature and are also greedy. They have many needs as food, clothing, shelter, cooperation and sharing with the other members of the society. For meeting these needs for their existence the human-beings have developed and, have been still developing, many social organisations and institutions like family, religious institutions, community and educational institutions. The development of the future citizens and guardians is very necessary, which can only be possible through sound educational system in the country. Also, for sound socio-economic development it is necessary to inculcate sociability, morality, religiosity, spirituality in the members of the society which can also be done through sound educational system. The man, has also developed a system of unity in bio-diversity through the institution of marriage. Through the institution of marriage coming of the new off-springs becomes possible which makes the social existence possible. The children become young and in due course of time become the future guardians of the society and the nation. The future guardians need some necessary things like food, clothes and shelter which are necessary for their existence. And for all these a viable socio-economic development is necessary which can only be done through a sound educational structure.

Socio-economic developments are inter-related. This can only be possible through education, be it familial education or non-formal education or formal education. As such, socio-economic developments are closely inter-related. Neither social development, which has wider spectrum as cultural development, can only be possible without many aesthetic and social activities, nor economic development can be possible without epistemic development of the individual. Neither economy is possible without education nor education can be acquired without money, which is a main source of economy. The word economy is a derivation of Latin and Greek words—'economia' and 'eikonomia' meaning, 'management of property', 'application of labour or any instrument of labour'. Now the concept of economy has a very wider meaning. There is a cutthroat competition in every field of economy. So economical epistemacy is very necessary which can play a vital role in every field of human life. So, it is necessary to educate our youngers about economy and, school and college education can do this easily. Concept of economy covers four aspects: (*a*) production, (*b*) consumption, (*c*) demand, and (*d*) supply and knowledge of all these can boost economy. If the production is more the supply will be more and products will be cheaper. If the production is less the demand will be more and the goods will be dearer. All these aspects are covered by education. Through appropriate education a person can know to manage his/her household. Old Indian education used to educate the youngers in this regard. Now, the school education, as well as, higher education lay emphasis on teaching the subject contents in order to prepare the students to come out in flying colours in examinations. Also no work habits are developed in the students in educational institutions and also in families due to examination phobia.

Also, like economic development, the social development of the youngers is very necessary, which is ignored at both stages at home and at school as well as at colleges. The social development of the youngers who are our future guardians has a wide spectrum. They should be properly educated to live a sane homogenic social life. For this, one has to develop good living life patterns—as to be social kind and considerable to the fellow social beings, to behave with them to be cooperative and sharing with them, to be honest and not greedy. In spite of rational beings the human beings are greedy. To check the greedy nature some good life attitudes and habits are, to be developed—as 'early to bed early to rise', 'to make the youngers aware about ontological aspects of human life' as 'to be and not to be', to develop religiosity, homogeneity and spirituality to live a simple life and avoid hedonism and to enculturate the youngers for making them dedicated to the national culture. This is most essential because our national culture has been totally fractured due to cultural diffusion and resultant acculturation. Neither the parents of the youngers, as they remain very busy in money earning. Due to this they have become totally polytheistic and hedonistic. They have hardly any time to do regular religious prayers. They only do periodical *kirtans* and *bhajans*. And many of them arrange periodic '*bhojs*' lunches. Also, the educational institutions only devote to subject content teaching and prepare the students for annual examinations. As such, both social and economic development of the youngers are totally ignored at basic levels, that is, at home, at educational institutions. The main social agency, the joint family system has also been totally crumbled. Also, this cannot be denied that the socio-economic development of the youngers is most essential for a sound social life. In the present period of science and technology industrialisation came into being and the economy is linked with the industrial production. Education can do this.

Education is a crucial type of investment for the exploitation of modern industry and economy. In an advanced industrial society it is necessary that the education system should be in close relationship with industry and its related social aspects. In a mechanical productive process, capital bureaucratic liaison for its maintenance and, an effective communication system and social rapport for its proliferation are necessary.

Modern industrial societies are distinguished in their structure and development forms in comparable complexities, institutionalising of innovations, large-scale scientific researches in socio-economic growth. The occupational structures are by and large diversified which require highly qualified workforce for employment at all levels. Therefore, education attains an unprecedented economic importance as a source of technological innovations and for development and related social latitudes. As such educational structure needs vast infrastructure for training for occupation recruitment. The traditional functions of social differentiation were based on caste structure has been replaced by formal industrial training which entailed cutthroat competition in the society. Mass industrialisation has also changed the status of caste based labour force. Now the formal education and consequent formal industrial education is to cater the requirement of employment.

As such education has now become an investment for economy as a whole, and old forms of education and non-formal education, training in occupational guilds now have totally become redundant due to new economic face. This has also changed the status of the teacher and functions of the educational institutes. Educational set ups are now transformed according to the new age, neo-political structure and secularism. This has changed all of the traditional sociological, economical, religious, spiritual and axiological norms. Now the *Guru* is no more. The present teacher is now a poor public servant, who is neither a religious, spiritual and nor sociological torch-bearer in the society as, the old *Guru* was. The present teacher is forced to pass on subject contents knowledge to the students for passing out the examinations. The present teacher has nothing to do with inculcation of good life habits and life building and enculturation. The old teacher, the *Guru* used to do all these. Due to hedonism the present teacher is denied his/her due social status in the society.

Now, the man is in the rat-race of money earning. Social institutions like joint family, community relationships and social relationship as a whole have come down. Due to money earning the human sociability has come down to a low ebb. Money acquisition efforts have entailed social conflicts, mitigation of man, human personal relationship, non-sociability, personal grudge, no respect for elders. These have become endemic in the modern industrial society, which shows that education has also become microscopically as an industrial tool in relation to total materially structured society. Less attention is given to the fact that microscopically structured education makes man mechanical, which is not at all helpful in building an interactive, as well as, social sharing way of human life which is very essential for a sane society. The role of the teacher remains restricted to microscopically system of subject content for good examination results, which has nothing to do with inculcating good life habits and axiological norms in the students, which are very necessary for enculturation and life building, character building through good human attitudes, which are necessary for harmonious social living and; social integration, do not get proper attention of the teacher. The teachers work as a tools in the modern educational structure. They do not do anything regarding enculturation. Microscopically designed teaching methodologies for educational opportunities only exhibit elitist and populist theories of educational opportunities which confer each other. There is a controversy about what proportion of population is benefited by the present system of formal education imparted in schools and universities. At microscopic level, there is a parallel class struggle for education between upper castes and lower castes, between classical and modern curricula, between intellectuals and common social milieu and, between elites and ordinary persons. There is a cutthroat competitions for admissions in the institutions of higher learning.

According to Peter F. Ducker an abundant and increasing supply of highly educated personnel is a pre-requisite condition for social and economic development in the world now-a-days. It is a requisite condition for national survival. Uneducated masses are becoming an economic liability. They are considered unproductive. Therefore, all members of the society must be educated, so as to grow, progress and survive. There is a sudden change regarding the meaning of education and also knowledge for the betterment of society. For upward economic growth, upward mobility and for social sanity, creating a viable potential in the members of the society rightly educated persons is social necessity. And the roles of educational institutions, their teachers, educational administrators is increasingly become important for this purpose.

There is a complete history of man within sixty or seventy years. Until the beginning of 20th century there were handful of educated people. Now, it is believed and to some extent it is also an axiomatic truth that man having little education will find it difficult to survive in the modern technological age. He is likely to loose his traditional methods of earning. And due to modernisation, all cottage industries, which had a hoary past either have totally disappeared or on the verge of total disappearance. Tools like potter's wheel, carpenter's framed saw (फरनाई), turning wheel and black smith's old forging and tempering techniques are disappearing. Not only these, with the introduction of modern techniques and modern software system, the man will also be deprived of his writing skills. In other words, it would not be wrong to say that modern education is growing to promote scientific techniques as, use of computer discourage manual work, which is the need of the day in the present demographic explosive conditions.

For the economic development the utilisation of human, mental as we as manual resources is must for which the proper development of human resources is necessary, which can only be possible if all people are educated well. As such, expansion of education is a due necessity for economic development, that too entails differentiation. The expansion of education in Athens in Pericles times (approximately 550 B.C.) rested on slavery. Artistic and intellectual splendour of Italian Renaissance depended on sharp debasement of economic and social positions of peasants and artisans. In India, artisans and hand workers were also considered low by higher castes though they were the builders of the Indian culture. Still if a hand worker shines and proves himself epistemic, his past is always tagged with him. This trend is not good for socio-economic development of the country. There should not be any caste bias in educational fields. Utopian scientific projects like nuclear capability of erstwhile USSR recently have rendered Russian people nowhere. At home, we can see the expansion unthoughtful institutions of higher education and research has brought misery to the downtrodden and opened hedonistic avenues for those who were rich and now are becoming richer.

The idealist tried to break this tendency by combining manual work, which is necessary for economic growth, with academic field of education. Though Homer had pleaded for placing the plough in education for promoting this trend, but the Greek oligarchy was for retaining class hierarchy i.e., nobles, philosophers, soldiers and artisans, like Indian Varna system. Jefferson's concept of higher education was for those who deserved. At home in India, we see caste system a hierarchical social stratification, developed out of merit based Varna system. Some greedy people of upper Varna had converted into birth based caste system. Ved Vyasa who had survived for 157 years, it is said, had consolidated the birth based caste system in India. The expansion of unthought institutions of higher learning and research has brought misery to the downtrodden lower castes; these opened hedonistic avenues for those who are rich and now are becoming richer.

The speed of educational expansion varies. We find that ratio of school going children in USA was 1:8, today it is 4:5 proportion of the school going population of the children. The ratio of those who are engaged in hand work was 3:100. Now, it is more (18:100). Adult education is increasing. Educational explosion has been more erstwhile in USSR. Earlier, there the basic literacy was confined to small majority. Now, education is a patent force there. So, it cannot be denied that education is not a capital resource to economy in modern industrial society. And education serves as a foundation stone for higher education which is necessary for all sorts of economy.

In Switzerland and Mexico the secondary education is universal. No expenditure is deferred on school education. In the contemporary society productivity, which generates economy, revolves around the work which requires knowledge which is gained through vision, perception, conception, which entail concepts. Generally the work is based on thinking, reasoning, comprehension, which are the functions of the mind. After these work can be done, only hand cannot do the work. In the present economic spectrum it appears that there are greater demand for the educated skilled workers, who make the productivity of consumer goods in the society. The educated people are the capital of a developed society. So the development of educated people is most important, their number, quality and utilisation are most meaningful index of wealth producing capacity of a country. And in this production the school education is the epicentre where productivity rests. Both the stages of education are important in which teachers play a vital role. So the teacher education is also very important.

IMPACT ON SOCIETY

Automation is a rapid sublimation caused by knowledge and machine. Automation lies in specific machinery, technical ideas and skills. Automation should be known first in school of formal education to the age group of 12-16 years, having expectations to work and do related manual work jobs. Our future workforce should have the capacity to accept what they can do properly, and apply their knowledge. Those who do not have capacity to accept and do complicated jobs should be prepared for doing skilled jobs. For them, training in the jobs of fitting, fabrication and assembling will be difficult. Fallacy lies that we try to make every job meaningful for everybody, thinking that functions of every work are common and universal and can be handled by everybody. This is done under the cover of common employment. Individual differences and personal specific capacities and potentialities are often ignored. The teachers can work as guides to the students in this regard. They should check the students doing undesirable works, and promote the viability of specific jobs.

The educational revolution has had an equal impact on work, work culture, economy, international trade having an epigamic (to take off for upward mobility) move for economic competition. The educational development, above all, has become a central problem of the poor countries. Many poor countries spend a large amount of money on education. In USA one-fifth of their youngers do not get complete higher education. Out of these some even do not complete high school education. In India most of the parents desire that their wards should complete university or technical education, irrespective of the fact that most of them remain unemployed. Our school education is such that it does not invoke any interest for hand work. The school should do it. It can be done by introducing some artistic creative activities in schools curriculum. In addition to this some co-curricular activities should be done in school programme.

The educational inequality is a serious intra-social as well as economic problem. This sort of inequality is increasing day by day, greater and greater. The rich is becoming richer and richer, and the poor is becoming poor and poorer. There is a danger that in long-run it will push the society to total social disharmony which may encourage division in the society, by disunity, theological furry bringing agony and anarchy in the society.

Educational Competition

"The battle of Eton was fought in the field of Eton due to class struggle". The school master defeated France in 1870 A.D. With the launching of sputnik it became clear that the high scientific education controls its defence preparedness, its technology and economic potentialities. So the educational development becomes top priorities of national policy of the countries these days. And the institutions of education—the schools, colleges, technical institutions become the architects for achieving educational gains.

The Pressure for Economic Changes

Due to industrialisation and modernisation, which entailed hedonism and consumerism, the standards of living of higher sections of the society have sharply risen. This entailed inflation, progressive taxation by the state, desire and lurch to machine made things, and adoption of alien ways of living, resulting in acute acculturation, hedonism and consumerism. So there is compulsion to have school children as early as possible and thereafter higher education so as to enable the youngers to fall in the line of competition. Hedonistic materialistic desires made it necessary for the youngers to be ready for getting higher education as early as possible for getting suitable jobs. As such, the present man should be mentally prepared to be economically prepared is a socially recognised notion and a viable necessity. So the present day school education as it is the edifice for further higher education is supposed to prepare the youngers economically viable. Being a well-qualified is an urgent necessity due to employment requirements and, to meet the cutthroat competition in the job market. For getting a job a person should have knowledge, skills and performing abilities. Demographic explosion is another reason of competition in job market.

IMPACT OF TECHNOLOGY ON EDUCATION

Importance of educational qualification is the latest manifestation of the employment scenario on which the whole edifice of industrial development is built. There is an enormous demographic increase in the world. It is said that 1,30,000 new faces are emerging in the world population everyday. We can say that the size of Derby town comes every day. Half of the world population is at starvation level. And in India, in other Asian countries and in African countries it is much lower. Energy consumption has also increased in the world. It is highest in USA. In India and other African countries it is also lower. There are chances of energy shortage in the world due to population increase. It is said that China, some African and Asian countries and also India are contributing to the demographic explosion. Theology in some Muslim countries, and to some extent in some Christian catholic pockets in some countries are potent of population increase. It is because of orthodoxy due to some old beliefs. In Iran, there was a blacksmith who lived for 155 years. He married seven times and had a family of 121 children and grand children. His youngest grand daughter is still alive and is in thirties. So due to demographic explosion there is shortage of food, water energy and also of shelter. And this has affected the economic development of the nations. This problem can only be solved if a man becomes conscious of realities. And this can only be possible if a man is truly educated and is able to realise what is wrong and what is true? The school education can be an instrument for educating the future guardians about true socio-economic realities.

The scientists are engaged to find out what can be the substitutes of food and energy? But such an approach is not sufficient, until and unless the man is truly educated to be able to do self-realisation and self-introspection. Until this is done, the clouds of conflicts, uncertainty and non-working will continue, and the socio-economic development of the human society will be badly affected. Corruption, terrorism will whip the innocent people. The animal nature of the human beings will play its cards which will affect the economic development of the country. The utmost need of the day is to make the man a true rational being who could discover or trace his undue greed, religious fanaticism and dogmatism which needed to bringing sanity in the society as necessary for the sane socio-economic development in the society. Proper education both at school and at higher level can achieved this aim. Of course, there is a need of producing scientists, technologists, technicians and skilled workers who could raise the economy of the society. But this should not be done at the cost of social homogeneity, morality, humanity and social sanity. The school, as well as, higher educational institutions should take into consideration all these facts.

Technological Change and Educational Consequences

The first phase of industrialisation up to World War I shows that three different occupational groups existed, more or less, corresponding to the phases of technological development as, (*a*) skilled workers, (*b*) unskilled workers, and (*c*) clerical and managerial personnels, were required. Social prestige of these groups reflected closely in their importance in production and trading. Now the situation is altogether changed because of advance technology. A worker is the slave of machine these days. He cannot take any initiative. A worker is provided raw materials, he operates the machine and works as a mere operator. He operates the machine as he operates his cycle. Also, the worker is alienated by the owner of the machines used in an industrial unit.

EDUCATIONAL DEVELOPMENT AND ECONOMIC ASPECTS

We are living in a time when knowledge is exploding. One has to acquire more knowledge, more techniques, skills and more fabricating abilities, then only one can think of economic gains. So gaining of more knowledge is the only prime cry of the day. Without knowledge one cannot think of better economic development. So, the development of human resources is the utmost necessity in the present industrial age. And human resource development can be possible with better viable educational opportunities. The school education is the prime source of the development of human resources, as without it higher education cannot be gained. Through appropriate school education a youngster can proceed for further advanced education and can gain socio-economic gains. Real education should transmit or generate good human work attitudes, cultural traits, values, spirit of diligence and sincerity in the youngers. With all these qualities, a person can also develop good work habits, which can make him an economically viable person. These must be first and foremost priorities of the school as well as of higher education. The school and higher education must check cultural diffusion and acculturation which hinder the all-round socio-economic development of the nation. The first priority of the education should be to prepare the students economically viable citizens to lead a sane social life. Our education is lagging behind in this important educational function. On the economic front our educational aim should be preparing the students economically well. But our school and higher education aims at preparing the students for white-collar jobs. This is tantamount to the dream of Lord Macaulay who had imposed alien formal system of education for producing clerks for British India Company Government and for acculturating the Indians. On the social cultural front our present school and higher education is still doing acculturation of our youngers who are future guardians. It should be checked by those who are in power.

As an economy develops, the need for experts, that is, managerial staff, highly skilled, skilled and semi-skilled technicians and for helping hands increases geometrically. Consequently, there appears an increasing demand of education which could produce such workforce. Increase in economy is necessary for better living standards. Therefore, educational development is necessary which should be according to the needs of rapidity. The school education should play a prominent role in this regard, as it is a prominent let-out for higher education. Due to demographic explosion there is an enormous increase in enrolment in schools. Every section of the society desires that their children should get admission first in the school and thereafter get university education. So the university enrolments have reached on the high peaks. Many commercial educational institutions have also emerged. Due to unaffordable expenses the lower castes people miss higher education which is necessary for the national socio-economic development. Only elite class people's children can get higher education. Now-a-days education is an investment and consumption for survival.

Human beings have been surviving since times immemorial in spite of their animal nature which is tainted with greed and lust for xenophilism, which is done by acquisition of many material things. This greed factor of human beings, though has ever been dominant, but has always been modified and corrected by those human beings who have been rewarded by the nature or Almighty God with rationality and social sanity. In olden times, every society had such rational elements who used (being rational) to guide the other human beings. They used to impose some social restraints through religious sermons on irrational social elements. These rational elements being used to study, speculate, idealise and propitiate new knowledge in the society through thinking, reasoning, contemplating and comprehending the social structure and its problems. They used to lay down certain social norms and rules. As in India, good and sane actions (नैतिककर्म), *dharma* (धर्म) that is, actions done as per religious rules, *adharma* (अधर्म), that is, actions against religious tenets, morality. Actions done against morality were called immoral actions (अनैतिक कार्य). These were the suo motto base (आधार) of the Indian society, which are still followed, to some extent, though acculturation has changed the social situation. These were the manifestations of Indian education. The *Gurus* (teachers) used to do a lot in rationalising the human society through religious sermons for making the Indian society a sane society. If such religious sermons were ignored, and some undesirable social activities were done, the rulers used to punish the defaulters. So, in the olden times, the trauma of greed was under control because of Indian old system of education.

Now-a-days, the economics of corruption has become rampant in the society—be it a Government office or higher seat of learning or mustard oil shop, one cannot get any work done without greasing the palm of the authority. There is no clarity in the appointments of teachers. The meritorious candidates are generally ignored due to nepotism and favouritism. Our markets are prone to adulteration. The recent adulteration in mustard oil had taken a large number of lives of innocent people. The present man wants to be richer and richer by unfair and foul means. This is happening because of our acculturation. Many of our politicians are facing court cases but they are occupying the administrative chairs. Many politicians support the criminals who are living quite safe. It can be concluded that corruption has become a common social feature these days which is derailing our sane socio-economic development. As such there is a need to look into this social evil. Our education system can do a lot in this regard. Everybody is fully aware what is happening in the society but we have become so immune that we do not open our mouth. A state of anarchy is emerging. Atmosphere of loot, robberies, chain snatching and cases of rapes are reported by our newspapers daily. All these events affect our economy. Our educational institutions, be it school or university or technical education, should look to this problem along with socio-economic development. There is a need of political will to bring our socio-economic development on the right track in society to improve the economy based on sanity. Stringent political actions and also social will are needed.

However, the school education is the edifice of all type of education which are necessary for economic development. Therefore, it is necessary to take necessary steps for the improvement of national socio-economic development through education.

14

Examination System in Education

Human beings are rational beings. From the early age they are trained and educated for living a sane and sustainable social life for better living. For better living, the human beings have to earn and for that they have to do some activities. And for the promotion, development and advancement of viable human activities, the human beings are trained and educated. They are also encouraged to do some activities which may prove to be helpful to them. For educating the youngers, the Government has opened so many schools and educational institutions in which the youngers are trained and educated. This is essential for the life building of the youngers.

In the present industrial age the man has invented many new things for his use. Since the nature of man, in spite of rational being is greedy accumulative. The present man has become totally consumeristic, hedonistic, and xenophilic. All this has created a cutthroat competition in every field of work in the society. Sixty years back, Delhi's population was about five to six lakhs. Now it is about one crore fifty two lakhs. It is estimated that by 2021 A.D. Delhi's population will cross the figure of 2 crores and twenty five lakhs. Sixty years ago Delhi had only about 10 senior secondary and secondary schools. Now the number of schools has crossed the figure approximately of three thousands. In addition to these there are many coaching shops for different examinations. The present schools have to educate all children of increased population. These children are examined by the authorised examining bodies and are certified so that they may stand in queue of competition. Now-a-days the better examination results is the crown of present school or higher education. The education authorities, especially the schools authorities lay too much stress on good examination results and the students and the parents bear the brunt of it. The scientific development and consequent industrialisation and commercialisation have entailed a social change which has brought undue competition in the society. The students are educated to face this social situation and they are examined. As such, good examination results have become the soul of present formal system of education. In the past there was no examination neither in Gurukula education nor in non-formal system of hereditary education. All educational institutions used to devote on life building of the youngers. For that they used to inculcate good life attitudes in the youngers for saneful social living. Many of our present thinkers have bitterly criticised the present structure of examination system because of its bad social effects. But the examination is going in full swing in our school education, as well as, in higher education. Committing of suicides by the school and college students have become a common social practice. Last year one mother had also committed suicide because her daughter had not done well in her secondary school examination. This year (2006) also approximately one dozen students have committed suicides because of their poor examination results. In spite of all this the examination system is going on.

Social change occurred in the society due to scientific development and consequent industrialisation necessitated educational adaptability throughout the world. The original educational norms of life building were changed to competitive norms, as industrial infrastructure required knowledgeable, skilled and proficient workforce. For finding out such workforce some measures for evaluating the proficiency the examination was introduced, which was necessary. Therefore, proper and regular judgement of educational achievements of the students became necessary. And this is done through the examination system. The modern system of formal education has been designed to meet the demands of modern post-industrial infrastructural workforce, which entailed evaluation, assessment and examination system. As such, the examination system became necessary from the first class and goes up to the last class. The students are promoted from the lower class to higher class on the basis of examination. And at the final stage of school or college education the students are examined by an examination body and are certified so as to proceed further. As such, the school or college formal education is totally examination oriented education. The teachers, both at school and university level, are also evaluated for the preparation of good examination results. Other educational activities like inculcations of good life habits and enculturation either are generally done in name sake or totally ignored.

The examination has forms as internal examination and external examination, subjective examination or objective examination for which evaluation and assessment procedures are adopted. If we look etymologically, the concept of 'evaluation' is the development of the word 'value', which is a derivation of the Latin word 'valere' meaning 'worth'. The word evaluation means to find out the numerical validity of a think or an action or an appraisal of state of affairs. As such, the word 'evaluation' means an act of finding out worth of an action. Likewise, the word 'assess' is a derivation from the Latin word 'assisdeo' meaning to 'set aside' or 'to find out value'. The word 'examine' is a derivation from the Latin word 'examino' meaning 'to assess', 'to bring out', 'to observe carefully', 'to look into', 'to question', 'to consider all aspects', 'to interrogate a witness' and 'to find out educational worth and capabilities'. The act of examining is called examination, which is also a derivation from the Latin word 'Examinus'. The word 'examinee' is also a derivation from the Latin word 'examinitum', meaning who is examined.

The genesis of 'evaluation' and 'examination' centres around human activities, as already mentioned above. Every action always entails a reaction. Most common characteristics, common to all normal human beings, is to assess the results of their actions. With various needs or objectives in our minds we desire to know the validity of our activities, and these activities are assessed. If the results are favourable, we continue the activities, otherwise we reformulate the activities or drop if the results are unfavourable. Since the dawn of the society the man has ever been doing his activities on these premises. A farmer tills the land, sows the seeds with a hope that the result would be good crop. An engineer plans and execute a road bridge hoping that it would facilitate easy road traffic. Likewise, all human activities are done hoping good results. So, the human activities are continuously done and examined and if the results are good and favourable, these are continued and often are not reformulated. All human activities always entail good or bad results. So the human activities, including examination activities are continuously assessed and examined. As such, continuous educational examination and examination of human activities yield good results. Sociologists, philosophers and scientists proceed through the assessment and evaluation of their thought processes and contribute in their fields.

Teaching, is and has ever been a foremost human activity done on mass scale with certain stipulated aims and objectives and consequent results which are ascertained through evaluation, assessment, measurement and examination which are conducted on certain principles and rules and regulations. Firstly, we have certain principles basing on certain objectives in mind which motivate us to do certain activities for certain ends. Secondly, the activities are continuously assessed for the degree or standard of success one can obtain. Thirdly, the pace of improvement occurs in the process of activity as a result of assessment or examinations.

The process of teaching is a specialised activity, involving the stimulus performances of three tasks (*a*) maintaining the class environment alive, (*b*) providing adequate learning experiences appropriate to the changing needs of the pupils, and (*c*) implementing the experiences in which the teacher is an active participant. For the convenience of the first task, the environment management is necessary, the second is managing, learning and, the third is instructing or teaching.

The teacher deals with the conscious beings, as his/her clients. His clients are not ignorant clients, as that of a medical man or legal man or of a priest. The teacher moulds his/her conscious clients. He/she moulds the pupils or students by giving them a good shape or a form in their mental, spiritual, moral and aesthetic capabilities by doing a lot of work and setting up examples. As such, the activities of teachers are like that of an artist, which always excels than the activities of a doctor or lawyer or a priest who are recognised as professionists by the versatile thinkers in the field of sociology and philosophy.

The aims and objectives of education are many (*a*) mental development, (*b*) physical development, (*c*) emotional development, (*d*) academic development, (*e*) spiritual development, (*f*) cultural development, (*g*) aesthetic development, and (*h*) social development, and the teacher is expected to achieve all these. But now-a-days the schools are required to provide all subject instructional activities done compulsorily for good shining examining results. In many cases these activities are not carried out properly because of too much stress on good examination results. There is a misconception that teaching should be examination oriented. In such a situation the main aim of the education either sidetracked or ignored and teaching of examination subjects remain an hi-fi activity for good annual examination results. As such, the examination becomes a versatile hindrance in the field of real education. And present school and university education centres around only for good examination results. And due to this all other necessary education either forgotten or totally sidetracked. The fear of examination results looms large in the minds of the teachers, educational administrators, students, parents (especially mothers) and other family members. Examination psyche has become so dangerous that many students and sometimes some mothers end their lives by committing suicides. J.J. Rousseau had said that when the child is born, he/she is free but finds himself or herself in chains and this dictum proves to be true for the school going children as their parents apply too much pressure on students for securing good marks in their annual examinations. This leaves the educational world in a lurch. Many times, the teachers and the schools in which they are working, if do not show good examination results, are punished. The examination system, which is generally external examination, breeds corruption. Many coaching shops are running a lucrative business. Also sometimes these coaching shops try to cheat the students and their parents by introducing pseudo false examination papers. Sometimes the examination papers are leaked even at the examining body level. Intelligent, just and honest paper setters are discarded and sidetracked at the behest of some interested persons who want to use the examiners as a tool for good results of their institutions. Such persons, generally have close links with the examining bodies. As such, the examination, through which a large number of students are supposed to be assessed is found defective as (*a*) often many question papers are generally found of sub-standard level, (*b*) examinations are only held in few selected studies, (*c*) cases of cheating doing copying and impersonation are also generally noticed, (*d*) important areas of education as character development, inculcation of good life habits, moral development and enculturation are totally ignored due to examination system, (*e*) the teachers, who teach the students generally are not involved in examination system, and (*f*) there is no provision for examining the teaching faculty members, that is teachers, lecturers, readers, professors, policy makers and principals. They are left out of the evaluation process activities.

It is also said that without evaluation and examination the quality of teaching and the resultant standards of education cannot be improved. According to Toreston Hussen, the quality of teaching in schools depends upon its effectiveness which could be ascertained on the availability of accurate and detailed objectives of evaluating of teaching. According to him focus should be laid on evaluation of teaching rather than on teachers and interactive teaching or on process of self-learning by the students.

So a comprehensive criterion is to be developed for evaluating. A criterion is an aspect or a dimension of a desired quality to be evaluated or to be assessed. Such a criterion should be empowered to check the arbitrary steps of evaluation or assessment, which are noticed in many cases. Evaluation in education is a method of judging educational objectives. So the criterion of evaluation of teaching and resultant education should be based on four distinct types of achievements (*a*) respective gains to be achieved out of teaching, (*b*) behaviour of the teacher while teaching the students, (*c*) behaviour of the students during the course of teaching, and (*d*) experience, skills and knowledge, the students acquired through teaching. The behaviour of the teachers, employed by them, during teaching should be observed informally using some kind of rating scales by the headmasters or vice-principals and principals of the schools. This criterion should also be applicable in colleges, universities and other institutes at higher learning. If possible students opinion should also be obtained in this regard. Usually, what generally happens that only the students are evaluated, assessed and not doing his/her duty well and there is no criteria to evaluate the teacher, whether she or he is devoted to teaching profession or not. Similarly, if a teacher is devoted and committed to teaching profession, he or she is not recognised or praised? Generally the efforts of the devoted teachers go unnoticed. Parents and public are very keen to know the examination results of their wards and not about the performance of the teachers.

Performance to be done by the teacher requires that (*a*) the teacher should make so many discussions during teaching instantively everyday. The quality of discussions is always indicative of good quality of teaching, (*b*) the purpose of teaching should be to motivate the students for self-learning, (*c*) knowledge orientations depend upon teachers efforts. And it seems logical to evaluate teaching on the basis of its outcome. As the function of the teacher seems to be focussed around the production of learning by providing experience, which is likely to be result oriented learning, therefore, it seems logical to evaluate teaching on the basis of pupils' attitudes, behaviours and efforts to learn following teachers contribution in classroom teaching. Since, the pupil's behaviour is the outcome of the teacher's behaviour, the teacher's behaviour also needs to be observed and assessed.

Evaluation

To evaluate is to ascertain a viable process or action. Thus educational evaluation involves the passing of judgement on the degree of worthwhileness of teaching process or providing the learning experiences. Evaluation involves the purposive assessment of behaviour caused by teaching tasks. Performance of assessment entails or involves three steps all are essential.

(*a*) *Standard tasks or set of tasks*:

- (*i*) the candidate i.e., the pupil must demonstrate the professional ability or quality, so as the candidate is able to demonstrate,
- (*ii*) there should be a mechanism of discrimination or self-assessment in the candidates (students) about their appropriate elements of performance,
- (*iii*) the evaluation task set for the students must be equal (same paper, same project and same assignments).

(*b*) Outcome of the evaluation must be recorded.

(*c*) There should be a set standard of scoring.

(*d*) Elicitation should be the aim. Relevant behaviour showed by the teacher should be recorded.

(*e*) The tasks, the students likely to perform must be recorded.

Basis of Scoring

The scoring task should be clearly specified so as to find out the changes occurred in students' minds. There should be equivalent tasks for internal assessment. Random or unspecified procedure should not be applied for this. It should be done through obtaining records of learning. Rating scales should be adopted by the teacher. Ralph Taylor said that the teacher should observe the students systematically and regularly. Ralph Taylor, who is considered father of educational evaluation, assessment and measurement. These have commonly in educational testing, though these are not the same. None of these in synonymous. These three areas of applications are considered different. But these areas of applications are continuous in nature, whereas the examination is taken once or twice in an academic year.

Measurement

Measurement assigns a numerical quantity to instruments like spectrometer, electrometer, hydrometer, vernier calliper, measuring tape, thermometer and stop watch etc. These can be used to determine height, length, race and temperature so on and so forth. Many intellectual and related capacities or other qualities of intellectual related aspects are measured directly or indirectly. The educational measurements are logically designed and are used to measure such dimensions, as level of intelligence (I.Q.), ability to apply a given principle in a variety of situations. Measurement is rarely carried out for its own sake. It may be more regarded as necessary for doing research also. Though it is included in assessment and evaluation, it is considered mini-science of physiological measurements and psychometers. For intelligent measurement special intelligent tests and apparatus are required which are so designed.

B.H. Choppires has described the different approaches for mental measurement and some of their principles. A number of basic psychometric concepts are relevant for the uses in the tests used for evaluation. These are as such—item analysis and objective tests. Reliability of test results depends upon validity, guessing, inferring, correlation and confidence matching. Assessment is also used for application to people. It is used for grading (formally and non-formally) examining, certifying and so on and so forth. Student's achievement in a particular course may be examined. When such an assessment or evaluation is carried on en-mass in a wider area at the end of the term or season, it is termed as an examination—say annual examination or half yearly or quarterly examination. Throughout the world, educational systems find it appropriate to find out the record of students achievements placing them in grades or class or commenting about the students. Such an assessment is based on formal evidence of ability. We can say that the examination system in all educational systems throughout the world is an universal common feature, though it has its own demerits and merits too. The term evaluation in educational system is used to refer to such programmes, such as co-curricular activities as inculcation of desirable life habits and enculturation programmes, organisational variables, like art and crafts and other festive events on which some extra curricular activities are arranged. Also for epistemic development some research work is carried on which requires evaluation.

If we look to the sociological aspects of evaluation and examination system, we came to the conclusion that the examination system does more harm than benefit to the society. It breeds corruption, make the individual self-centred and maglomaniac. It also kills the enculturation processes, which is necessary for the development of national culture: students, parents, family members, teachers, society and the educational administration become mad after the annual examination results. Other educational objectives, which are very important for the life building are totally ignored for the sake of good shining examination results. Sometimes, the validity of examination comes under the clouds of doubts. Essay type of examination which was prominent in yester years, and still is in existence to some extent fails to test the student's ability. If the students attempt to write some good content, sometimes the examiner ignores to read all material written by the students. Objective type test papers are difficult to be prepared so their reliability is also doubtful. Only very few intelligent students fair well in objective type test or examination. Objective type tests are very common for all types of recruitment and entrance examinations. Whether the existing system of examination serves the social needs or it requires a change are the upper most questions in the minds of not only those who are only responsible for the improvement of education in our country, but also for those whose children are studying in Government or aided schools and in other educational institutions. Prof. N. Hussain observed that the existing system of examination began to bring negative results. The University Commission (1948-

50) headed by S. Radhakrishnan described it as an evil. The Secondary Education Commission headed by Dr. Mudaliar described the examination system as a dead weight on our educational structure. The Education Commission headed by Dr. D.S. Kothari described it as a defective system and suggested drastic reforms for the current examination system. Oxford University, U.K. had introduced external examination only in 1958 A.D. with an idea that it would motivate both the students and the teachers, but this did not happen. Gunar Myrdal in his book "Challenges of the World Poverty" described the examination system as a legacy of colonial rule. Charles Colton said, "Today the examinations are formidable, even the best prepared are greatest fools, may ask more than wisest person can answer". The examination system can only benefit those who can afford to get their children prepared and those who cannot afford are not benefited. The examination system has been very harmful to those who learn non-formally and become skilled technician but are ignored by the employees in the absence of certification.

The present whole educational programme centres around good examination results. The school or higher educational administration keeps a vigilant eye on school administration regarding the annual examination results. If the school examination results are not satisfactory, the school central administration scolds and tightens the school administration. Then the principals and headmasters of the schools warn the school teachers. As such, generally the teachers remain busy in preparing the students for good examination results. The teachers do not get time to do any other educational activities like, inculcation of good life attitudes, enculturation of students and for these doing co-curricular and extra-curricular activities like sports, social work and art and craft activities. Good examination result is the only cry in the corridors of educational institutions, in the galis of the villages, *mohallas* of the towns and in the streets of the cities. Mothers and fathers of the students usually play a dictorial roles and force their children to read as much as can be possible for securing highest marks in annual examinations. Even they do not allow their children to go out of home to mix up and play with their peer group. Also they forbid their children to do any house work. Even the children are forbidden to wash their *'kachha'*, *'banyan'* and 'towel' after taking bath, so that they can study more and more. Mothers try to provide them every sort of fast and junky foods so as to study more and more. As a matter of fact the parents make their children hedonistic and work evaders. As such, work culture which has been the soul of our culture is being mitigated under the examination oriented alienistic formal system of education. In olden times there was no examination system in India neither in Gurukulas nor in Madarsas and nor in non-formal education and the products of old system of education used to be highly epistemic, knowledgeable, social, religious, spiritual and highly skilled. They used to be cooperative and involved in common cause.

Therefore, keeping all these social as well as other aspects in view, there is an urgent need for examination reforms at all levels in our educational structure. This is necessary to brighten our education safe. First of all it is necessary to consider whether the present system of examination should be replaced by some other evaluation system or some of its aspects should be retained. If the present type of examination system is to continue, some steps, such as training of examination paper setters for replacement of essay type of examination question paper by a balanced paper setting should be taken. There should be a provision for some sort of internal examination. The paper setters and examiners should follow an ethical code like that of teaching professional ethics. Steps should be taken to eliminate the selective study by the students through guidebooks, which is usually done by the students for better examination results. There should be a provision for checking the cheating like copying in examination, paper leakage and pilferage for influencing the examiners. The students should be keenly advised to do self-study and not to do tuitions at any cost. They should be prepared to do self-assessment. There should be qualitative certification in place of quantitative certification. There should be ability based appointment procedure in Government departments instead of present certificate based appointments. Unfair means applied in appointment procedure should be strictly checked. Instead of periodical evaluation there should be a continuous assessment system without favour in educational system. This will evoke study habits in the students. Also, there should not be gender bias in the field of education and employment.

The teacher has to play a vital role in teaching, educating the students and life building of future guardians. So he/she should be given a proper place in students evaluation and assessment. Though it will take a lot of time of the teacher but he/she should do it earnestly, sincerely and judiciously. The school authorities should have faith and confidence in teacher. The national education scape can not be improved without reformation in education system.

15

Family and Education

The family is the most important social institutions developed by the human-beings since the inception of the human society. It is the family which produces human beings and make the existence of the society possible. The family is a derivation from the Latin word 'familia'—meaning a household, 'a body of persons who live together in one house under a common roof and under one head', 'parents and children'. The children are those who descend from common progenitor. They are distinguished with parents or grand-parents. Also family means a 'race', 'a kindred linage with the ancestors', 'a noble descent', 'a type of person who perform a common service as slaves do'. The term family has also a wider meaning as a 'family of noble descent', 'a family of criminals' etc. etc. For human beings and other living beings the institution of family is the progenitor of life. It is true about the other living beings also. The unity in human bio-diversity makes the existence of family possible. The male and female members are two different biological wholes. They are united through the institution of marriage for living together life long. It is nothing but an 'unity in bio-diversity'. They both live together life long. They maintain sexual relations. With the result the female partner gives births to youngers and she is called mother. The male partner is called father. As a matter of fact the institution of marriage which makes possible the birth of the youngers is a social licence of sexual relations. The married couples live long together to maintain viable sexual relations and give birth to the youngers who become future guardians and members of the society. The youngers after their births are brought up by parents and other family members. They are brought up and educated by the family members by inculcating some desirable good life habits and attitudes, which are necessary for rational sane social living. The family members used to inculcate good life habits and attitudes as 'early to bed, early to rise', 'to live a simple and honest life', 'to be self-introspective and diligent', 'to respect elders and fair sex' and 'to love youngers and animal life'. All this is done through familial education which is the foundation of life building.

Family can play a vital role in educating of the youngers. Actually the roots of education of the youngers lie in the family. In the past, the genesis of the education of the youngers was enshrined in familial education throughout the world. Most of the ancient world's civilisations like Greek, Hebrew, Indian and Chinese civilisations were basically the outcomes of familial education. And in familial education the mother used to play a prominent role. Besides this, grandparents, uncles, siblings, members of the extended families and the elderly members of the community used to play an important role till recent past, in nurturing and preparing the youngers for sane social living. They used to inculcate the desirable necessary life attitudes in the children. Such attitudes used to generate desirable social, moral, ethical and cultural values like, cooperation, sharing, tolerance, respecting elders and a sense of spirituality in the young children. The familial education was a sort of "*Panch Mukhi Siksha*"—a five-faced education. It contained, (*a*) to prepare the youngers to know about what is good and what is bad? (*b*) to prepare the youngers to know about sane religiosity and spirituality, (*c*) to develop a good sane character in the children, (*d*) to apprise the children about greed and self-centredness and how to avoid these by simple living and high thinking, and (*e*) to prepare the children to adopt good life attitudes as, desirable good habits, thinking, reasoning and comprehending, sharing and cooperation. All these used to prepare the children to be responsible future citizens who could respect the elders, women and to be responsible sane individuals.

It can be assumed that familial education used to be the foundation of life buildings of the youngers in the past. In India, after getting the familial education at home, the youngers of higher castes—the Brahmans and Kshatriyas used to be sent to the Gurukula Ashramas to gain further higher education regarding epistemacy, spirituality, homogeneity, axiology, astrology and sociability. As a matter of fact the Gurukula Ashramas were also like very big joint families, where the *Shishyas* used to live together under the common roof of Gurukula Ashrama. This was done to ward off too much parental love, which was considered dangerous for the youngers, and to make the youngers disciplined. At Gurukulas the *Shishyas* and the *Gurus* used to take very simple vegetarian food. There was no provision of tasty junky and fast foods. The *Shishyas* (students) used to sleep early in the night and rise early in the morning. In many cases this was not possible while living with the parents in the family. After this, after going or natural call, the *Shishyas* used to take bath, do yoga and thereafter they used to perform *'Yajna'* and do *'Sandhya'*. The *Shishyas* used to be taught to be true, honest and to live a simple life, to be sociable, religious and spiritual throughout their lives. The *Gurus* used to teach the *Shishyas* to be cooperative, honest, reverential to elders and women and always think of common good. And the youngers of other artisan and working castes used to learn the skills of the family vocations from their family elders non-formally. They also used to acquire good life attitudes and moral values from their elders. Also, they used to learn social customs, traditions and cultural traits through simple living which was totally non-materialistic. The families used to live a very simple life. 'Simple living and high thinking, 'early to bed early to rise', to be honest and truthful', 'to be punctual and diligent' were the basic rules of Indian family and familial education. These used to be inculcated through familial education first at home and later on at Gurukula Ashramas. Hedonism, consumerism and xenophilism were often found in the ruling class. These tendencies were not found in general public. These were the qualities of Indian education. And family was the main agency of education.

Now the situation has gone totally topsy-turvy in all fields of social life, and family life has been badly affected, with the result that the familial education has been badly affected. This has occurred due to long cultural diffusion which has resulted in killing acculturation. Now the situation of familial education has gone in opposite direction. There is no more *'Panch Mukhi Siksha'* (five-faced education) which was imparted through familial education, the *Aikal Mukhi* (One faced) or formal education which is totally examination oriented has become prominent. In all schools and other educational institutions the students are taught for passing out examinations, that too in flying colours. As such, the prime aim of all types of educations—be it schools, or colleges or universities or technical institutions—is to prepare the students for examinations with an aim that the students should pass the examinations in flying colours. Since the schools are the bases of all sorts of education like higher education, enculturation and life building but the school lay emphasis on teaching for good examination results. With the result private public schools have become good earning enterprises. And good examination results of the schools and other educational institutions have become their crowns. There are many public schools in the country which charge school fee in lakhs. Only the affluent families can afford to admit their children in such commercial schools. In the past, the Gurukula Ashramas used to provide not only free education, but also free boarding and lodging to the youngers. The Gurukula Ashramas used to inculcate good life attitudes for life building of the youngers. Now, in the present system of alienistic formal education there is no provision of inculcation of good life habits and enculturation for national cultural development which are necessary for the life building. The educational institutions and also parents are also mad for the good shining results of the students.

Since good examination results pave the way for higher education which is necessary for employment, so all schools want that their students should fair well in their annual examinations, so that they may add some feathers in the crowns of the school. As such, main focus of teaching activities centres around good examination results and not on life building for socio-economic development. There is no place in schools and other educational institutions for inculcating good life habits and attitudes like sanity, morality, axiology, truthfulness, respecting elders and fair sex. All schools devote all school time for the preparation of good examination results. Authorities also force the teachers to do examination oriented teaching. So they do not have time to do any socio-economic activity, inculcation of good habits and do enculturation. Not only the teachers but the parents also try hard to achieve this objective. They arrange private tuitions for their children. Both the mother and the father do not leave any stone unturned in this regard. Many of them are not qualified and eligible but try to teach their children the school subjects. They force their children not to do any house work so that they may study as much as possible and come in flying colours in their annual examinations. The parents of the children also do not allow them to play with their peer group. Especially the mothers of the school going children are very crazy for shining good examination results. They also do not allow their school going children to take a glass of water for drinking themselves. Many mothers do not allow their children to take their clothes like underwears and towels in the bathroom and, washing of such clothes is a distant action. The mothers hang these clothes in the bathroom themselves. As such, due to examination phobia the children are debarred to do any of their personal work, which inculcate in them 'no work habits' by the family. Such a social phenomenon proves to be dangerous for the children for their future work in their life. Such a tendency proves to be very dangerous specially for their girls as they are anta-property (पराया-धन). They may face very awkward situations in their lives after their marriages. Many of them are often murdered by their in-laws for not doing required homework.

The parents often do grease the palms and stomachs of their children for motivating them to study more and more for good examination results. Often the mothers prepare junky fast foods and items like Pizzas, Burgers, Samosas, Patties, Potato Tikkies, Dahi Bhallas and Dalbhaji for their children for motivating them to study more and more. The parents also give good pocket money to their children, which they sometimes spend on undesirable eating items. Due to over eating many children develop obesity which becomes very dangerous for the children. Many children become lazy. As such, the present families, instead of life building of their kids, spoil them. No good life attitudes, desirable work habits, moral values and sociability are developed in the youngers by many families. They only acquire luxurious habits and become hedonistic. They are not apprised by the parents that everything is in flux and they will have also to face change in their future life. Mothers of the children desire that their children should shine in future. But they do not realise and assess the potentialities of their own and of their children. Similar is the condition in schools and in colleges also. Equal education for all is the aim of all educational institutions irrespective of the potentialities of the students, their parents and teachers. This is all happening due to change in the mindset of families because of acculturation. People have almost lost their faith in simple living and high thinking. Materialism, hedonism, consumerism and xenophilism, which always entail greed, have changed the life styles of families. Today's families aspire luxurious life. And all these make the families unaware about their responsibilities about the required familial education.

The families are now so involved in materialism and hedonism and it is necessary to make the present families aware about the effects of materialism and hedonism on the socio-economic development of their children which is the prime aim of familial education. This can be done by social organisations and schools also. Then only the families can impart familial education and can help the children in their socio-economic development. The parents should not be mad after school examination results. They should realise that education is much more than mere examination results. The parents should also take some steps for enculturation of the youngers. The parents should also advise the schools to take some steps for enculturation of the students. This can be done by organising some co-curricular activities. Now-a-days the school education is only limited up to the preparation for examination. The examination fear psyche often takes the lives of some students. The parents should know this fact also. The families should also inculcate work habits. They should also involve their kids in their family vocations. The work habits are necessary for the socio-economic development of the children.

Now the situation of family life has gone totally topsy-turvy. Earlier the families were spiritual and religious. The family members used to believe in monotheism. The family members used to pray Almighty God daily. In Muslims the people used to pray five times a day. Now due to acculturation all families have become hedonistic and xenophilic. Both the parents of the youngers remain busy in rat-race of money earning. They have adopted 'carvac' and Calvinistic ethics 'earn more, enjoy and be merry'. This mental set, has broken the India's idealist socialist institution of the 'joint family system'. In place of it nuclear family system has taken place. Being continuously remaining busy in money earning, generally the family renounce monotheism and adopt henotheism and polytheism. As such, religiously and spirituality also say good bye to such families. Such families try to earn as much as possible. The members of such families become totally materialistic and xenophilic. And for material gains such families arrange *bhajans* and *kirtans* periodically—either yearly or half yearly. Many of them arrange community lunches (भोज). The daily prayers are no more seen in the nuclear families. Such families follow generally

Calvinistic ethics 'earn throughout the week and go to church once on Sunday'. Many ladies play vital role in breaking the joint families. For them their own children are important for them. This self-centredness has totally crippled the familial education. The children do not pay regard to the family elders. Even many of the present young generation do not like to talk to their elders. In such a situation there is no familial education. And in absence of familial education there cannot be socio-economic development of the youngers. Nuclear families only make the children hedonistic. Modern electronic media—TV, radio and VCR have added fuel to the fire and there is no chance of enculturation of the youngers in the present nuclear families. As such, socio-economic development of the youngers is very difficult. Whereas the youngers should be given opportunities to develop all-round skills.

16

Education for All
(Sarva Siksha Abhiyan)

Saneful, harmonious, purposeful and prosperous socio-economic development of all human-beings is very necessary and for that better enmass utilisation of human resources is most essential. For this purpose proper education for all is a dire social necessity for every society. There exist many races, castes and creeds and ethnic groups in all human societies. These groups often have variant life patterns, ways of living, attitudes and also have specific skills and expertise to perform specific duties. Such groups are stratified in castes in India who do their hereditary vocations. Until and unless the talents and capabilities of the members, and future members of the society are fully developed and well-utilised, there can neither be socio-economic development of the people nor social mobility of the society as a whole. And national economic development can never be possible. If any section of the society, that is, an ethnic group in a society remains uneducated there cannot be any national development in the nation. This can be done by upward socio-economic mobility of all social groups of the society, which can only be possible if all social groups get a chance of proper education, training and skills acquisition. So, proper educational opportunities for all members of the society is dire necessity for the better health and prosperity of the whole nation.

If poverty, ill health, illiteracy and social disunity exist in any section of the society or religious groups or in any ethnic group or groups of the society exist, these may prove not only co-terminus but cancerous not only for the health of few but for the whole society. The extremism and terrorism are result of lack of proper sane education. As such, for the proper viable rational sane development and welfare of the whole nation, there is a need for proper education which may mould the lives of the future guardians who may become sane, religious and spiritual persons. A religious and spiritual person is one who always thinks of common good. Taking lives of innocent people in the garb of religious dogmatism can never be said religiosity and spirituality. This is nothing but barbarism. The rationalistic education of the youngers can only be the solutions to social disharmony and barbarism. This cannot be achieved by mere slogan mongering. This can be done by better serious efforts of human resources development which should be based on rationality development in the future guardians of the nation. So proper education of the youngers is most essential. Proper human resources development can also be possible if proper avenues of education could be provided to all citizens of the nation equally. Providing equal opportunities for desirable human resources development for all can be a boon for national progress. If any section of the society lags behind or even few members of the society remain deficient in rightful of earning of their livelihood and fall pray or short of required living standards or not getting chance to apply and utilise their talents and skills, they will feel ignored and, will remain frustrated. This will devastate the spirit of homogeneity, commonality and brotherhood in the society. It will harm the unity of the nation. And ultimately such members of the society may turn to crimes and become criminals. And it would not be good for the health of the whole nation.

India is a multi-racial, multi-religious and multi-cultural society. There are many castes, creeds, sects, ethnic groups and religious followers in India, which reflect social diversity. Even though in the past, because of common spirit of tolerance there was a social harmony. Now this social harmony is badly affected by human material desires and consequent hedonism which emerged due to cultural diffusion and resultant acculturation. So, there is an urgent need of 'unity in the diversity' in the entire country. The entire social milieu because of caste based social structure differs due to the concept of purity and pollution. The higher castes still enjoy some hereditary privileges. Whereas, some lower castes suffer due to some inbuilt birth based caste status and degradation. As such, there is a need for education for all. Some castes are reaping the fruits of higher castes, whereas some lower castes are victims of social degradation. To meet this situation education for all is necessary.

According to Prof. M.N. Sriniwas caste is a horizontal solidarity of some ethnic groups. Whereas community is a vertical group in which all members of the society mix up and cooperate for common good. Out-casting and degrading of some castes in Indian society through the norms of purity and pollution and thereby imposition of some social restrictions according to versatility of caste status, in the past and to some extent in the present age also, had and has been a common feature. And due to this the Indian society has to adopt a form of social segregation among castes. This had and, has affected the programme of education for all. In the past, the wards of the upper castes—the Brahmans and Kshatriyas were allowed to get education in Gurukula Ashramas. Due to economic backwardness the lower castes were deprived of education. Even these castes were deprived to share common feasts on the occasion of marriage ceremonies. The upper castes and lower castes used to adopt a segregate inhabitation. In spite of education the lower castes used to satisfy themselves with their birth based occupations. As such, due to lack of educational opportunities there could not be upward mobility of backward castes. In other words it was due to no education to lower castes. It is also true that the present educational structure is designed for education for all. But social homogeneity, enculturation and life building process are missing in it. These were done in Indian old Gurukula education. Of course, the present educational infrastructure is designed for education for all but some people of higher and lower castes are not fully utilising or enjoying it.

India had paid a heavy cost for social heterogeneity, degradation and personal feuds in the past. The Rajas and Maharajas always fought amongst themselves for self-interests and pride. Due to lack of proper education, the Indian society always remained segregated and divided in higher castes and lower castes, which entailed mistrust amongst them. The foreigners took advantage of this situation and reaped the harvest of Indian natural, as well as human resources fully. They kept the Indians slaves more than one thousand years. Had all Indians would have been given equal opportunities of education for socio-economic development for all, this ugly situation would not have emerged. We should learn a lesson from this awkward ugly social situation occurred in the past Indian history. Now we should try to provide equal educational opportunities to all sections of the society irrespective of various castes, creeds and religious sects. Then only the present generation would be saved from the agony of disunity, self-centredness and hedonistic situations which are the gifts of western cultural diffusion and consequent acculturation. Every Indian citizen should get equal educational opportunities in every field according to his/her taste, desire and mental capabilities.

Education should not be limited up to the knowledge of 3Rs. True education has a wide and varied spectrum. For this it is necessary that our youngers should be educated properly according to their individual differences. Of course our present school education is open to all. And it can be said a source of education for all irrespective of castes, creeds and ethnicity. But the commercialisation of school education has closed the doors for "education for all". There are schools of which the doors are totally closed for the poor castes. The commercialisation of school education is also the gift of acculturation. There should be a provision that the students of all poor class or castes should be allowed to take admission in any school or in any educational institutions. These educational institutions should impart comprehensive education which should not only be examination oriented. The education should include comprehensive basic elements of education such as, inculcation of good life habits—speaking true, sharing, brotherhood, respect for elders and women, sociability, punctuality, diligency, morality, work habits, love for the nation, character building and doing enculturation of the students. No doubt, now-a-days everybody is entitled for school as well as higher education which not provided in olden times but, the present education is not education in real sense as it is examination oriented and is limited to teaching of few subjects. There is no provision for life building education, which requires inculcation of good life habits. Our present system of formal education is an alien system of education and it does not fit according to our social needs. It centres around examination results. As such, instructions are only given in 3Rs. It breeds competition, which always entails corruption. It does not have any place for inculcation of good life habits and for enculturation. With the result acculturation has taken deep roots in India, as a result all old social ethos have gone. Only there is an emphasis on the preparation of the students for good examination results. A desire of material greed is increasing day by day in the society, which brought corruption.

The institution of school and other educational institutions cannot be blamed for such a bad social situation. The educational institutions have to implement the policies chalked out by the Government. The Government educational policies are generally examination oriented. As such, the teachers basically remain busy in preparing the students for annual examinations. So, the teachers do not get time for doing enculturation of the students. This can only be possible if the teachers are motivated and given time to do so. Without inculcation of good life habits, which can only be possible through viable enculturation, true education can never be possible. True education is self-learning, life building and preparing the youngers for sane social living, which is not done in true sense now. And it can be said that education for all is denied partly. If this all is not done, and the youngers are taught a few subjects blindly, it would not be wrong to say that the youngers will remain uneducated. Therefore, it would not be wrong to assume that without inculcation good habits in youngers—like sociability, morality, truthfulness, sharing and cooperation, good behaviour and character development, which is only possible through inculcation of good life habits, without which education for all cannot be possible. For this end all should contribute. The true education should start from family and community. Thereafter, the school should educate the students in true sense, teaching them 3Rs and also inculcating them through good life habits and attitudes.

As a matter of fact, the programme of "education for all" was anticipated by our leaders before independence. It was initiated in the Constitution of Republic of India, implemented on 26th January, 1950. The Constitution of Republic of India aimed at primary education for all children up to the 14 years of age. The builders of the Constitution of India had visualised "education for all by educating the youngers up to the age of 14. They had thought that if all youngers are educated at primary level compulsorily, they will surely continue education further. This aim of education for all youngers was to be achieved up to 26th January, 1960. But still this aim of "education for all" remains a distant dream. Still many of our younger generation remain uneducated. For this, there may be many reasons. And for this the Government alone cannot be blamed. There may be reasons for it. Demographic explosion is one of the prime reasons. Of course, it was very difficult for the state to provide funds for "education for all". But the state tried its best in this regard by opening many educational institutions. The parents, community, religious organisations are also responsible for this drawback. In the past many generous people, members of the community used to contribute for 'education for all'. There was one Late Swami Kalyan Dev Ji, who lived for 129 years. He had contributed a lot in 'education for all'. After taking *sanyas* at the age of 8, he had devoted his whole life for the promotion of 'education for all', with the help of rich persons. He had opened 331 educational institutions in all fields in Western U.P. and Haryana. He had also opened S.D. Post Graduate College, Muzaffarnagar, where he lived in his old age. He was looked after by the management committee of the college. He had died in the college campus. He was also honoured by the President of India with Padam Shree. Earlier Swami Shradhanand Ji had opened the famous Gurukul Ashram in Kangri, Haridwar, Uttrakhand. Like this many generous people contributed in the field of 'education for all'. In the village of the writer Maharshi Harish Chandra Ji had opened a middle school which is now a renowned Rashtriya Co-educational Inter College in Uttrakhand.

Also, onus goes to the parents for the 'education for all'. They should not hesitate in educating their youngers. But it generally does not happen. The state has opened many schools but many parents engage their children in child labour. Their economic backwardness forces them to do so. Also many parents do not educate their daughters. They do not send them to school thinking that, the girls are 'anta property' (पराया धन). They believe that an 'anta property' should not be educated as they have to go to another homes. This situation is generally found in rural areas. In cities crimes like molestations, teasing and rapes are increasing day by day. And many parents of the girls being afraid of such crimes do not want to send their girls to schools. This problem should be handed by the Government. Also the Government should make "education for all" compulsory.

The Government has also started 'schemes of education for all'. But the covert aim of the programme appears to be a preparation of 'Vote Bank' building for the political party in power. Because some committees are formed on the bases of castes, creeds and religions. In spite of its backward castes and communities should be provided coaching facilities. In any case there should not be tempering with the merit. There should be education for all without bias then only 'education for all' programme can be successful.

17

The Teacher

For the implementation of curriculum, to be followed by an educational institution, there is a need of a sound educational infrastructure for the educational institution. There should be a spacious building for an educational institute, which should have sufficient spacious well-equipped classroom. Every classroom should have a chalk-board, a store room for storing teaching aids and good display bulletin boards. It should also have well-equipped library, art room, workshop for crafts, a play ground, a canteen, office rooms and office staff etc. etc. But the main key functionaries of any educational infrastructure are the teachers. Without the teachers an educational institution cannot function at all. And it can be said that the teachers are the livers of any educational institutions who make the functioning of the educational institution possible. So, it is very necessary that an educational institution, be it a school or any college or technical institution or an university should have intelligent, qualified, diligent, sincere, proficient and dedicated teachers. So it is very necessary to highlight the qualities of a good teacher. If the educational authorities are not fully aware about the necessary qualities of a teacher, neither the implementation of curriculum of the school or any other educational institution nor the pre-conceived educational aims can be implemented and achieved. As such, this is very necessary for any educational institution to make the teachers aware about their viable roles. Then only true educational aims can be achieved.

The personality of the teacher has many facets. Since the emergence of human beings and consequent evolution of human society or societies in the world, the teacher has ever been playing a vital role as a constructive moulder and upbringer of the youngers. The teacher has ever been educating the youngers to lead a good socio-economic and sane cultural life. And the men have ever been creating cultures and civilisations. And it is the teacher who has ever been contributing in this process. So, the teacher has ever been respected by all in the society. The teacher has ever been doing the noble work of upbringing the youngers by educating them in all spheres of life, that is, in socialisation, moralisation, enculturation, in training in appropriate skills for earning livelihood. So the teaching profession was ever considered a noble profession in olden times. In olden times, the teacher used to be a religious preacher. He never desired material gains, so he was non-inclinative too. Being sympathetic to his disciples he had ever sympathetic feelings of love and affection towards the students. So, the teacher had always a close rapport with the students. In reciprocation the students also respected their teachers (*Gurus*) and always considered them of high esteem equating them as their elders at par with the father. The teacher (*Guru*) was respected by all including the ruler or king of the country in all societies. As such, the teacher has ever been a prime, specific functionary in educating and upbringing the youngsters.

> ''गुरु, गोविन्द दोनों खड़े काके लागूँ पाँव।
> बलिहारी गुरु आपने, गोविन्द दियो मिलाये।।'' —सन्त कबीर
> "The teacher and the Almighty both are standing to whom I should bow, thanks to the teacher who enabled to meet the Lord" — *Sant Kabir*

> गुरु बिन जग अंधियारा। —सन्त कबीर
> "There is darkness without the *Guru*" —Sant Kabir

The teacher is the builder of the nation, so it is necessary that all concerned, the school teachers, school authorities, the society as a whole, politicians, parents and students should know about the roles and responsibilities of the teacher.

The teacher has ever been doing noble epistemic social work in the society by moulding and upbringing the youngers, by educating them about all aspects of life, that is socialisation, moralisation, training them to acquire skills for earning for livelihood and inculcating in them good desirable life habits. And the teacher has ever been enculturating the students. So the teaching profession was considered a noble profession in olden times. In olden times the teacher was the monotheistic religious preacher. He was non-inclinative and never aspired any material gain. He was very epistemic also. He used to impart education only as charity and donation. Only he wanted something for his substance. Being sympathetic to his disciples he used to shower sympathetic love on his disciples. He used to have a close rapport with them. In reciprocation, the students also, always respected their *Guru* (teacher) and considered him unique personality and equated him with their fathers. The teacher was respected by all including the ruler or king of the country in all societies. As such, in olden days the teacher used to be a learned and esteemed person. He used to observe spirituality, religiosity and teaching professional ethics. He used to believe in simple living and high thinking in non-inclinativeness and used to live a non-hedonistic simple life. The teacher, either used to live generally in Gurukula Ashram or in self-ashram in jungles. The philosophy of the *Guru* (teacher) was to mould the lives of the youngers for a sane social living. As such, the teacher has ever been a specific functionary in educating, moulding and upbringing the youngers. In olden times, the *Gurus* (teachers) were teaching in Gurukula Ashramas which were considered the moulding houses of the youngers. Some of the Gurukulas, were named as moulding places like Taxila (now in Pakistan).

In the present corporate driven socio-economic structure the choices of career are many. So teaching is not considered a good profession. But according to a British recent scholar Ted Wragg the teaching is a noble profession. In India many scholars considered teaching as the noblest profession. Dr. Sarvapalli Radhakrishnan considered teaching as the most auspicious noble profession. The teaching profession was his first love, and whatever position he held whether as Vice-President or President of the Indian Republic or as an ambassador, Dr. Radhakrishnan earnestly remained a teacher. As a tribute to Dr. Radhakrishnan his birthday is observed on 5th September as Teacher's Day in India. He was very kind and affectionate to his students. One of his students named Mr. Albert Coomer, who had done B.A. (Hon.) Philosophy at Cambridge University, London, was so much impressed by his love, affection and generosity that he decided to meet his teacher (*Guru*) Dr. S. Radhakrishnan when he was Vice-President of India. He crossed the British Channel. And after this decided to go to

India on foot. He was looted eight times up to Khyber pass. When he entered in Pakistan he was given a hearty reception. From Pakistan he crossed the Wagha Border and came to India. He stayed in Golden Temple at Amritsar for few days. From there he came to Delhi. In India also he was given a hearty reception. He stayed with Dr. Radhakrishnan about a fortnight. He decided to visit the religious places on foot and see the landscape of India. He started his journey from New Delhi on foot. He stayed one night in village Duhai, Dist. Ghaziabad, U.P. from there he proceeded further. When he crossed Modinagar and entered Govindpuri, a town established for refugees came from Pakistan. There was a "Training-*cum*-Production Centre" for the refugees. There were four courses (*a*) Radio Repairing, (*b*) Electrician, (*c*) Sheet Metal, and (*d*) Carpentry. The writer of this book was working as Carpentry Instructor. Mr. Albert Coomer when visited this training-*cum*-production centre, he entered in it and sought the permission of the superintendent of centre to see it. He saw all classes and finally entered in the carpentry class. The writer, who was carpentry instructor, gave him a stool to sit, offered him water and asked him whether he would like to eat something. He replied "anything can be offered as he was hungry". The writer (carpentry instructor) and Shri K.N. Lohani, the then Sheet Metal Instructor were living together, sent Mr. Albert Coomer to their residence along with their attendant Shri Kothari. Mr. Kothari was directed to cook the food and offer to Mr. Albert Coomer. Mr. Albert Coomer stayed for two nights with them. They gave him due hospitability. On the third day Mr. Albert Coomer started his journey to Swarglok Ashram, Rishikesh on foot. While going he expressed that his teacher, Dr. S. Radhakrishnan was one of the noblest teacher at Cambridge University, London. He also expressed gratitude to the Indians and Pakistanis for the sane hospitability he was given.

Now, due to the boon in industrial infrastructure, as development of information technology industry, industrial engineering technology, fashion technology and management sector opened more options for the fresh graduates. They prefer quicker and better financial rewards. And due to this emerging of soft white collar jobs, the noble teaching profession got a setback. Our youths prefer jobs which could give them more salary to live a hedonistic life. Only those who do not get a chance of employment in new emerging industries only look to the teaching profession. Also the teaching is seen as pastime (to pass time) and not as a profession. There are many teachers in schools and in universities who are always engaged in some business and they do teaching for passing out their time and getting salary. So teaching is considered as boring and not a creative activity. The present teacher is totally different from the old Indian teacher (*Guru*). This situation has been developed due to textbooks oriented teaching, which is only examination oriented. Better shining examination result is the ethos of the present day teaching be it in schools or in colleges, which leaves very little time for interaction between the teachers and the students. As Guru Rabindra Nath Tagore said that "in the present days teaching is done in mechanical ways and the students are prepared as nuts and bolts are produced in factories". When a disinterested teacher get a chance of employment in some Government organisation or industry he/she says goodbye to teaching.

In such a situation, there is an urgent need to resuscitate the teaching profession to make it first choice of Gen-Next. Some say that the movements like 'Sarva Siksha Abhiyan' will help in resuscitation of the status of the teachers. But it will not be sufficient. This can only be done by changing the mindsets of youths who would like to become teachers. They should be made aware about the nobility of the teaching profession. The teachers should be well paid, so that they may not aspire to any other extra work or part time work to earn money to meet their hedonistic needs. The society, the students and bureaucrats should respect the teachers.

Now the socio-economic structure of the modern society has altogether changed due to killing acculturation. The old notion of 'simple living and high thinking' is no more. This happened due to human greedy nature, mechanisation and industrialisation. The earlier man was religious, monotheistic and spiritualistic. He used to believe in common good. The modern man is henotheistic, materialistic, hedonistic, acquisitive, xenophilic. The earlier social system was considered homogenic. Now the present Indian social system has become totally heterogenic. Instead of caste system the class structure, which is the copy of the western heterogenic feudalistic class structure, is becoming dominant. The rich person wants to talk only with rich person. Since the teacher is poor in the present empiricist hedonistic age, he/she does not get due respect and regard in the society. It can only be possible if people are educated about the social viability of the teacher.

According to Greek Philosopher, Hereclitus change in every social sphere and phenomenon as well as in physical life is must, the change in the present status of the teacher shall also come in due course of time. As such, awareness about the teaching profession is necessary for that. The individuality of the teacher has many facets. From the evolution of human beings and consequent emergence of the human society, the teacher has ever been playing a constructive role. He has been teaching, inculcating and enculturating the youngers to live a sane social living. He has created the culture and civilisation. And due to this the teacher has been always ranked high and, was always respected by all in the society.

It is an accepted fact that the teacher has ever been doing a noble work in the society. He/she has ever been upbringing the youngers through educating them about all aspects and spheres of life, that is, through socialisation, moralisation, character building and in gaining skills for earning for existence. The teacher has also been inculcating good habits in the students and enculturating them. So the teaching profession was considered a noble profession in olden days. In olden day the teacher (*Guru*) was the preacher of religiosity and spirituality to his *Shishyas* (students). Through this he was generating morality and sociability in the students. After this he used to teach other subjects. Thus, the Indian teacher has ever been proficient in the areas of teaching religion and all other subjects like Sanskrit language, mathematics, astronomy, philosophy and sociology. He used to be very sympathetic, kind and sincere to his disciples (students). He used to have a very close rapport with them. As such, the teacher has ever been a prime functionary in educating, moulding and upbringing the youngers.

Education of the youngers existed in all times in all societies. And the teacher has ever been a main prime functionary in this pursuit. Now, because of scientific revolution and consequent industrialisation and resultant urbanisation, modernisation, resulted in dys-functioning of old values. Old value system and ways of living have more or less disappeared. Of course, due to democratic system education of the youngers got a boost. The demographic explosion changed the social scenario of the world.

Human greed made the human-beings accultured. Men become materialistic and hedonistic. Of course, the number of school going children enormously increased, but then sensitivity towards social values totally decreased. Affluency has made the youngers also totally consumeristic and hedonistic. They have totally forgotten viable social values. They even do not pay respect even to their elders. So, it is necessary to reform our present existing educational system and prepare the teachers to carry on such reforms logically and successfully. Due to decrease in child mortality, the demographic scenario of the world totally changed. Number of the school going children enormously increased. So the number of educational institutions like schools, technical universities and universities also enormously increased. When there is an expansion in any sphere of social activity, there is a fear of falling down of standards. So the fear of fall in standard of teaching is likely to occur. As such to meet this problem there occurs a lot of change in teaching methodology which is to be followed by the teachers. As such the teaching process has to adapt new techniques of presentation in the classrooms which are based on elicitations. For this end, the teacher has to provide perceptual experiences to the students for self-learning. When conservative clergy was prominent in teaching, conservative methods like one way verbal communication were used. The teacher was the giver and the students were the receivers. Now, due to the development of science and technology many new progressive methods of teaching have emerged. This has increased the responsibility of the teacher as he/she has to follow new teaching methods. So, it is necessary to make the pupil-teachers fully aware about all new teaching methods. This can only be done if the would be teacher is also aware about teaching professional ethics. The teacher training institutes should make the pupil-teachers aware about teaching professional ethics.

If we peep into the etymology of the word 'teach' out of which the word teacher has emerged, we find that it has wide and varied meanings, which indicate that the teaching which is done by the teacher has also wide and varied spectrum. The word 'teach' is derived from Anglo-Saxon word 'teccon' which means 'to teach', 'to show', 'to punish', 'to command', 'to instruct', 'to point out'. Its equivalent Greek 'dickngnic' means 'to impart', 'to instruct', 'to guide', 'to train', 'to tell', 'to show', 'to practice', 'to demonstrate' and 'to give instructions' for doing 'business', 'to do preaching', 'to act as Minister of gospel etc. etc.' The Sanskrit word 'Sikh' means 'to upbring' and '*Siksha*' is a process of upbringing. The word 'vidh' means a method of self-learning which is tantamount to education. All this is done through a process of teaching, which is done by the teacher. Therefore, one who teaches has to supply various different teaching methods and techniques for educating the younger generation. Telling, narrating, showing, instructing, training, demonstrating, guiding, questioning and eliciting are the methods, a teacher uses during teaching in the present times. And above all these innovating, motivating, sympathising through establishing a congenial rapport with students are necessary, without which the students cannot move forward towards self-learning, which is true education.

In the present socio-economic, cultural and political conditions in the society the teacher's job has become very complex. It needs a thorough study of prevalent socio-economic, cultural and political study of the society and also study of the teaching profession existed in olden days in India.

In olden days the *Gurus* (teachers) were the pivots of the society for the life development of the youngers and for the sound socio-economic and cultural development of the nation. The *Guru* (teacher) was preacher first and the teacher later. In our old Brahmanical and Vedic system the teaching was carried on in Rishi Ashramas and Gurukula Ashramas. Only the proficient religious teachers, proficient in religiosity and spirituality were preferred to teach. Their day used to start with religious preaching, meditation and yoga and thereby motivating the *Shishyas* (students) to be religious and spiritual. They used to tell the students about *dharma* (धर्म), *adharma* (अधर्म), *netikta* (नैतिकता), *anetikta* (अनैतिकता), *nyay* (न्याय), *anyay* (अन्याय), sociability (सामाजिकता), and to be a worker (कर्ता) and thereby preparing them for saneful social living. They also used to make the students aware about '*maya*' (माया), *amaya* (अमाया) and preparing the students to discard greed and acquisitiveness. And this way, they used to prepare the future guardians for saneful social living. The *Gurus* (teachers) used to motivate the *Shishyas* (students) to live a simple religious life based on the principle of "simple living and high thinking". These principles were explicitly elucidated through teaching. The teaching was based on the exposition of nature as the Gurukulas

Ashramas and Rishi Ashramas were situated on river banks in jungles far off from the students' houses. This was done for shifting the parental love to the social love. Also, the students were given a sufficient chance for elicitation by arranging regular *'vad-vivad'* discussion and through the seminars *'samvad'* between the Gurus (teachers) and *Shishyas* (students). This used to promote thinking, reasoning and analysing and finally learning in students. Such type of teaching was based on conservative method of teaching and was purely aimed at life building so that the future guardians of the nation may live a sane social life in their future lives.

The teacher, in olden times, was called *'Guru'* which means 'heavy'. The student was called *'Shishya'*. The relation between the *Guru* (teacher) and *Shishya* (student) was like that of father and son. The *Shishya* used to acquire knowledge from the *Guru*. Rishis used to give religious sermons and teach the *Shishyas* in their Rishi Ashramas. Through the religious sermons, *Rishis* and *Munis* used to inculcate life values as sociability, truthfulness, social-cooperation in the adults also. *Rishis* and *Munis* used to live in dense jungles (forests) on the river banks. Their way of living was very simple based on renouncement of greed and acquisitiveness. Mostly the *Rishi* and *Munis* used to lead such life in their *Banprasth* Ashram and *Sanayas* Ashram. They used to lay emphasis on religious prayers, simple living and high thinking. In Rishi Ashrams many princes used to live for getting education. The *Rishi* also used to treat their disciples as their sons and daughters. The ladies and girls used to come in day time to listen the sermon of the *Rishis*. In Buddhist monasteries in India and abroad; in Muslim Madarsas in Middle East and; in Christian Church Missionary Schools, the education was imparted on the same lines as in India. The teachers were religious preachers first and knowledge givers thereafter. As such, the teaching was co-relative or bi-polar. In olden times the teachers had always open ears and soft heart towards the students. The teachers in all these institutions had very little materialistic desires and were non-inclinative. The teaching was a sacred and donatory pious job. So the teachers considered teaching as *'Sudharma'* (सुधर्मा) (pious duty) through donating knowledge (ज्ञान) to the younger generation.

In olden days the aim of education was to establish a sane, honest, unhedonistic, social, moral and cooperative society in the nation, and for these the *Gurus* used to inculcate these qualities in their disciples (pupils). It is also noticed that the Gurukulas used to admit the *Shishyas* from rich and poor families. Ujaini Gurukula Ashramas was one of such example, where rich Krishna Yadava, a Rajput and Sudama, a poor Brahman boy were studying together in Maharshi Sandipani Ujaini Ashram. Likewise King Dasharatha's sons—Ram Chandra, Lakshmana, Bharata and Shatrughana had to renounce their royal family comforts and lived in Rishi Vashishtha's ashram for getting proper education. In Gurukula instructions were also given in *'Tap-Sadhna'* (तप साधना), austerity, public welfare (लोक उत्थान), good manners and self-control. All these are totally absent in present aliensitic formal system of education. Another aim of old Indian education was to spread sane social education through religious sermons given to masses. The imagination of 'Sam Raj' or equality-based administration was gained by Ram Chandra in Rishi Vashishta's Ashram, which he tried to materialise later on as 'Ram Raj'.

Many Gurukulas in olden times were nationally and internationally recognised as Nalanda (Rajgiri) in Bihar, Vikram Shila (Bhagalpur) in Bihar, Vallabhi in Kathiawad (Gujarat), Taxila (now in N.W.F.P. Pakistan), Gandhar (now in Afghanistan) etc. etc. were such Gurukulas where students used to flock from far off places like China, Thailand, Indonesia, Greece, Japan, Iran (Aryana) and Sri Lanka for studying Indian religions (Hinduism and Buddhism) and culture. The teachers of these Vishwa-vidyalayas (Gurukulas) had produced imminent thinkers and teachers like Chanakya who had imagined great India. Nalanda had teachers like Kumaril Bhatt on whose lines the Shankaracharya laid a foundation of Indian monotheistic culture. The teachers produced by these universities travelled to far distant countries like China, Thailand, Vietnam, Japan, Indonesia and Sri Lanka. Ujjain, Kanchipuram, Amravati, Adityapuram were the Gurukulas where the teacher's aim was to educate the people to make them cultured. Gurukula Aryanakapuram had consolidated the Indian culture and monotheistic religion which fostered sociability and morality in Indians. And main or prime stalwarts were the teachers of these Gurukulas (universities) and Rishi Ashramas who had promoted Indian culture.

All religious places like Badrinath, Kedarnath, Rishikesh, Haridwar, Prayag, Mathura, Kashi, Patliputra, Puri, Bhubaneswar, Ujjain, etc. etc. were the *'Tirth Sthals'* where their disciples used to give *'parvachans'* on the religiosity, spirituality and sociability to the people during their stay at these *'Tirth Sthals'*. As such, people living in the vicinity of religious places used to be educated. Gurukulas and religious mathas like Nalanda and Taxila were functioning like open universities where everybody from India and abroad could get admission and get education by the teachers. The education, boarding and lodging were free. No fee and board and lodging fees were charged. As such, the education in olden times was different from the present times. Now the present education system is very costly and very few people have assess to it.

In recent times, Gurukul Kangri, Kankhul Haridwar, established by Late Shri Maharshi Sardhanandji, Sanskriti Vishwa Vidyalaya Shanti Kunj, situated on Haridwar-Rishikesh Road, Rishi Patanjali Yogapeeth (University), Bahadra Bad, Gurukul Narseen, Dist. Haridwar are functioning on the old Indian education pattern. The teachers in these institutions are like the *Gurus* of old Gurukula Ashram. Also some Gurukulas are still functioning on the old pattern in the country. Also there are some educational institutions like Shantiniketan, Bolpur, West Bengal and some Rishi Valley schools established by Shri J. Krishnamoorthy are working for the revival of Indian culture and for stopping acculturation. The teachers in these institutions are doing wonderful jobs for the retrieval of Indian culture and the prestige of the Indian teaching profession.

As Hereclitus said that everything is in flux, so the Indian society is also changing from spiritual to materialistic and hedonistic society, because of so-called industrialisation, urbanisation, westernisation, modernisation, and consequent hedonism and consumerism which happened due to cultural diffusion and acculturation, now is a completely changed society. This situation has not only occurred in India, all other societies also have changed due to fast active communication procedure, better travel conditions and better interaction between people to people in the whole world. Our present educational infrastructure —the schools, technical institutions like I.T.Is., polytechnics, engineering colleges and universities are alien gifts which added the cultural diffusion and acculturation. The teachers played a vital role in this social change, because they have also been moulded on alienistic pattern and they have been the prime functionaries in the educational institutions. The present teacher's role in the present formal system of education is only to teach school subjects which can be said a mere formality which diverts the students from the national culture to the alien culture. The present teacher is a tool in the hands of the administrators, for achieving the desired stipulated ends of the formal education, which is aimed at to give a particular shape to our future guardians. Earlier, the aim of old education was a common enterprise of parents, elders, teachers, community, society and the country. The states, in the past were always striving for the common good. So, also the teachers were called *Gurus* who always thought of common good. Now the states have also complete control over the education with an aim to give equal opportunity to all irrespective of individual differences. All students are required to study all subjects and appear at annual examination. In other words the present education is imparted en-mass to the students who are produced on mass scale like consumer goods are produced in factories. And the teacher in the mass operation or production is like an operator of the die machine which produces consumer goods for common use. Guru Rabindra Nath Tagore correctly said that our present educational structure is functioning like a production factory producing consumer goods. The teacher has no option but to obey what is desired by the state, as education is an instrument of state.

The state wants to give maximum information and knowledge equally to all younger generation of the state irrespective of their taste and abilities. Due to this enculturation of the students is ignored. Every teacher is supposed to be proficient in one or two teaching subjects. The state and its educational bureaucrats or educationists decide what to teach, how to teach and when to teach? The bureaucrats after deciding this demarcate the subject content and prepare curriculum for it for the academic session, which generally starts from the first week of July and ends on the last day of March every year. And at the end of the session the students are examined at the annual examination and certified and promoted to next higher class. This is necessary because our alienistic formal system of formal education gives top priority to annual examination which should show good shining examination results. This creates blatant competition in the society. Our old system of education did not have any place for examination.

Our teacher is bound to observe some formalities, which will be mentioned under the heading 'Teaching'. Only it can be said that present teacher has to work in mechanical way which eludes him/her of his/her prime duty of enculturation of the future guardians. Due to hedonism the parents of the students generally remain in the rat-race of money earning, they also cannot enculturating joint family system has also been crumbled. So our educationist should examine the whole situation and should take right action.

18

The Teachers

The teachers constitute a big academic community of teaching profession throughout the world. There are large number of state run schools, aided schools, private public schools, coaching schools and other educational institutions which employ a big number of teachers for teaching various subjects, art activities and physical education activities to the students. They teach them subjects in which the students are examined. In olden times the teachers (*Gurus*) used to teach in Gurukula Ashramas who were quite different from the present teachers. They were dedicated teachers. The main aim of their teaching was educating and, life building of their *Shishyas* (disciples). They used to follow the teaching ethics very sincerely. They were true epistemic and knowledgeable, very sincere to their disciples (students) and were totally non-inclinative, as they were free from greed, self-centredness and materialistic, hedonistic aspirations. They were religious, spiritualistic and social. They used to inculcate good life attitudes in their *Shishyas* as—speaking true, to be friendly, sharing and cooperative, social, axiological to be monotheistic religious and spiritual and, dedicated to the society and to the nation. The main life attitudes they used to inculcate were to believe in simple living and high thinking, to be sincere for the common good, early to bed early to rise makes a man, healthy wealthy and wise, to do regular exercise and yoga, to do yajna and to take simple vegetarian food in Gurukula kitchen. Also the *Gurus* used to live with their disciples under common roof in Gurukula Ashramas. The *Gurus* (teachers) used to believe in simple living and high thinking. They had a good rapport with their disciples. And they were highly respected in the society. On the whole, it would not be wrong to conclude that our *Gurus* (teachers) were ideal persons who used to believe in epistemacy, that is, knowledge gaining, religiosity, spirituality and sociability which they used to donate to their disciples throughout their lives freely without inclination.

On the contrary the present teachers are quite different from the old teachers (*Gurus*). They are public servants and have to follow the norms, rules and regulations prescribed for the Government servants. They are employed by the agencies which run the schools and other educational institutions. These are instruments of the state as, the state has full control over all of the educational institutions. As such, the present teachers come under hook of the state control. They are required to reach the school or educational institutions on stipulated time and go back when the prescribed time is over. They have to teach the students in six periods out of eight periods formally. They have to prepare the students for passing out examination in flying colours, as per prescribed curriculum. In addition to regular teaching period, if any teacher goes on leave, his/her teaching periods are assigned as arrangement periods to other teachers. As such, the present teachers have to do teaching in mechanical way. Also the teachers have to do some clerical work, as maintaining of teacher's diary, preparation of lesson plans and examining the students' homework. Every teacher has to be class in-charge of one class and he/she has to maintain the records of the students studying in that class. Besides these, the teachers have to look after co-curricular activities which are often arranged in the schools. In comparison to school teachers, the college lecture readers and professors have less teaching load. As such, it can be concluded that the teachers in schools are often overloaded with teaching.

As the social status of the teacher is concerned, now-a-days the social status of the teacher is at the lowest ebb. The teachers are not well paid in comparison to the staff in Government offices, Government organisations and in public undertakings. So the teachers are considered a poor community in the society. Due to western cultural diffusion and consequent acculturation every human-being used to desire 'earn, drink, eat and be marry'. The whole society has adopted 'carvac' and Calvinistic philosophy of 'earn, eat, drink and be marry'. So the human greed has touched new heights. Materialism has become a common social feature. It has entrenched in every nook and corner of the society. Everyone aspire to be rich, hedonistic, consumeristic and xenophilic. As the teacher gets limited salary, he/she is considered a poor and helpless person. Even many girls do not like to marry with the boy teachers. In the middle of sixties of the twentieth century there was a poor handsome Brahman boy. He was first class M.Sc. Physics from Agra University. He was doing B.Ed. from C.I.E., Delhi University and was student of the writer. There was also a Brahman girl who was also doing B.Ed., who desired that her elder sister, who was B.Sc. General, be married with the boy. She approached the writer to convince the boy for the matrimonial proposal. The writer consulted the boy, obtained the opinion of his uncle who agreed. The boy also agreed. And finally, the writer on a Sunday went to the house of the girl in R.K. Puram, New Delhi to see the parents. Her father was a section officer in the Ministry of Home Affairs. Her both parents had agreed for the matrimonial proposal. The girl was not so beautiful as the boy was. Her eyes were not balanced (भैंगी). The writer thought to reject the girl. But when her parents asked her about the matrimonial proposal, she openly said that "She would not marry with a teacher". I thanked the girl.

Likewise, the teachers because of their little pay packets are considered inferiors in the society in comparison to other persons who earn money by fair and foul means. To meet the hedonistic demands of their families, the teachers also try to earn money. They do tuitions and also do some other petty extra part-time jobs. The families, wherein the teachers do tuitions consider the teachers inferior. They forget that the teachers are epistemic and knowledge givers to the youngers. The parents of the kids to whom a teacher teaches through tuitions in their homes do not give proper respect to the teacher. They call him either 'Mr. teacher' or 'Master ji". They consider the teacher as a part-time servant. So, the teacher is not given proper respect in the society as was given to the *Guru* in olden days. It is also true the present teacher is not like a *Guru*. The present teacher is bound with the formality, whereas, the old teacher was roped in epistemacy, religiosity, spiritually, sociability, non-inclinativeness. He used to believe in simplicity. The present teacher aspire to be hedonistic.

The another social factor which, also makes the teacher immune about the human social respectability is the virus of acculturation. Acculturation is the product of western cultural diffusion with the Indian culture. It has made the man conscious of western culture, its ways of living and class structure. In the western society the heterogeneity is a paramount social feature, under which the human beings are categorised or socially stratified as rich persons or 'barons' and poor persons or 'serfs'. Due to cultural diffusion and acculturation this western social trend has taken its deep roots in the Indian society. Now, Indian rich persons always desire to have social relations only with the persons of their status. A car owner always would like to have relations with a car owner. The Indian teachers also do so. In the schools the art teacher, craft teacher and physical education teacher are considered inferior by their fellow teachers. Similar is the situation in colleges and universities. A teacher who does hard work is considered inferior by his/her fellow colleagues. Emphasis on subjects teaching under formal system of education, in which the students are examined, may be the another reason of discrimination by some teachers against their fellow teachers. Such situation never existed in Indian old system of education.

Because of demographic explosion in the country and due to Indian constitutional provision for equal education for all, there has been an enormous expansion educational infrastructure. Many primary, middle, secondary, senior secondary schools, colleges, universities, Indian Institutes of Technology, agricultural institutes, management institutes and medical institutes have been opened throughout the country by the Government. So, there has been a great demand of teachers. Due to non-availability of qualified and trained persons in respective fields, there has been shortage of qualified teachers at all levels. Not only in schools but in many premier educational institutes, universities and technical institutes, there have been the shortage of teachers. As such, many of the premier educational institutions are failing to follow the guidelines laid down by the regulatory educational authorities like University Grants Commission (UGC), All India Council for Technical Education (AICTE) and National Council for Teacher Education (NCTE). Now, the Government has decided to implement 27 per cent of reservation for other backward castes (OBC's) in higher institutions of learning, more teachers would be needed from the next academic year (2007-2008).

In many states, there are lots of vacancies of teachers in primary schools as well as in secondary schools. Filling these vacant posts of the teachers take a lot of time. Similar is the position in many departments of the universities, colleges and in technical institutions of higher and, also in other institutions of higher learning. The paucity of qualified teachers is also felt in professional technical institutions. Guru Govind Singh Indraprastha University (G.G.S.I.P.U.) has around 150 faculty members (as reported in *Times of India* dated 03.07.2006) for, approximately 2500 students studying in University's in-house schools but when it comes to its affiliated institutions is far worse.

Almost 17 of its private affiliated institutions do not have between 32 per cent to 75 per cent of the faculty strength. As reported in T.O.I., these are 20 to 25 such institutions which do not have adequately required teaching staff. As a matter of fact an institution should have adequate teaching staff before the commencement of the next session. Some renounced educationists have suggested that there should be a cadre ratio of teaching faculty 1:2:6 of professors, readers and lecturers. Several institutions of G.G.S.I.P.U. are lacking this ratio.

At the Indian Institute of Technology, the situation is reported better. At the Indian Institute of Technology, Delhi, which is considered a benchmark of the technical institutions, the situation is marginally better. Out of 571 sanctioned posts 427 have been filled. The teacher-student ratio is 1:9:5. Many fresh graduates of I.I.T. get around 2:5 times salary of a faculty member. This trend gives an indication that I.I.T. graduates hardly join teaching profession. More or less, similar is the position in all other six I.I.Ts. of India. Also, the I.I.M. in India is also sailing in the same boat.

Even Delhi University's College of Engineering (D.C.E.) fails to meet the A.I.C.T.E. guidelines regarding faculty and student ratio far from 10:1 for premier institutes like I.I.Ts. and the 15:1 for ordinary engineering colleges, the D.C.E. has a teacher-student ratio of 20:1. It has even included teachers employed on deputation by other institutions. Such teachers are reported as included in the faculty. It is also reported that some vacant posts are likely to be filled through Union Public Service Commission.

A shortage of teaching staff often leads to unfinished or hurried covering of course under the prescribed curriculum. This always entails inadequate attention to the individual student's needs. This not only hampers the students' learning but also overburdens those replacing the missing colleges. Many faculty members complain that this type of over teaching work does not spare time to do research work and development in their teaching work. Several institutions try to get the teaching work done by guest lectures, but these institutions do not realise that having permanent teaching faculty members is always better.

Availability of more options in the growing economy, which provide better pay package in the corporate sector is the main reason of evading the teaching profession by the brilliant students. Besides teacher shortage is growing phenomena in higher educational institutions, the teacher absentation is also prevalent in Government run primary schools. A recent World Bank Report revealed that around 25 per cent primary school teachers, specially in rural areas remain absent themselves from teaching work. Most of the primary school teachers teach in the nearby schools of their villages. First they do their homework as—agricultural work and feeding the cattle in the morning. And after this they go to the schools, where they take rest. They take teaching very lightly. They do not try to add to their knowledge. Similar is the situation in rural secondary and senior secondary schools or intermediate colleges. The teachers working in these institutes, hardly utilise school library. They hardly use progressive methods of teaching and use of the teaching aids. "Most excellent education is which begins with eyes. It is a recovery what we possessed. It is recovered with our senses Plato said. But the teachers working in rural areas treat teaching as a mere formality. Also, there is Chinese adage "what we hear, we forget, and what we see, we remember." But in rural schools generally the teachers pass on verbal information. There is no provision for sense perception in teaching. Hardly, there is provision for co-curricular activities and discourses in rural schools. This is why the students of these schools fail to express or do some creative activity.

Similar condition prevails in some urban schools. The teachers in urban localities do tuitions. Generally some science and mathematics teachers do too many tuitions. They get tired. When they go to schools they fail to devote to their teaching duty in schools. Many teachers keep themselves in some part-time commercial activities. They also fail to discharge their just teaching duties. Not only the school teachers but some faculty members in the colleges and university do some hidden part time duties and fail to discharge required teaching duties.

As such, due to hedonistic aspirations generally the younger generation who get education in colleges and universities aspire to get jobs either in Government departments or in public undertakings where they could earn more. When they do not get the jobs of their choice they turn to teaching profession. And they seek admission in teacher's training colleges for doing either B.Ed. or B.T. After completing the teacher training generally they are employed in schools as teachers. But they continue their efforts to seek the jobs of their dreams. And when they get a job of their choice, they say goodbye to teaching. It is, therefore, very necessary that the education of the teachers should analyse this fact deeply. They should select the candidates who are interested in teaching profession. Generally, now-a-days, the teaches educationists give importance to the teaching subjects for examination. Potentialities of the candidates regarding inculcation of good life habits and doing enculturation are totally ignored. As such, total potentialities of teacher trainees are not searched. The educational administrators should look into all these aspects for having good teachers for schools. Recently survey was conducted by World Bank by paying unexpected visits to over 3700 schools in 20 Indian states, it was found that the teachers were chronically absent. Maharashtra, Gujarat and Madhya Pradesh had relatively low rates of absenteeism among teachers. But Kerala which has achieved 100 per cent literacy rate faces the crisis of absenteeism rate of 21.2 per cent. Similarly the economically prosperous state of Punjab reported 34.4 per cent absenteeism. Even in Jharkhand around 42 per cent and nearly 38 per cent teachers in Bihar are missing from their classrooms.

The report, however, had another significant finding that teachers are unlikely to be fined for being absent, only one in 3000 head teachers or headmasters fine a teacher for repeated absenteeism. Better pay does not stop lower absenteeism, the research revealed. Old teachers, more educated ones and head teachers or headmasters have better salaries but are also absent more frequently according to the related research paper.

India's budget 2006-2007 allocated Rs. 155 crore for teacher training, while the budgetary allocation for primary was increased by 4000 crore to 15367 crore. The salary structure of the teacher has improved over the years but problem persists because of basic infrastructure needs to be improved. The drop out level is also high among students.

Even the reports recommended that the working conditions have greater influence on teacher absenteeism than pay. There is a clear association between better infrastructure and lower absence, if the facilities like proper toilets and a roof, teacher will be more enthusiastic about going to work. The survey was conducted in six countries—Bangladesh, Ecuador, India, Indonesia, Peru and Uganda which revealed similar results. In the face students intake increasing by 53 per cent the Government is advised to raise the retirement age for teachers to 65 years. It was also suggested to re-employ the healthy retired teachers. The state is also funding for coaching the students of weaker sections which require the experienced teachers.

The teaching profession can only be improved by proper training of teachers, which requires suitable selection of the candidate for teachers training, the pupil suitable trained in all aspects of education. It should not be restricted up to training in subject teaching. All other aspects of education as inculcation of good life habits like sociability, morality and cooperation and enculturation should be taught to the pupil-teachers.

TEACHER'S TRAINING

In olden times the population of the human-beings was limited so there were limited educational institutions, which were run by social organisations. As such, there was no demand for formally trained teachers. And there was a saying that, "teacher is born and not trained". So in the olden days the teachers were not formally trained as, they are trained now-a-days. Now, the formal training is an educational necessity for imparting education in formal way. In the past the teachers were sincere, earnest, dedicated and had inner consciousness and desire for teaching. It was also believed that *Vidya Dan* (विध्या दान), that is, knowledge donation was best sacred, auspicious donation, as it was done for the social upliftment. Therefore, in olden days in India all epistemic persons wanted to donate their knowledge for social upliftment. They used to take teaching profession as their life long profession. They needed not any training for teaching. They used to carry on teaching throughout their lives without any material gain or inclination. They used to follow the teaching professional ethical codes—(*a*) They always used to add to their knowledge and as proficiency; (*b*) They used to remain very kind and sincere to their disciples (students). They used to maintain very close rapport with their disciples (students) and maintain with them parental relationship. They (*Gurus*) used to treat them as their own sons; (*c*) They (*Gurus*) were purely non-inclinative. The teachers in olden times were called *Gurus*. A *Guru* meant 'heavy', not in weight but in knowledge. The chhatras (students) used to treat their *Gurus* as their fathers. There were no teacher training institutes or schools as existed now-a-days. Also education was imparted in Gurukula Ashramas situated in the jungles on the banks of rivers, far away from the student homes. This was done to isolate the students from their parents, so that the students could be spared from too much of parental love and may get education in sociability, religiosity, spirituality and in other life attitudes for saneful living.

Also, the education was bifurcated into Gurukula education, for educating the students in religiosity, spirituality, simplicity and sociability. In Gurukula Ashramas only two Varnas—Brahmans and Kshatriyas were admitted. The other two Varnas—Vaishyas and *Sudras* used to get education in their family vocations in non-formal way on hereditary lines. The Gurukula Ashramas taught formal education to some extent but, the students were educated in familial ways as the Gurukulas were big families like joint families. In non-formal education, the youngers used to do apprenticeship with their elders for learning their family occupations. As such, their elders used to be their teachers who also did not need any training. This system of non-formal education in technical trades continued till the alien system of formal education got total acceptance in Indian society and the youths were sat to be trained in technical trades in industrial training institutes formally.

With the passage of time some factors, like sociological, economical, political, demographic and theological changed. Due to increase in human population there has been a demographic explosion not only in India but in the whole world. This entailed many changes which required many things. The necessities for many things developed science and technology, as necessity is the mother of invention. Consequently there has been industrial development which entailed urbanisation, modernisation and sanskritisation. All these entailed hedonism, consumerism and xenophilism. These developments necessitated broad-based education. This social phenomenon boosted educational development not only India but in the whole world. The expansion of industries and trade required many expert hands for which education was necessary. Therefore, steps were taken to educate all youngers first by the industrialists and later on by the Governments. The formal system of education came into being. The schools were established first by the industrialists and later on by the Governments. All this required many teachers. The earlier concept of *Gyan Dan* (ज्ञान दान) became redundant, and the teaching became a source of white collar jobs. Many youths desired to take up teaching as honourable vocation for earning livelihood. As such teaching in schools, colleges, universities and technical institutes became an honourable profession for earning livelihood. As such, teaching got a social recognition as a honourable profession, though not as it was in Gurukulas in olden days.

For preparing through training, suitable qualified teachers many teacher training institutes like normal schools, emerged during the British period. Later on, a good number of teaching institutes increased. These institutes used to train the teachers of various levels—as nursery school teachers, primary school teachers, secondary school teachers, senior secondary school teachers and technical training institute teachers. Since the teachers are considered life builders and moulders of the youngers hailing from different social, economic and cultural backgrounds, it becomes necessary to prepare the future teachers to educate the youngers about social, economic and cultural inequality, so as to prepare them to fight all these social evils. For achieving this end it becomes necessary to apprise the teacher trainees about all philosophical, sociological, axiological, psychological and historical aspects of education. As such, it became necessary for the teacher trainees to know about (*a*) philosophical aspects of education, (*b*) sociological aspects of education, (*c*) psychological aspects of education, (*d*) history of education, (*e*) methodologies of teaching used in educating the youngers, and (*f*) some specific educational areas of education. All these come under the theoretical arenas of teacher education. These theoretical aspects are generally taught to teacher trainees, in teacher training institutes formally.

But there are some other important sociological, economical, cultural, theological and political aspects about which the teacher training generally remain unaware. And, they fail to make the students about some killing social evils. Until and unless the future teachers are made aware about these aspects, neither they can inculcate desirable necessary life attitudes in the students, nor they can counter the virus of acculturation by enculturating the students properly. This is necessary to be done for making the youngers as responsible sane future citizens.

The desirable sociological aspects which should be inculcated in the students are the development of viable sociability, cooperation, sharing, helping the needy, respecting the elders and fair sex, loving the youngers and animal life, social unity, integrity, homogeneity, to live peacefully in the family, maintaining 'unity in bio-diversity'. All these aspects have been widely damaged by the virus of acculturation. Therefore, it is also necessary to make the teacher trainees aware about the virus of acculturation, so that in future they may educate the students about acculturation. It is the teachers who can do this, as the parents are mad after hedonism which is the result of acculturation. Preparation of the students for proper economic development is also necessary. For this, development of proper work habits is very necessary. Earlier, this was done through familial education. Now, the parents are mad for the good shining examination results, and they only force their kids to study and study. They are unable to inculcate work habits in their youngers. The culture is the soul of any society or nation. If the culture of any society or nation crumbled, the society or nation will become weak and fractured. The culture of any nation is the embodiment of social traits, traditions, behaviour, art and craft, ways of living, etc. etc. When the numbers of a society try to shift to alien forms of culture traits, the culture of the nations crumbles. Also majority of the world population are victim of theology. Religious dogmatism generates extremism and terrorism of which many innocent people become victims. Therefore, it is necessary to make the future teachers aware about dogmatic theology and its bad effects. Likewise, awareness about the political system is also very necessary. There are various political systems as—anarchy, monarchy, diarchy, theology based Governments and democracy, exist in the world. Anarchy is a system of Government has no proper rules for the governance. Monarchy is a rule by one person. Diarchy is a rule by few people. A religious based Government is purely religious Government and a democracy is a "rule by the people for the people". In a democracy there is a complete freedom of speech, working and saneful living for all.

As such, the teacher training institutes should make the pupil-teachers aware all types of political set-ups, so that they may make the students aware about these aspects.

Only theoretical knowledge does not yield viable practical results. All theoretical knowledge always entails some practical activities also, because it is doing which sustains life. So also, philosophical—theoretical knowledge in teaching profession makes the logical teaching possible. Teaching also requires practices (*a*) practical teaching, (*b*) use of audio-visual aids, (*c*) doing co-curricular and extra-curricular activities, and (*d*) doing artistic creative activities. So while training teachers, the pupil-teachers should be apprised about all educational, philosophical, sociological and psychological theories. They should be given training in all teaching aspects as mentioned above. The teacher training institutes give 'practice teaching training' to pupil-teachers and, ignore other aspects of practical training. As such, during the course of teacher training following pedagogic aspects should be covered.

EDUCATIONAL THEORY

The following areas should be covered under the Educational Theory :

Educational theory in teacher training, either it is of graduate level (B.Ed. or B.T.) or under graduate level (C.T. or J.B.T. or Diploma in Teaching) usually covers the following theory papers. But one of the most theoretical aspect, that is, sociological theory is not taught. Knowledge of sociological aspects is most important. The organisers of the teacher training courses should look into this aspect also earnestly.

Philosophy of Education—Paper I

From the very beginning many thinkers have been presenting various philosophical views. Some presented rationalistic views. On the basis of which philosophic views of various social structures have emerged in the world. And on the basis of social structures various educational systems emerged out of the philosophies of the respective societies. Since the teacher is supposed to mould the lives of the future guardians, he also must be made aware about all of the philosophical aspects, as he is supposed to innovate and motivate thinking, reasoning and analysing in the students. Under the philosophy of education the pupil-teacher should be made aware about the philosophies advanced by Hegel (Idealist), René Descartes (Rationalist), John Locke (Empiricist), John Dewy (Pragmatist), Froebel (Emotionalist), Pestalozzi (Emotionalist), and Comenius (Educational Technologist) and also about Indian thinkers like J. Krishnamoorthy, Vivekananda, Rabindra Nath Tagore, and M.K. Gandhi. The pupil-teachers should be made aware about the social structure and its most important aspects. As effects of social stratification which is caste based are not good. Effects of cultural diffusion and acculturation on Indian society are bad. Also other social aspects as necessity of proper socialisation, morality, work culture, killing hedonism and materialism should be included in educational theory which are still ignored. These aspects may be covered under Paper I.

Psychology of Education—Paper II

Psychology of education is very important for educating the youngers. Psychology is a wide discipline. Under the education some important topics of the psychology about which the teacher training should be taught are: (*a*) human behaviour, and personality development (*b*) human psyche, (*c*) theories of learning, (*d*) steps to be taken for eliciting students catharsis, (*e*) steps to be taken for knowing the students catharsis, and (*f*) doing some action researches while teaching like preparing case studies etc.

History of Education—Paper III

Every aspect of society has a historical background. Until and unless one knows the past events he/she cannot proceed amicably. It is, therefore, necessary to know about the educational history of the country in which one is living. For the teacher, knowledge of the educational as well as of socio-economic, cultural and political conditions is very necessary. Because, without the historical knowledge of these phenomena the teacher cannot proceed on the right teaching track. If we look into our past educational history, Indian Brahmanical Gurukula Ashram education was an ideal system of education for life building. The *Gurus* (teachers) used to inculcate good life attitudes through socialising and enculturating the students. Due to caste based social stratification the Gurukula education was only given to two upper castes—Brahmans and Khastriyas. Even the ladies of the two upper castes were denied Gurukula education. The history of education makes the pupil-teachers aware about the total educational development like the imposition of formal system of education by the British Government on India. This imposition has killed our national culture. As such, the teacher trainees must be aware about all of the educational, cultural, socio-economic and political aspects. Then only the teacher can proceed well.

Methodologies of Teaching—Paper IV

Knowledge of methodologies of teaching is very important for the teacher. The teacher's client—the students are conscious beings. They have some inner potentialities and taking out these potentialities is called 'education'. As a spade is used for digging out some underground hidden wealth, the teacher is supposed to use appropriate teaching methods to take out the hidden potentialities or innate ideas of the students. These methods may include narration about the topic to be taught to make the students aware about the topic, and thereafter use of bi-polar communication. This can be possible if teaching is entailed with the teaching aids and consequent questioning. This can make elicitations possible from the students. For all this the teacher has to do lesson planning and proceed accordingly. The pupil-teachers are supposed to teach two teaching subjects in schools. Therefore, they should be trained in teaching two subjects. The practice teaching training and related activities should be given proper attention in the teacher training institutes, so that, the pupil-teachers may be properly trained. In many teacher training institutes which are running on commercial lines, the practice teaching is a mere routine formality. The pupil-teachers are not trained in using the most important teaching tools like black-board and other teaching aids. This should be done very carefully and sincerely.

Special Educational Area—Paper V

The modern scientific period has put forward many problems

before man. For facing these problems there is a need for special knowledge in the educational fields such as (*a*) Educational and vocational guidance, (*b*) Basic education, (*c*) Library education, (*d*) Aesthetic education, (*e*) Audio-visual education, (*f*) Social education, (*g*) Art and craft education, (*h*) Physical education, (*i*) History of education, (*j*) Women education, and (*k*) Juvenile education. etc. etc. Some students have specific interests in this regard. Each student should choose one field of his choice and should learn it.

THE PRACTICAL TRAINING OF THE TEACHER

Teacher training is a professional course like other professional courses as engineering, medicine, art and crafts etc. etc. The teacher training also needs an intensive practical training like as in other practical fields. A teacher who is properly trained in practical activities as, practice teaching use audio-visual aids, arranging of co-curricular and extra-curricular activities can only be a successful teacher. Such teacher can add wings in the crown of teaching. And this can only be expected from a teacher who is dedicated to teaching profession.

University Education Commission noted that one of the major deficiency in our teaching programme is inadequate practical training given to the pupil-teachers. Very little time and attention is given to it. Also, whatsoever practical training is given too little weightage. There are so many areas which need adequate practical training in teacher training are not at all thought in many teacher training institutions. As such, the condition of teaching in many schools which employ such practically untrained teachers become more and more worse. Many commercial teachers training institutes have emerged in the country which totally ignore practical training in some important activities, though these activities are most essential for teaching. So, in addition to practice teaching all sorts of practical activities should be taught to the pupil-teachers in teacher training institutes.

What is required is that there should be sufficient opportunities for the pupil, teachers, in teacher training institutes, for doing multiple tasks of practical nature which are necessary for the enculturation of the students. The practical training should not be restricted to practice teaching only. During the practice teaching the fellow teachers of the practice teaching school can also be involved in some practical work. They can guide the pupil-teachers in various kinds of practical work to be done in schools. During the course of practice teaching pupil-teachers should be trained in lesson planning. The concept of lesson planning has emerged out of the term planning. First of all the concept of planning had emerged in Soviet Union called U.S.S.R. after throwing out the Czars. The newly emerged Communist Government prepared first five year plan for the economic and military development. Thereafter, the concept of planning became an universal phenomenon. As pupil-teachers are trained to teach two subjects in the school, they should be trained to prepare lesson plans for two subjects. There is a specified proforma of the lesson plan. The main features of the lesson plan are: (*a*) lesson No., (*b*) topic to be taught or developed during the course of teaching, (*c*) period number, (*d*) class, (*e*) objectives of teaching, (*f*) teaching device to be used, (*g*) methodology of teaching to be used, (*h*) methods of recapitulation, (*i*) progressive method of teaching, and (*j*) method communication to be used. The teacher should start teaching with an elicitative narration which could ignite an eagerness in the minds of the students to learn. And this should follow presentation which may entail questioning for viable elicitations. For the development of the lesson proper development should be done. The elicited points should be written on the black-board. And there should be recapitulation through questioning. And if necessary proper homework should be given to the students.

The pupil-teachers should be guided by the teachers incharge of practical activities. The supervisor, who is supervising the practice teaching should have a close watch on practice teaching activities of the pupil-teachers. He/she should see whether, the pupil-teachers are being properly guided by the subject lectures. Whether the lesson plans have been properly checked. Whether the pupil-teachers are using appropriate teaching aids properly. The visual-aids lecturer should also guide the students for preparing the teaching aids. There should also be criticism, observation of the lesson development at least one in each subject daily. The pupil-teachers are generally trained in two teaching subjects, so there should be one criticism lesson daily during practice teaching which should be observed by all pupil-teachers. The school authorities, where the practice of teaching is being conducted, should earnestly cooperate with the practice teaching supervisor and with the teacher trainees. They should make arrangements for conducting experiments. They should allow the pupil-teachers to use the school library and visual aids, science laboratory if there is any. The school authorities should also help the pupil-teachers to prepare the projects for using in teaching in heuristic teaching methods. The teacher trainees should do it at least once a week. If it is not possible, once a week, at least once a month. The school authorities should also encourage the pupil-teachers to become good school teachers in future by adopting sincere and diligent ways of working. The principal of the school should invite the pupil-teachers to see the co-curricular activities arranged on special occasion in the school. If the pupil-teachers are interested they should be allowed to use the school playground for games and yoga. The principal and the vice-principal of the school should make the pupil-teachers aware about the difficulties of the students in the school and should also motivate the pupil-teachers to help the students in future.

The practice teaching should be given adequate weightage. The pupil-teachers should be properly guided in lesson planning and teaching in heuristic way. The practice teaching supervisor should also be devoted to practice teaching. He/she should also be fully aware about the practice teaching operations. In many teachers training colleges many practice teaching supervisors are not fully devoted to their duties. They go to the practice teaching schools late and come earlier. Sometimes many practice teaching supervisors are not fully aware about the teaching methodologies, ways of communication should be used in teaching and about the use of audio-visual aids. Such persons should not be assigned the duties of supervision of practice teaching. The practice teaching supervisor must be fully aware teaching methodologies, use of desirable way of communication in teaching and knowledge of teaching subjects.

In addition to all this the pupil-teachers must be made aware about culture, cultural diffusion as it result acculturation and to meet the situations doing enculturation. The teacher training colleges where the pupil-teachers are trained should arrange cultural programmes periodically, and all pupil-teachers should take part in these compulsorily. The teacher training colleges must make the pupil-teachers aware how the school should be equipped for arranging cultural activities, art and craft activities and physical education activities. The colleges should also motivate the pupil-teacher to keep the cleanliness and sanitary conditions good in the schools. The pupil-teachers should be encouraged to make use of the school library nicely. They should be trained how the school syllabus and school time table be prepared.

IDEAL ROLES OF THE TEACHERS

Swami Vivekananda said that "the main aim of education is the wholesome development of the individual". Father of the nation, Late Shri M.K. Gandhi said that "education is drawing out of the best from the individual". Late Prof. E.A. Pires said that "the education should inculcate ideas in the individual for making him/herself conscious human beings. The individual should be kind to him/her fellow beings. His/her soul should discern common spiritual good. Without good idea a man/woman can never be a good person. Therefore, essence of education should be self-discovery, self-direction and to find out ones own limitations. The goal of education should be wholesome and integrative development of individual's personality and self-built character and ideal development one's personality. So, the teacher should always cherish and develop sane, unique and important ideals in all students."

It is necessary to give etymological explanation of the term "ideal", first of all. The word ideal is an adverb of the word 'idea'. The word 'idea' is a derivation from the Greek word 'Idus', meaning the mental form or appearance of "a person", "a thing", "a kind of species", "a root", "a mode thinking in mind", that which is comprehended by intellectual faculties in philosophical terms. An idea is generally aimed at to designate subjective notions with or without objective validity. An idea is a thought acceptable, appreciable and applicable belief by majority of the people. These are schools of thoughts and philosophy like idealism, realism, naturalism, empiricism, socialism, dogmatism, xenophilism, capitalism, favouritism etc. etc. based on specific ideas. Idealism is one such philosophical school which is based on common good. Acting according to one's inner consciousness, believing in religiosity and spirituality for common interests are good, without any personal gain or inclination is a form of action which may be an action based on idealism. As such, the term 'ideal' is that 'form' of actions which is noble, good for all and is always non-inclinative. There are Governments' which have ideal constitutions. Ideal thinking generally, always entails beliefs which are circumscribed around the wish for common good and not doing things which may harm or hurt others in the society. An ideal person is one who has always good ideas and, works for the common good. Such person is considered an ideal man in the society. He is liked and loved by the majority of the people. So, an ideal man is an embodiment of goodness. An ideal person should be a fully developed personality. He should possess the following human qualities:

1. A perfect admirable character,
2. An integrated personality which should always entails
   (*a*) balanced behaviour,
   (*b*) non-inclinativeness, non-self-centredness and greed freeness,
   (*c*) deep desire for common good,
   (*d*) respect to elders and fair sex,
   (*e*) an intense desire to help the weak, poor, ill children and fair sex,
   (*f*) to love siblings and younger children, and
   (*g*) to believe in simple living and high thinking.

An ideal personality should be worth respecting by all in the society. Sanity, sociability, morality, truthfulness, spirituality and living for common good should be the life motto of an ideal person. A fully developed ideal man/woman is only possible if a person develops sociability, mentality having sensitivity for self-introspection, having sensitivity for truthfulness, aestheticity, justice, love, affection, cooperation, tolerance, non-violence, non-gender bias thinking, reasoning, comprehending and a sense of kinship sharing. In modern age of industrialisation, which entailed hedonism and modernisation which forced the man to renounce simple living and high thinking. This made the man too much greedy, self-centred, utilitarian, hedonistic, xenophilic and maglomaniac. Due to this social idealism has been, more or less, lost by most of the people. Instead of being idealist, the modern man has become totally pragmatic and remains busy in the rat-race of material gains. The old religious beliefs based on spirituality and monotheism have been replaced by henotheism, polytheism and tantrism which are practiced for personal gains. Daily prayers are generally being discarded due to busy materialistic life of the man. These have been replaced by periodical *satsangs* on the pattern of Western Calvinistic philosophy of exploitation of natural resources for material gains and praying in church once a week on Sunday. For material gains the modern man/woman does not have time, even time for the enculturation of their own kids, kith and kins. It is seen that the wife does not hesitate in killing her legal partner—the husband for personal enjoyment. Son does not hesitate in killing his own father for gaining family's property. Neighbourly relations have almost been vanished due to unsociability of man. Now the old caste structure is being replaced by Western class structure. The old norms of homogenic social living are vanishing day by day. Neighbourly familial social relations have almost been vanished. Now the old norms of social living are vanishing day by day. An elite person does not want to maintain relations with neighbourly elite because of megalomaniasm. An owner of a car always does not like to take to a person having a bicycle, though he may be an intelligent, diligent, honest and an ideal person. Now he is considered a fool by the well-established and economically settled persons. Due to the rat-race of money earning for material mobility, the modern will of person including the professionals for doing periodical *kirtans* and *bhajans*. This trend has more or less eliminated sociability, morality and ethnicity from the society. As such, idealism is no more in the society. The present man has become totally self-centred, egoistic, greedy, acquisitive and meglomaniac. This is because of acculturation and our present formal system of education which has no place to inculcate sanity and idealism in the students.

Our present system of formal education only breeds love for material gains which entails cutthroat competition in the society. It lacks axiology, socialisation and moralisation which is the soul of integrated homogenic ideal social life. The corruption has become so rampant in the society that there is not any field which can be said free of corruption. Incidents of loot, cheating, dacoities, burglaries, snatching, pick-pocketing have become a common social feature. Acculturation has made the people totally blind about the national culture. Seventy years back there was fear of wolves and other beasts in the country side fields. Now the jungle wolves and other beast have disappeared and more and more human wolves and beasts are found in abundance in both rural and urban areas. Kidnappings of young children, businessmen, young girls for ransom have become a common feature throughout the country. Man has become an animal, as cases of rape even of old women and young girls have become a common feature in the society. And an unfortunate thing is that often many criminals doing such un-social heinous crimes are shielded by the politicians for building their vote banks.

In such a pathetic social situation, there is a need of an urgent need of idealism in our lives. But there is no congenial social atmosphere in the society for inculcating ideals in our younger generation. Because of ostentatious and xenophilic life styles, the joint family system has, more or less been crumbled down. In place of joint family system, nuclear families have emerged. The joint family system was the best source to create or inculcate idealism in the youngers. The joint families were the prime source of familial education in the Indian society. Now both the parents are in the rat-race of money earning. They do not have time for familial education and for inculcating good ideal habits in the youngers. So, they generally ignore their youngers. The socialisation and moralisation which used to start at home and, the family members used to do it, is missing now. Where are the younger ones are going is neither the concern of the parents, nor of community nor of society? The rulers always look to the consolidation of their governance. Parents and the community generally expect schools to do everything for the younger generation, that is, education and inculcation of good habits—socialisation, moralisation. Also the schools and the institutions of higher learning should prepare the future guardians for competitions. The teachers are bound to devote themselves for preparing the students for annual examination so as to enable them to face the competitions for getting jobs. The teachers do not have time to inculcate good life attitudes in the students and enculturate them. If a younger becomes a criminal generally the school in which he/she is studying or studied is blamed and not the parents. So, the moulding of the minds of the youngers by inculcating good life habits is neither done at home nor at school, nor at college, which is the prime need of the day. Only inculcation of good ideas can save our youngers and society for materialistic fever which has gripped our society very badly. The materialistic trends are robbing the national culture and are increasing the elements of acculturation. In fact the school teachers are over occupied in competitive struggle for preparing the students for shining examination results. The teachers do not get time to do inculcating of good life habits and doing enculturation activities. But, in spite of busy teaching programme, the teachers have to arrange some co-curricular activities for doing the enculturation of the students, which should be given more time by the school administrators.

The teachers are the nation builders, trend setters, and character builders of the youngers. If we peep into our past history of Brahmanic education system, we find that our old teachers were idealistic personalities. They were well read, epistemic, monotheistic, religioistic, spiritualistic personalities. They were dedicated to teaching profession. The old teachers (*Gurus*) were always eager to add their knowledge, so they were epistemic. They were also sincere and kind to their *Shishyas* (disciples) and were non-inclinative. They used to act for spiritual and social gains. They never thought of their personal gains and enjoyment. They always respected elders and fair sex. The main objective of teaching in olden times was life building through inculcation of good life habits such as socialisation, moralisation and economic upliftment of the people.

The old teachers used to follow the teaching professional ethical code seriously. Now the situation has totally changed. It can be said topsy-turvy to old situation. Now the teachers are public servants, whereas in the past the *Gurus* were true professionists, idealists, religionists and spiritualists, so they were highly respected in the society. The present teachers, because of their low economic gains are not respected by the economically affluent members of the society. But, the present teachers should not forget the ideal roles preformed by their predecessors—the old Indian *Gurus* (teachers).

It is the teacher who can raise the people from social degradation. The teacher has cherish and aspire a well-balanced self-personality. If a teacher has a well-balanced personality, then he/she can mould the personalities of the pupils by presenting himself/herself as an ideal model before them. The teacher should constantly build himself/herself to be a constant helper of the students. This can only be possible if he/she has a sympathetic ear towards the pupils. The teacher should listen and understand the problems of the pupils and then should respond to their problems sympathetically. The teacher should see that the pupil is not mentally disturbed, and is spiritually bold. Therefore, the teacher should try to take steps to prepare the young pupils as fully developed human beings. The full development of pupils can only be possible, if inculcation is done for their social, economic and moral development at earlier stage. For this end the teachers should have a sensitivity about truthfulness, aestheticity, justice, law, goodness, love and a sense of kinship and he/she should educate the pupils about these. With these qualities an individual can become a true sane ideal citizen, who will aspire for the common good and will dedicate to the national development. The teachers should also enculturate the pupils.

No teacher can be said to have a real ideal role of teaching profession, if he/she is not inspired by the idealism. The teacher can only play the ideal role of the teaching profession if he/she is fully aware about the teaching professional ethical codes, which are as under:

1. A profession is a relationship between an expert and an ignorant client. Of course, the teacher is supposed to be an expert in the subject he is teaching, but his/her client, the student, is not an ignorant client like that of a medical man or a lawyer or a priest. So the teacher has to be expert and proficient in subject he is going to teach. He has to deal with the conscious clients. So, he/she has to continue his/her studies continuously for becoming proficient in the subject he/she is going to teach. The teacher should analyse the psyche of the pupils in order to handle them.
2. Therefore, a teacher must continue his studies so that he/she may be proficient in the subject he/she is teaching.
3. The teacher should be very sincere to his/her clients, that is, students, he is going to teach. If the teacher is not inspired by the ideals of teaching profession and is not dedicated to the pupils and society, he/she can never mould the future guardians. This can be done when a teacher possess:
   (*a*) an ideal good character.
   (*b*) a sense of sympathy and kindness towards the pupils.
   (*c*) a sense of self-introspection and restraint.

(*d*) a sense of epistemacy and desire for gaining more and more knowledge and practical experience in creative activities.

(*e*) a teacher should sympathetically appreciative and supporter of multi-faceted life situations. He should face all life situations courageously.

(*f*) a teacher should be non-inclinative.

In addition to these, the teacher should be sympathetic to animal life also. He/she should always keep in mind that as a builder or moulder of future guardians, his/her services are essential for the society and nation as a whole. These should be discharged with sincere dedication. The teacher should also keep in mind that his duties are not limited within the four walls of the school alone. These go beyond the school. He/she is the moulder, builder and enlighten of the whole nation. Therefore, a teacher has to be most intelligent, diligent, sincere and social minded citizen. As such, a teacher should be broad-minded, kind hearted and socially active person.

A teacher must strictly follow the code of teaching professional ethics which requires epistemacy, sincerity and non-inclinativeness towards the pupils and to the society as a whole. He/she should not have any bias towards his/her fellow colleagues. The teacher should not commercialise the teaching profession. He/she should not do tuitions. Instead, the teacher should innovate and motivate the students for self-learning. The teacher should create appropriate conditions for self-learning and upbringing. The teacher should sincerely cooperate with his/her colleagues. The teacher should never be megalomaniac, that is, having or belief of knowing everything. If a fellow colleague advises the teacher he/she should not ignore it. If a teacher maglomaniac he/she can never be good teacher, because he/she will not try to know more and add to his/her knowledge This dictum does not apply only to the teaching profession, but it also applies to all other vocations. For example, if a cabinet maker or a fabricator thinks that he is the master of area of action, his maglomony will block his thinking, reasoning, and analysing. This ultimately will put a halt on his/her creative activities. So a teacher should always keep his/her area of action open for thinking, reasoning, analysing and criticism. A teacher should not be afraid of criticism by his/her students and colleagues. Rather, the teacher should welcome and appreciate open criticism and suggestions.

This will open the doors of his/her brain and lead to self-introspection and thinking. The teacher should apply progressive teaching methods during teaching such as heuristic method, project method, discussion method, etc. etc. which could innovate, motivate and stimulate the students to thinking, reasoning, analysing and comprehending. This will help the students in self-learning. For this process the use of teaching aids is necessary during teaching. The teaching aids can initiate the teacher-taught interaction which will lead to elicitations. The teacher should be liberal. He/she should allow the students to discuss openly all other matters as social, political, moral, upward mobility, social integration and present social condition due to acculturation. He/she should also do some enculturation activities. The teacher should use his/her leisure time for the development of aestheticity.

The culture of any country is its soul. If the culture of a nation disappears, the nation also disappears like a human body dies when its soul (जीवात्मा) leaves it. Therefore, for protecting a wide variety of national interests the teacher must be fully aware about the elements of national culture, and should also learn all cultural activities. Then the teacher will be able to enculturate the students.

The culture of any country is its soul. If the culture of any country disappears, the nation also dies like a human body dies when its soul (जीवात्मा) leaves it. Therefore, for having a wide variety of wholesome interests the teacher should know fully about the national culture and should learn the enculturation activities. Then only the teacher can enculturate the students.

The democracy is the slogan of the day. In a democratic form of Government many people, if not all, participate. A democratic government, "is a government by the people, for the people". Because of human animal greedy nature, many political leaders make democracy as their property. And for keeping their hold intact to remain in power, they even do not hesitate to criminalise the political institutions. The teacher has a great responsibility in this regard. He/she should inculcate democratic norms in the students for developing beliefs in democratic institutions. The teacher should prepare the future citizens for ideal democratic living, making them aware about criminal dens and other criminals, also and to be ready to fight such bad, criminal elements.

This can be done through co-curricular activities, group discussions, seminars, workshops and symposiums. The school administration should initiate all these. The teacher should make the students aware of versatility of sociability, truthfulness, cooperation, honesty, regularity in life, such as "early to bed, early to rise makes a man healthy and wise", and "simple living and high thinking". The teacher should also motivate the pupils to be regular and punctual. The teacher should also inculcate some habits for good saneful living. Also, all these can be inculcated through co-curricular activities arranged in the school.

Teaching is a creative process like that of doing creative activities of arts and crafts. The teacher should always apply creative process in teaching the pupils which may result in educating them. This will cultivate the creative spirit in the pupils. And few of them will be creative thinkers, creative artists and other professionalists. The teacher should always keep in his/her mind the great *Gurus* (teachers) of olden times while teaching. He/she should also know about great personalities like Swami Vivekananda, Swami Dayanand Saraswati, Father of the Nation, Shri M.K. Gandhi etc. etc. He/she should pay reverence to such great persons, of and tell on during teaching. This will help in character building of the students. The teacher should always keep a good rapport with the students and their parents. The teacher should also apprise the students about modernisation and acculturation which occurred due to Western cultural diffusion with Indian culture.

Finally, it would not be illogical to assume that the versatility of the ideal roles of the teachers is well-recognised and well-established. The modern industrial materialistic age is loaded with greed, self-interestedness and corruption. It entails many social evils. And, extremism, terrorism and corruption are the recent embodiments of social evils. These are the manifestations of social disparity in the community due to poverty. Poverty is the result of social disparity, unemployment, religious dogmatism. These are premises which hurt the democratic process. The premises of the liberal democracy are fraternity and brotherhood, equality and liberty. In the present material age, there is no chance of sociability, so all these are fractured. Only the teacher can re-establish these by educating the youngers in right directions. And for doing so the teacher should observe honesty, fraternity, sincerity to the students, simplicity, sociability, proficiency in the teaching subjects, truthfulness and dedication to the teaching profession.

One of the important duty of the teacher is to test and examine the students performance periodically. Therefore, the pupil-teachers while under training should be trained in examining the students. For doing this they should know how to prepare the periodic test and examination papers? They must know about the categories of examining tools and types of tests like subjective test or objective test and they must learn to prepare the respective papers. They should also learn how to check the answer sheets and answer books. If the pupil-teachers learn all these during their training, they shall be able to discharge all of their required duties after being appointed teachers in schools.

Another important factor of the teacher training is to train the pupil-teachers in co-curricular activities and extra-curricular activities, because without these activities there cannot be enculturation of the students in the schools. The process of enculturation, as a matter of fact has been badly affected due to western cultural diffusion. It has totally acculturated the people. Earlier enculturation process used to start from home. The family members used to enculturate the youngers. Earlier there were joint families. Now the joint family system has been totally crumbled, and nuclear family system has taken its place. Both the parents remain busy in the rat-race of money earning. They do not have time to enculturate their children. They are mad after hedonism. As such, the school teachers are supposed to do enculturation of the students also in addition to teaching the students for good examination results. The enculturation of the students can only be done by arranging regular periodic co-curricular activities along with academic activities. For arranging the co-curricular activities, doing artistic activities is necessary. According to Sigmund Freud, the artistic activities are very necessary for the development of sane personality of the youngers. In addition to the co-curricular activities, extra-curricular activities like games, sports, social services and upkeep of the school compound are necessary. These programmes should be arranged house-wise and should be judged by an expert committee. The winning house should be honoured and rewarded. This will boost the co-curricular and extra-curricular activities in an educational institute and thereby the students will be benefited to the maximum.

Games and sports play an important role in socialisation, development of health care habits and sound personality development. The games and sports also come under the extra-curricular activities. If we look to the younger children, we find that they are very much interested in games. Every child wants to play with his/her peer group. But it is regretted to note that there is hardly provision for games in very few teachers training colleges. If some college has a provision of games, there the physical education teacher tries to ignore the games activities. He/she generally tries to shift to another discipline. It is because the games activities, like other manual work activities as art and craft activities are looked upon with contempt by other teachers. This is due to the fact that our education is totally subject teaching based. This is the reason teachers teaching games and crafts adopted a sort of sanskritisation and try to shift to subject teaching fields. The teachers teaching games, art and craft should be treated at par with other teachers at schools and teacher training institutes.

Another important field of extra-curricular activities is hand work. Though hand work one can do creative artistic work and bring aestheticity in the society. By doing hand work students can express or release these emotions which is important according to Sigmund Freud. The hand work can create a spirit of sociability and cooperation in students. This helps in personality development. A spirit of sociability and morality is very necessary for sane social living. So training in hand work as doing painting, craftwork, sculpture, making mobiles, doing alpana and rangoli and also arranging displays with mobiles and making posters should be given to the pupil-teachers in teacher training colleges. For doing so art and craft clubs should be formed and pupil-teachers should be motivated and encouraged to take part in these clubs.

Regular effective programme of using audio-visual aids in teaching is very necessary for good education. As such, there should be a compulsory training programme in visual education for all B.Ed./B.T., B.Ed.Ed. and for nursery and primary school teachers. Along with this the use of different materials/medias are for making charts, models, diagrams, flash-cards, etc. etc. is necessary. The pupil-teachers should be made aware about these. For making various teaching aids different materials can be used. Visual education is necessary for the use of bi-polar communication in teaching. So the pupil-teachers should be trained in making a variety of charts, maps, flash-cards, models, diagrams, posters, transparencies and scrap book which can be used in teaching. Also, the pupil-teachers should be made aware about the versatility of chalk-board (black-board), roller chalk-board, in teaching. The pupil-teacher should be made aware about the proper use and maintenance of the chalk-board. Also, other audio-visual aids like film strips, slides, use of epidiascope, film projectors should be taught to the pupil-teachers. But it is observed that many teachers training colleges do not apprise the students even about chalk-boards or black-boards. Also, it is true that through non-verbal bi-polar communication, which can only be possible through the use of teaching aids sound teaching cannot be possible. Until and unless the opportunities for thinking, reasoning and analysing, which can be possible through analysing, proper education can never be possible. This can be done by using teaching aids.

In the present age, scientific generalisation of human development and behaviour needs balancing. Therefore, the pupil-teachers should be trained to analyse these aspects of the students during practice teaching. This needs some psychological equipments like I.Q. testing equipments which should be available in teacher training institutes for use by the pupil-teachers. The pupil-teachers should be trained for using these instruments. This will help the pupil-teachers in analysing the students in school when they are appointed as teachers. Also, the pupil-teachers should be encouraged to be innovative. They should be fully apprised about the importance of the teaching profession. And they should be prepared to follow the teaching professional ethics seriously.

In the olden days, the teachers were given due respect in the society which is not given in the present times. The hedonism and consumerism in the society, is the main reason. The teachers have also become inclinative. They devote time for the inclinative purposes. They do tuitions (not all). Many give preference to do their homework, as agriculture, and give teaching second preference. Such teachers should realise this professional drawback for the improvement of their teaching career.

Theory and practice must go hand in glove. The practice teaching should get due weightage. At least 25 lessons in one subject should be taught during the practice teaching. As such, for two subjects there should be 50 lessons. Sufficient weightage should be given to internal assessment. The internal assessment should be compulsory not only in teacher training colleges but also in schools and colleges. It should be also in theory papers as it is done in Central Institute of Education, University of Delhi, as given below:

Theory 500 Marks				*Practical 500 Marks*	
				All Internal Assessment	
Paper	Total Marks	Internal Assessment	External Assessment		
Paper I	100	25%	75%	Practice (i) Subject	125
Paper II	100	25%	75%	Practice (ii) Subject	125
Paper III	100	25%	75%	Total	250
Paper IV (Two Teaching	(i) 50	30%	70%	(i) Tutorials	50
Subjects)	(ii) 50	30%	70%	(ii) Psychology Practicals	40
Paper V	100	25	75%	(iii) Visual Education	55
Total Marks	500	130	370	(iv) School Assignments	55
				(v) Co-curricular Activities	50
				All Internal Assessment	500
N.B.:	Total internal assessment 63%, and external examination 37%				
	Theory 500 marks, Practical 500 marks, Total Marks 1000 marks				

Besides these, there are other areas of practical training such as training in maintaining school records, knowledge, about the school functions such as foundation day, parents day, national days, alumni day, orientation day, valedictory day function for the final year students, school evaluation system, teachers day, days of eminent persons, holy club, art club etc. etc. The pupil-teachers should be made aware about all these during their teacher training course. Evaluation of physical health care, social work, co-curricular and extra-curricular activities is very necessary. Above all these arranging of morning assembly is also very necessary. All these should be done by especially appointed committees. The pupil-teacher should be made aware about all these activities during their training.

The question arises whether all these aspects of practical activities can be achieved easily during the pupils-teachers' training? Answer these can be achieved easily if the teacher working at teacher training institute and pupils are sincere and dedicated. But, it is seen that sometimes few teachers at the teacher training institutes and, also few pupil-teachers are not found sincere and dedicated to the practical activities. Some teachers take the practical activities very lightly. They only believe in theoretical academic knowledge, which also they do as a mere formality. Also some pupil-teachers are not interested in teaching profession. Their interests are in some other lucrative jobs. They only decided to join teaching as an alternative as a last resort. And whenever they would get a chance they would say goodbye to teaching. As such, they do not have any interest in teacher training too. Such pupil-teachers can be said as 'anta-property' of the teaching profession as the girls are to their parents.

As such, only suitable candidates should be selected for training in teacher training institutes. For that a logical selection process should be adopted for selecting the pupil-teachers. Now-a-days the selection of the pupil-teacher is subject biased. Only the candidates who are proficient in teaching subjects are selected. The reason for this emphasised on examination results. Whereas the education has a wide spectrum. Education is a life building process. And this fact is not taken into consideration while selecting the pupil-teachers. Only the subjects which are to be taught are taken into consideration. Other capabilities of the candidates should be find out. This cannot be done by finding out subject teaching capabilities. About 45 years back it was done in Central Institute of Education under the guidance of Late Dr. E.A. Pierce, the then Principal of C.I.E. The aspirant pupil-teachers had to do cultural programmes, social activities and to participate in games activities at least for three days. Late Shri H.A. Gerde, K.D. Bakshi and Late Meharchand used to conduct these programmes. The writer used to help in stage setting.

19

Educational Teaching Method

Any kinds of activity, be it social, economic, theological, cultural and educational entails a functioning processes. Even the human life, which has a long continuum entails a process. After unity in bio-diversity a child is born, brought up, educated, encultured and prepared for sane social living. As living beings and human beings pass through various stages. The educational activity entails many processes including teaching. As such, any system contains many facets. Likewise education is also a perennial life long system which entails many processes and teaching methods. The educational system is also affected by biological, social, economic, cultural, theological and political factors, which affect the human life also. As such, for successful implementation for any type educational process, it is necessary to study the past history of educational system of the country and, also to visualise the country's present sociological, economic, cultural, political and theological perspectives of the society. Then only appropriate educational process and relating teaching methods can be thought of and adopted.

As the processes of education has already been mentioned earlier are many and varied. But in the present materialistic and hedonistic age when due to demographic explosion the socio-economic and cultural scenarios of the world have totally changed, and many youngers are to be educated for happy living, many new educational institutions like schools, industrial schools, management schools and universities have emerged. The old processes of education like familial education, informal education and non-formal education have become ineffective for educating the youngers. Another reason for this is that parents of the youngers have become materialistic and hedonistic, they do not have time to pay due attention to their children, because they remain busy in the rat-race of money earning. This trend has also caused the dys-functioning of the joint family system. Now only, the formal system of education has become an universal phenomena. As already mentioned, the present formal education is to give a platform to all students irrespective of their taste, liking and mental abilities. This is supposed to be done through teaching. The teaching is a process in which a knowledgeable person, that is, teacher, passes his acquired knowledge to a person or persons who does or do not know about this knowledge. Since the teaching methods are used for educating the youngers, these should be so designed which could motivate the students for self-learning. Because, self-learning can be said true education. in other words teaching in formal system of education should be designed for self-learning by the students. As such, teaching for self-learning has a wide and varied spectrum which needs planning and proper implementation. Therefore, it is necessary that the teachers should be trained accordingly, so that they may do effective teaching. Following steps should be taken for effective teaching. The teachers should also follow these:

LESSON PLANNING

For effective proper teaching there is a need of proper advance lesson planning. The teacher has to teach one lesson in one period. Therefore, the lesson which is to be taught should be planned in advance. And such planning is called 'Lesson Planning'. Concept of planning was first adopted in U.S.S.R. after 1917 A.D. after communist revolution. After this, concept of planning spread throughout the world in all fields. Like planning in other fields, lesson planning for teaching is also not an easy job. The teacher is required to teach the stipulated content, as shown in the curriculum for the academic year. So the teacher first has to divide the full year subject content first in three terms or units, which is called 'unit plan'. Further, the unit plan is divided month-wise. These are called monthly teaching unit plans. And finally the monthly unit plan is divided day-wise. The first term of the school starts in the first week of April every year and ends in the middle of October on the occasion of Dusshera holiday. But it is observed that the school teaching takes its full form in the first week of July every year. In April and up to middle of May, before the summer vacation, generally the process of fresh admission continues. The second term of the school starts after Dusshera holidays and ends by the last week of December. The third and last term starts from second January and ends on 31st March.

While planning a lesson plan the teacher is supposed to indicate the (1) topic of the content to be taught to the students in the class, (2) age groups of the students, (3) date, (4) period number, (5) lesson plan number, (6) duration of the period, and (7) general and specific objectives of the topic to be taught. Also the teacher is required to mention (*a*) particular way of presentation of teaching, (*b*) procedure of introduction of the topic to be taught—either by a reference to previous knowledge or by pointing the current socio-economic or culture problems prevalent in the society. Since the teacher is supposed to adopt a progressive method of teaching, he/she will have to mention the particular method of teaching and the teaching aids to be used during teaching for making out elicitations from the students. The teacher is not supposed to be a mere informer or narrator. His/her aim should be that the students should learn themselves. As such, the whole process of teaching should be on creating an atmosphere for a healthy interaction between the teacher and the students which may contribute to self-learning and sound education. So the questioning, from both sides, and thereby points clinching and recording these on chalk-board (black-board) through the students' responses should be the main aim of teaching. For this end questioning and cross questioning for reinforcement is necessary. Thereafter, recapitulation should find a place in a lesson plan and its development. And finally some home assignment should be given to the students. The format of the lesson plan should be as under:

Lesson Plan No. …………..

1. Name of the School….. 2. Class…. 3. Period….
4. Name of the Teacher …………………………..
5. Topic to be taught ………………..
6. Age group …………… 7. Date ……………………
8. Objectives of Teaching ……………………………..
9. Teaching method to be applied ……………………..
10. Method of introduction of the topic ………………..
11. Teaching aids to be used for bi-polar communication
……………………………………………………
12. Presentation ……………………………………….

Questioning	Elicitation and supplementation by the teacher
"	"
"	"
"	"

13. Recapitulation to be done by questioning related to the subject content taught. The teacher should be to involve all students in this process.
14. Home assignment

In view of the fact that every teacher is required to teach in six periods, out of eight periods, in a day. Generally, it is seen that in many schools chalk-boards (black-boards) are so defective that it is very difficult to write on these black-boards. Necessary teaching aids are also not available in most of schools and even in some higher institutions of education. In such a situation teaching continuously in six periods becomes tiresome and boring. And teaching does not become successful. The teacher is blamed for that. In some schools, the number of teachers is small. In such a situation when a teacher goes on leave, his/her teaching is given to another teachers as arrangement periods, which the teachers have to take in addition to their assigned teaching periods. In many cases, in many schools, there are teachers who are not proficient in their field of teaching - as some unskilled craft instructors, yoga teachers and physical education teachers. It is because many of them are appointed from reserved quota. Such teachers pass their time either doing some work or pleasing the authorities. Their inefficiency also affects the other teachers who also stop working sincerely, and as a result the teaching in the school, as a whole, is badly affected.

If counted in numbers, the teaching is the worlds' biggest profession. In 1980 A.D. it was estimated that there were 30,000,000 teachers in the world. Now, due to demographic explosion, the number has crossed 40,000,000. Though roles and function of the teacher might differ from country to country.

Because, the nature of teaching activities depends upon the age group being taught, the role of the teachers widely differ, so also their categorisation. These categories in early 1980 A.D. had appropriate ratio — 57 per cent at primary, secondary and at senior secondary level, 9 per cent percent at the university level. And the rest in other institutions.

As regards status of the teacher in the society, teaching is given average to higher status in the society. It also depends upon educational qualification, training, experience, contribution in the field of education and rapport with the parents and the students. But, in spite of all this the teacher is not well paid yet. Decline in the status of the teacher is due to materialism and hedonism. Those who have become rich consider teacher as purchasable. They engage the teacher for tutoring their children. And the teachers who do tuitions are not well-treated. As such, the teacher should always use progressive teaching methods which could elicit knowledge from the students. Such teaching methods are termed as heuristic methods. And for these bi-polar communication is to be used. Such teaching methods will motivate the students to self-learning.

20

Social Stratification and Education

If we look etymological to the concept of 'social stratification', we find the word stratification is the development of the word 'strait', which is a derivation of the Latin word 'strictus' meaning 'to draw right', 'a narrow path', 'not wide', 'a passage of water to sea in two lanes'. As such, 'social stratification' is a process of placing the members of the society in different categories or group according to social needs or requirements or 'social feasibility'. Various bases of social stratification are found in the world.

A society is a composite whole of human beings, that is, of men and women. A man and woman are united by the institution of marriage. It is an 'unity of bio-diversity'. Of course, they are biologically 'male' and 'female', but they live together lifelong and they produce the future members of the society, which makes the social existence possible. A human body is a biological whole, in which all body parts function harmoniously together and keep the human body alive. If any part of the body becomes dys-functional the whole human body becomes crippled. And in many cases the human body dies. But the members of the society are separate biological wholes. All have individual differences because of varied mental and bodily capacities. As such, the human beings have different bodily capacities and desires. So they do different kinds of works and jobs. On the basis of their work culture, generally the members of the society are socially structured. Some societies stratify on the economic conditions as rich and poor. The Western societies are generally stratified on these principles. And, generally there are two classes 'rich' and 'poor'. The rich people are termed as 'barons' and poor people are termed as 'workers' or 'serfs'. As such, economic conditions based social stratification is termed as 'heterogeneous social stratification and is not considered as human social stratification, though heterogeneity is found in all societies. This affects the education of the people.

The human-beings are gifted by Almighty God with marvellous body structure. The man and woman have bigger brains to think, reason and analyse. The man/woman has an appropriate torso with flexible and moveable hands and legs, with which the man/woman can move, walk observe the natural phenomenon and can think and act. As such, the human beings are called rational beings who can act after rationalising things. On the contrary other living beings as—animals, birds, insects and bees are not considered rational beings. But, the human-beings have also been adorned, with the bad elements of greed, self-centredness and acquisitiveness. Due to this bad natural gifts, that is, greed, self-centredness and acquisitiveness the social stratification has been badly affected in almost all societies. And there have been killing social disparities in the societies. Some have become very rich and some remained very poor. And this state of disparities has been the prime base of social stratification throughout the world. In some societies religious beliefs have also become the source of social stratification. And all this has also affected education of the members of the society.

Indian society is the oldest in the world. Its religion, culture and civilisation are also very old. In the past India also had some greedy rulers. Also, it had many rationalist thinkers who always thought of common good. They always tried to control the human greed and self-centredness through religiosity, spirituality and sociability which they always tried to establish through the religious discourses. The old seers of India also had tried to stratify the human society on the pattern of human body. They had thought that as the human biological whole is a well-composed whole and functions harmoniously if the social stratification is done on this pattern. The social structure will remain homogeneous and will function smoothly. Lord Krishna has also endorsed the social stratification on the bases of human body in *Shrimad Bhagavad Gita*. So Maharishi Manu had suggested such social stratification which was implemented by the rulers. And the Indian society was stratified on the pattern of human biological whole as (*a*) human head, (*b*) human torso, (*c*) legs, and (*d*) feet. They had visualised that as human body, as a biological whole remain united till its death, if Indian society is stratified on this pattern, it will remain united forever. And this kind of social stratification was named 'Varna system' (वर्ण पद्धति). Those, who were supposed to do mental activities were called 'Brahmans', like head of the society, those who were supposed to defend the country were called 'Kshatriyas' like torso and hands of the human body, those who used to do agriculture, business activities and catering of cows and other animals were called 'Vaishyas' like legs. And all these Varnas were called the 'divijas' or twice born. And the fourth Varna who were not able to do all these works and used to serve all the three Varnas were called 'Sudras'. The Varna system originally was merit based. If any member of any Varna showed improvement in his performance he could have upper mobility. Likewise if any member of any upper three Varnas used to show lackness in his performance, he was supposed to be dipped to lower Varna. As such, proficiency in the work area used to lead to upward mobility in 'Varna' system. In due course of time before '*Mahabharata*' period some greedy saints (name not mentioned) converted the Varna system, to birth based caste system for giving advantage to his family members whose number was great. And this birth based caste system is still in existence. The birth based caste system has merits and demerits. The demerits are more than merits. And it is certain that the development of education of the people has been affected due to Indian birth based social stratification. Some important effects of it are given below:

Birth based caste social stratification came into existence due to human greed, self-interestedness and desire for exploitation of the week by the strong. Those who had converted the Varna system to birth based caste system had done so far their personal benefit and for the benefit of their future generation. Nature has created every one with specific potentialities. Hereditary potentialities also always differ. Everybody cannot be equally intelligent to his/her parents or ancestors. So putting everybody in heredity cadre on the basis of birth can neither be logical nor can be justified. It was impossible for the off-springs to be epistemically equal in Brahmans to their father and elders. So, the assumption that every child of a Brahman will be epistemic and, will study *Vedas, Upanishads,* Shrutis and epics etc. etc. was wrong. But under caste system, every off-spring, rather all off-spring of Brahmans were and still are considered epistemic and knowledgeable, though they are incompetent to read and learn Sanskrit. In their young age they will have to do some lower category jobs, but they are considered crowns of the society and are duly respected. They are given top place on the cot to sit. So the birth based caste system has entailed many social evils which have badly affected many intelligent children of the lower castes. Many so-called lower castes had have to face social degradation in the society. The upper castes have brought dirty social situations like 'purity' and 'pollution'. Purity and pollution has brought the ugly social face of untouchability in the society. A Brahman consider himself as the purest and worth of respecting person. Though, many of them commit heinous social crimes which are not committed by an untouchable. Even though such persons enjoy respectable recognition in the society. As such, the birth based caste social stratification has brought social disunity and disharmony in the society. In south, in Karnataka upper castes even avoid the shadow of lower castes. Generally in rural areas the scheduled castes reside in the outskirts of the villages. In the village of the Wrier one-third of the population was of scheduled castes. They were allotted one well to draw water to the scheduled castes. It was a very difficult job as the village is a big village. The trio-freedom fighters Late Shri Maharshi Harish Chand ji, Babu Malkhan Singh ji, Pt. Babu Ram Sharma Munde collected the scheduled castes and forced them to draw water from all twelve wells of the village. But the village Pandits instantly purified all twelve wells by dropping Ganga water and forced all thakurs of the village not to allow scheduled castes to draw water from the village wells. The sweepers were to beg water. As such, caste based social stratification has also killed the 'will power' (मनोबल) of the lower castes. On the whole they did not have agricultural land. They remained poor, and made up their mindset not to send their children to schools. After the independence their mindset changed to some extent and their children could get elementary to secondary education. They could not afford to admit their wards in colleges and universities. As such, the lower castes remained constantly backward in the field of education.

The Kshatriyas were the ruling caste of the country. The Brahmans used to be their advisers in the field of ruling. So, they always respected Brahmans. They also walked on the footsteps of Brahmans and always followed their footsteps of 'purity and pollution' which harmed the lower castes to large extent in the field of education. Though Kshatriyas (Rajputs) are farmers. They depend on agriculture for their existence. But they also behave in caste based social stratification.

The Vaishyas is a business class. They are extensively doing business. Their ethnical relationship is also limited to Brahmans and Kshatriyas (Rajputs). Generally the vocations of the Vaishyas is business and commerce.

All service castes are called Sudras. Their social relationship is based on caste structure. They are not considered as 'divijas'. The upper castes consider the lower castes as impure or dirty. So they do not take even water from their hands. They are not allowed to sit in the line of upper castes while taking lunch or dinner in marriage parties. As the Sudras or lower castes are considered as degraded community. Brahmans and other upper castes do not take food cooked by them. This social segregation has affected the social mobility of the lower castes as they could not get proper education as upper castes could get.

The upper caste Brahmans are supposed to read religious scriptures—all four *Vedas,* 121 *Upanishads,* all Brahmans, Arynakas, all epics and *Shrimad Bhagavad Gita* continuously and seriously. They are all supposed to live a very simple austerous life. They are supposed to renounce materialistic hedonism, consumerism and xenophilism. Being simple, religious, spiritualistic and epistemic, they were fit for doing rituals at special occasions. They had to perform marriage ceremonies. But now the situation has gone topsy-turvy. Many of them are unable to perform ritualistic ceremonies. At one or two or three occasions the writer had witnessed such odd situations when Panditjis doing rituals were asked to sit aside and the rituals were performed by local people who used to be Arya Samajis. But still the Panditjis are given high place in the society, even though many of them are not well-educated.

The caste social structure has also affected the Indian matrimonial structure. Every caste has to marry their sons or daughters in their own castes, though they avoid their totems (गौत्र). Inter-caste marriages are considered social crime. And at many such occasions the village Panchayats and local people behave awkwardly such people whose youngers break the barriers of castes in arranging matrimony. A Greek Philosopher, Hereclitus said that every situation change with time, the Indian matrimonial structure will also change with the passage of time.

The upper caste Brahmans generally do not like to see other caste people to do ritual performances. They anticipate if other castes are allowed to perform religious ritualistic performances, they will be set aside, and their earning of livelihood will nullified. As such, they started campaign to declare that only Brahmans are eligible to do religious ritualistic performances. The religious ritualistic performances done by other castes are not pure, so these are not acceptable by Almighty God. They also tried to declare such performances are as profane. In this context, all creative hand workers, that is, renowned citizens, though they were 'adi Brahmans' were declared Sudras. Therefore, it can be assumed that birth based caste social stratification damaged the Indian social structure and crippled the educational opportunities of the lower castes. The lower castes could not get proper education due to killing caste bias, so their social mobility could not be possible. Only the lower caste could try to get their children educated. The main purpose of the British Government was to consolidate their rule in India. For this aim they had visualised acculturation as the main tool. For this end they had introduced Western type of English formal education. By doing so, they could prepare a white collar office work force. They opened the doors of education for all irrespective of caste and creed. But in this venture only upper castes could harvest the educational crop. Lower castes could not be benefited.

It can also not be denied that caste based social stratification did not benefit the Indian people. It has also its own merits. It could provide an ethnical segmental division of the society, through which a sound community cooperative life could be possible. It has no links with class based social structure. Castes could create a homogeneous atmosphere in the society. Higher castes and lower castes mingle themselves and cooperate in their social living, in spite of the ethos of 'purity and pollution'. This is why Karl Marx had also praised the Indian caste based social structure. Till now, the castes follow their hereditical vocations in non-formal system of education which had got international praise. When the British India Government was going to impose British type of formal education on India, many members of the then Viceroy's Council had appreciated the caste-based non-formal education and also opposed the imposition of formal education. The then British Governor of erstwhile Punjab, Lahore had bluntly opposed the imposing of English type of formal education. He had argued that it would kill the Indian caste based non-formal education, which he said was one of the best system of skill acquisition through non-formal education in the world. The state is not required to spend any amount on non-formal education. As such, non-formal education was and still is the gift of caste based social stratification.

The castes in India used to have their own caste panchayats (though these are not seen these days). These panchayats used to deal with:

(*i*) Creation of professional etiquettes regarding caste vocations for professional gains in the youngers.
(*ii*) Setting rules and qualification for entry in caste panchayats.
(*iii*) Deciding the norms for acquisition of hereditary skills and teaching methods, and also setting remuneration norms.
(*iv*) Setting conditions for employment which may not hurt the fellow caste brothers.
(*v*) Setting rules of vocational ethics and imposing fine on the violation of vocational ethics as expulsion etc.
(*vi*) Dealing with many offences pertaining to eating, drinking, violation of caste rules.
(*vii*) Deciding rules regarding maintenance of caste stability and imposing fines in this regard.
(*viii*) Imposition of fine on sedition, undue behaviour with elderly ladies and with the married women.
(*ix*) Punishing for bad misbehaviour with the daughter-in-laws by the in-laws.
(*x*) To check the violation of matrimonial laws.

The caste panchayats used to lay emphasis to be very fair in dealing with the married women as, refusal of sending a married daughter and daughter-in-law, refusing to accept a woman as wife. Also the caste panchayats used to punish on payment of debt petty assaults on married wife, encroaching upon others children, killing a cow, insulting a Brahman and violating the caste customs and rules.

The entire community differs from caste to caste. According to Professor M.N. Srinivas, caste is a horizontal solidarity whereas community is a vertical solidarity, caste panchayats used to impose fine for violation of the caste rules. The punishment used to be fine in the form the feast to be given to members of the caste. The caste panchayats also used to impose fine as outcasting, by side tracking from *hukkapani* (हुक्का पानी), that is, water drinking and smoking *hukka*. The caste panchayats had some religious expectations, to pray Almighty God daily, to follow customs of marriage, to do rituals. Low castes remain in more proximity to each other. Upper castes used to impose restrictions regarding feeding and social intercourse who will accept food from whom? There are (*i*) divijas (twice born) are those who decide from whom cooked food can be taken and from whose hands water can be taken. There was a system of *kachcha* and *pakka* foods. The upper castes used to take pucca food as *puri-paratha* from certain lower castes. In lower castes there was no restrictions for taking water expecting from one or two lower castes, but for cooked foods. The caste system has some civil and religious disabilities, such as ecological segregation (चमारों, बलिहारों की बस्ती अलग), use of separate street by the Scheduled Castes, denial of entry in temples, service castes, (चमार, बलिहार) cannot render services to all, refusal of entry of Scheduled Castes in Peshwa house in Maharashtra in the evening from 3.00 P.M. to 6.00 P.M. In Tamil Nadu, a Scheduled Caste is prohibited to ride on the horse back, in many southern Indian states the Brahmans cannot pass through the low caste streets as Brahmans bows only to Brahman. In Punjab a sweeper cannot walk in the street with sweeping sticks and, in Northern India in some parts of a Brahman meets a Sudra he is not entitled for food. There were some restrictions regarding occupation such as no one can pressurise the calling below one's caste, no accepting the degrading occupation. The Brahmans were supposed to do three functions as, priestly, occupying offices in Government departments, to serve in military. Tilling of land was considered disgraceful. Only Kanaujia Brahmans were allowed to do tilling of land. Also in Rajasthan the Brahmans allowed to do every work. Endogamy was also restricted. Some specific sub-castes used to do matrimony in their sub-castes.

Indian old and new systems of education have totally failed to check these socio-economic and cultural evils, which had bifurcated the Indian society in the past so badly that we could not stand united in the hour of need against the foreigners when they invaded and occupied India, and who had made us slaves and ruled the country for more than one thousand years. The upper caste creamy layer of the Indian society remained totally immune to these socio-economic and cultural problems of the country which affected the unity and integrity of the Indian nation.

The acculturation which occurred due to western culture diffusion in Indian culture, was the gift of our foreign rulers. It converted the Indian social structure from birth based caste stratification to hedonistic class structure of the western style. A social class in any position of a community is marked by economic status—rich and poor. A class system or structure of a society involves:

1. A hierarchy of economic status;
2. Recognition of superior or inferior through social stratification;
3. Having some degree of permanently in social structure;
4. Observance of some specific cultural symbols. The class social structure has also some ethical and social factors, which can be termed as:
   Subjective factors as:
   (*a*) one believes to follow some life rules as not to steal, etc. to work for eat and be merry,
   (*b*) Use of specific language as use of English,
   (*c*) To live in a specific locality,
   (*d*) To maintain an income level,
   (*e*) To get the youngers educated,
   (*f*) To maintain cohesiveness level with the people of their status. A car owner would like to talk with a car owner. It can be assumed that the sense of status in social structure is entirely sustained by economic, religion and political power and distinctive mode of life is maintained according to the class culture.

Partial tillage of the social caste structure to social class structure in the Indian society made monopoly of rich and elite class over education. Only those who can afford to pay the hi-fi tuition fees can send their children to hi-fi education institutions, that is, to pubic schools. The running of the public schools has been totally commercialised. Running of such schools has become a source of easy earning money. The public schools are run by many of the persons who are not fully educated. In the field of business there is cutthroat competition. And in running the commercialised schools and educational institutions there is no competition. So many businessmen like to open public schools and institutions which become their permanent source of income. In the past many generous businessmen used to donate for opening educational institutions. They used to do it for common good on charity basis without any inclination. They used to believe in caste structure and not in class structure. Now-a-days many such commercial educational institutions have emerged in the country with covert business establishment. These institutions charge high fees which is unaffordable for the poor backward castes. So the scope of viable education is limited to rich class, and doors of such educational institutions always remain closed for the poor backward castes. So the children of the poor castes remain deprived of proper education. Of course, there are many Government schools, which are not considered equal to public schools. Due to the opening of many industrial training institutes in the country the non-formal education, which was once the main source of gaining skills in the family vocations has been wiped out, as certification is the only source of employment these days. Because, the youngers of the artisan, castes do not have certificates of getting training in spite of being highly skilled, they are refused employment in Government and private establishments. They remain unemployed.

As the Greek thinker Hereclitus said that everything, physical or social phenomenon is in flux. So the rigid caste system also will surely change. But the Indian politician can be blamed for keeping the caste based social stratification intact for preserving their vote banks. The politician raise the caste issue and try again and again and keep the caste consciousness alive. It is they who had appointed Mandal Commission, which had recommended some reservation for the Scheduled Castes, Scheduled Tribes and also for other backward castes. The Indian Government headed by Shri V.P. Singh had tried to implement the recommendations of the Mandal Commission. But it was strongly opposed by upper castes. Many Government buildings, like Meerut Railway Station, N.R. were badly damaged. So the implementation was dropped at that time. Now the U.P.A. Government again has proposed to implement the recommendation of Mandal Commission. It has been again opposed by the upper castes on the plea that educational development can only be possible on merit basis. They have forgotten that intelligence and diligence is not the only property of the upper castes. Anybody can be intelligent, epistemic and a contributor from any caste. The upward mobility of lower castes through proper education is becoming a distant dream in the Indian society. And the education development of all backward castes has been a serious academic crisis as upper castes have been continuously opposing the reservation facilities for the lower castes which is necessary for their upward liftment.

Many famous sociologists like Andre Betelle had earlier wrote that inequality can be studied not only in mode of existence but also in a mode of consciousness and, that in traditional systems these inequalities are closely related to inequalities among castes. Now he is blaming the Government for reservation of lower castes in educational institutions. He blames politicians about caste reservation which may vitiate the educational institutions. The caste based reservation issue does not seen to be a political crisis any more. It became a deep academic crisis marked by the fast surfacing biases of the intellectual class. The rot that has set in Indian academic can be traced to the history of modern education. History of education in India is replete with incidents of imperialists using policies to enslave the natives.

The East India Company and later the British Government believed in 'divide and rule'. They instituted a system where a handful of upper castes (divijas—twice born) could have an absolute control over the majority. The formal education system, that was imposed on us and, finally we inherited it from the British never represented neither in the Indian society nor Indian culture. The educational dispatches launched by the British Government clearly prove this. One of the dispatches said that education, culture and civilisation may descend from the higher classes to inferior classes. It would never ascend from the lower classes. Mindset of some contemporary intellectuals reflects this trend initiated by the British colonisers.

Jothirao Phule started the fight against the caste exclusion in our educational system. His book titled *'Slavery'* to the maratha world appeared by storm in 1873. It was Phule who told to the Hunter Commission in 1882 that the British were collecting revenue from Sudras (*Dalits*) to educate upper caste Brahmans. Thus, he claimed that it was atrocious and, the remedy he suggested was universalisation of primary education. Later his disciple Dr. B.R. Ambedkar demanded equality of educational opportunity from Simon Commission in 1928 A.D. It is from his memorandum one discovers the enrolment of lower castes in colleges was zero in 1882 A.D. and just one per cent in 1923-24 A.D. These facts have never been discussed in our mainstream discourses. The economist K.S. Chalam brought out the nature of apartheid in education.

University education in India has retained by and large as upper caste prerogative. Caste prejudice continued to exist in our universities in the first half of the 20th century A.D. due to no representation of lower castes. There are stories of how universities used to search the sacred threads (जनेव) (as described by Raja Sekhar Vindhru T.O.I. dated 1.6.2006) of the students to find out the identity of the students belonging to upper castes. The present anti-quota agitations are a continuance of the legacy of imperialists and few self-centred individuals. It is said that the social scientists are working for equal education for all. The Indian scholars are busy in side-tracking the lower castes in the field of education.

Education is a vehicle of change. What kind of change and progress can we anticipate in the education system which is tagged with stereo types of the few scholars. There are only few scholars who publicly talk about social inclusion. How long do we expect universities to flourish and compete, as long we keep them as islands of caste prejudices and vanities. So it is necessary that the educational institutions should be free from caste enclaves. All castes should be given equal chances for education. It is also true that all do not have equal mental capabilities. The weaker section of the any castes should be helped for getting admission. For this the weaker section of any caste should be helped through preparatory classes.

It is also true that a caste or community is availing some concessions either in the field of education or in employment, the particular community or caste members are benefited. But it affects the national development. The Scheduled Castes get 15 per cent reservation in the field of education and employment. But it is observed that the performance of many of them does not remain as good as of general category. Likewise Scheduled Tribes get 7.5% reservation like Scheduled Castes. Many of them became creamy layers of their castes. While giving such concessions the creamy layer of Scheduled Castes and Scheduled Tribes should not be given such concessions.

The other backward castes are many. Many of them are very rich. They have lot of agricultural land and other avenues. In backward castes, poor artisan castes, service castes should be given concessions. Amongst these castes there are many rich who constitute a creamy layer. They should be kept out of reservation in factories. The reservation facilities, be it in the field of education or employment, should be based on economic backwardness.

21

Education and Social Change in India

Every human society has to perform the task of transmitting its accumulated stock of knowledge, skills, beliefs, customs, cultural traits and wisdom from one generation to another and, such transmission may be called education. Such transmission motivate the youngers to self-learning which is true education. In this sense, there is educational process found in primitive tribal societies which do not possess scripts for their language, or have distinct category of teachers. The institutions of family as, joint family, extended families, ethnic kin groups and peer groups perform the basic act of education and do socialisation. The quantum of knowledge through such transmission, of course is small, but it innovates and motivates the youngers to learn more. This process leads to social change. In India and other civilised countries, there existed, from the very beginning some formal institutions for the transmission of accumulated knowledge. The social stratification of the Indian society was also reflected in its education, in both categories—the Brahmans as teachers and youngers of the upper castes as students and, artisans as teachers and their youngers as their students under non-formal systems of education. This tendency continued generally during the British rule when the educational system began increasingly to be more open. A crucial feature of modern Indian society is rapidly changing the educational system, and some of the consequences of this changing can be seen in the famous results which have serious implications for the whole Indian society.

Many developed as well as developing countries have invested good amount of money on their educational institutions. These educational institutions, are many, diversified and stratified, and entrance in these institutions is done on merit basis rather than on status considerations. Since amount of education is indispensable to the exercise of leadership roles and, in theory it is open to those who have ability and desire. The education provides indispensable avenues of social upward mobility of large number of individuals of higher caste groups as well as to lower caste groups. This fact, for modern or developed societies and for developing societies makes possible a radical transmission of desirable social values, attitudes and cultural traits in vast number of people. First democracy based on adult franchise, as well as, programmes of industrialisation, commercialisation and scientific agriculture make it almost, essential for every one to have a minimum of education, which in term affects radically their habits, beliefs, life attitudes and values, second, in many advanced and modernised countries, compulsory education has been introduced for making advanced 'welfare state'. It opened the gates of higher education for majority of the people.

The makers of Indian Constitution had included in the Constitution 'compulsory primary education', which aimed at to achieve it up to 1960 A.D., but could not be achieved till today. Indian ruling elite desired universal education as remedy for country's killing ills. According to the 1961 census the number of literates was 240 out of 1000 people. After this the number of educated persons increased. The number of rural children in classes I to V on 31st December was over 38 millions of which over 25 millions were boys and over 13 millions were girls. The number of urban children in the same classes was over 10 millions of which 6 millions were boys and over 4 millions were girls. In due course of time enrolment of the students increased at all levels. The number of graduates produced annually by the Indian universities was over one lakh.

It is necessary to draw to the dual and somewhat conflicting functions of education, especially as it is usual that one ignores another. The educational system of a country is usually looked upon as the principal instrument for the production of leaders in every walk of life. And it is believed that they will play a critical role in bringing the socio-economic development and modernisation in the country. This seemed to have happened in the case of India and, many may regard the sizeable, westernised Indian elites as the most sizeable important result of British rule.

Independence has resulted in a sharpened awareness role of the elites, and its frightening implications in the context of the magnitude, complexity and intractability of the problems the country is facing. Our educational institutions right from schools to higher educational institutions should produce the leaders who are fully aware about the socio-economic and cultural problems of the country. These educational institutions should inculcate right attitude for working and for the environment. These are necessary for generating patriotism for the country.

The second educational function stems out from the organic nature of nexus between the educational system and wider social system and its structure. The former cannot but reproduce within itself the essential characteristics of the latter. This point is significant as its implications run counter to some facile assumptions made by the politicians and reformers regarding the role and ability of the educated to transform their society. How such transformation can be brought out if the educational system is not viable. But for the equalities a sound system is necessary. The educational system cannot remain pure and unsullied if the wider section of the society is not. When the wider society is corrupt, it is likely that vice-chancellors, principals, teachers, students and even the administrative staff are going to be chosen on consideration of other aspects than ability, qualification and right aptitudes. The acculturation which made man money minded and mutilated religiosity, spirituality and simplicity is the prime reason for this kind of corruption. Progress in the educational system requires the educational qualities other than the purely academic or intellectual. In other words the system requires the individual qualities other than the purely academic or intellectual. In other words the educational system should have been developed for devices necessary for rooting out inefficiency, favouritism and corruption from the society. A corrupt and inefficient society cannot bring necessary social change. A good viable education system is necessary for rooting out all these from the society.

Coming to specific points, if able students and teachers are excluded from universities on the grounds of criteria such as caste, religion, language, domicile and, if only political influence becomes a sole criterion in the promotion and appointment of teachers to higher positions, the resultant atmosphere of the universities and other institutions be impaired. Such situation is not frequent, it is becoming a common feature in the society. Inter-relationship between educational institutions and society, as existed in olden days is necessary.

In olden days all educational institutions of higher learning as Nalanda, Taxila, Vallabhi and Ujjaini etc. etc. were run by the society. There was no state control over these institutions of learning. So interrelationship between educational system and the wider society is an educational necessity for viable social change. A change is must. Greek thinker Hereclitus said, A changing society makes new demands for which a viable educational system is necessary. Without proper educational system a social change can never be possible Educational system, before the World War II, was tailored for the aspirations of a relatively small, privileged and largely urban section of the population which used to be prepared for white-collar employment in the government departments or enter in other professions. In independent India, however, lakhs of people, especially from under-privileged sections of the society, are seeking education not only to gain economic mobility but to gain social and political mobility. Education has always been an important means for individual to emancipate themselves from the tyrannies and indignities of the lost caste system. This is why the backward castes always desire to educate their youngers.

Changes of a fundamental kind have occurred in Indian sub-continent during the one hundred and fifty years of British rule. During British rule a sense of self-consciousness emerged at several levels ranging from village, caste, sect., religion, towns to the entire country. Increased self-consciousness meant a sensitivity to criticism from outsides, a desire to discard outdated customs, institutions, ideas and beliefs which lowered the groups prestige before outsiders, and to adopt features which were necessary to enhance their prestige. The new sense of self-consciousness also led to the founding of schools, colleges, hostels, orphanages, housing cooperatively and other social welfare institutions. In understanding these types of social activities people were influenced deeply by the Christian missionaries. The Rama Krishna Mission, Dayanand Anglo-Vedic Sansthan, Sanatan Dharam Sansthan, Khalsa Panth played a vital role in establishing several educational institutions. Also the Aligarh-Muslim University, the Banaras Hindu University and the Lingayat (now Karnataka)

Education Society of Peninsular India were established to improve the socio-economic conditions of the respective groups. Besides these, individual castes such as Brahmans, Rajputs, Jats, Nadars (नादर) raised schools, colleges and hostels and, resources were raised mainly from members of the castes concerned. It is necessary to add here that when a religious group or sect started an educational institution, it did not think of excluding any student on denominational ground. Preference was given to the members of the religion, sect or ethnic group or caste, also they in many case enjoyed fee concessions but there was no attempt to exclude others. In the selection of staff all preference was given to members of the sect. However, the institutions could not help becoming of religious sect and caste loyalty. When the products of these institutions entered or joined the government service they could not help or act as the promoters of the interests of their groups. Religious dogmatism promoted communal and caste politics.

The desire of upward mobility for capturing power and popularity helped the educational development. The backward castes realised clearly that power was indispensable for their socio-economic upward upliftment which was not possible without proper education. Therefore, they thought of educational facilities. The knowledge of backward classes movement is indispensable for the spread of education. Two, more or less, distinct phases may be traced, which were used for caste mobility. In the first phase, an individual caste tried to claim a higher caste status that was often conceded by other castes in local hierarchy. This was preceded by change in life style through sanskritisation. The caste concerned even changed its name for achieving higher caste status. This was an effort of changing caste identity. The second effort was to bring change for social mobility, for that the castes secular credentials, which were essential for attaining high status, political power and education. For these sanskritisation also became essential for lower castes. The mode of sanskritisation was important for gaining higher status in caste structure and for attaining desirable social change for upper social mobility in social stratification. Sanskritisation needs to be adopted some life styles of upper castes, ways of religiosity and certain amount of cultural traits of westernisation in order to be acceptable by all social milieu. It can be said that sanskritisation involves the rejection of the position traditionally accorded to the caste, realisation of the position desired for upper status. And adoption of ways of living of the upper castes as (*a*) reading of religious books regularly, (*b*) doing puja and yajna regularly, (*c*) eating vegetarian food, (*d*) wearing sacred thread and for all this regularity in life—early to bed, early to rise and to take bath are necessary. All this implies self-awareness, a spirit of defending the caste and its leaders and also upward mobility in economic affairs and improvement in living conditions. It also needs greater contacts with other castes. And for all these aspects of 'sanskritisation' proper education plays a vital role.

In the context of collective social mobility, then, sanskritisation has been relegated to the position of an appendage to the things that are more central. It is logical to infer from the above process that the overall social system has undergone a considerable degree of secularisation since the beginning of 20th century. The immediate context of this significant development is interesting. It could also happen due to the development of educational opportunities. It was the outcome of the decision of the British rulers to transfer power gradually to Indians, and at the same time to protect the interests of religious, ethnic, and minorities, and also unprivileged sections of Hindu society, through the system of 'communal electorate' and reservation of seats in legislative and local self-governing bodies. About the measures introduced under the Montagu-Chelmsford Reforms 1919 to protect the minority interests, Berridale Kaith said, "It was reluctantly felt necessary to continue communal electorate for Muslims and grant the Europeans minority status to Anglo-Indians where their number was considered for such action in Madras alone. Anglo-Indians in Bengal, Europeans in all provinces, except Punjab, Central Province and Assam, for land holders and for commerce and industry were given this status. And further compilation arose in the necessity of reserving seats for non-Brahmans in Madras in view of the predominance there of Brahmans, who though 3 to 4 per cent of the total population/electorate, had secured practically complete representation in the legislative. The reservation proved needless.

The caste mobility was seen in peninsular India from roughly 1910 to 1960. The backward castes movement in South India brought about this change. It happened due to education, which lead to the understanding of the cultural, social and economic upward mobility which brought total social change in South India. Education could sharpen self-awareness among the backward castes and made them conscious for more education.

The backward castes movement was the result of social discrimination against the backward castes. Firstly, the existence of a small body of Brahmans (not exceeding 3 or 4% of the total population) owning land in rural areas, who had tradition of learning and a distinctive style of life tradition of their own. They used to observe the social evil of 'purity and pollution'. They were the first to take advantage of English education and, as a result enjoy a near monopoly of employment on government posts, and politics. These were the main reason of the unity and collectivity of non-Brahman castes. These non-Brahman castes formed a collective group of backward castes for fighting the monopoly Brahmans. These backward castes became conscious about proper education. These castes got their youngs educated, who in due course of time captured the political power and continuously are occupying state administration. It is a "grab all" category uniting all non-Brahman Hindus, Muslims, Christians and Anglo-Indians. Since Madras (present Tamil Nadu) in those days was a composite province, castes speaking different languages—Tamil, Telugu, Malayalam, Kannada and Tulu were involved in the non-Brahman movement. During the discussions preceding the introduction of Montagu-Chemlsford Reforms, all these groups demanded reservation of seats in the legislatures, executive council and a Government posts. The Brahmans never realised the bad effects of their irrational, illogical and universal blind observance of "purity and pollution". These groups had the strong support of the British administrators who were opposed to the nationalist movement which was dominated by the Brahmans. Though Northern India was no so awkward as it was South. The principle of reservation one introduced in the legislative came to be extended every where—to local governing bodies, to posts in the Governments, in colleges, to scholarships and fee concession. It happened due to the rigidity of "purity and pollution" which ultimately resulted in the division of the country at the time of independence. The British believed in 'divide and rule' and 'caste quotas' got widespread acceptance, which boosted education as without education nothing was possible. The caste quota system was introduced in Gram Panchayats also. In fact the Indian

Constitution was amended in early fifties vide Article 15(4) in order to safeguard the principle of caste quota. It was only in 1960s that the principle of reservation of posts and seats in educational institutions to the backward castes and classes was accepted in addition to Scheduled Castes and Tribes. This was done under the twin pressures of the Home Ministry of the Government of India and judiciary decisions.

The backward castes movement of South India activated every one including the poorest amongst the Scheduled Castes, and the capture of political power was indispensable to socio-economic mobility. It should be remembered in this connection that the self-respect movement by the non-Brahman leader Shri E.V. Ramaswamy Naicker in 1925, caught the imagination of the people by attempts to erase the word "Brahman" from declaring sign boards above shops like "Brahman Coffee Hotel", to use pure Tamil in place of mixed Sanskrit, to prevent the singing of Telugu songs before the Tamil audience, to break the image of popular deity Ganpati, to burn the copies of Tamil classic Ramayana, written by the great poet Kambar; and finally to show contempt towards Brahmans by abusing them, teaming their sacred thread and cutting off their 'Shikha' (चोटी). This also entailed conflicts between upper caste 'Brahmans' and lower castes and also between lower castes.

The backward caste movement was the result of education which created self-conscious among the non-Brahmans not only in South India but in North India also the spirit of self-consciousness in the lower backward amongst them. It created a pool of educated men in backward lower castes who become aggressive spokesmen for their castes and for the movement as a whole. In other words, education made them very able and aggressive against the upper castes who were exploiting them through the wrong concept of 'purity and pollution' and to 'churn up' poor illiterate and low status group of low castes who had long reconciled to their social degradation by the upper castes. It changed their aspirations and prepared them for participation in the political process. It had the character of cultural revolution. But it could not stop western cultural diffusion which brought acculturation.

Nothing comparable to South India backward caste movement occurred in North India. This raises question whether the North

Indian backward castes remain uneducated? Caste structure is a pan-Indian social structure. Then why South Indian backward castes came forward to challenge the upper caste Brahmans? This is because they more suppressed and were more educated. The North Indian lower castes belonged to different ethnic groups. They could not be united, so could not bring a social change as South Indian backward castes did.

One of the reasons for the absence of backward castes movement is that the position of Brahmans in North was not comparable to that of Brahmans in the South. The cultural differences between the Brahmans and other lower castes were not significant, nor were the pre-eminent in Western education and new occupations. Some castes such as Kayasthas, Rajputs and Vaishyas seem to have been more prominent than the Brahmans. Also two or three castes besides Brahmans were also significant. These castes were Kayasthas, Kshatriyas and Vaishyas. So, no single group was so conscious by its success. They were all combined to beat the inequalities.

It is well-known that the people of Calcutta (Kolkata) got western education and thought and also in commerce because the English people started governance from Calcutta. The intermingling of Bengali's with the Bihari, Oriyas and Assamese resulted in diffusion of Bengali culture which entailed the unity and amity in the region. The shifting of the capital of India from Calcutta to Delhi in 1911 also helped in the spread of Bengali inteligencia to the towns and cities of U.P. and Punjab. But exploitation of lower castes continued. In brief, it would be fair to conclude that the educated Bengalis called 'bhadralok' who were strongly represented in the administration and in the professions, enjoyed power. But due caste phobia of this area was divided in five distinct entities one of which East Bengal had become part of Pakistan.

As such, it can be concluded that education has brought social change in every field of human life. Because of Western English education the Indians could unite. They started political movements and gained national independence. Earlier the main aim of social human life was to be religious and spiritual. Man used to believe in simple living and high thinking for common good. Because of education the men gained proficiency in many fields. Now they are able to earn livelihood and enjoy life. 'Earn more and enjoy more' has become the human life aim. Many of the men became elites which entailed alienation, segregation and self-centredness. Due to western type of education the present man has become totally accultured. The class structure has taken the place of caste structure. The institution of joint family has been crumbled. Family relationships have totally gone. Now the present man has become totally self-centred. Earlier the Indian education aimed at preparing the younger for living a sane social life. The present social aim has totally faded away social homogeneity, integrity and cooperation.

22

Effects of Gender Bias in Education

All human-beings and other living beings as animals, beasts, birds, insects and bees, etc. are bio-diversified, that is, have different genders and are called males and females. And 'unity in bio-diversity', that is, union of males and females, both in human-beings and other living beings, make their existence possible. Demographic figures of males and females are more or less equal. The man and woman are united through the institution of marriage and they live together life long. They have sex and produce the younger ones. In human-beings, they are very few who are infertile and non-breeding. They are called 'Hizde' (हिजड़े), and Kinner in Punjab. Human-beings both do more or less equal duties and are entitled for equal rights. But many girls are denied education facilities due to gender bias.

The term 'gender bias' is a combination of two words 'gender' and 'bias'. The word gender is a derivation from 'French' and 'Latin' words — 'generi' and 'genus', meaning, a 'kind' or 'sort' or 'a sex', 'a male or female', or 'a category of differentiation of living beings', or 'of human beings'. All males are 'mascular genders' and all females are 'familial genders'. Both have retrospective sex organs to capitulate to have sex and breed. One has to give another has to accept. The unity of male and female is 'unity in bio-diversity' reproduction which makes social existence possible. Males and females in human-beings, in spite of being bodily topsy-turvy, live together lifelong and in hand and glove contribute and reproduce future members of the society who make social living possible. The word 'bias' is also derivation of 'French' and 'Latin' words 'biasis' and 'biafix' meaning 'weight or load tilted to one side', 'prejudice', 'to treat in a startling manner', or 'oligarchy'.

Both the males and the females are different genders, who have different topsy-turvy body structures to discharge different life roles. The body of the male is broader at his shoulders. He is supposed to do difficult manual work. The body of the female is broader at her hips as she is supposed to bear a child and keep the child in her womb for nine months. The topsy-turvy bodies of males and females are indicative of their different life roles. The union of male and female is must. Without their union human life is not possible in the world. As such, because of their union the males and females should get equal rights and opportunities to grow and to sustain in their lives. But, generally in many cases it does not happen. Women, being bodily weaker than men are generally not well-treated by men in all societies. In some sections of the human beings, throughout the world, women are beaten and tortured by their life partners. Generally, it is seen that there is a gender bias against the women. As such, the women are not well-treated throughout the world, in many cases. And there are some social reasons for this universal spread of gender bias. A few of these are mentioned below:

Patriarchal Social Structure

Generally all social structures, excepting a very few, where matriarchal structure is found in the world, are patriarchal. In a patriarchal social structure men play a vital role in family management. So, they generally remain dominant in household affairs. The women being bodily weaker than men are not generally treated by men, rather they are often tortured by their husbands. *The Times of India*, dated 23.7.2005 reported in *Delhi Times* that a husband started beating his wife on the first day after their union and continued beating her till she went back to her parents. This is not a solitary case of beating, torture and harassment of a wife by her husband. Many such cases are noted in all societies. In a patriarchal society, the girls are born and brought up by their parents. When they become young they are married with the young boys of other families. The institution of marriage is an institution of binding together a young girl and a young boy. Though marriage an 'unity in bio-diversity' is materialised. The girls after their marriage say goodbye to their parents and live their parental homes forever. They go with their husbands to the house of their in-laws and live there lifelong. So the girls are always considered anta-property (पराया धन). This is why many parents of the girls slip their parental duty and do not treat the girls well equally to their boys. The girls are considered inferior to the boys and are not given attention and care as given to the boys. Though, now in many educated families, the girls' education is given prime importance. The girls are socially equal. From the very beginning the girls have been respected in their parental families. In all sections of the society the virgin girls have ever been respected not only by their parents and family members but by the whole community. Some elders even do not eat the cooked food by the virgin girls. In India most of the rivers are named after the names of girls. These rivers are Ganga, Yamuna, Gomti, Godavari, Krishna, Triveni and Tapti etc. etc. Not only in India, in Sri Lanka, a river, on which bank Colombo, the capital of Sri Lanka is situated is named as 'Kalyani' river. Many goddesses like Vaishno Devi, Chandumain Devi, Kali etc. etc. are worshipped in India. But, mostly girls of the poor families are denied school education. It is estimated that about ten per cent girls of such families are enable to see the gates of the village primary schools. Many parents made their mindset that the girls will have to go to another homes, so they are 'anta-property' (पराया धन) and there is no use to get them educated. Many parents got afraid of some bad social elements, so they do not dare to send their girls outside homes. Many think the girls will have to be housewives and will look after their household and children they should be trained in the management of house in the family.

Marriage and Dowry System

Marriage is a culturally approved relationship of a man and a woman who are biological topsy-turvy. So marriage is a process of 'unity in bio-diversity'. Marriage leads to parenthood. It is the genesis of family, community and society. It legalises the sexual relationship between wife and husband which is a requisite requirement for pregnancy for the birth of a child. So marriage is must for existence. Though marriage is a matri-centre, which consists of father, mother, children and other family members like grand parents, uncles and aunts. This kind of 'unity in bio-diversity' is a common feature. All living beings—human beings, animals do this kind of 'unity in bio-diversity' for existence. But only human-beings, being rational beings, do such unity under sane social, culturally established social norms.

In India, under such socially and culturally established norms, the priests prepare rules for the marriage of the young boys and girls which is arranged according to astrologer's advice. The priest asks if anybody has objection to the proposed marriage. Marriage ritual ceremony starts. Bride's father washes the grooms feet. The priest recites the holy hymn-mantras. A sacred fire (अग्निहोत्री) is arranged. The priest recites holy mantra equating the groom equal to Lord Vishnu. The bride's father presents his daughter in grooms' lap (कन्यादान) and finally gives his daughter as a gift to the groom binding them for living together lifelong happily. The groom wears three sacred threads (जनेऊ) symbolic to three pledges — love and affection, protection and permanent life long union of bride and bridegroom. Bride's sari is tied with groom's patka. Couple go around the sacred fire (हवन कुंड) seven times. The marriage is solemnised. And the present audience greet them by reciting an *arti* (आरती) called *manglacharan* (मंगलाचरण). Audience present at the marriage ceremony jointly pray for the long and prosperous life of the couple. They shower rice and barley over the couple. And the bride goes to the house of the groom permanently. This is why the girls are considered 'anta property'. Though in the beginning the bride stays for few days. Her brothers bring her back. Again the astrologer decides for her *gona* (गोना) or nuptial ties. After this the bride goes with her husband's house permanently. All this ritualistic procedure confirm that the bride-groom is put on higher paddle and the bride is put on lower level. The bridegroom is considered as protector of his wife or placed at a giving end, and the bride is put on a receiving end. This shows a clear 'gender bias' against the fair sex. But the Indian marriage system is considered best in the world. Many western couples come to India for arranging their marriages as per Indian rituals. They believe that if they married in Indian way there will not be the agony of diverse. The writer had witnessed such views. In August, 1964, Late Prof. P.K. Roy, the then Principal, Central Institute of Education, Delhi, had deputed the writer to work with a USAID team headed by Dr. Arthur William Earl and learn to prepare the teaching aids and use these in teaching for self-learning. After completing the six months period working with the USAID twice a week on Tuesdays and Thursdays. The writer invited Dr. Arthur

William Earl at his residence for tea. The writer had presented him a wooden sculpture prepared by the writer. As a reciprocation Dr. Arthur William Earl had invited him to his residence at 5 Golf Links, New Delhi on the coming Sunday. The writer accepted the invitation. He went to his residence on the coming Sunday. As Dr. Arthur William Earl had to go to the church. He asked his wife to offer the water, tea and refreshment. While having refreshment and tea, Mrs. Arthur William Earl asked the writer, "Please tell me what is the reason, the Indian marriages are permanent". The writer put a counter question 'why she was asking this question'? She replied that she was divorced three times earlier and Dr. Arthur William Earl was her fourth husband. She was fed up with the divorcing tendency. So Indian marriage was considered, and is considered a pious system of 'unity in bio-diversity' in the world.

But dowry system has always added some very bad evils in the Indian 'unity in bio-diversity. It has totally crippled the women education. Bridegrooms' parents not only expect but demand huge dowry from the bride's parents, who in turn do not spend too much on girls' education. So dowry system had added fuel to the 'gender bias' in the Indian society. In olden days, the dowry system was not prevalent in India. Like this many other countries also did not have dowry system. The word 'dowry' is the derivation from the Latin word 'dower' meaning a gift given to a bride at the time of her marriage. In the West, in European countries, there was a social custom to give gifts to the girls at the time of their marriage. People used to buy beautiful artistic handicraft items from the Indian handicraft traders who used to sell Indian handicraft items in European countries. These Indian handicraft traders brought the idea of 'dower' from the Western countries. They had also spread the idea of 'dower' in Arabian countries and also in India. Now, the dowry system has become a killing, social evil. The Arabians and the Indians started giving 'dowers' to their daughters on the occasion of their marriages. Now, the dowry has become a killing virus for the fair sex. And the parents of the girls are responsible for this killing social evil. All Indians, irrespective of castes and creeds, have to give dowry on the occasion of the marriages of their daughters. The dowry system has tilted the resources of the girls parents totally topsy-turvy. Because of the rules of marriage the girls are to be married in other family where they are supposed to live life long. The girls parents always try to find a very suitable boy for their daughters. This is why they always try to give suitable dowry. And the groom's parents put a dowry demand before the marriage is settled. And the situation has become so dangerous that the dowry demand has become a common social feature. Since the girls are 'anta-property', they have to be married and sent to another homes, the parents of the girls have to manage the dowry at any cost. Even after giving the dowry on the occasion of marriage of their daughters and their parents face very dangerous situations. If the dowry thrust is not satisfied, the in-laws may continue to harass their daughter-in-laws for bringing more and more dowry. And due to this many daughter-in-laws are brutally murdered. As such, many parents consider having a daughter is a great unhappening. After the birth of daughter, an atmosphere of sorrow is observed in many families, because due to the menace of dowry girl babies are considered a great financial burden. Due to this reason many girl babies are eliminated due to foeticide. And those who allow the girls to take birth consider it inauspicious happening by the Divine authority. They do not celebrate the births of the girls as are celebrated on the occasion of the boys. It can also not be denied that the girls, that is, the further women are the genesis of the human society, but they are the victims of gender bias. And dowry is one of important reason of this gender bias, which affects girls' education badly.

Institution of Marriage

In Indian human society in the past the marriage of the boys and girls were arranged in a simple manner through *Gandharva Vivah* (गंधर्व विवाह) by the parents of both sides. This system was generally prevalent in the whole poor and middle castes of the society. The marriage of a boy and a girl is decided by the parents of both sides. While deciding 'unity in bio-diversity' the totems (गोत्र) of mothers and fathers of both sides used to be different. The groom side, used not to demand any dowry. After the settlement, both sides used to go nearby Rishi Ashramas for solemnising the marriage rituals. The girls' side used to arrange a very simple vegetarian *bhoj* (लंगर) in Rishi Ashrama. After solemnising the marriage ceremony, the audience used to bless the newly married couple with a recitation of *manglacharan* (मंगलाचरण) and used to give a coin as a gift to the girl. After this the audience used to do a common prayer for the long prosperous happy life of the couple and, for leading an auspicious model married life. And after the marriage ceremony, the groom side used to treat the bride as their own important family member. As such, there was no gender bias at all. Now, the greed of dowry has made the situation topsy-turvy.

Life Roles

All living beings, be it animals, beasts, birds, insects, bees or human beings, that is, men and women have to play some specific life roles. They play these roles gender-wise. All fair or familial genders, that is women, have to play familial roles, generally as bearing the children, bringing them up and to manage the household affairs. Both man and woman used to cooperate in playing these life roles. They live together throughout their lives. But, in other living beings this does not happen. Their union is very short, only for reproduction. In human beings, the women specifically play familial roles, and majority of them remain within the four walls of the house. The men supposed to do muscular roles. They are supposed to earn for sustaining the family. As such, the family roles performed by women are not considered as important as that of men. They are considered weaker than the men. But in the present hedonistic age many women do earning and play familial roles also. But the man being stronger rarely help his wife in family role. And many do not help their wives. This is nothing but gender bias.

Human Psyche

Human psyche also plays a very positive role in establishing and perpetuating gender bias in human-beings that is, bias against women by men. The Almighty God has made both men and women as rational beings. They both can think, rationalise and act logically. But the nature or the Almighty God has empowered the human-beings with greed and self-centredness. Generally majority of the human-beings, excepting very few, become mad for the self-interests, for meeting hedonistic desires, these entail greed. And very limits for attainment of their desires. They cross all borders for attaining their self-interests. Man can go against woman and, woman also can go to any extent against her life partners. Very shameful happenings occur in the society due to greedy psyche of the human beings. As man is physically well-built and is stronger than woman, he usually tries to exploit the woman being weaker than him. Many men exploit women by applying unusual, unsocial and barbarous behaviour towards their life partners. Not only this, many barbarous (jungli) men do not hesitate in raping their own daughters and daughter-in-laws and women of old age. In cities like Delhi it is very risky for women of all ages to go out of their houses. Recently a seventy years old woman was raped by a twenty-three years old boy. Rapes and molestations, especially of young women and minor girls have become a common feature in the present hedonistic-materialistic society. All this can be termed nothing but 'gender bias' against women by men. In the present patriarchal social structure, girls being weak and 'anta property' (पराया धन), female is married to a male life partners and are thrown in their in-laws' houses like bio-garbage. After the marriage, generally the girls are abandoned. Nobody tries to be kind, affectionate and remember their girls. *The Times of India* dated 23.7.2005 reported that a mother had left her four years of daughter in Deccan Express at Church Gate Railway Station in Mumbai. When the train was being shunted for being placed in a railway yard, after sometime, the girl started weeping. A cooley heard the crying baby girl. He picked up the girl and took her to the Station Superintendent, who sent the girl to child care department in the Sir J.J. Hospital, Mumbai. Such treatment shows gender bias against women by women. So, especially the girls are becoming victims of gender bias from the very beginning. First they are not well-treated in their parental homes and later on they face similar problems in their new homes, that is, in their house of in-laws (ससुराल). There is an urgent need to meet this fallacy. This can be done through proper education of both males and females of the society.

Role of Education to Face the Gender Bias

Gender bias against woman by man is a very serious chronic problem. It is a social evil. It can neither be rooted out by enforcement of civil laws nor by social decrees. It can only be rooted out by changing the mindsets of both man and woman. They should be fully made aware about this social evil. This can only be done by educating them about the present 'gender bias' against the women by men in the society and about its killing implications on Indian culture and civilisation. The education should start at initial stage of education, that is, through familial education and during school teaching. The school teaching due to examination system is overloaded with the teaching of few students, and enculturation of the students is generally ignored. Mere subjects teaching cannot bring social change. Complete epistemological knowledge concerning sociological, economical, political, axiological and teleological arenas pertaining to 'gender bias' is required for both men and women. Above all these women should be made aware about the evil effects of 'gender bias'. A few aspects of gender bias are given below:

(a) Sociological Aspects of Gender Bias

Sociologically both men and women are two parts of a sociological unit, which we call family. Their biological union, which is an 'unity in bio-diversity', is for happy lifelong living and producing new human beings, the future members of the society. As such, the union of man and woman is most important. The genesis of human beings lies in both. Both the roles of woman are important as she is the birth giver and sustainers of the future guardians. As such, the woman is the equal partner of the human social unit called family, then why should there be gender bias against woman by man? The man and woman should know about their social rights. This should be done at all levels right from familial up to higher level. They should also be educated about their life roles.

(b) Economical Aspects of Gender Bias

From the very beginning the man is considered most viable to earn and contribute in household sustenance. As such, he is considered fit to earn for the maintenance of the family. And the woman is supposed to manage and run household. Because the man earns, he considers himself superior than woman. But, now in many families, this situation has totally changed. The women are not behind men in earning. Even though their male partners consider themselves superior to their female partners. They do not cooperate in the household work. In spite of earning the ladies to do all household work, which is very burdensome. In such a situation the gender bias is illegal.

(c) Political Aspects of Gender Bias

Due to gender bias the women are generally devoid of their political rights by men. Very few women get chance to become members of political bodies like Gram Panchayats, municipalities, municipal corporations, state assemblies and Parliament, which are temples of our democracy. The women should be given a chance to become members of these bodies according to their demographic picture. For so many years there has been a hue and cry that women should get at least 33 per cent seats in these bodies. But still, it appears a mere show. Also, there is a whispering in the society for empowerment of women, which also appears a mere show. Indian demographic scape shows that women are equal in numbers to men. Therefore, there should not be any kind of discrimination against women community, which can be a sad gender bias.

(d) Axiological Aspects and Gender Bias

Axiology is the science of ethics and morality which entails, sanity, morality, sociability, social homogeneity and above all good behaviour, love and affection, sharing and cooperation. For all these mothers should inculcate good life attitudes in their children through familial education. They should innovate and motivate their children to develop good life habits, work habits, sane socio-cultural traits and good sound behaviour. The children should be motivated to speak true, to avoid unnecessary greed, to respect the elders and the fair sex. The girls should be prepared to follow all these life attitudes in their new permanent homes, that is *sasural* (ससुराल). The youngers should be asked to respect their siblings. Simple living and high thinking should be the base of inculcation of good life attitudes. Equality should also be given due importance. After this familial education the school also educate the youngers about these axiological attitudes about including women.

(e) Teleological, Knowledge and Gender Bias

Until and unless the youngers know the teleological, that is truth about the living beings and flora and fauna, that all these are the creation of the Almighty God. The Almighty God is present in all, in all living beings in the form of soul (जीवात्मा) which is part of the bigger soul (परमात्मा). As such all living beings are equal in this physical world. Everybody is immortal. Therefore one should not harress or exploit or ignore anybody. Teleologically the gender bias is against the Divine authority, that is, Almighty God. As such, all women should be equally treated and respected. They should not be discriminated at any stage. The youngers should be educated about this teleological truths from the very beginning at home and later on at educational institutions through related co-curricular activities. The gender bias, be it against woman or man is illogical and it should be avoided.

(f) Self-Defencing

And finally the women should be trained in self-defencing at schools and colleges levels by the physical education teachers. They should train the girls in karatas, jogging and self-defencing techniques, so that, they may combat the criminals.

23

Enculturation through Education

Enculturation is a process of cultural development through inculcation of good life habits, like good life attitudes, work-habits, good behaviour, aestheticity, good character, customs, love and affection and dedication to the nation, perpetuation of these and preservation of the national culture. National culture of any nation is said to be the soul of nation. Any nation without its own culture cannot survive. So it is very necessary to preserve the national culture of any nation. Also the culture is likely to face many challenges which may be caused due to cultural diffusion, which always entails acculturation. Therefore, it is very necessary to enculturate the younger generation very perfectly and sincerely. For doing enculturation, the complete knowledge about culture and its related concepts like cultural diffusion, sources of cultural diffusion which result in acculturation is very necessary. This also follow the methods to check the cultural diffusion and resultant acculturation. All this is very necessary to protect the national culture. As such, it is very necessary to know about all these aspects in detail.

Culture—Its Evolution

According to Ralph Linton, "the culture is the embodiment of good sane human behaviour, sound character, customs, sociability, social traditions, cultural traditions and traits and artistic art and craft activities". All these enable the human-beings to lead good saneful social living and finally to the development of civilisation of the nation. Good culture of a nation makes the nation civilised.

The word 'culture' is a derivation from the Latin words 'cultura' and 'cultus', which mean 'care', 'cultivation', 'fostering', 'adornment to worship'. Both words are used in functional sense. Since the Indian culture is the oldest in the world its equivalent Sanskrit word 'Sanskriti' was used, and is still used in India. In functional sense, the word 'cultura' refers to agriculture, that is, tilling of the land. The origin of the word 'cultura' is supposed to be very old when tilling of the land might have been started by man for producing some 'crops' for human use. And for the good harvest of the crops when worship of the God was referred to as "Agricultura Devi' or 'Agricultural God', as usually the man used to worship some super power for the fulfillment of his needs.

Cicero described culture as 'cultura animi', that is, cultivation of human mind. In this sense there are various attributable functional uses of the words 'cultura' and 'cultus', which fused into general and substantive term 'culture'. And people now find 'culture' as contrary to 'barbarism'—a change from attributive to social significance. In the specific conditions, the man who, in spite of being rational, becomes irrational for his personal ends and self-interest ignores the social trends. This trend becomes a killer of culture.

The term culture becomes synonymous to and, interchangeable with terms, such as, 'humanitus' meaning humanity and 'civilas' meaning civility, urbanite meaning urbanity and ruralites meaning rurality. In Germany, the term 'Kultua', evolved from German philosophical term 'Biding' or Binding. Now the concept of culture evolved from 16th century A.D. on the ground territorial states. In this regard the political thinkers gave their opinions about the national denominations of specific customs, style of life and institutions regarding culture. John Bodin (a French thinker) thought that different Republics contributed in the development of respective culture. Montesquie and Voltaire thought that the styles of life and ways of living contributed in the development of specific cultures. Anthropologists adopted the term culture in specific sense for the tribal groups they explored. As the evolution of specific culture has a vast history and culture seems as a general state and stage of human existence. It carries a value commutation which is considered equivalent to superiority over state of plain culture—over barbarism and beastalism. In the past, it was an intellectuals and moral criticism to measure the worth and dignity of the individual and people. And culture was considered tantamount to the development and for the progress and betterment of human conditions. Development of culture means unwrapping and evolution of certain new means of unfolding.

Aristotle regarded organic nature—the vegetal, the animal and the human nature as consecutive evolutionary stages which occur as periodical reoccurrences. The idea of historic evolution did not exist before the Hellenistic period. Jews visualised man's unconscious state and found conscious state Christianity believes that divine saviour lead to divine solutions. And finally when at the end of middle age when the rule of Christian dogma crumbled. Through the scientific, rational, technological and industrial development, human living conditions improved. Christian protestant movement and Calvinism developed human belief in historical development, improved human living conditions which boosted respective culture. Since the beginning of 19th and later on 20th century, man saw dark reverse due to expanding rational enlightenment, growing collectivism and dehumanisation which industrialisation entailed. These also entailed abrupt stamp of humanity because of rationalised barbarism. Other factors which disrupted the proper development of culture were historical hypertrophy of historians which occurred under the scientific positivism, as all criterion of facts lost. Spengler and Toynbee were most conspicuous of anti-historical and anti-evolutionary trends.

Emile Durkhiem and Levy Brudle, anthropologists too adopted anti-evolutionary attitudes due to radical positivism. But the concept of evolution regarding culture development could not be given up. There is a confusion between evolution and progress. Progress implies a value statement, which means improvement. Evolution denotes a plainly factual progress an advancement only of material conditions, but also of happiness and morality of actions done according to reason. Biological theories identified evolution with progress. Huxley says that human individual is the final perfection of evolution. Now-a-days we eliminate the notion of progress from the concept of evolution. Recent scientific findings show that nature is continuous process. This thesis goes against the anti-revolutionist movement. Axistonomy is historical science. Biological science is a continuous progress of a biological whole. History of life is like a tree, like growth of multifarious ramifications. Gap between organic and inorganic is crumbling.

It is evolution which evolved mean from the cradle of amreba and produced personalities like Buddha, Jesus, Dante, Shakespeare, Newton and Eienstein. Then what is evolution? Gaylord Simpson said that the tendency of human life is to expand by filling all the available spaces in liveable environment and, doing improvement in adaptations, control over environment, increasing structural complications and progress in individualisation etc. etc. The cultural evolution has to play a definite role in the development of culture. Man is the highest animal. Being rational, he is capable to visualise and to do judgment what is good or bad for living, inheritance and learning the man can decide. Jullus Huxley says that "the human being not only is but will continue to be the highest product of evolution". He defines, "Evolution is an increase in complexity, in organisation, self-regulation and greater knowledge".

Evolution appears as a gradual, consistent extension of scope, extension range of human-being with all differentiations interpretations of experiences, a process of inter-orientation, transformation of internal and external extensive contents into internal intense organism. Stoics called evolution two process 'diastole' and 'systole'.

Human life is such a biological whole consisting concentration, internalisation, introspection of physical elements, successive element of molecules, cells, having a continuous process of living through transformation. Gaylord Simpson says that all plants are human. Life develops through internalisation of metabolics and formation of internal nervous system. Integration goes hand in glove with differentiations.

The Relation Between Individual and Group in the Process of Evolution

There remains closer connections between the individual and the society. The individual is part of the society. So human existence is a multi-level affair. And culture plays a dominant role in this regard. Historical survey of human culture shows that:

(*i*) Culture is a human living condition which implies a value (what is cultivated in man or woman).

(*ii*) A value based life of people as Kroeber says it is a totality of customs based life of people.
(*iii*) Anthropologists say culture is an ethnic entity—pure, simple and modern.
(*iv*) Leo Frobenius says that culture is regional meta-ethnic entity. It is pure and simple.

All these evolutionary (I, II, III and IV) stages have different evolutionary aspects reflect human self-realisation. These are diverse organic coherence of ethnic groups, pre-suppose, Judeo-Christianity realisation of common humanity. Human evolution itself has developed the ethnic communities with specific cultures. The decline of culture always entails disintegration and decline. And those people who do not see other people prospering always try to infringe in other culture. They try to acculturate the concerned people through cultural diffusion. The English rulers had tried to do this in India for keeping the Indians their faithful slaves forever. And for this end they had imposed formal education on Indians in 1833 A.D.

CULTURE AND CIVILISATION

Morgan believed that human society, since the emergence of human race, passed through three stages:

(*a*) Beginning with savagery,
(*b*) Going through barbarism, and
(*c*) Coming to the civilisation.

Culminating stage came with the growth of cities, emergence of writing, development of metallurgy, science and technology so on and so forth. The use of the term civilisation has been, and is generally followed by all anthropologists, who contrast—pre-urban, pre-literate society with civilised society. The civilised society represents a particular type of culture. German idealists and some American sociologists differentiate between culture and civilisation differently. Culture is regarded as:

"the moral, spiritual and intellectual attainment of man. It stands for symbols and values. It is the primary and basic thing. It is inside us and is what we are. It may register progress and decline".

Civilisation is secondary element. It is something which is outside us and, consists of technology material culture and social institutions. It is a sum total instrument dejecting material development of cultural life. It is that what we have and, we well-accumulate it and, it never progress or decline by itself.

Cultural Traits and Cultural Complex

When culture is taken to mean the way of life, it is obvious to believe that there are some elements in the cultural whole like—say prayer, rituals observance of good life habits—as belief in simple living and high thinking, believing in social customs for social homogeneity and making of some useful things for human use are called cultural traits. If some cultural traits combine together to produce a meaningful congery, which may be within the total or whole culture then this is called 'cultural complex'. A cultural complex is an institution. It is the outcome of interaction between several social institutions. Culture complex has also been as the pattern of inter-relation of several cultural traits.

Theories of Cultural Growth

How do the cultural growth come to be and how do they come to have similar cultural traits and complexes? Earlier theories about culture mainly concerned with two main problems—evolutionism and anthropology as a modern science born with the faith of evolutionary theory. Darwin and Spencer both sought to establish evolution as life breadth of all phenomena under the evolutionary impact under the pioneers like Tylor, Morgan and others who devoted themselves to the study of the evolution of human society and culture. It was believed from the points of human psyche that man everywhere was considered the same with same problems and same solutions of these. However, variation of environments would however register themselves in variations of institutions as found in various cultures. Thus, there are cultural groups through evolution—from simpler towards complex and different types.

Convergent Evolution

If the two culture, similar traits or institutions exhibit the similar traits or institutions, the same are referred to as cases of convergent evolution, as agricultural evolution. Morgan gives a kind of conjectural reasoning while turning to the contents of culture. Assuming the legally enforced monogamy was considered the highest stage of highest marital bond, he supposed the evolutionary process started from a stage of hypothetical proximity, which have gone through group marriages, polyandry, voluntary monogamy and polygamy. And due to mental bound various types of family were also evolved out of class or ethnic groups through the stages of marital and patriarchcal reckoning into bi-lateral family. Also thinkers studied evolutionary convergence in other fields which are related to culture. Tylor studied evolution in the field of religion. He regarded animistic polytheism the earliest and simplest form of religion which has become polytheism and ultimately monotheism in due course of time. Hudson traced the evolution of 'form', from an early stage through geometric to symbolic and abstract forms. Levy Bruhal also traced the modern logic from a primitive tribal logic.

Cultural Diffusion

Cultural diffusion is a process of intermingling of one particular culture or its cultural traits, to another culture. There is a process of cultural diffusion. Due to evolutionary measures the cultural traits always evolve independently and due to cultural similarities which are the result convergent evolution many manifestations emerge which merge with the cultural traits of other culture. The cultural is like the whirlpool (लहर) created in a water tank by throwing a stone in it. When some new cultural traits emerge in a particular culture, these traits spread not only in nearby areas but also in distant areas. When tobacco was grown in Brazil and people started smoking, Queen Elizabeth I of England prohibited smoking in England. Also many other countries prohibited smoking but in spite of restrictions the smoking spread throughout the world. For, cultural diffusion needs no special training or motivation. Only better ways of communication which create better ways of interaction between people of different countries create an atmosphere of cultural diffusion. The cultural diffusion does not require a donor only it needs a receiver. And role of receiver is more important. The cultural diffusion includes fairly three processes: (1) presentation of new cultural elements to a society,

(2) the acceptance of these elements by the members of the society, and (3) acceptance and integration of these alien cultural elements by the members of the receiving society. Such presentations of cultural traits sometimes aimed at to gain the loyalties from the receiving societies. Many imperialist countries had done cultural diffusion of their cultural traits to the culture of the people of their occupied countries. The cultural diffusion of Western English culture traits to Indian cultural traits was done to gain the obedience and loyalty of Indian people for keeping the Indians as slaves forever. So the presentation for the cultural diffusion sometimes is pre-planned and well-thought diplomacy, which is done in a manner that the receivers and could never anticipate that the cultural diffusion may kill their culture through acculturation. This tragedy happened with the Indians as they got themselves accultured, and the alienistic system of formal education played a distinctive role in this regard.

Many social thinkers have presented different theories about cultural diffusion. Some German thinkers and writers presented a theory of culture diffusion. Their theory consists belief in evolution tempered with diffusion, which is called 'kultrukreise' meaning cultural circle, cultural district. They believed that the scholar always depended on evidence of material culture. British thinker Tylor said that civilisation is like a plant that often propagates and independently grow.

Cultural Integration

Radcliff Brown said that functionalism makes the culture a meaningful whole. There is an inner consistency in a culture, or in other words cultures are integrated wholes. Malinowski make use of Tylor's definition of culture. But does not mean it as a super organic reality as Tylor did. To Malinowski culture is an instrument which enables man to secure his bio-psychic survival and subsequently a higher mental and intellectual survival. Therefore, each aspect of a culture, whether it is economic, social, religious or language or epistemic gain which is rooted in the needs of human beings. They are interrelated to each other through common ground like human needs. Therefore, Malinowski does not believe in loose survival. The evolutionists often believe in functionless cultural traits as survival and hangover from the past. Malinowski ridiculed this as inability to search for survival in cultures. There is nothing in culture that it is integrated. No single cultural trait has its meaning by itself unless it is seen in the context of a whole. Similarly cultural diffusion is a new manner which brings change in the original culture of the society. When an alien cultural is diffused it creates the obstacles in maintaining the original cultural traits and, creates hurdle in cultural integration, that is one aspect of the cultural changes, which changes the whole structure of the national culture. Malinowski believed in cultural pluralism. Every culture grows in responses to local responses which depend upon the bio-psychic needs of the people. And culture is to be judged in terms of these and absolute values. Adequacy in terms of local needs is the characteristics of well-integrated culture in the light of prevailing culture. But Malinowski fails when he does not provide a well-integrated conception of culture.

Radcliff Brown is more concerned with the survival of the society. A society cannot survive without its own culture. And integration is both an ideal and reality. If such cultural integration breaks it will result in the dys-functioning of the society. There will be no society. The function of every single group is not only our individualistic need but is requirement of the social whole, that is, society.

Patterns of Culture

Ruth Benedict drawing inspiration from her field of aesthetics, said that "the integration in culture is brought about by the embodiment of contrast into permanent or semi-permanent design which she called pattern, within the culture. She said that there would be style of each large social segment, and these segmented styles would come together into a super style which moulds the whole culture. And this is called 'cultural configuration'. All cultural styles are harmonious blending into 'blending configuration.' And it exhibit harmony in the culture. She calls it genesis of culture which brings about integration of a cultural form.

M.E. Opler has put forward the concept of 'theme' while explaining cultural integration. Motivation is necessary for various themes. Themes do go with types. Radcliff Brown emphasis on the styles of life. He says that good styles of life are the constituent of good human conduct. Radfield emphasis comparison of life styles for good conduct and character which is necessary for a sound culture for a society or a nation.

Cultural Lag

If any member of the society or a section of the society is unaware and, lacks some patterns of the culture of the society, it will be called a 'cultural lag'. Cultural lag generally becomes a hurdle in bringing social cohesion and integration in the society. Many members of the society sometimes are not fully or totally aware about the cultural traits and national culture as they are not educated about these. As such, there is an urgent need to educate the youngers about the national culture and its cultural traits at very early stage in the family through familial education and later on in the school through co-curricular activities.

ACCULTURATION

Acculturation is a process of adopting the cultural traits and patterns of an alien culture for meeting one's materialistic hedonistic needs ignoring the national culture. The process of acculturation is like a "rat-trap" in which a rat is trapped only with a piece of bread. Generally acculturation of the members of a society or nation is done for a specific purpose through the process of cultural diffusion. But generally it is done for the specific objectives. Some capitalist and empiricist countries still do so for keeping their superiority over the poor and underdevelopment countries. Such countries use acculturation for creating their permanent markets for selling their industrial products. In the past, when such countries had captured some countries, they did so for keeping such countries as slaves and loyal subjects forever. The British East India Company Government did so in India for keeping the Indians loyal slaves to them. They governed India about two hundred years. And for acculturating Indians they used a wonderful cultural diffusion method. On the advice of Lord Macaulay they imposed the British System of Formal Education in 1833 A.D. on Indians which has totally accultured almost all Indians.

Also the poor under developed countries willingly accepted acculturation thinking that this would relieve them from poverty and economic backwardness. This happened because of human greedy nature. The human-beings are considered rational beings in comparison to other living being. The Almighty God has rewarded the human-being with specific biological faculties. A human-being has been rewarded with a bigger head to think, reason, analyse and comprehend. He/she has been rewarded with moving hands attached with a strong torso to act and invent many useful things for the use of all human-beings. With these Divine rewards the man could exploit the natural resources for human use and could progress well. And the man has been rewarded with fact and standing posture. Due to this man could walk and find many things for his use. But above all these Almighty God has also rewarded man with greed and self-centredness, due to which the man became acquisitive, greedy and exploitative, which encouraged exploitation of the human-beings. All these encouraged the acculturation.

Effects of Acculturation on Indian Society

Acculturation has very badly affected and, is still affecting, the Indian society. The Indian society is on the verge of dys-functioning, as its every aspect has been changed. The Indian culture and civilisation are the oldest in the world. Due to its culture, the Indian society was liked throughout the world. The main features of Indian culture were—sociability depicting love, hospitability and affection, humanity, religiosity, spirituality, simple living and high thinking, homogeneity, cooperation, sharing and saneful social living. All these social-cultural aspects are missing from the Indian society now. The social institutions like joint family, community and relatives were the main bases of Indian society. Now the joint family system has been totally broken due to acculturation which has entailed greed and self-centredness. In place of joint families the nuclear families have emerged. Earlier, at the time of 'unity in bio-diversity', that is, marriage of the boy and girl, the parents of the girl used to educate her girl to live amicably in her new home in logical way in family harmony. As such, the Indian society was homogenic society in comparison to heterogenic society. Now the brides come with a dream of separate nuclear family. They are educated to do so by their mothers and other family ladies. Just after the marriage a bride want to establish a separate nuclear home. In joint family, the elders used to educate and enculturate their grand children. Now the grand parents are totally discarded and thrown out of house like bio-garbage. Neither they are looked after by their sons and daughter-in-laws nor by the grand children. Generally, both the husband and wife earn to meet their hedonistic needs. They have totally become consumeristic. They do not have time to take care of their young children, educating and enculturating them under familial education is a distant dream. So the present nuclear families are unable to discharge their familial education duties. The young children are not even motivated to be social. Earlier the joint family members used to be monotheistic, religious and spiritual. They used to offer or do daily prayers. Now, throughout the day they both remain busy in earning money. They count the money late in the night. So they go to bed very late and also rise very late next day. So they do not have time to do *pooja-archana* or *sandhya*. There is nobody to look after the younger children in the family, and they sent them to day care schools. After 2 or 3 years of age such children are admitted in nursery schools. The prime aim of the nuclear families is to see their young children coming out in flying colours in their school examinations. As such, the parents pressurise their younger children to read, read and study continuously. Even they do not permit their children to do any homework. They are exempted even washing their *kachha banyan* and towel after taking bath. In other words, the present parents are mad after good examination results. The parents even do not allow the children to go out of home, after coming from the school, for playing with their peer group. As such, neither the present generation become sociable, homogenic, cooperative and sharing nor they acquire work habits from the parents and members of society. They parents also remain so busy that they do not find time to talk with their close neighbours. All this is happening due to blind acculturation.

This social change has occurred due to acculturation. In Europe the boys and girls leave their parental homes just after adolescent age and live like the youngers of the animals and birds. Once, the writer, along with his wife and daughter, was going from Delhi to Puri via Calcutta. While catching Puri Express from Howrah Railway Station, the two German girls came and sat along with us as their birth reservation was in same coach. They travelled from

Howrah Railway Station to Puri Railway Station. During this time the writer asked about their family and country. And the girls revealed that they had left their parents after the age of 17 years. They were earning and self-supporting themselves. But in India similar was not the situation. The younger generation used to maintain parental relationship life long. Now, due to cultural diffusion and consequent acculturation this situation has also changed in India also. There are many girls who have adopted modelling profession, whereas their parents do not like such occupation. Close kith and kins and their youngers and their children do not like to talk with the family elders even in their old age.

Due to acculturation the present Indian society has totally become hedonistic, consumeristic and self-centred, more or less, tantamount to 'carvacs' (चारवाक-चारु) of Mahabharata period. 'Earn, eat and be marry' is the prime aim of present Indian society. And our present alienistic system of formal education is the epicentre of acculturation in India. It is totally based on Western culture. Western culture is tantamount to Indian 'carvac' atheistic philosophy. It is also based on Calvinistic protestant Christian philosophy. St. Calvin had advised the protestant Christians to 'earn throughout week and enjoy life. He had advised them to go to the church once on Sundays'. The present system of formal education is only aimed at to achieve material gains. It has no place for inculcating good life attitudes in the students and thereby enculturating them. Due to acculturation the religiosity and spirituality has also been wiped out from the Indian society. Generally the people remain busy in the rat-race of money earning. Due to greed social evils like cheating, deceiving and corruption have become common features of the society. Now the Indian business class has also adopted the Calvinistic principle. They earn throughout the week, take rest on one day and arrange *'kirtan'* and *'ratjaga'* probably once a year in which the *'pooja-archana'* is also done by a *poojari*. As such, the acculturation has affected the Indian society in all fields. It has made the man totally ignorant about Indian culture. Money makers are found everywhere in the society. And our present system of formal education boosts this trend. There remains no sociability, humanity, religiosity, cooperation and cohesion in the society at all. Only competition is found everywhere. And this situation has happened due to killing acculturation. And our present system of education has no provision to combat acculturation through enculturation.

Enculturation through Education

As already mentioned, enculturation is a process of culture development and its preservation. The process of enculturation should start from family which is not possible because the present Indian families, expecting very few, remain busy in the rat-race of money earning. Most of the families are quite unaware about the national culture and its traits. Can this awkward situation be allowed to continue? Answer is no. Then, how the youngers of the nation can be encultured? Enculturation of the youngers is not an easy job. It should be a joint venture of the family, society and education. Social, religious organisation and bodies should also take this initiative. They should educate all members of the society about national culture, its development through enculturation. This should be done through a mass movement of enculturation and by educating the people about the virus of acculturation. The efforts should be made for the revival of Indian joint family system. The joint family can effectively enculturate the younger generation. The enculturation should start from the family.

When the younger generation start going to school for education, the educational authorities should do enculturation of the students. But this is not possible until and unless the examination phobia is reduced. Only passing out examination is not education. The education has a wider spectrum. It is a life building process. Only teaching of some subjects, like sciences, mathematics and humanities cannot be said education. Education is much more. It should inculcate some good life attitudes as 'simple living and high thinking', 'early to bed early to rise', 'to be punctual', 'to learn to do hand work', 'to be diligent and honest', 'to respect elders and fair sex', and 'to love youngers and animal life'. But all these are absent from our present alienistic formal system of education. The examination pressure on students and teachers should be reduced, and educational institutions, administrators, teachers and other supporting staff should be made aware about the importance of national culture and, bad effects of cultural diffusion and acculturation.

They should be motivated about enculturation and also about necessary activities like model character of the teacher and about arranging co-curricular activities.

24

Co-Curricular Activities

In the present age of science and technology, educational programme in all educational institutes is generally based on imparting knowledge, through teaching of some subjects like physics, chemistry, biology, botany, mathematics and humanities subjects like languages, history, political science, economics and sociology etc. etc. For teaching these a stipulated yearly curriculum is prepared for the whole session in advance, and teaching is done by the teachers accordingly, which is considered education. And the students are examined in the subjects which are taught. As such, our present formal system of education is purely examination oriented. As a matter of fact the teaching of the subjects to the students is only done for the preparation of the examination, which cannot be called education at all. Education is much more. It has a wider spectrum. It should be self-learning, for which teaching should be used as a tool, and an arena of life building. But the aim of life building during teaching is totally ignored. It is because of the phobia of examination. In olden days, under the vedic and Brahmanical education imparted in Gurukula Ashramas, the basic aim of education was life building of the *Shishyas* (students). And the whole education was planned to do the life building of the *Shishyas* (students). The *Gurus* used to inculcate desirable necessary life attitudes as—early to bed, early to rise, to do all life activities like going for natural call at right time, taking bath at fixed time, to do yoga for their health care, to attend yajna daily and after taking refreshment to go with the *Gurus* and sit under a tree for getting education. After completing the education at Gurukula the *Shishyas* were required to lead a sane family life (गृहस्थाश्रम) and, while living in family teaching people about social sanity.

But now our present educational system devote mainly on teaching of subjects in which the students are examined and later on are awarded certificates. Our educational administrators, parents and social milieu are mad after good examination result. Some parents lay too much stress on perennial study for good examination results. Many make their kids mentally and emotionally disturbed. With the result many future guardians commit suicides. In our old system of education, there was no examination. The students were judged through discussions and symposiums, that is, *vad-vivad* (वाद-विवाद). Our present examination based education system has totally changed the socio-economic and cultural spectrum of the country and also fate of the youngers. Our present system of education has also accultured the Indian society totally, which has mitigated the social traits, customs, traditions, social institutions like joint family. Therefore, it is very necessary to enculturate the youngers, that is, students which can be done through the use of co-curricular activities in educational institutions.

Culture of any country is its soul. Cultural whole is a configuration of many human activities like human behaviour, traditions, customs, social traits and total social life. The term 'culture' is a derivation from the Latin word 'cultura', which was developed out of Latin word 'calo' meaning a 'colum' or a constructed stand or pillar on which the weight of the building is put. Culture also means a tillage or a cultivation of land, or training in a particular field, or inculcation of some good life, habits for developing a discipline by which man's moral, social or intellectual nature is developed or moulded. The result of such training or development is enlightenment which may lead a saneful living of ideal persons. And such process of cultural development is called enculturation, specifically when country's own culture is developed. But when, national culture, development is ignored and another nations' alien culture is adopted through culture diffusion that process of cultural formation is called acculturation. And for stopping acculturation enculturation of the people is very necessary. Many countries became target of cultural diffusion very easily. But many countries like China, Japan and Korea tried to preserve their culture though they also adopted certain features of other cultural feature like dresses of other countries.

Ralph Linton says that for majority of the people, culture plays the role of a guide. It lays norms of behaviour, sociability, morality and sane cooperative reciprocity which are necessary for the survival of human-beings. Human survival cannot be possible without culture. Culture is liberator of man from undesirable human activities. It liberates men from biological determinism such as greed, self-centredness and acquisitiveness. These lead a man to corruption. If a person is to be benefited from the society he is to confirm and follow the accepted social norms of the society. Culture liberates as well as enslaves man. If the culture is developed and formed on sane social principles, equality, sanity and cooperation it will definitely help the individuals. On the other hand, if the base of the culture is materialistic and it promotes greed and self-centredness, it will be a exploitative culture and will harm a section of the society. The Western culture in which majority of Indians have been accultured does not suite to Indian society. Due to acculturation there emerged many social stigmas in the Indian society. When the parents of the youngsters have adopted norms of the Western culture and have totally accultured themselves it has become necessary to enculturate the youngers. Because, the parents of the students generally remain busy in their business activities, it is not possible for them to enculturate their youngers through familial education, the responsibility of enculturating the students has fallen on the teachers in the present socio-economic situation. But enculturating the students by the teachers is a challenging job, when the whole formal system of education is examination oriented. It can only be done through organising the related co-curricular activities.

It is a culture through which civilisation of the nation is developed. The civilisation is formed through which the citizens are civilised from rude and barbarous behaviour and is a sewage of life to an ideal sane social life. Though the human-beings are considered rational beings. Even though they have acquisitive by nature so, they are to be civilised. A civilised person is one who also cares for his fellow beings. In many materialistic societies it is hardly done. In order to make a person sane it is to go beyond books. Going to school should no longer be limited to book reading only. It should go beyond book reading. The students should be involved in many co-curricular activities like dramas, debates, art activities, excursions, picnics, river rafting, swimming, dancing and knowing the national culture. Only reading and reading not only makes the students unsocial but also makes them dull. They feel bored of teaching. It is, therefore, necessary to provide complete education to the students which could only be possible through co-curricular activities. Such activities provide opportunities to the students for expression which releases their emotions. The parents should also find out such schools which provide co-curricular activities and also extra-curricular activities. Generally the school curriculum does not have any mention about such activities. The curriculum planners should give a place to these in the curriculum. Through these activitics a student can be enlightened about sociability, axiology, culture, cultural diffusion and acculturation. Therefore, it is necessary to arrange co-curricular activities and extra-curricular activities based on civil enlightening which can be done by inculcating good life attitudes, social customs, social and cultural traits, artistic activities, cultural activities like visual arts, folk arts, dance, drama, music and social work. Therefore, it is necessary to arrange co-curricular and extra-curricular systematically and regularly for enculturation of the students in schools and in all other educational institutions.

A nation which looses its culture looses everything even independence. In the past the colonisers always tried to fracture the cultures of their colonies for keeping their grip on these permanently. So they always acculturated their subjects. On the whole it can be said that through acculturation they could retain their hold for a longer time. The British East India Company Government did so in India. And we Indians paid a heavy price for acculturation. India was divided in 1947 due to this reason.

Morgan believed that since the emergence of human society the man passed through three stages:

(*a*) In the beginning through savagery,
(*b*) Thereafter going through barbarism due to human greed and self-centredness, and
(*c*) Coming to the civilisation which could be possible through the development of respective cultures.

Culminating stage came with the growth of cities, emergence of speech, development of writing, development of metallurgy, science and technology so on and so forth, which paved the ways for the development of culture and civilisations. The anthropologists use the term civilisation in contrast to pre-urban, pre-literate out of which the urban society emerged. Every civilisation represents a particular type of culture. A German idealist and some American sociologists differentiate between culture and civilisation differently.

A culture is regarded as 'moral, spiritual, social and intellectual attainment of man'. It stands for symbols and values. A culture is a primary and basic embodiment of values and shows what actually human beings are. It may exhibit human axiology, sociability, necessary social values, human progress, harmony and homogeneity. A true culture is always non-inclinative and, is for the common good. Whereas a civilisation is a secondary face of culture. It is something which depicts inclinativeness. In other words, a civilisation may be said a socio-material culture which emerges out of science and technology and related social institutions. A civilisation is a sum total of instrument of cultural life. It is what we have and we will never accumulate, and never kill progress or decline.

CULTURAL TRAITS AND CULTURE COMPLEX

When culture is taken to mean the way of life, it is obvious that within this whole there are elements like, prayers, rituals, making of tools for exploring and exploiting natural resources and behaving well with all. Each of these are called cultural traits. If some cultural traits are combined together to produce a meaningful consciousness or social aspect this will be a segment within total culture, which is called cultural complex. A cultural complex is an institution. It is an outcome of interaction between several institutions. Cultural complex has also been defined as the pattern of inter-relations of cultural traits.

Theories of Cultural Growth

How do the cultural traits come to be and, how these have similar cultural traits and patterns which are called cultural complexes.

Earlier theories about culture occurred with two main problems:

1. *Evolutionism*: Anthropology as a modern science was born with the birth of evolutionary theory. Darwin and Spencer, both sought to establish evolution as a life breath of all phenomena. Under evolutionary impact earlier pioneers like Tylor, Morgan and others devoted themselves to the study of evolution of human society and culture. It was believed from the psychic make up, that is, the man everywhere was the same, so were the same problems and same solutions. Variation of environment and climatic conditions would, however, depicted various cultural traits in various cultures. Thus, cultures grow through evolution—from simpler towards complex and differential types.
2. *Convergent Evolutions*: If two cultures exhibit similar traits or institutions, the same referred to as cases of convergent evolution. Example: Agriculture had evolved in Southern, Eastern and South Eastern and Northern Zones on the similar patterns.

Prominent evolutionary theorists argued:

1. *Morgan postulated three stages:*

(*a*) Man lived in savage society which had an older period. Older period predicted the invention of pottery. It was a period of barbarism.
(*b*) Middle period had a demonstration of animal feeding, cultivation of land, breeding plants, saving corn and irrigation. It was a middle period of barbarism.
(*c*) And the later period was innovative. During this period development of alphabets, search of iron ore, tools and writing come into being.

Morgan gives a kind of congenial reasoning while turning to the contents of culture. Assuming the legality enforced by monogamy was the highest stage of marital bonds, he assumed that it is started due to evolution process due to hypothetical stage of proximity, which might have emerged through group marriages in the form of polyandry, voluntary monogamy and polygamy.

Due to marital bonds various types of families might have emerged. Out of which patriarchal families might have emerged. Out of which the class developed, through which patriarchal families might have been perpetuated.

2. Tylor carried out similar study of the growth of the religion. He regarded animistism, the animistic polytheism to have been the darkest and simplest form of religion. Thereafter intermediary stages of higher polytheistic thinking might have lead to monotheism.

3. Hudson traced the art forms from an early stage through geometric forms to symbolic and abstract forms.

4. Levy Brahel also tried to find the evolution of modern logic. He asserted that the primitives were not conscious of implications of contradictions. So they were underdeveloped in finding the comparison to present ones, their mentality was pre-logical mentality.

As such, it is believed that the evolutionists have made a significant contribution to our understanding of cultural traits, cultural complexes and cultural development.

Process of Cultural Transmission

For enculturation some cultural transmission and transformation processes are to be applied. But in the present age of materialism and hedonism the parents are unable to transmit the cultural traits due to some personal reasons. This is to be done by the teachers, who can do it through arranging the co-curricular activities in schools. The major cultural transmission processes are:

(*a*) Assimilation of thoughts, social customs and values, cultural traits through marginal contacts between the teachers and the students.

(*b*) Assimilation of religious values through regular *poojas, sandhyas, yajnas* and *kirtans* in the family. But these are missing in the family. Our educational institutions come under the scanner of secularism. But the inculcation of morality is very necessary for a sane social life. The morality can also be inculcated through related co-curricular activities and morning assembly discourses.

(*c*) Arranging cultural programmes on special occasions will enculturate the students and will assimilate the cultural development.
(*d*) Socialisation should be done by encouraging the youngsters to mix up with their peer group and to respect the elders and fair sex. The arranging of co-curricular activities opens the doors of socialisation of the youngers. The parents should allow their children to mix up with their peer group.
(*e*) Presentation of ideal behaviour by the elders, parents and the teachers before the youngers.
(*f*) Encouraging the students to be extroverts.
(*g*) To be truthful, honest and idealist open in behaviour. For this openness is to be adopted.

There are two aspects of culture:

(a) Material Aspect of Culture

Material aspect of culture is consumption oriented. It entails more goods production, better techniques of production and desire for acquisition and hoarding. It makes the man hedonistic. Industrialisation could be possible due to the development of science and technology. Material culture has added fuel to the human greed. It has made the man individualistic, acquisitive, self-indulgent, and self-centred. Main aim of the materialistic culture is to make the man luxurious, hedonistic and consumeristic. The men and women who follow materialistic culture are bound to follow alienation. They do not want to maintain good cordial relation even with their own family members. And many of us have become accultured by adopting Western culture.

(b) Non-Material Aspects of Culture

Whereas, non-material culture is mental and epistemic, normative and value oriented. Under the non-materialistic culture the man is generally interested and involved in social customs, traits, norms, values, cooperation sociability and cultural development. Such person remains humanistic and truly social. Indian culture and also cultures of many eastern countries are non-materialistic culture. But due to human greed and cultural diffusion acculturation has taken place largely in these countries. Acculturation has made the men and women totally self-centred and greedy. So all old social values and cultural traits have been vanished. Institutions like joint family and community and also sociability and social cohesion have been crumbled. And due to this many social stigmas have emerged in the society.

This cultural contradiction has led to cultural lag. Now, we Indians want to proceed on Western materialistic path and achieve all materialistic gains. Such material gains also require certain values. Such values are contrary to the values of non-materialist culture. We Indians still stick to our old values, social customs and cultural traits. But contradictions between materialistic gains and aspirations make the individuals more greedy and hedonistic. With the result old value system which centres around 'simple living and high thinking', belief in fraternity and love developed a cultural lag. This divides the society in two sections (1) who run after material gains at the cost of social harmony, homogeneity and cooperation and (2) those who believe in simplicity, cooperation, brotherhood, social harmony and homogeneity, sharing and integrity. They try to renounce greed, acquisitiveness, self-centredness through religiosity and spirituality. Instead of material aspiration they try to understand theological aspects of human life and do not try to gain too much social gains. The people and their cultures are differentiated by their cultural lags. Some have scientific outlook which leads them to materialism and hedonism. Whereas some have religious and spiritual outlook, both are topsy-turvy as scientific outlook demands rationality and modern attitude as:

(*i*) Love for science, initiativeness and inventiveness,
(*ii*) Hate for dogmatism and traditionalism,
(*iii*) Development of attitude for search of material means for material and hedonistic gains,
(*iv*) Specialisation, skill acquisition and expertise, and
(*v*) Development of attitude for verification.

On the other hand religious attitudes demand to believe in a pious social beliefs, customs, ideals, attitudes, cultural traits, sociability, harmony, homogeneity, cooperation and spirituality.

Both scientific and religious attitudes and beliefs do not go together. What is happening in our country that we want to be scientific as well as religious also. Both are contradictory. Such an attitude is not compatible for being sane, as well as, modern. This brings a cultural lag. So an adjustment between these is necessary which can be brought by observing the religiousity and spirituality.

Pre-requisite conditions for economic growth are:

(*i*) Rationality,
(*ii*) Scientific attitude,
(*iii*) Initiative and keen desire to do some thing,
(*iv*) Specialisation in a particular field,
(*v*) Sincerity, diligency and proper attitudes,
(*vi*) To believe in work culture,
(*vii*) Money economy and barter system,
(*viii*) To develop its national goals,
(*ix*) Skilled manpower, and
(*x*) Ideal expert management.

As such, knowledge of national culture should be given to the youngers during the course of school education. Since culture is a multiple whole—a configuration and embodiment of many artistic activities, human behaviour, traditions, customs, social values and cultural traits, it cannot be taught as a school subject, as other subjects are taught. It can be built up or developed through enculturation or by developing the cultural traits of the national culture. This cannot be done by any single social agency alone. So the cultural development, in the present materialistic hedonistic atmosphere which generally creates many cultural lags, is not an easy job. But enculturation of the younger cannot evaded. It is very necessary for the health of the whole nation. The enculturation of the youngers should be a joint venture. It should be done by the social agencies like family, joint family if it exists, extended families, community, school and other educational institutions. It should be initiated through marginal contacts, first at the family, extended families and community and later at the school and educational institutions levels. At family and community levels the religious discourses are very helpful in inculcating good life attitudes, which may develop sociability, religiosity, spirituality, morality, good behaviour and sound character in the future guardians. These may enculturate the youngers. For the development of these personal contacts through good rapport with sympathetic eyes and ears are very necessary. Above all for these the students should be continuously made aware about the socio-economic, political, cultural and axiological conditions of the nation which have been badly affected by cultural lag caused due to the virus of acculturation, if not at family level or community level at least at the school level. Also the students at the school level should be apprised about the teleological position of the man/woman. Everybody is mortal in this world. Then why should one individual exploit other? The students should know about the social sanity. They should be apprised about the material culture and spiritual culture. For this they should also be apprised about the Indian old education system. And this way present materialistic culture can be rooted out of the country. Because of human greed the contemporary human-being are acting in barbarous way, which is very dangerous for the social existence. This is happening due to the virus of acculturation. It is necessary to make the young generation aware how the present cultural lag affected the Indian institutions like joint family, relatives, educational institutions. The cultural lag has promoted the cultural diffusion which entailed the killing acculturation. Now-a-days almost all parents, family members and youngers have been accultured due to greed and self-centredness They all adopted Western hedonistic life styles. They are unable to enculturate their children. Therefore, auspicious duty of enculturation falls on the teachers of the educational institutions, who are at present engrilled in examination oriented system of teaching programme. The educational institutions often ignore enculturation of the students due to good examination results. As such, enculturation of the students at educational institutions is also a challenging job. How to meet this challenge? Where there is a will there is a way. In the present accultured socio-economic conditions, the enculturation of the youngers is must. And this most auspicious duty of acculturation can only be done by the teachers. For this, it is necessary that all teachers must be educated about all cultural aspects. They must be made aware about all aspects of the national culture. First of all this should be done at the teachers training institutions. The school authorities should also be very conscious and serious about the national culture. They should know all cultural aspects including cultural lags and their serious effects on the health of the nation. If possible the whole society be made aware about the national culture.

Happiness through Enculturation

The enculturating of the students is necessary for leading to happiness. The happiness is neither gained through material gains nor merely depending on others. The happiness is only gained through preparing the youngers to be happy in life. The former U.S.A. President, Abraham Lincoln once said that "people are happy as they make up their minds to be happy in the present world". But the present world is interested in instant solutions of the human life problems which are laced with greed. There is no place for self-introspection neither in the society nor in educational programmes. Only achieving the material gains is considered happiness. And our present system of formal education is based on gaining the economic gains, which can only be possible through good shining examination results.

The Government and many other agencies make propaganda through mass-media for showing that they want to see the people happy. They considered it a best technique to propagate happiness. But money cannot buy happiness. Only inner consciousness optimism and keen desire can bring happiness. Some people feel that doing something for the needy people can bring happiness to the needy as well as for the people who do something for others. It gives them emotional and spiritual happiness. The deeper sense of contentment of doing something for others always entails happiness. The highest form of happiness lies in inner freedom. So happiness can never be materialistic. If somebody guides or helps in the time of distress to anyone it will bring happiness to both. National happiness is much more important which can be achieved through national culture.

As such for the holistic development of youngers (students) there should be then all round developments. Any teacher can teach the students to secure good marks but happiness in life cannot brought without inculcating good life values. If good life values are inculcated in students they can be happy throughout their lives, which can be done through enculturating them in Indian culture.

A teacher hardly can pass on less than of his/her knowledge. But if the students are encultured properly they can be prepared for a happy sane social life, and they will do self-learning.

The school and other educational institutions can do enculturation of the students by arranging some cultural, social dramatic, and artistic activities which may promote and build national culture. Some of these activities are as under:

1. Thought for the Day. In school or college building some display bulletin boards should be installed at the appropriate places, such as verandas or corridors from where the students generally pass. On some moving chalk-boards some quotations about national culture should be written.
2. Morning Assembly. In the morning assembly, some talks should be delivered on national culture, if not daily at least once a week.
3. The co-curricular activities should be so planned that there should be a cultural programme once a week on the last day of the week.
4. Some religious festivities of different religions as Janmashtmi, Diwali, Id-ul-Fitr, Milad-un-Nabi, Guru Nanak Day, Basant Panchami and Christmas Day should be arranged regularly and cultural programmes should be arranged.
5. The Teachers Day should be arranged on 5th September every year.
6. Parents-Teachers Day should be organised once in a year.
7. For the incoming students the orientation programme should be arranged and, cultural programme should also be arranged.
8. Like Orientation Day the valedictory programme should be arranged for the outgoing students.
9. The school and educational institutions should constitute (*a*) art club, (*b*) crafts and hobby club, (*c*) sports club and (*d*) social services club and decoration club. These clubs should be monitored by the experienced teachers. The deserving candidates should be rewarded.
10. Some eminent persons should be invited to give lectures on culture at special workshops and symposiums. Decoration and cleanliness should be given importance.

25

Extra-Curricular Activities

Extra-curricular activities are such activities which neither come under school or educational institutions, regular prescribed teaching programme nor come under the arena of co-curricular activities. These activities cover (*a*) games and sports, (*b*) other special festivities like arranging lungar or common dinner or lunch, arranging some common gatherings like melas for encouraging sociability, (*c*) arranging picnics, (*d*) arranging educational tours and excursions, (*e*) arranging social work activities, and (*f*) arranging some social programmes. Extra-curricular activities are useful in inculcating good life habits in the students as (*a*) good work habits, (*b*) sociability, (*c*) brotherhood and fraternity, (*d*) diligency, (*e*) working for the better of all etc. etc. Such inculcation of good habits and exposure to a wide social and physical arena ultimately enculturate the students. It also relieves the students from the virus of greed, self-centredness and hedonism. They start thinking of common good. They also start self-learning. The Greek Philosopher, Plato said "that most excellent education is that which begins with eyes. It is a recovery what we already possessed and recover with our senses". Also there is a Chinese adage, "what we see, we remember and what we hear we forget". The education has a wide spectrum. There are many things about which we must know. But we cannot know them exactly without seeing these things. And there are many things we cannot see. Neither their pictures nor photographs, nor models, diagrams and diaroma give clear picture or scenario of these things. And in many cases it becomes very difficult for the teacher to describe the clear perspective of such things. Such things can be taught, through arranging the extra-curricular activities, easily.

Therefore, there is an urgent necessity of exposures of the extra-curricular activities to the students. Some of these are mentioned as under

(*a*) Games and Sports

The knowledge and proficiency in games, sports and yoga is very essential for the good health of the students who are our future guardians. If an individual does not care for his/her health, he/she cannot remain healthy. The Greek Philosopher, Hereclitus said that every physical and social phenomenon is continuously in flux. The man is born as a baby boy, becomes youth, young, he faces many life stages and finally dies. If a man/woman, during his/her life time, does not follow some good desirable norms for keeping himself/herself healthy, he/she cannot remain healthy and may face very disastrous health hazards. Therefore, it is very essential to educate the youngers in health care techniques. Now-a-days the parents do not have time to do health exercises due to their economic pursuits for hedonistic enjoyments. Therefore, it is essential that the educational programme of the youngers should compulsorily entail a health care programme. And this can be done under the games and sports programme. The education authorities should give due attention to this aspect. But it is seen that it does not happen usually. In many schools that health education is ignored due to the examination phobia. So, in many schools sports and games teaching does not exist at all. In some schools and educational institutions where it does exist, it is not properly done. The reason for this is the professional bias against the physical education teacher. He/she is considered as non-epistemic and inferior teacher by his/her fellow teachers. So, the physical education teacher finds himself degraded and isolated. He/she gets himself/herself emotionally disturbed and take teaching games and sports as mere formality. So the games and sports should be given due weightage in educational programme. Another reason for the professional bias is that physical and sports education is not an examination subject. In spite of this health education can for more important examination result, so the students should be good trained in games and sports as—Kabbadi, Mukkabazi, Wrestling, Cricket, Hockey, Gymnastics, Karate, and Swimming etc. etc. The students should be given a chance to learn games and sports of his choice. They should be taught yoga compulsorily. Also, the students should be inspired to adopt regular life habits as early to bed early to rise, to take regular bath and to avoid junky fast foods. In the present hedonistic age the mothers spoil the lives of their children by providing junky fast foods. So that the students should be rewarded for good performance. Other teachers should not skip the students' games and sports programmes. They should involve themselves in games and sports on special occasions.

(*b*) Other Festivities

Sociability of the youngers is most important for inculcation a sense of fraternity, brotherhood, sharing and cooperation in them. Without sociability the youngers cannot develop themselves as sane citizens, and the society cannot function as an ideal social institution. But, now-a-days, it is observed that members of the society hardly speak with their fellow-beings due to hedonistic temper, human greed and self-centredness, which are becoming common feature in the society. Therefore, it is very necessary to inculcate a sense of sociability in the future guardians who are studying in schools. The present parents cannot do this due to their hedonistic consumeristic temper which also entails egoism. Even, they do not encourage their children to talk with their own kith and kins and elders. This is why the Indian society is becoming unsocial day by day. This temper has broken the institution of joint family. The schools and other educational institutions are the builders of the nation. These educational institutions are the moulders of the youngers who are our future guardians. As such, during the academic session of these institutions, there should be provision of arranging some special festivities in which all students, teaching staff and other staff could participate jointly and could contribute in the festivities. In Indian culture there are three or four occasions like Guru Nanak Birth Day, Goverdhan Day, Christmas Day and Basant Panchmi (Saraswati Day) are such occasions on which students can jointly participate for celebrating these days. On these days common food is cooked for all. And the students should do it irrespective of caste and creeds and the staff should also participate on the occasions. Also some melas should also be arranged. By arranging such extra-curricular activities the students will be socialised.

(c) Arranging Picnics

Present system of formal education is based on teaching some subjects for appearing in annual examination. As such, it is purely examination oriented scheme of education. And no other educational activities like inculcation of good life habits, enculturation have a place in it. As such both the teachers and the students get bored and tired. Therefore, it is very necessary to give them a reprieve from boredom of continuous teaching. For this an easiest method is to arrange picnics for the students and the teachers in different groups. These picnics should be arranged at least once in a term of the academic session. Visiting a beautiful place, staying there throughout the day, having lunch together and arranging some cultural programme are the main features of a picnic. The school or educational institutions authorities should appoint a extra-curricular activities committee which should plan a picnic in advance, which should arrange transportation, arrangement for common tea and refreshment. After the picnic there should be a follow-up discussion pertaining to picnic activities and about the place where the picnic was arranged.

(d) Educational Tour and Excursion

There are many places in the country, which are not only famous in India but throughout the world, for their historical, cultural, geographical and religious features. In India, such places are—Agra, Fatehpur Sikri, Mathura, Varanasi, Prayag in U.P., Mount Abu, Jaipur, Ajmer, Nathdwara in Rajasthan, Bhubaneswar, Konark and Puri in Orissa, Amritsar in Punjab, Srinagar, Jammu, Vaishno Devi in Jammu and Kashmir, Haridwar, Rishikesh, Chardham and Nainital in Uttrakhand, Chennai, Rameshwaram and Madurai in Tamil Nadu, Shimla in Himachal Pradesh, Kurukshetra in Haryana, Patna, Bodh Gaya, Nalanda in Bihar, Kolkata in West Bengal, etc. etc. Because, these places are of rare importance the teachers and the students generally remain very eager to visit such places of unique importance. The teacher cannot tell about such places by telling or by showing their replicas, through pictures, charts, models or diaromas. Only by visiting such places detailed physical and climatic panorama can be seen. And social conditions of the people can be known. As such, an educational tour to one such place once a year is most essential for the epistemic health of the students. Such educational tours should be planned and managed in advance by the expert teachers. There should be a detailed follow-up discussion after the tour. The students should note down important points.

(*e*) Work Activities—Work Culture

It can be assumed that our present formal education system does not have any place for developing work habits in our youngers, so there is no work culture development. This because too much importance is given to good examination results. And the teachers are pressurised to prepare the students for good examination results. Also the parents pressurise their children for good shining examination results. They, especially, many mothers do not allow their children to do any housework. The contemporary children are not allowed to pick up *kachha banyan*, while going to bathroom. They are not allowed to wash their undergarments. As such, the work habits are not inculcated to the children in their homes. In our schools the children are not given any opportunity to do work due to examination phobia. In Indian old system of education the *Shishyas* (students) were required to do some sort of hard work as fuel collection for the Gurukula kitchens and cutting of grass for Gurukula cows. Under non-formal system of education all artisans and working castes used to train their youngers in their family vocations. Now the main emphasis remains on books—books and their study. In *Shrimad Bhagavad Gita*, Lord Krishna laid emphasis on 'Karam yoga' or work culture. Therefore, it is necessary there should be a provision for work activities, for developing work culture, in schools. This can be done by teaching art and craft activities in the schools, so that the students may learn to do work.

(*f*) Social Work

To help each other is the main function of a society. It keeps the society alive. This is done through social work. The social work should be done sincerely with a non-inclinative temper as in some eastern societies done where the people believe in teleological truth, that everyone is mortal, and every human beings soul (जीवात्मा) is part of bigger 'soul' (परमात्मा) or Almighty God. So all are equal and deserve equal treatment. All should be nicely treated and helped in the hour of need and distress. This kind of social ethos is found in many monotheistic and spiritualistic countries. India was and still is, one of the monotheistic and spiritualistic countries in the world where social service was done in spiritualistic and in non-inclinative way. Sixty or seventy years back if a person fell ill, whole *Mohalla* used to take care of him. Now this temper of social service has totally changed due to materialistic and hedonistic temper of human beings, which occurred due to acculturation.

On the other hand, in some western societies, the teleological approach is quite different. They believe in "earn more enjoy more". So instead of doing service in non-inclinative way, they do service in inclinative way. Such societies have heterogenic social structure, that is, class structure, in which a section of society is very rich called 'barons' and some are very poor called 'serfs'. These western societies mostly follow 'calvinistic' ethics "Earn throughout the week and enjoy life. And go to church once a week on Sunday". Such people are protestant Christians.

Social service is necessary for any society. But due to western cultural diffusion, we Indians have been totally accultured. So, we have become totally inclinative, greedy, hedonistic, self-centred. We do not care even our close neighbours. We Indians who were once sane and idealist are going to be barbarous. Due to human greed many evils have emerged in the society. The corruption, cheating, thefts, loots, snatching, kidnapping for ransom, molestation and rapes have become a common social features. All important social institutions like joint family system have been totally crumbled. These all are happening due to human greed and self-centredness. For stopping all these evil a spirit of commonality and cooperation is very necessary. A spirit of social service can put a halt on all unsocial activities. The present parents who are living in nuclear families cannot do this because they are totally accultured and, have become totally hedonistics and consumeristics. Only schools and other educational institutions can do it. These educational institutions should make their mindset to do so. These institutes should motivate the teachers for educating the students for doing social work in their lives. This will make the future guardians (students) social and humane. The students should take round of the locality and try to find the difficulties of the men and women . They should help them in educating their children and also elders.

26

Creativity in Education for Aestheticity

Physical world is the gift of Almighty God. Physical world is the embodiment of varied flora and fauna which have very beautiful, attractive and delighted forms. All human beings are parts of the physical world. They are rational beings. So, they are capable of enjoying the natural beauty of all physical flora and fauna. This kind of eagerness in human-beings is called 'a sense of aestheticity.' The concept of aestheticity is the development out of the concept of 'aesthetics' which means 'theory of fine arts and a sense of beauty'. The word aesthetics has been developed out of the word aesthetic, which is a derivation from Greek word 'aesthesis', which means 'theory of fine arts and beauty'. Also aesthetics means a sense, which deals with beauty or beautiful things or artefacts or a taste of judging or analysing the beautiful things.

If an individual does not a sense of viewing, recognising and enjoying beauty of physical phenomena, he or she cannot be said a rational being. Such person cannot be equated with a rational being. Many animals have some perceptional capacity. They have a sensibility to recognise beautiful things. Even many birds express their emotions by creative works by fabricating their nets (*ghoslas*). Also an individual can express his emotions by doing creative works and fabricating beautiful useful things. This is called a sense of 'aestheticity' or ability of recognising beautiful aspects of physical things. As such, a sense of aestheticity is a vital human necessity. Through a sense of aestheticity in an individual can create many new beautiful things and who becomes an inventor. But then there occurs a situation in human life which makes an individual immune towards life situations and mute towards aestheticity. This happens because of laziness in life. In the present hedonistic and consumeristic age many parents shower too much of love over their children and make them lazy, sleepery-lazy and inactive. There is an adage "too much of love is always poisonous". This is why during old system of education, the youngers were sent to Gurukula Ashramas, which were away from their homes, to save them from unnecessary parental love.

Now, this is not possible. Because of affluency the mothers shower too much of love over their children and spoil them. For making the youngers active, creative and aesthetic, it is very necessary to educate them about art and craft activities. It is necessary for making the youngers sociable, cooperative and diligents. The area of art has a wide spectrum. There are three or four branches of art that is, (*a*) fine arts, (*b*) applied art or commercial art, (*c*) sculpture, and (*d*) other creative arts as wooden sculpture or stone sculpture. All these branches of arts need practice in free hand drawing, sketching, figure drawing, knowledge of perspective and anatomy, portraiture, landscaping, designing, composition and illustration. For making paintings and commercial art composition, knowledge of art materials required for making oil and water colour painting, is necessary. Applied art contains poster making, making of illustrations etc. etc. Making of wooden sculpture requires the knowledge about woods and tools required for making sculptures, soft woods or hard woods and their seasoning procedures. Therefore, it is necessary that the students should be properly educated and should be adequately apprised about the art theories and art practices.

Creativity is not only essential but is an utmost necessity of human life. Because it gives an astonishing newness to all human activities and develop a sense of aestheticity in human beings. Aestheticity promotes thinking, reasoning, analysing and motivates to acting in a creative manner, which leads to inventiveness. All these promote epistemacy, proficiency and sanity in human-beings. Without epistemacy, the human beings are like animals and are irrationals. It is epistemacy which always entails, thinking, reasoning, analysing, and comprehending which leads to learning. All these makes a man/woman a rational being different from other living/beings. It is, therefore, necessary to inculcate a sense, desire, and an urge for creativity in all youngers and also in adult human-beings. So the educational procedure to be adopted for teaching should be so designed which may create a sense of creativity in all fields of human life. Creativity is not the outcome of hard work. It can only be possible when mental and manual activities go hand in glove. Art activities always require mental and manual activities in human life. A human-being without a sense of creativity is like an animal. It is the sense of creativity which makes an individual different from an animal. So, it is very necessary to inculcate a sense of creativity in youngers while teaching and educating them. The school education should always have a place, in school curriculum for generating an urge to do creative works. Creativity leads to art.

For doing creative activities, which are termed as artistic activities, the knowledge of the 'concept of art' is necessary. The word 'Art' is a derivation from the Latin word 'Ars', which means doing something 'useful', which should be beautiful and delightful. Various thinkers have defined art in different ways. Some of the important references or descriptions about art are given below very briefly.

1. *Plato*: According to Plato, art is an activity or a careful creation, which requires a careful theory and practice while doing it (Ref. 10th book of Republic). According to Plato art can only be possible through practice which requires imitation.
2. *Aristotle*: According to Aristotle, art is one of the science, as are Physics, Philosophy. Art provides beautiful things for aesthetical use.
3. *Aquinas*: According to Aquinas, "for the creation of right things art is way of thinking".
4. *Lessing*: According to Lessing, every work of art has the principles for doing it.
5. *Hegel*: Hegel described different aspects of art. These are 'symbolic', 'classical', and 'romantic'. According to him, art is an absolute shining.
6. *Schopenhauer*: According to Schopenhauer, "music is the biggest art".
7. *Nietzsche*: According to Nietzsche, art is the manifestation of spiritual soul.
8. *John Dewey*: According to John Dewey, art is an experience like any other experiences. With the knowledge of art, creation of beautiful artefacts, things and architecture can

be possible. Aesthetic sense can only be possible through the knowledge of art. Aesthetics sense implies a sensible experience about the beautiful and delightful things. Because aesthetic things are always beautiful, so these always enculturate the human-beings.

9. The concept of aesthetics was also given by Baumgailen. Also, Herbert Read used the term aesthetics. Many philosophers and thinkers have further put forward their views as given below:
10. *Platinius*: Art is associated with beauty and creates splendour.
11. *Jaqnnus Maritan*: Beauty as transcendental, a concrete embodiment and is pleasing to the intellect. It is something more of Divine.
12. *Shaftburry & Huthson*: Art is the result of inner sense and sensitivity to harmony.
13. *Immanuel Kant*: Art is a sense of harmony in whatever is produced.
14. *Borsangot*: Borsangot was follower of Hegel. He described art as a concrete universal phenomenon.
15. *Thomas Aquinas*: Beautiful art objects are completely integrated and have perfection.
16. *Croce*: Art in which we find beauty is a specific act of imagination. It is a complete intuition.
17. *Tolstoy*: Art is an impression of emotions.
18. *Santayam:* Art is an objectified pleasure.
19. *Fredreg Scheller*: Basic category of life allowing morality and feelings are to be existent in art.
20. *Collingwood*: Art is concerned to reality of things and their historicity.
21. *Edward Bullough*: Art represents psychological distances.
22. *H.S. Langfield*: Art is a tentative activity within self and experience.
23. *Sigmund Freud*. Art is an inner drama of the human soul which occur due to repressed emotions which forces man/woman to create.
24. *Roger Pry*: Aesthetic emotions leads to artistic activity.
25. *Ortega Y. Gasset*: Dehumanisation due to modernisation forces man to create and construct new understandings.
26. *Theodor Lipps*: Art is expressed in objects.

27. *Sushan & Langer*: Art is a presentation of unconscious symbols.
28. *Clive*: Art is a significant form of human actions.
29. *Herbert Read*: Amongst all thinkers who put forward their views on art, Herbert Read tried to define art. He said that art is a metaphysical concept—an organic and measurable phenomenon. Art is deeply involved in human actions, perceptions, thought and contemplation. Not as much, a growing principle adopted to life, it is a governing mechanism. This mechanism is culture and civilisation which tries to balance human the social life.
30. Mrs. S.K. Langer said that art is a creative activity which has been done for the first time for one's personal satisfaction without any inclination.
31. Guru Rabindra Nath Tagore said that art is the manifestation of realising of transcendental reality. He said that there is a duality of 'person'. One is physical person who is temporary—comes and goes. Another is metaphysical or transcendental. Person who is permanent and is all pervasive. When a person is rewarded by Almighty God before he becomes grateful to the Divine Authority. Emotions arise in the physical person and he/she tries to express his/her emotions through creative artistic activity. All sculptures, images of Devi, Devtas, wall paintings and murals, relief sculptures found in temples are the testimonies of such art.
32. J. Krishnamoorthy said that art is a tool for enculturation.

As such, theories of art activities can be classified as (1) metaphysical theory as defined by Guru Rabindra Nath Tagore. So, Indian art can be said metaphysical art, (2) psychological theory of art advanced by Sigmund Freud, who was a renowned medical man. After doing M.D. in medicine from Vienna University, he started treating persons in Vienna suffering from fits. He observed that the repressed emotions are the reason of fits. He came to the conclusion that these repressed emotions are like an ice piece in the water of which a small portion can be seen and, no repressed emotion can be seen. These emotions are (*a*) fully repressed, (*b*) semi-repressed, and (*c*) partly repressed emotions. Sigmund Freud felt that if these fully repressed and semi-repressed are not taken out from the affected individual, these can be very dangerous. There can be two ways of taking out their repressed emotions either by giving an opportunity to the suffering person for doing some creative work or let him or her to face the illness. Doing creative work is an ideal and proper option. The second may be a killing option. Therefore, Sigmund Freud had recommended compulsory art activities for all youths. And the art education should be introduced in all educational institutions. He had also written two books on fits (1) 'Dora' and (2) 'Wolf' (two case studies of fits patients in psuedo-names). And on the basis of these case studies advanced the theory of education many artists adopted the principles of activity in art education. Painters like Picasso did painting applying this principle. Social modern Western paintings represent social heterogeneity. And Indian art activities represent divinity and spontaneity on modern paintings done on the principles of Western thinking that art is that which has been created for the first time is generally based on social heterogeneity.

Art is one of those activities, which represent soil, physical things, flora and fauna which are always found around us. And, art is something we not only find in museums and in art galleries or in old cities like Rome, Paris and Rameshwaram etc. etc. Art presents everything, it delights our senses and desires. There is a hierarchy in art. Many artistic qualities make the work of art of highest standard or type or quality. The work of art which does not appeal to the senses is not good. An aesthetic element is already present in perception itself.

The senses are so universal, so open to all kinds of perceptions which entails impressions interwoven with one another. It exchanges with senses ringing at every second, motivating a person to do something now which is called art. This is an universal human phenomenon. So school or college education should not ignore art, and should try to promote creative activities along with teaching other subjects.

What is art in true sense? To begin with it can be said that a work of art is something, which we call 'Form'. Form is a simple and small word. It is a derivation from the Greek word 'forma' meaning a shape. If someone plays a game well or runs well or does everything well, we can say that he or she is in good form. We mean that his/her body is trim, active, he or she acts quickly and efficiently. We also use this word for artistic activities like painting, moulding, fabricating, dancing, acting and singing etc.

etc. In comparison to other activities, the concept of form is well-connected with artistic activities. We also use the word 'form' as 'forming the cricket club', hobby club, art club, and nature study club etc. etc. The word 'form' means shape. Sometimes a 'form' is created in natural way as drops of dew makes a form, due to wind storm sand forms a den. The form actually means to take a new shape.

What does form mean in art? The shape of a work art is called 'art form' which is generally given by a deliberate action. Such action is the result of emotions. It does not matter whether it is a building or a statue or a poem or a painting or a sonata all these take specific specialised shapes which are called forms of art. The artist is not only a person who creates art forms, but the persons who composes music, writes poetry, makes furniture, prepares new cookies, designs, new clothes or dresses, etc. etc. are all form given.

A good form in art is that which pleases senses. The best works of art are those which have good forms. Then what are the conditions which help in making good forms? These conditions are which give to our senses most pleasure, not only to one sense but in two or more senses and finally to reservoir of all senses, which is our mind. This creates a sense of aestheticity in the mind of a person.

But what pleases one person many displease another. Then what is the touchstone outside the human peculiarities of human beings. This is the touchstone which exists in nature. And by nature, we mean the whole organic process of human life, its movements, that is, the process of human organised whole, which makes the existence of an individual possible.

The nature is so imminent and multiformal, that at first sight, it seems to be difficult to select any general or universal features, which may be touchstone for the form of things, we are going to analyse. Usually the artists do not seek such a touchstone. They sense it and find it instinctively. They try to provide art elements in the work of art, which exist in nature.

What are forms in nature? These are present in the vast space of the nature, that is, universe. These are interconnected and are found in microscopic cells and molecules of the matter, and given them a new shapes virtually, which are called 'forms'.

Many centuries ago Pythagoras and Plato had already found in many numbers of the clues of the nature of the universe and the mystery of natural beauty. Science and philosophy have undergone many transformation since then, but final result is that, the number is the basis of all forms, which matter assumes whether organic or inorganic in kind. That is, to say that the growth of particular things in particular shapes is determined by forces acting in accordance with certain inevitable mathematical and mechanical laws.

The bees cells might be taken as an example. Each cell is a honeycomb figured and has a form. It is very close to approach to a mathematical figure. Mathematics is the basis of measurements and proportions which are the basis of good form. When we call something beautiful, we recognise that certain mathematical proportions give rise to emotions in us which are normally associated with the work of art. Likewise many other examples can be cited which give rise to forms.

There are many symmetrical forms in nature, which we might see—like pelvis, bones of legs, hand bones, pairs of ribs in human body are examples. There is every reason to believe so not only in structure, but also in actual form. It is assumed that the bones are a mathematical solution to the problem regarding stress and strain in body. The modern railway and road bridges are result of geometrical form, which gives the shape to the bridge and protect these from stress and strain. Symmetry can be seen by observing anatomical structures. This is all due to naturalism as well as rationality and mathematical features.

Herbert Read said there is not only form in nature which is operational due to mathematical laws. According to Aristotle and Bertrand Russell (History of Philosophy) form is a shape given to matter. Bertrand Russel said (1) we start with marble for making a statue, here marble is matter with shape or form given is sculpture, (2) if a carpenter makes a replica out of a wooden piece, the wooden piece is matter and replica is a form. It is the virtue of form that matter is converted into something which looks creative and is useful and, is a usable substance. A thing is made by bounding or composing the matter together through a form. Form gives unity to a portion of the matter, and this unity is usually teleological but also is compositional and sometimes, it is virtual in two dimensional forms. Forms are substantial though materials are not universal. Things increase in actuality by form which is created in matter. Without form the matter is useless.

A sculpture made by the sculpture has a unity which is derived from its shape which actually is a form. The essential feature is a virtue which is the form of the body. Soul makes the body an organic whole having a purpose as an unit (Herbert Read, pp. 187-189). Finally, we can say that art is the ultimate structure which fulfils and embodies a shape or a form developed by the artist by means of appropriate material. And it can be said that form is the essence of a piece of work of art.

NATURE OF ART

Proportion

Nature is main source of manipulation for the artist. But a deliberate initiation of natural form for things like vessels, dishes etc. etc. emerge like shape of animals, leaves and fruits etc. etc. Of course such initiations are intelligent and diligent efforts but do not deserve appreciation as such initiative will be considered imitation. And imitation is not considered art. An imitation can never be worth of appreciation in the field of creativity which is the soul of art. Natural things develop spontaneousity and have basic laws of physics and mathematics. Take for example a pear shaped figure—a form derived from a fruit—pear, which has all tendencies which make the jug beautiful and utilitarian. Like this all organisms in nature are confirmed to the proportion, thus have curious mathematical properties. Ideal situation for the artist is that he/she should learn the principles of proportion and division from nature.

Composition

Getting inspired by the ideas of Herbert Read, that nature is the main source of artistic activities, I believe that the elements of 'composition', which are essential characteristics of any art work, are also derived from nature. Nature has opposite elements, also as bio-diversity in living beings, which makes the existence possible of living beings through unity in bio-diversity, without which the existence of the living can never be possible. For example, males and females are two opposites who are topsy-turvy, biologically and naturally. But when they are united it makes their living fruitful. It makes human social existence possible because they jointly produce their new off-springs. In other words social existence is only possible through their union. There are other things in the nature which are not only biologically supplementary as botanical things are, but these things exist and enhance the beauty of the nature. These things are beautiful and also enhance the creativity. Such things are found in abundance in natural flora and fauna. Like that artist composes many things which entail creativity and enhance art. As a human organic whole contains many body parts like head, hands and legs etc. which have bones, nerves, muscles, flesh, blood and skin etc. etc.; an art work is also made by joining like lines, perspective, rhythm, colour and hues, balance and proportion. By joining all these, a virtual element is created in the work of art which makes it attractive, beautiful and delightful. And a form is created through all these elements and this process is called 'composition'.

In the present industrial individualistic and materialistic age the man has become totally hedonistic, self-centred, greedy, materialistic and xenophilic. And for achieving all these, the man has totally become money minded. Old social values like simple living high thinking, doing work and respecting elders and fair sex have totally been vanished from the society. For the materialistic ends we have become totally materialistic. And for achieving the materialistic and hedonistic ends we have become greedy, self-centred and unsocial.

Therefore, it is necessary to review our examination based system of formal education and to adopt a socially progressive pattern of school and higher system of education soon. The introduction of creativity in education for aestheticity can be very useful for realising the dreams of social cohesion, because art and crafts activities makes man socially cooperative. So the artistic activities for school and higher education is a dire necessity in the present materialistic and hedonistic age. Herbert Read related the artistic activities in education as very essential activities. He said that the artistic activities can lead to the achievement of education which is to foster the individualistic, and social growth in each human being, at the same time harmonising the individuality and personality of the individual for the development of organic unity of the social group to which individual belongs. So according to Herbert Read art activities in education is a necessity. Likewise,

Frank Loyed Wright said, that art is a discipline of sense, that is, it is skilful, selective and intensive. To deny the artistic activities, the opportunities will be dangerous, that is, tantamount to deprive the individual's soul of beauty, aestheticity and sense of pleasure and enjoyment.

Because, the artistic activities mould the psyche of the child and makes him/her cooperative social beings, these should be given a proper place in school and higher education programmes. Every child has some inborn creative capacities and qualities. These should be nurtured and tapped in the early formative years of the child, then he/she can only be a balanced sane personality, who will be responsible, cooperative, sharing, social, intelligent and diligent person. Child's personality can only be moulded and developed as a balanced personality if his/her creative urges be tapped for his/her all round development. When language was not developed art symbols were the only source of communication. Art has been developed in various ways and forms—as realism forms of impressionism, expressionism, cubism, suralism and romanticism, etc. etc. Education is knowledge gained through old and new experiences. Art helps in this process. It also helps in educating through teaching aids.

Types of Artistic Activities and their Application

1. *Sketching*: For learning art sketching should be taught to the students. Sketching should be done of different flora and fauna. For doing sketching B1 or B2 or HB pencil should be used. Sketching should be done on white cartidge paper. While sketching, pencil should be hold correctly and proportion and perspective aspects should be taken into consideration.
2. *Still Life Drawing*: After learning sketching, the students should learn to make still life drawing. Proportion and perspective aspects should be applied while doing still life drawing.
3. *Landscaping*: After learning doing still 'life drawing' the students should be given chances of doing landscape drawing. Landscaping is making drawing of big area of land. Like landscape, seascape and nightscapes can also be made.

4. *Painting*: (oil and water colour) painting is done for making murals, portraits, folk social scenes and for making pictures on stained glass.
5. *Collage Painting*: Collage painting is done by using cut pieces and supplementing these with paints.
6. *Designing*: Making creative designs of greeting cards, wears, greeting cards and of usable things etc. etc.
7. *Graphic Arts*: Doing print making and making applied arts.
8. Applied or Commercial Art are doing textile design, furniture design, making posters, hoardings, costume design, doing make-ups, stage setting for dramatics, making illustrations for books etc.
9. *Decoration*: Making designs for doing Alpna, Rangoli and movable.
10. *Lighting*: Lighting is done for shadow plays and for showing various kinds of effects as storm, rain, nightscapes, etc. etc.
11. *Photography*: Photography is done for film making, film strips, slides etc. etc.
12. *Display*: Displaying artistic creations on special occasions such as Foundation Day, Alumni Day, Parents Day and Teachers Day, etc. etc.
13. *Exhibition*: The art objects done by the students should be collected and preserved in exhibition room.
14. House and Class Room Decoration should also be done through black-board illustrations and through flaunnel board get together and melas also.

In addition to the above art work there is immense scope of doing art activities as doing sculpture—in low relief and high relief, sculpture in round or in three dimensional, preservation of ancient movements and works of art and making teaching aids for teaching.

The inculcation of creativity in students, teaching of art and consequent doing of creative activities is the soul of school and higher education. Every educational institution should have provision for teaching art to the students. The art should be taught regularly and should be given equal weightage as given to other subjects. Generally it is seen that examination subjects are given importance in the present system of formal education and subjects like art and other like physical education, sports, social and cultural activities are ignored. Education is recovery of latent knowledge. For this recovery artistic activities are most important. Artistic activities always motivate the students to think and reason. These always remove boredom, release emotions and build a sound personality. But it is observed that artistic activities in schools, colleges and also in teachers training colleges are generally ignored. Not only this the art and craft teachers are generally considered inferior to other teachers who teach other subject. As such, there is an academic bias against manual work. This is due to our examination system which is only subjects based. This situation is not only common feature in our Indian society but it is found in other societies also. At least during the present democratic regime this practice should be discontinued. There should be a soul searching in this regard and art and craft teachers should be given their due status; and their services should be fully utilised for proper education of the students. For this all teachers of the educational institutions should take active part in artistic creative activities. These activities are so many, which can help the students in their career building. Such activities can improve the image of the educational institutions. Though these activities have already been mentioned earlier, there is no harm to repeat these activities again. The artistic creative activity can boost the co-curricular activities. On special occasions like national days, parents day, alumni day, teachers day, foundation day and valedictory etc. etc. decoration should be done by doing rangoli and alpana. Like this special programmes should be arranged in which artistic activities should be done. All teachers should organise and participate in such programme and should train the students. The artistic activities can prepare the students to be creative, inventive and enterprenuing in their future life. These can develop everything aesthetically. The present system of our formal education has more or less killed our work culture in the society. The work culture can be revived through artistic activities in education system. As such, artistic activities are necessary for the life building of our youngers. Artistic activities can help in the preparation of the teaching aids.

Onus for the artistic pursuit lies with the educational administrators. They should know the worth of the artistic activities fully and should take necessary steps for art education in all educational institutions. Every school should have an art room and a craft room or workshop. Necessary equipments, tools and raw materials should also be provided. And finally the art teacher and craft teacher should dedicate themselves to creativities in education. They should earnestly cooperate in organising all functions in the school or college. They should also preserve creative works done by the students and display these in exhibition room. The best creative students should be justly assessed and rewarded. And art and craft activities should be given due weightage in school or college annual assessment.

27

Teaching Aids in Education

Plato said that "excellent education is that which begins with eyes. It is a recovery of which we possessed previously and recover it with our senses". There is a Chinese adage "we remember what we see and forget what we hear". Also many thinkers like Comenius, John Locke, John Dewey, J.J. Rousseau laid emphasis on sensory experience for learning. As such, sensory experiences are key to learning. Due to intensive industrialisation and consequent spread of formal education in schools and colleges the teaching is done in mechanical way, aiming to mould all of the students in the same cast, that is, to secure highest marks in annual examination. Gurudev Rabindra Nath Tagore had rightly described the present alienistic Indian formal system of education, a mechanical process of education. So our schools and other institutions of education still follow the conflict model of teaching. Good examination results is the dominant aspiration of schools and other educational institutions and, also of the parents and the teachers. So, the students are pressurised to do intensive preparation for the annual examinations. The curriculum for teaching is so designed that the students come in flying colours in their annual examinations. All students are required to study the prescribed subjects in spite of their tastes and abilities. Individual differences of the students are totally ignored. The teachers are required to teach the same subject contents to all students whether the students are interested or not. The teacher has to teach in six periods out of total eight periods. In addition to this society expects that the teachers should also inculcate good life attitudes in order to enculturate them. In addition to all this the teachers are required to do some additional jobs as evaluation of the students work, to attend some extension services, seminars and to do some office work relating to classroom teaching. As such, under such a situation the school and college education and teaching has become a very challenging job for both the male and female teachers. Also the demographic explosion had added fuel to this fire of education. And due to heavy teaching and teaching related workload in order to cover the whole course, the teachers are generally forced to adopt 'conflict teaching model' whereby mere information is poured on the students through 'one way communication'. And the real process of education often is ignored. As such, to meet this illogical teaching situation and, for providing true education the use of two-way communication through the use of teaching aids has become very necessary.

Education, the teacher, teaching methods, and the teaching aids are correlated. Though these are supplementary to each other, these have different meanings also. The teaching has emerged out of the word 'Taccon', a Greek word, meaning, 'to instruct', 'to impart', 'to pass on what one knows'. The word 'education' is a derivation from the Latin word, 'educare' meaning to 'bring out' 'to grow up', to take out'. Teaching is usually done by a knowledgeable person. He/she possess knowledge and passes it to a person (or persons) who does not know about it. Education and teaching are two different concepts contrary to each other. In teaching the teacher who knows the subject-matter, passes it to a younger (or youngers) who does not know it. But education is a process through which one tries to know himself or herself. If the teaching does not innovate and motivate the students for self-learning it can never be said education. Mere passing of information makes the students passive, inactive, introvert and non-expressive because mere passing of information does not innovate the students to think, reason and comprehend and to self-learning. In the modern sense the education has varied meanings. It is a process of upbringing of the youngers. It is an instrument of change which leads an individual to modernity. It is an instrument of upward mobility in socio-economic, cultural, political and in epistemic fields. Karl Marx said that education is used by the strong to exploit the weak. Education is also used for ushering the religion by the theocrats. Prof. M.N. Srinivas said that education is a transformation of accumulated knowledge. Many sociologists said that the education is a vehicle of enculturation, acculturation, cultural diffusion and socialisation, so on and so forth. As such, it may be assumed that education is a process of development of innate human potentialities and capabilities, what are already within the human biological whole or entity of a person.

Teaching and education both are complimentary and supplementary to each other. Education is not possible without teaching and, teaching is useless if it is not educating the students through self-learning which can only be possible by igniting the students through the use of teaching aids. The use of teaching aids makes two way communication possible. The communication is done through various symbols as given below:

1. gestures,
2. through spoken and written words (non-discursive and discursive),
3. by showing concrete things,
4. through contrived experiences,
5. through pictures, photographs, illustrations, maps and flash-cards etc. etc.,
6. through projections,
7. through displays, decorations and exhibitions.

Teaching is basically done through two kinds of symbols:

(*a*) Non-discursive symbols, that is, verbal, words-spoken and written,

(*b*) Discursive symbols, that is, non-verbal media like concrete things or contrived experiences of concrete things, through maps, pictures, charts, illustrations, flash-cards, models diagrams and maps etc. etc.

In teaching both kinds of communications, that is (1) verbal or non-discursive, and (2) non-verbal or discursive symbols are used. Then only teaching lead to educating. In olden times, conservative methods of teaching were used. The teaching was aimed at to pass on cultural heritage for moral socialisation for saneful social living. The teacher (*Guru*) used to be an authority. He used to have proficiency in all these fields. He used to observe teaching professional ethics. He was non-inclinative. He used to pass on information on the above mentioned areas verbally to his disciples (*Shishyas*), the students in Gurukula Ashramas for their life building. As such, the teaching was basically teacher oriented. The students used to accept what the teacher used to tell them. But in some countries the situation was different, as it was in India and China. In India, in Gurukulas there used to be lengthy session of debates and discussions [*Vad* (वाद) and *Vivad* (विवाद)] between the teachers (*Gurus*) and *Shishyas*. This was an important educational activity in Indian old system of education. In China, teaching was based on showing of things. There is an important Chinese adage "what we hear we forget and what we see we remember". In other countries teaching was done basically through non-discursive verbal one-way communication. Teaching done verbally does not lead to education, which is only possible through self-learning and knowledge formation. Teaching verbally merely remains information.

From the olden times thinkers have been continuously supporting the use of discursive symbols along with the non-discursive symbols of communication in teaching. Socrates said 'perception is the better source of knowledge'. Plato said 'knowledge is only possible through perception, comprehension and understanding'. Aristotle said 'that knowledge is only possible through the study of matter. Rene' Desecrates said 'every person has some innate ideas, these ideas should be tapped through thinking, reasoning and comprehending'. Thinking can only be possible through perception of concrete things or their contrived images. John Locke rejected this assumption of rationality put forward by Rene' Desecrates, he had put forward under the assumption of innate ideas. John Locke said that the child has no such innate ideas at the time of his/her birth. The child is mere a biological whole at the time of his/her birth. As he/she grows his/her sense organs also grow. Initially, the mind of the child is like a 'Tabula Rasa' (empty slate). And the child starts writing on his/her mental slate (Tabula Rasa) through perception (*per se*). John Locke advocated that the human sense perception is the only source of knowledge. Therefore, he pleaded that sensory experience in teaching as "hardening". He/she should be forced to go out while snow is falling. Likewise J.J. Rousseau, who was propounder of naturalism said that "the child is born free but he/she finds himself/herself in chains". The society imposes many social restrictions on the child and forces the child to obey". For learning the child should be given chances to perceive the natural phenomena. Following these assumptions many thinkers advocated for the sensory experiences for real education. A.J. Ayre said that 'true education is that which can be verified'. David Hume said 'dogmatism should not have any place in education'. Comenius was the first person who thought of the use of pictures in teaching. He also had suggested that the books should also be illustrated. He introduced the didactic method of teaching, out of which heuristic methods of teaching emerged. He had written two books on teaching aids (1) Orbis Pictus (teaching with the help of pictures), and (2) Didactus teaching through methods which could elicit information from the students. Froebel said that child's curiosity for knowing should be exploited. M.K. Gandhi said that "all the best should be taken out from the child through hand work". John Dewey laid emphasis on pragmatism in education. He advocated pragmatism in education which could only be possible through sensory experiences. Captain Robin Cook was the first person who utilised his artistic skills in making teaching aids, which he used in a grammar school in London. Gurudev Rabindra Nath Tagore laid stress on nature and freedom, and also on simplicity. And for achieving all these aims he had established Viswa Bharti University at Bolpur in Bengal. Fed up with the bookish and informative education through one way teaching, which promoted Western cultural diffusion and consequent acculturation, J. Krishnamoorthy had established many Rishi Schools on the pattern of Gurukula Ashramas on the river banks in jungles in Andhra Pradesh and Rajghat Schools on the right bank of the river Ganga near Varanasi. He was fed up with the formal type of education imposed on India by the East India Company British Government. And many thinkers laid stress on the use of audio-visual aids in teaching.

The process of education should always be a 'didactic process' without which self-learning cannot be possible. The self-learning actually is education. If teaching does not motivate the students for self-learning, and it is done through one way communication, it will make the students dummy passive receivers, who can never try to think, reason, analyse and comprehend. Such students will be introvert and non-expressive. Such persons can never be creative thinkers. As such, self-learning is very necessary for the youngers to become inventors in future. So teaching, whether it is done in schools or colleges should always entail use of audio-visual aids so to motivate the students to think, reason, analyse, comprehend, understand and, finally to learn and express. All great men were prone to thinking and learning. They were using 'didactic approach'. Didactics is a method of teaching in which bi-polar communication method is applied and efforts are made to have maximum interaction between the teacher and the taughts. This can only be possible when the teacher applies progressive method of teaching such as heuristic method, project method, discussion method and demonstration method etc. etc. These methods can only be applied when teaching audio-visual aids are used very effectively and sincerely during the course of lesson development. All great men like Goethe, Homer, Milton, Shakespeare, Schopenhauer, Rene Desecrates, G.E. Moor, Immanuel Kant, Hegel, Neitze etc. in the West and Kalidas, Tulsidas, Surdas, Kabir, Guru Nanak, Swami Dayanand Saraswati, Rabindra Nath Tagore, Vivekananda, Ramakrishna Paramhans, Ramanujam, J. Krishnamoorthy and C.V. Raman etc. in India could educate themselves through didactic approach, that is, self-learning. Likewise all great thinkers in the field of sociology, philosophy and physical sciences applied didactic approach in educating themselves.

As such, teachers' approach while teaching in classroom should be to create a didactic atmosphere for eliciting knowledge from the students. It can only possible by using appropriate teaching aids. The use of teaching aids during teaching can lead the students to self-learning and make teaching progressive.

As such during the course of teaching, the teacher should keep in mind the pedagogic aspects. The word 'pedagogic' is a combination of two Greek words 'peda' which means, 'child' and 'gogic', which means 'concerning'. As such, the teacher should apply suitable approach for the development of the child or younger. For pedagogic understanding three elements should be studied:

(*i*) Pedagogic epistemological stand points,
(*ii*) Pedagogic psychological stand points, and
(*iii*) Pedagogic personalistic stand points.

Epistemological stand points refer to the epistemological conditions which can promote self-learning and can lead to knowledge development. How can the child be motivated to learn and how? What teaching aids can be useful in this pursuit. And how can these aids be prepared? The teacher must have knowledge of the related epistemic situations for proper teaching. The teacher should try to know the psychological conditions of the classroom students, in order to promote learning by the students. He/she should try to know the psyche of individual student. This can be possible by establishing individual close rapport with each students. The teacher should have a close sympathetic ear. To make the pupils psychologically sound to the brain, the child should be understood as an individual. He/she should be loved and should be respected. He/she should be stimulated, innovated, motivated and encouraged. Pedagogic understanding implies and aims at knowing the unknown.

Audio-visual aids provide sensory experiences, which are the bases of knowledge. There are five senses—(1) Visual (eyes), (2) Aura (ears), (3) Olfactory (nose), (4) Gustatory (tongue), and (5) Tactile (skin). They are called gateways of knowledge. To begin with thinking is necessary which is generated by concrete experiences. Learning occurs due to concrete experiences. And these lead to learning as these appeal to senses. As such, there is a strong case for using audio-visual teaching aids by the teacher during the course of teaching.

Though all of the five senses are important for learning. But in many cases, particular sensory experience is most suitable for learning and knowing, though stress is generally laid on aural and visual senses because without these two senses, teaching and learning are not possible. If a teacher does not use verbal communication and only use non-verbal communication, the students do not understand. If verbal and non-verbal communications are used simultaneously then only learning becomes possible. Since verbal communication is non-discursive, it does not evoke thinking and reasoning which are necessary for learning and knowing. Whereas, non-verbal communication, which is done through the use of audio-visual aids, which is discursive, is useful in self-learning since this evoke thinking and reasoning.

Use of audio-visual aids in teaching always makes teaching easy. It makes the students active. They respond in the classroom and learn quickly. So these accelerate the rate of learning and increase the span of retention. More self-learning, quick learning and larger retention is the slogan of audio-visual technologists. Sixty or seventy years ago the teaching in almost all educational institutions was basically done through verbal communication. Now the entire field of education in urban areas is more or less supported by audio-visual education, and teaching is aimed at self-learning. But in rural areas, the schools do not use teaching aids. It is because, generally the teachers in rural schools first do their homework and skip doing teaching properly. This is why our rural youths are not well-educated in comparison to urban youths. Due to the advancement of science and technology progressive methods of teaching have become mandatory for the teachers. It is, therefore has also become mandatory for the schools. It is, therefore, has become necessary that the teacher should be fully aware about the audio-visual aids and the techniques and methods of their use so that the students could learn effectively and could increase their span of retention. More learning, quick learning and larger retention is the need of the day in the present age of science and technology.

As sensory experiences are bases of effective learning and knowledge development. Edger Dale (USA) suggested a cone of experience which can help in providing a series of sensory experiences and which can help in providing of learning through the use of audio-visual aids.

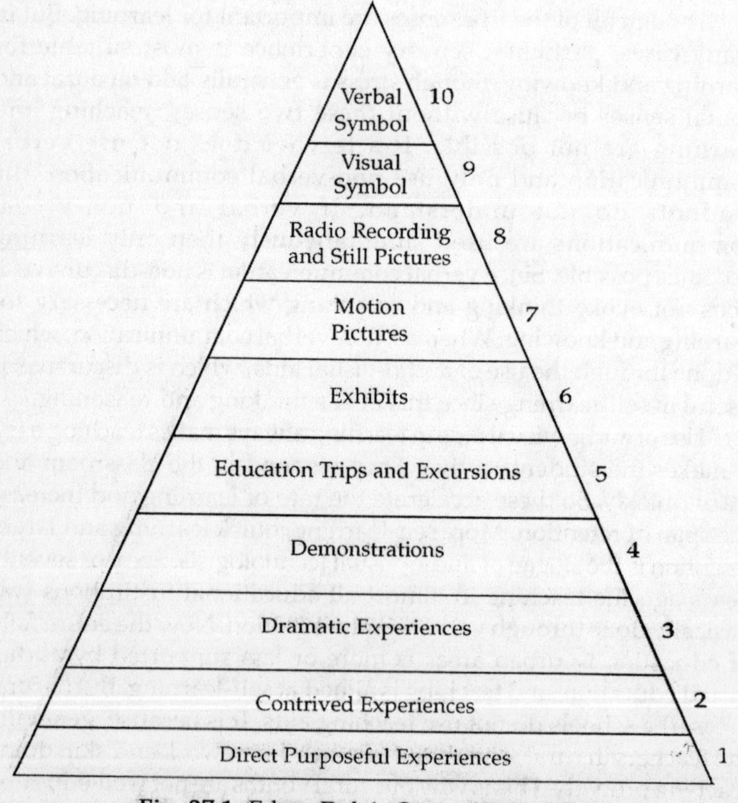

Fig. 27.1: Edger Dale's Cone of Experience

Though all of the five senses are important in learning, stress is laid on aural and visual senses as these are widely used in classroom teaching. Every object cannot be shown in real form in the classroom teaching. In the absence of actual things their pictures or photos, replicas or models or diaromas are shown by the teacher in the classroom. The teaching aids or audio-visual aids sometimes give dual perspective and create confusion. A three dimensional model or diaroma of a thing is also a source of per-se (perception) like that of a picture. It can be touched also. Broadly speaking the teaching aids, which are called audio-visual aids can be divided into two categories: (1) projected aids, and (2) non-projected aids. Though projected aids are the image of real things, which arc projected on a screen with the projections. Films, filmstrips, slides and other transparencies come under this category. Non-projected aids constitute the bulk of audio-visual aids. The projected and non-projected aids can be classified as Fig. 27.2.

In projected aids the images are projected on a screen with the help of projectors. Films, filmstrips, slides and other transparencies come under this category. Non-project aids constitute the bulk of audio-visual aids. Pictures, photographs, graphs, maps are major visual-aids. Also chalk-board (named as black-board), bulletin board, tag board etc. etc. come under this category. Display boards, diaromas, globes, human skeleton and models come under the category of experiences giving teaching aids.

UTILISATION OF AUDIO-VISUAL AIDS

Even the most effective teaching aids may become ineffective in the hands of an inexperienced and non-serious teacher. Right use of right material at the right place on right occasion constitute four 'Rs' which are the right steps for the right use of teaching—aids that can lead to proper education. The teacher while using the audio-visual aids during teaching must keep in mind (1) educational outcome or expected elicitations from the students, (2) nature and complexity of the subject to be taught or developed, (3) methodology of teaching to be applied, (4) related experience are to be given to the students, and (5) appropriate audio-visual aids to be used should be decided accordingly to the complexity and objectives of teaching. How can the audio-visual aids be related to the lesson development, should be

Types of Audio-Visual Aids

Projected Aids

1. Copying Units and Projected aids
   - (*i*) Epidioscope
   - (*ii*) Electro-photostate machine
   - (*iii*) Film Strip Projector
   - (*iv*) Slide Projector
   - (*v*) Opaque Projector
   - (*vi*) Overhead Projector
   - (*vii*) Film Strips
   - (*viii*) Slides
   - (*ix*) T.V.
   - (*x*) Video and V.C.R.
   - (*xi*) Telescope
   - (*xii*) Sterescope
   - (*xiii*) Magic Lantern
   - (*xiv*) Live Film Projector
   - (*xv*) Slide Cassettes

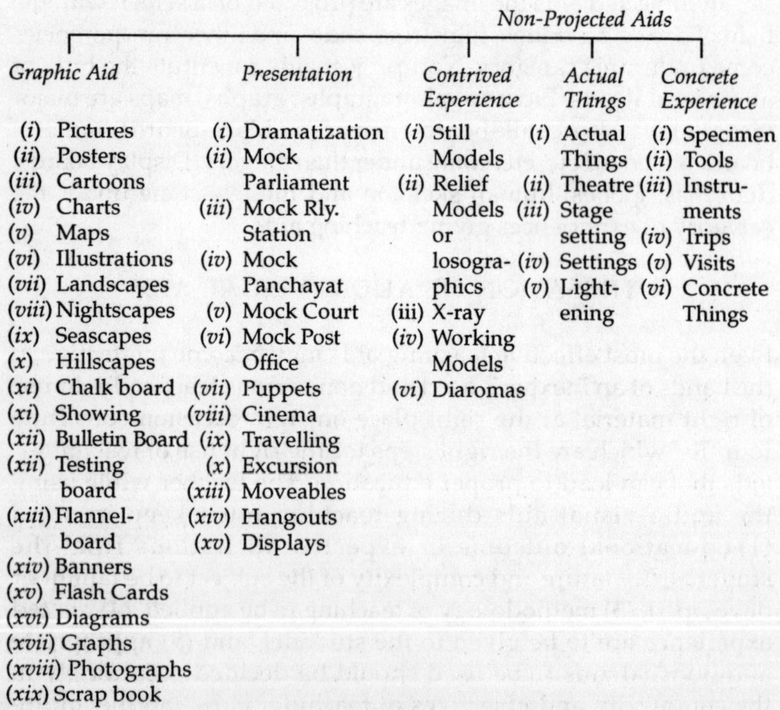

Fig. 27.2: Types of Audio-Visual Aids

decided according to the needs of the students? There are different scopes of the use of teaching aids. The teacher should not use more than one teaching aid at one time. This will create confusion in the minds of the students. In order to avoid the trouble of displaying charts, models and maps etc. again and again some teachers display all charts before they start teaching. This is not a correct procedure, as the students get confused with such unnecessary, untimely mass display. An appropriate teaching aid should be displayed at an appropriate time.

While using the projected aids like films, filmstrips, slides and transparencies etc. the teacher should give an introductory talk to the students about the material before he/she is going to use during teaching. Also after the projection of such aids there should be a follow-up discussion. Films of 8 mm, 16 mm, 35 mm and 70 mm are prepared for projection. But generally films of 8 mm and 16 mm size are used for educational purposes. In Indian schools 16 mm film are used widely. A 16 mm sound film has (wholes) pockets on one margin, and sound track on the other side. Therefore, in 16 mm sound projector the pockets should have claws on the one side only. 16 mm silent film has pocket holes on both sides of film. It needs a silent projector also. Therefore, a 16 mm slide or silent film should be inserted in 16 mm silent projector. Therefore, a 16 mm film should not be inserted in 16 mm silent projector, as its both sides will spoil the film and the film will be totally spoiled. Only a sound projector should be used for sound films.

Advantages of Motion Pictures in Teaching

These are audio, as well as, visual aids, thus appealing to (1) both the senses at the same time, (2) because of their presentation is done on a limited screen in total or in semi-darkness, attracts the students to see the presentation, (3) the pupils generally try to identify with the events presented on the screen, the presentation appeals to the emotions of the pupils, (4) the presentation enables the students to observe the objects, places and events not ordinarily seen in their lives. The film presentations are close to the life situations, as such their presentations contribute to life realism. But the film projectors and films are costly. Films on so many topics may not be easily available. The teachers sometimes use the films for mere relaxation and rest from teaching. In such a situation the use of films is generally done only for entertainment and not for instructional purpose. Many teachers, usually do not know how to operate the film projectors and use films. This makes them dependent on others who are few in numbers. In spite of all these limitations, the films, that are motion pictures or T.V. programme, are very useful, purposeful and powerful audio-visual aids for teaching. A teacher using these aids should arrange a follow-up programme after the film or T.V. programme. All students should be guided to note down important points while they visualising the programme and follow-up programme should cover all these points.

Filmstrips

Filmstrips are useful teaching aids. A film, one foot to three foot long is used for preparing the filmstrips. It may have thirty to fifty still pictures. These pictures are framed. There are two sizes of filmstrips frames—18 mm and 24 mm. A film strip is adaptable to projector of both kinds of frames (as these are framed). The filmstrips are cheap and easily transportable. Filmstrips can be shot on camera, and can be framed at home according to the size of the film projector. For storing the filmstrips card board racks should be made at home. Filmstrips can be projected easily for a desirable time, again and again.

Slides

Slides are made from 35 mm films (2″ × 2″). Slides are photographic slides. Glass slides either may be hand made or photographic slides. The 2″ × 2″ slides can also be projected using a film strip projector after fixing in the slides gate.

The teachers can only prepare slides with 3.25″ × 3.25″ or 2″ × 2″ glass plates using Indian ink or cellophane paper having printed or written matter. Semi-transparent glass can also be used for preparing the slides. One surface of the glass should be coated with a solution or gelatine. Writing should be done on the surface. Thereafter, it should be covered with another glass plate of the same size and glued using moisture resistant glue. The slides are flexible teaching aids, that is their sequence is not fixed. The teacher can arrange these serially according to their needs. This is the major advantage of slides over filmstrips. Slides need more storage space. The glass slides are breakable. The teacher has to be very cautious while putting the glass slides into slide gates avoiding vertical and lateral inversion during projection.

NON-PROJECTED AIDS

Graphic aids are powerful media for teaching and learning. Through their visualisation the graphic aids simplify ideas and concepts. Conventional symbols are used in the graphic teaching aids. They represent judicial form of drawings, illustrations, graphics, pictures and also written words. These graphic aids are usually two-dimensional and many of these can be projected through opaque projector (epidiascope). As already mentioned, charts, posters, diagrams, maps and flash-cards are some of the important graphic aids. In addition to these illustrations, graphs, photographs, cartoons and maps are some graphic aids. Some of the graphic aids are mentioned below briefly.

Chart: "A chart is a combination of graphic material and pictorial media, especially designed to present the subject content and, thereby, elicit information from the students". Charts are useful to show relationships, classification of content by means of pictorial media, figures or statistics to present the subject content systematically, creating problems for stimulating the students to think, reason, comprehend and to respond. As such, a chart is an appropriate tool to catch elicitations from the students. Charts can be classified as tree chart, flow chart, time chart etc. etc. The word 'chart' is derivation from the Greek word 'charta' meaning a 'plan of action'. And sea pirates, dacoits, burglars used to make chart for their action plans. Comenius was the first thinker to think of educational Chart. After him Captain Cook, who was serving in British army in Australia materialised the dreams of Comenius.

Poster: A poster is a pictorial device designed to communicate and attract attention to a fact or an idea, an image, a social event, an economic development, a political event or an image to catch the attention of the masses quickly and more effectively. In other words, the posters are generally used to make a wide spread publicity. A poster can be useful in communicating community's common interest either at public places or in classroom teaching. Big posters installed on roadsides are called 'hoardings'.

Diagram: A diagram is an explanatory drawing. It highlights the inter-relationship through lines, geometrical figures, forms and symbols.

Graph: A graph represents a qualitative data including comparisons and relationships which are clearly shown through graphs.

Cartoons: A cartoon is a metaphysical presentation in the form of tainted illustration depicting a picture.

Comics: The children like comics. Comics are useful in teaching language, socio-economic and political conditions and affairs.

Maps: Maps vary in types and forms. In education maps are usually used in teaching history, geography, economics and political science in schools.

Photographs: Photographs or pictures pasted on a thick cartridge paper or card board are shown in the classroom teaching. If the photographs are big, big sheets of paper or card should be used. These should not be used for a prolonged time.

Flash-cards: A flash-card is a small compact picturised card. A flash-card is used to apprise the students in the classroom about the new physical phenomena, new ideas or concepts. The flash-cards are generally very useful in introducing new words or things to the young pupils.

Chalk-Board: Chalk-boards are generally called black-boards as mostly black surface chalk-boards are used in classroom teaching. The chalk-boards are extensively used in teaching. A class is incomplete without a chalk-board. The chalk-board is the oldest and simplest visual teaching aid. The chalk-board was developed during the Christian protestant religious movement launched by Martin Luther in Germany. The Catholics were very strict and they did not allow any protest against the religious orthodoxy. The followers of Martin Luther had adopted a hideout protest method. They wrought their views on the empty walls in the night which was read by the people in the day. Later on this method was adopted by the Church schools in Europe. In due course of time, because of colonialism, the colonisers used the chalk-board in their missionary schools, which were established by them in their captured countries. They used it as a teaching aid. Now the use of chalk-board has become a universal phenomenon, and these are used in schools throughout the world. Now there are various kinds of chalk-boards as—wooden chalk-board, glass chalk-board, plywood chalk-board, cemented chalk-board, role-up chalk-board, sliding chalk-board and curtain chalk-boards etc. etc. A chalk-board or a black-board is an important teaching aid. It is a kind of teaching tools in the hands of the teacher. A teacher cannot proceed without a chalk-board in the classroom. But one of the agony is that many teachers are not fully aware about the desirable qualities of the chalk-board. This is because many teacher training institutes in the country do not give sufficient training to the pupil-teachers. Such institutes do not give importance to such an important teaching tool. Following are some basic important points regarding chalk-board which the teachers should keep using in his/her mind while using the chalk-board during teaching in the classroom:

1. The lower edge of the chalk-board (black-board) should be at the eye level of pupil's eyes.
2. There should not be reflection of glaring light on the chalk-board.
3. There should be six feet minimum distance between the chalk-board and the first row of the students.
4. The letters written on the chalk-board should be bold, straight and bright.
5. Overwriting, that is repeated writing and incomplete writing should not be done while doing chalk-board work.
6. Writing should be done slowly so as to give chance to the students to have a pace with the teacher.
7. The teacher should not stand before the chalk-board while teaching.
8. The pupils as well as, the teacher should not talk during teaching.
9. Any material should never be pasted or nailed on the surface of the chalk-board, as it will spoil the surface of the board.
10. The chalk-board is a trusted friend of the teacher, as well as of the students. It should always be given a friendly treatment. It should be properly dusted just after the chalk-board work is over. If the chalk-board is left undusted the coming teacher will be annoyed.
11. The chalk-board is a mistake rectifier. The teacher should not be got annoyed if any student clinches the mistake in chalk-board work. Rather he or she should be thankful to the student or students.

12. The students should be given sufficient time to cope with the teaching and note down all important points.
13. If possible the students should also be involved in (black-board work) chalk-board work.
14. The black-board or chalk-board should be dusted and painted regularly.
15. The teacher should use necessary accessories or material for doing chalk-board work as (*a*) good white and coloured chalks like Indian red, purple, yellow and blue etc. etc. Blue chalks are used for depicting oceans, (*b*) a chalk tray for keeping chalks and duster; (*c*) a piece of wet cloth; and (*d*) also some chalk-board equipments like templates, compass, square, right angled scale and an enlarger.
16. While starting chalk-board, the teacher should write date, class to be taught, period and topic.

A variety of techniques can be applied while doing chalk-board work. Templates are used for drawing geometrical and biological figures. Punching method is used for drawing maps. In this method a master map is first drawn, dots are punched on this marker map which can be used for making another map. Grid method is also used for drawing human figures. Role-up chalk-board is used for doing chalk-board work in advance. The teacher must be aware about chalk-board paint which is different than oil and enamel paint.

Display Boards

Display of educational material is very essential for student's self-learning. Display material is generally used for sociological, cultural and axiological development of the students. Our present examination oriented, alienistic formal system of education does not have any provision for the development of these qualities in the students. Because the present education system is totally examination oriented, the teachers generally remain busy in teaching the subjects for annual examinations. They do not give time for inculcating the axiological, cultural and sociological norms in the pupils. The parents of the students are gripped in money earning activities for meeting their hedonistic requirements. This aim can be achieved through the display techniques. It can be done by display material like, banners, useful sayings, paintings, artifacts, mobiles, etc. etc. For displaying such axiological matter, for the character building of the youngers, display material like chalk-boards, flaunnel boards, bulletin boards are extensively used.

For classroom display chalk-board can be used when it is not used for teaching. But generally for display a bulletin board is used. The bulletin board should be fixed on the classroom wall or on the walls of the educational institutions where there is a permanent passage. The lower edge of the bulletin board should be at the eye level of the students. As such, the bulletin boards in lower or nursery classes should be at the lower level. The bulletin boards are generally made of insulation boards, as these are very soft and may take drawing pins easily and display material can be fixed easily. Pictures, clippings, cartoons, paper cuttings and other materials on various topics can be displayed on bulletin board. Such educational material should be collected and kept ready for educational display. At a time only one specific theme like epistemic axiological, social, cultural or economic should be displayed. Pictures, photographs should be displayed on contrast coloured sheets or contrast coloured paper or on contrast coloured cloth. Lettering should be done wherever it is necessary. The students should be stimulated to do or follow necessary moral, social, cultural and economic activities through displays. The bulletin board display is useful in introducing, explaining and reviewing topics previously taught in the schools or colleges. Bulletin boards are useful for carrying out useful co-curricular and extra-curricular activities in educational institutions.

For doing or getting displays done by the students every teacher must be aware how to use epidiascope for enlarging small drawings on a full size drawing sheet. The teachers must know to project chalk-board, work transparencies on overhead projector while teaching the same topic in more than one section of the same class. It would be good if teachers learn how to use filmstrips and slide projector. Also, there are some activity aids like arranging mock Parliament, mock state assembly, excursion, educational tours, dramatisation, arranging melas and exhibitions, doing decoration at the time of special functions like orientations, teacher's day, national days, foundation day and valedictory day. On all these occasions displays can be arranged. Displays can play a very useful role in inculcating good life attitudes, habits and thereby character building and personality development.

But it is observed that in majority of the schools and colleges neither use the teaching aids are used during teaching nor proper displays are done. Only the teaching is done in mechanical way for examination.

As such use of teaching aids in teaching and displays are very necessary. The teaching aids are nerves of teaching for proper education. So, knowledge of teaching aids to the teacher is must. They should be well-informed about the teaching aids. This can be done if teachers training institutions properly educate the pupil-teachers. And after this the school authorities also give due attention and weightage to the use of teaching aids and display during teaching. The teachers should also involve the students in the preparation of teaching aids—like charts, maps, models and dioramas, etc. etc. With the use of teaching aids the educational standard can be improved and solo-track of formal education can be changed.

28

Morality, Religiosity, Spirituality and Secularism

Main aim of education should be to develop sanity and morality in youngers who are our future guardians. This is not possible without inculcation of sociability and a sense religiosity and spirituality in them. This is to be developed first in the family and later on in educational institutions. But in the present socio-economic and cultural atmosphere neither it is possible through school and college education, nor in families through familial education. The present families due to killing temper of greed, self-centredness greatly remain busy in money earning. Of course, it is true, that without earning an individual cannot sustain, live and exist in the society. But sustinance and living a hedonistic, consumeristic and materialistic, luxurious life are two different topsy-turvy ways of living. The living only for sustinance leads a man to simple living and high thinking which leads a man to sanity, morality, religiosity, spirituality, cooperation sharing, brotherhood and to common good. And luxurious hedonistic living always leads a man to greed, self-centeredness, nepotism, corruption and crimes. In the present social structure, generally the individual prefers to earn as much as possible and, ignores other life aspects as—to pray Almighty God, to behave well with the members of the society, to respect the elders and fair sex and to protect the weak, children, animals and natural flora and fauna. The present man/woman have no time to pray the Divine Authority who creates all living beings, flora and fauna and protect them. Generally the present families got the prayers done by the *pujaris* (priests) and that too periodically—once a year or twice a year. And on such occasions they arrange *'kirtans'* and *'bhajans'*, distribute *prasadas* and, some arrange *lungars* also. This situation has made the man purely henotheistic, polytheistic and believer in tanterism.

Actually this theocratic change has occurred due to constant Western cultural diffusion in Indian culture which has resulted in total acculturation of the Indian society. We Indians have totally become materialistic, consumeristic, and hedonistic. Our key social institutions, like joint family have been totally crumbled. Earlier, the families were more monotheistic. The elders used to pray the divine authority, that is, Almighty God daily. For that, 'early to bed early to rise' was necessary. Now, even the elders do not pray because of their involvement in money earning. Most of them earn throughout the day and when they come back to home they count the money late in the night. And for getting more money now they have become polytheistic, henotheistic and believer in tanterism. In other words, it can be said that they follow the western style of praying. St. Calvin had advised the western people to earn throughout the week and go to church, only once a week on Sunday for praying. In Islam five times prayer by offering namaz at five times is must. But many Muslims also remain busy in earning throughout the day. Simple living and high thinking, believing in the presence of Almighty God in the form of individual soul were the epicentres of morality in human beings. As such, the earlier the man was 'humane' and 'moral'. Now this is missing. In spite of the fact that the Indian society is multi-religious, multi-racial, multi-lingual and multi-cultural and due to tolerance which was the outcome of homogeneity and morality which kept the Indian society integrated. And 'unity in diversity' became the main feature of the Indian social structure of the Indian society. Earlier Indians were religious, spiritual, social and moral. They used to pray Almighty for the common good. Last five *mantras* of *Rigveda* are the proof of it. Now people use religion as an identity label, and they used to go to the temples, churches, mosques and Gurudwaras to seek some favour. According to Maulana Abdul Naorani religion is like an umbrella under which God protects to all. Religion should not ignite dogmatism. Swami Agnivesh said that the Almighty God is one. All religions believe in one God, then why should there should be diversity and disunity which create tensions. He further said that there should be sanity, sympathy, truthfulness and love in the society. Mrs. Aruna Roy said that everybody should speak against injustice.

Now the society is facing naxalism, extremism and menace of terrorism which is done in the name of religion. To face such challenges it is necessary to make our youngers sane citizens, which can be possible if they follow sane citizens, which can be possible if they follow morality. Inculcation of morality can never be possible without religiosity and spirituality.

Religious education is totally banned in our educational institutions. It is because that Indian society is a multi-religious society and, all religions have their own credentials. So religious teaching can never be possible and secularism has been imposed. Many committees and commissions for improving Indian education recommended that if religious education is not possible due to political reasons, at least morality should be inculcated to the youngers. This can only be possible if the youngers are made aware about the true aspects of religion. This can be done by reading about religions by the youngers. Also the school teachers should also tell them about social, moral and cultural aspects of the society. They should also generate a spirit of tolerance to all religions. Some co-curricular activities can be helpful in this regard. Some good aspects of religion as spirituality, love, affection and regard for all should be inculcated in the youngers.

Religion word is a French word, and is a derivation of Latin word 'Religio' meaning 'to care for', to respect, 'allied to', 'a feeling of reverence to supreme being', and 'to have a faith in the creator— the Almighty God. According to Durkhiem, "a religion is an integrated system of beliefs and practices related to sacred things, that is a superb identity which unite all in one moral community called a church for all who adhere to it. Sacred things are symbolised and not for necessarily desired ends".

For leading a sane daily life man has evolved certain mechanism like economic organisation, a technology for biological needs with his natural environment. Man developed language for communication, education, social organisation, political organisation. He also developed religion as an apprehension of a power which is a super power. Religion is the product of fewer— primitive societies. They had their own religious activity not different from that of civilised societies. Bouquet has said that Latin word, 'religio' which is itself derived from the root 'leg' means 'get-together' or count or observe or from root 'leg' which means to bind. In former sense the implication is belief and observance of signs of divine communication which binds together. Religion is for binding together.

BELIEFS AND RITUALS

All religions consist of mental attitude towards 'Super Natural Power'. This attitude manifests in the shape of beliefs and rituals. Some these are called myths. All religions—primitive and modern have this base of beliefs and rituals.

Rituals: Observing certain norms according to prescribed manner, as doing *sandhya* (सन्ध्या) designed to establish liaison between performing individual and their Super Natural Power or Powers.

Beliefs: Beliefs are charters of rituals performed or observed as rationalism or dogmatism. Difference between religion and higher religion is variety of philosophical speculation. The primitive man has not philosophical speculation regarding religion, but the presence of religion of one kind or other is there.

According to Jung religion is essential feature of human life without which attainment of full integration of human personality is not possible. The conception of exact nature of 'Super Natural Power' differs from society to society and from people to people. For some it is (*a*) ghost and spirit, (*b*) impersonal power, (*c*) a pantheon automorphic gods and goddesses, and (*d*) a single high power, that is Almighty God. Primitives generally distinguish between two component elements in the 'Super Natural' field (*a*) Sacred part and this Profane part. Religion is also described as sacred part-believing in Impersonal super power, and (*b*) Profane Part—as believing magic and tantrum. According to Durkheim sacred part is religion and profane part is magic or primitive science. Malinowosky however classified religion and sacred parts and science as profane.

Explanatory Theories About Religion

Anthropological theories of religion have been conjoined with examining (*a*) various conceptions of supernatural journey prevalent in different times, (*b*) to trace the evolution of religion, (*c*) recent theories concentrated on outlining the functions of religion.

Animism: Tyler said that the origin of the religion seems to have originated with the belief in the soul (anima), and the animism given has the theory of soul. Tyler's argument runs as follows:

Primitive man's experience in sleep or dream about other beings or being while awake he heard his voice, saw his reflections in water. The man thought there must be an unseen 'being' making the man dead. Tyler assumed such thing is human soul. Primitive man must have thought of two souls—one 'permanent' and other temporary. Indian religious philosophy is based on 'duality of the soul'. One is permanent omnipresent, indestructible, unseen divine authority which controls the upbringing and devastating the whole physical world and phenomena and, part of the divine authority is present in all living beings. The divine authority, that is, *Paramatma* or Almighty God is both creator and destroyer. The '*Paramatma's* part of which is present in all living beings is called 'soul' or '*Jeevatma*'. Till *Jeevatma* remains in the body of a living being, the living being survivers. So, every living being is mortal. Since, it is believed that Almighty God is in every living being, the Indian society has ever been homogenous in spite of rigid caste system. All human beings used to believe that they exist due to mercy of God who is the creator and sustainer, so all used to pay reverence and pray God which is the base of Indian religious system. Originally all Indians were monotheistic and used to pray the Almighty God regularly. This process is called *sandhya*. Since man being rational, is also greedy and acquisitive, he started praying other gods and goddeses, the man became henotheistic and polytheistic and he shifted from behaving in super power, that is, sacred aspect of religion to profane aspect of religion, which is called by the Westerners magic and by Indian 'tantarism'. This entails immorality and corruption. Different societies have religions having different view points. Some societies use religion as weapon to remain in power. Such societies are theocratic societies, and for them other religions of the world are meaningless. Some societies use religion for gaining economic power. But all believe in one and same Almighty God. Main aim of all religions is to protect humanity which can be done with morality.

The present religious trends appear to be dogmatic which can be said dys-functional. Dys-functionalism symbolises the connection between the dead and supernatural an awe, reverence towards the integrated and non-material spiritual beings. This is the core of primitive religion. Spiritual beings are not under our control, they need to be propitiated, then they will not harm. Ancestor worship was the earliest form of prayer, we Indian also worship our elders in 'Kanagtas'. Elder worship is the prime worship in China. But what is happening in the present hedonistic age in India, the son does not hesitate in killing father for gaining property. A 37 years old son killed on 9.9.06 his superintending engineer father in Pandav Nagar, Delhi for material gains. The youngers do not pay even respects to their parents and elders. What is the reason behind this ugly social face? They are not trained in morality and, because of materialism and hedonism they become totally immoral. And morality cannot be inculcated without religionsity and spirituality.

Religion is a wide subject and the writer is not competent to write about the religion. Religionsity can only be ignited or generated in youngers if they are educated about the theological truths—'all human beings are creations of the Almighty God, so they are all equal. They should treat all equally. All are mortal so they should not be greedy, acquisitive, materialistic, consumeristic and hedonistic. This sense of equality in youngers can make them humane and moral. They should be educated in religionsity and spirituality.

Religion has various concepts as 'ancestor worship', 'evolutionary concepts', 'animism', 'naturalism'. So religionsity cannot be taught but, can be attained through self-study. The students should be innovated, motivated and inspired for studying religious aspects by the teacher. Many youngers are born atheists, so the curtain of atheism should be withdrawn from their minds. This can be done by telling them some metaphysical teleological truths and aspects of human beings. They should also be inspired to read the religious contributions of some thinkers like Swami Vivekananda, Swami Dayanand Saraswati, Swami Agnivesh, Maulana Abdul Hamid Noorani and some religious texts like *Rigveda, Shrimad Bhagavad Gita, Bible, Quran, Upanishads*, etc. etc. The youngers should be encouraged to attend religious sermons.

Our present system of formal education is purely cent per cent alienistic. It was imposed by the British East India Company Government in 1833 A.D. on the advice of Lord Macaulay, the then law member in the Governor General's council. Main aim of this imposition was to kill the Indian culture through cultural diffusion and consequent acculturation. Our present system of education has nothing to do regarding enculturation and our society has been totally accultured which entailed many social crimes. As such, our present educational system should be aimed at to inculcate some axiological habits in our youngers along with preparing them to achieve economic gains. Morality and spirituality should be inculcated in youngers for making them future sane citizens of the country. This can only be done if the teachers are moral and spiritual and play an ideal role model before the students. The teacher should maintain a close rapport with the students having the sympathetic ears and eyes to the students. The teachers should be spiritualistic. Spirituality reflects the human being's spirit. It is the inner consciousness of a person. It leads a person to believe in equality and truthfulness. And spirituality can only be generated if the youngers are made aware about theology. A spiritual person can only be moral.

29

Role of Educators and Administrators in Making Education Panorama

For making any kind of scape (scenario), be it a land scape or seascape, or night scape, hill scape or a social scape or an education panorama some kind of knowledge about the concerned area and, also some skills and proficiency are required. Any kind of scape is generally made on the basis of ground realities and for depicting beauty. While making a land scape, the artist always tries to depict the physical ground realities of physical phenomenon and flora and fauna in his/her drawings. On the same lines all other scapes are made. An education panorama is like a land scape. It should contain all educational aspects pertaining to the socio-economic, cultural, biological, axiological conditions of the society and, epistemological and moral requirements for the society.

Our present Indian education panorama or educational system is the gift of our foreign rulers, that is, the British rulers who had imposed their formal system of education, of which the teaching of English language was the important part. It was imposed during the East India Company British Government by then the Governor General council. All other members were in favour of retaining Indian Gurukula education system as it was based to perpetuate the Indian culture. But Lord Macaulay's thinking was different. He had pleaded that if they had to keep their control over Indians, the Indian culture was to be eliminated. So for killing the Indian culture for keeping the Indian slaves for ever, the British Government had imposed the Western type system of formal education. Lord Macaulay's thinking has been so successful that we Indians have discarded our cultural traits, customs more or less totally. We try to live in Western style. We eat, drink, speak and dress in Western style. We try to be hedonistic instead of simple living. On many occasions it becomes very difficult to recognise genders. The boys try to adopt fashion and dressing in girls styles. One day, the writer was going to Agra Cantt Railway station in 'Dadar Express' from New Delhi. He could get a seat in general bogie, where a 'pseudo girl' was also sitting. The writer gave a full space to sit to this pseudo girl. When the writer got down at Agra Cantt Railway station pseudo girl also got down. The writer was surprised to know that the pseudo girl actually was a boy. He had long hairs. He was wearing a 'Salwar Kameez'. Like this, many girls try to become pseudo boy. As such, Lord Macaulay's thinking has been proved so successful that Indians have lost every aspect of their culture. We have been totally accultured, and Lord Macaulay might be enjoying in his grave and, might be eating Indian sweets like *'kalakand'* and *'burfi'*. Thank God, that the formal English type of education has also been beneficial to Indians. Due to English language we Indians could come closer and unite. We could fight the British imperialists and could attain independence. But this also cannot be denied that the present alienistic formal system of education has harmed Indians more. It killed our culture. We have been totally accultured. The acculturation has crossed its all limits. The human sense of acquisitiveness, greed and self-centredness have reached to the higher limits. The man who was once pure monotheistic, religious has now become totally pragmatic. And for achieving these ends, the man has become totally henotheistic, polytheistic and used to depend on tanterism. As such, the living and believing methods of man have totally changed. And this entailed corruption, nepotism, fraud, loot, thefts, molestations and rapes. And it can be concluded that cultural diffusion, which has resulted in total acculturation has badly damaged the Indian social structures and its institutions like joint family. All old social values like sociability, love and affection and simple living and high thinking have been badly damaged. Earlier, the youngers used to respect and take care of the elders seriously. Now, the youngers do not see even their own parents, seeing other elder is a distant dream. Only there is a love for acquisitiveness, greed and self-centredness. This trend entailed lot of crimes in the society. Due to greed and self-centredness the present man has forgotten the real meaning of religion, morality, sociability and sanity and, a kind of barbarism has taken place.

Of course our freedom fighters had fought the foreign rulers and got independence. But when they took the reigns of ruling power, they could not realise the evils, specially social evils, the foreigners had imposed on the Indian society. One of such evil was alienistic system of formal education they had imposed for killing the Indian culture. The present system of formal education is only examination oriented. It has totally crumbled our national culture and some important features of our social system. And the tragedy is that after 60 years of our independence we could not realise the bad effects of our present system of formal education. We are still immune to these bad effects. We are only mad after examination results. And our education and educational administrators are still blindly following the alien formal system of education, which does not suit to our social structure at all.

For proper education of the youngers, appropriate education-scape is necessary. And for the education and educational administrators first step should be to study the all aspects of the present educational system—whether the present system of formal education suits to tour national needs. They should try to visualise the national educational requirements and thereafter decide about the required educational needs. The educational system should be according to national, socio-economic, cultural, axiological and epistemological requirements. All these requirements are necessary. Any one area should not encroach other area. Our present system of education can be said 'epistemological' as it lays emphasis on examination results. But other areas as cultural and axiological are also important. Without inculcation of good habits for morality and without enculturation of our future guardians they cannot be sane citizens. Epistemology without sociability and sanity can be very dangerous for the health of the nation. As such the educators and administrators should come forward to improve our present educational system. They should convince our political leaders, who are governing the country, to improve our educational system. Sanity in education should go hand in glove with the teaching subjects. First and foremost reform in our education panorama should be to revive our culture. Culture of any country is its soul, so revival of culture is the utmost national necessity. Our national culture has been badly damaged by our present system. Epicentre of educational backwardness is our examination system which does not look to any other cultural or artistic activities to be taken place. In the past we did not have examination system. The examination system entailed certification which has brought cutthroat competition in the society. It has also killed non-formal heriditical system of education. And due to formal technical training and consequent certifications crores of artisans remain unemployed. The students do not pay respect to their parents elders, elder community members. They have become consumeristic. They only desire to take fast junky foods. Like all these many social evils have emerged. The educators and administrators should pay special attention to all these social problems. Our present education is a failure in creating a work culture. There is no provision for enculturation of the students. As such the educators and educational administrators should give special attention to the following educational aspects:

(*i*) The present examination system should be reformed. There should not be too much stress on examination.
(*ii*) The special attention should be given to artistic and craft activities.
(*iii*) Co-curricular activities relating to enculturation should be regularly arranged.
(*iv*) Extra-curricular actuaries like sports and games, should be arranged.
(*v*) Teacher-taught relations should be developed on Gurukula Ashramas pattern.
(*vi*) The educators and educational administrators should not function as bureaucrats but as guides and cooperative fellow beings.
(*vii*) There should be close rapport between teacher and students.
(*viii*) The administrators should also encourage the teachers to follow teaching professional ethics.

30

Conclusion

An education panorama (or educational scenrio) in any country generally has a wide spectrum and it is difficult to draw a conclusion about the viability of the existing educational structure. Only few aspects of it can be viewed and about which some opinions can be advanced. The present Indian education may be good for a particular section and, bad for another section of the society. But some aspects of the existing education scape are such about which majority of the people are fully aware. Top aspect of the present Indian educational structure is examination system. And it is the paramount feature of our present education panorama. So our educational structure has been designed to teach only few subjects for passing out examinations. And efforts are made that all students come in flying colours. Parents also desire that their wards should pass the annual examination after securing hi-fi marks. In the past there was no examination in India. It is the gift of our foreign rulers. At present the examination is the main suicide trigger in the country. The media reported that at least one youngster in the age group of 12-25 years commits suicide every week. Delhi Police records that in 75 per cent of the cases of examination stress acts as the suicide trigger. On 14th September, 2006 a girl named Khusboo age 20 years committed suicide in the office of the Central Board of Secondary Education, Preet Vihar, Delhi. Like this many promising youngers end their lives by committing suicides. Late Ms. Khusboo had failed three times in Class X examination. As such, education panorama is dominated by examination which is a killing evil in the society.

In the past there was neither examination system in Gurukula Ashram, nor Muslim Madarsas and nor in non-formal education imparted hereditically by the family elders. These systems of education used to educate the youngsters to prepare to live a sane socio-economic and cultural social life. As such, they used to do the life building of the youngers. In Gurukula Ashramas, as well as in Muslim Madarsas the students used to be trained and made proficient in religiosity, morality, sociability and social homogeneity. Under the non-formal system of the artisans used to train their youngers in their family vocations. They used to be highly skilled, proficient and sincere in their family trades. Indian non-formal system of education was one of the best system of technical training. But under the present technical trade training system in I.T.Is. no such trade efficiency is attained. The students are certified so, they get employment in factories and private establishments. The artisans who were trained by their elders are not given employment, and remained unemployed. This is the gift of our present education panorama, which is formal education.

Our present education panorama is such that it skips all life building activities. The teachers generally remain very busy in preparing the students for annual examinations. They cannot inculcate good life habits which may lead them to sane social living. The schools due to the examination phobia skip co-curricular activities, extra-curricular activities and social activities. The art and craft activities are done in the names sake. As such, there is no chance of aestheticity in our present education scape. Due to this, no work culture is created. The school authorities are also mad after the examination results. Our present system of education or education panorama triees to acculturate our youths. The school authorities prescribe western school dress for the students which motivates them towards western cultural traits. And this is dangerous for the development of national culture. Also the schools and other institutions do not have any prescribed enculturation programme. The public schools are far ahead in spreading acculturation in the country. Such schools serve or teach youngers of economically well-class only.

Acculturation by the educational institutions should be stopped, because it is very dangerous. It changes the mind set of the youngers. They want to be consumeristic and hedonistic. They do not learn sane behaviour. They do not learn how to behave in the society. Greed, egoism, self-centred are generated in them. The youngers do not learn how to respect elders. Due to acculturation, which is based on western culture the man generally remain busy in earning. And in the pursuit of learning they (men) do not get time to talk with nearest fellow beings and kith and kins. Because of acculturation Indian joint family system has been totally crumbled. And elders of the erstwhile joint families are considered as bio-garbage. Corruption, favouritism, nepotism, frauds, chain pulling have become common social feature. It is because of our education panorama. Our education system does not have any space for inculcating morality in the youngers. And the society is becoming uncivilised day by day.

The present education panorama's epistemological process is based on pouring of information. Generally the teaching is done through one way communication. The teacher lay emphasis on depending on guide books for preparation of examination. And due to this students evade reading books in library. The library is the store house of knowledge. The library gives a chance for self-learning. But hardly library is utilised by the students in the schools. This situation is more worse in rural schools where there are hardly well-equipped libraries. The teachers and the students hardly utilise library if there is any in the schools.

One of the tragic event of the present education panorama is that the teachers are not well-treated in the society. One of the main reasons for this teacher bias is that the teachers are not well-paid and are economically poor. Due to this the teachers are forced to do tuitions which also motivates the people to see the teachers a degraded class. In olden times the *Gurus* (teachers) were highly respected by the *Shishyas* and also by the members of the society. The *Gurus* used to follow teaching professional ethics very sincerely. They were epistemic, proficient, sincere to the students and non-inclinative. The present teachers should also follow teaching professional ethics.

On the whole, it can be concluded that our present education panorama does not meet our social requirements. It does not do life building. It does not have space or provision for inculcating good life habits in the younger and for inculcating them. It only creates cutthroat competitions in the socio-economic fields of the society. And examination system is the main reason for this ugly competition. Therefore, it is utmost necessary either to find an alternative of the examination or to find out some necessary steps for the reformation of the examination system. Merit based performance and evaluation can be one solution. It should be done through internation assessment.

Bibliography

Alum, Maktaba: *Quran* (Hindi and English Edition) Rampur, U.P.

Betielle Andre: *Caste: Old and New.*

Blakledge, David and Hind Barry: *Sociological Interpretation of Education.*

Cohen B.S.: *Indian Society and Culture.*

Desai I.P.: *Eliticism.*

Durkhiem Emile: *On Education.*

Etizoni Amitar: *Active Society* (Columbia University).

Encyclopaedia Britannica, London.

Fletcher: *Early Sociological Theories.*

F. Batch: *Alienation.*

Floud Jean, Halry A.H.: *Education and Social Structure.*

Fromn Eric: *Alienation and Sane Society.*

G.C. Honnman: *Social Behaviours—Its Elementary Forms.*

Halvey, Etizone: *Social Change.*

Hastings and Clark T.T.: *Encyclopaedia of Religion and Ethics.*

Harryanna M.: *The Essentials of Indian Philosophy.*

Hon Clifan: *Education Ideas.*

International Encyclopaedia of Education, New York.

Inequality and Social Change, Oxford University Press, Delhi.

Kabir Humayun: *Indian Philosophy of Education,* Asia Publishing House, New Delhi.

कृष्ण कुमार, Director N.C.E.R.T.: समाज और शिक्षा

Linton Ralph: *Culture.*

Locke John: *Essay on Human Understanding.*

Marx Karl, Engels and Fredrich: *Class Struggle.*

Merton: *Role of Intellectuals in Public Bureaucracy.*

National Policy on Education 1986, Ministry of Human Resources Development, Government of India.

Plato: *Dialogues—Phaedo, Republic and Meno.*

Porato: *Circular Ethics.*

Parsons Talcott: *The School, Class as Social System.*

Raymont Aron: *Sociology*.
Reading and Teaching to Think: *Times of India* 13.7.1994.
Shukla S.: *Socio-Economic Change and Teacher Education*.
Sriniwas M.N.: *Social Change and Sanskritisation*.
Suma : *Modernisation of Indian Education*.
Swami Dayanand Saraswati: *Satyarth Prakash*.
Timashelf Nicholas: *Social Theory—Nature Growth*.
Weber Max: On Education and Many Editorials from *Times of India*.

Index